Philip Smith

A Smaller Ancient History of the East

Philip Smith

A Smaller Ancient History of the East

ISBN/EAN: 9783744759496

Printed in Europe, USA, Canada, Australia, Japan

Cover: Foto ©ninafisch / pixelio.de

More available books at **www.hansebooks.com**

A SMALLER

ANCIENT HISTORY

OF

THE EAST.

FORM THE EARLIEST TIMES TO THE CONQUEST BY ALEXANDER THE GREAT.

INCLUDING EGYPT, ASSYRIA, BABYLONIA, MEDIA, PERSIA ASIA MINOR, AND PHŒNICIA.

By PHILIP SMITH, B.A.

ILLUSTRATED BY ENGRAVINGS ON WOOD.

LONDON:

JOHN MURRAY, ALBEMARLE STREET.

1871.

The right of Translation is reserved.

ASSYRIAN STANDARD.

LONDON: PRINTED BY WILLIAM CLOWES AND SONS, STAMFORD STREET, AND CHARING CROSS.

PREFACE.

———◆◇◆———

THIS is a book for the young, both in schools and families. It has a twofold purpose: to supply the learner with some information respecting the Eastern Nations, with which he comes in contact while reading the histories of Greece and Rome: and to set before the general reader a brief account of the course of ancient civilization in its earliest seats. Besides this general purpose, the book is specially designed to aid the study of the Scriptures, by placing in their true historical relations those allusions to Egypt, Assyria, Babylonia, Phœnicia, and the Medo-Persian Empire, which form the back-ground of the history of Israel from Abraham to Nehemiah. The present work is an indispensable adjunct of the 'Smaller Scripture History;' and the two have been written expressly to be used together.

The same authorities have been followed as in the 'Student's Ancient History of the East,' of which, however, this book is far from being a mere abridgment. It has been written with the special view of interesting the young readers for whom it is intended. The form of narrative is kept almost entirely free from discussion: the latter will be found in the larger work by those who wish to pursue the study of the subject. The picturesque stories of the ancient writers are given side by side with the results of recent discoveries; and the distinction is indicated, in preference to an attempt to substitute the latter for the former. Such an attempt is premature, till we know far more than we do at present of the contemporary native records; and the more

these are known, the more do we see the
served in the traditional stories. On eve
those stories should be made familiar to
ancient history.

Above all is it desirable, that such famili
with the exquisite stories embalmed in
language of Herodotus. Many of these, too
ing pages, and which any other form wo
expressly left to be read in the words of He
as a motive for the young student to acquir
them. It is not too much to say that, wi
liberal education can be complete; and th
beauty of his stories, for the value of his
ancient oriental history and manners, or for
Persian Wars—the reading of Herodotus in
adequate object for the study of Greek.

It remains to add, that this work aims at
with sufficient fulness to be clear and intere
string together the dry bones of a vast num
comparative completeness (for in so small
be comparative) has been studied in the divi
and even of the paragraphs; not without the
or family use, each chapter may generally fo
and every paragraph a single act of reading

A full analysis of the distinct points of in
in the work is given in the " Chronological
the form of which will enable the teacher to
Questions. The Chronology of each natio
own *data*. The reconciliation of these
Scripture is a work yet to be completed.

Rameses I.   Sete I.   Rameses II.

Names of Pharaohs of XIXth Dynasty.

CHRONOLOGICAL TABLE OF CONTENTS.

BOOK I.

EGYPT AND ETHIOPIA.

CHAPTER I.

THE LAND AND ITS RIVER.

	PAGE		PAGE
Egypt the Gift of the Nile	1	Its Isolation and Security	3
Sources of the River	1	Permanence of Character	3
The White, Blue, and Black Rivers	2	Beneficence of the River	4
The Island of Meroë	2	Inundation and Agriculture	4
The *Cataracts* in Ethiopia	2	Stimulus to Art and Science	5
Southern Boundary of Egypt	2	Means of Communication	5
The Arabian and Libyan Hills	2	Influence of the River and the Desert	
The Delta and Branches of the Nile	2	on the Moral and Religious Ideas	
Definition of EGYPT	3	of the Egyptians	6
Upper, Lower, and Middle Egypt	3	Belief in a Future State	6

CHAPTER II.

THE MONUMENTS OF EGYPT, AND THEIR HISTORICAL VALUE.

	PAGE		PAGE
Character of the Monuments	7	Egypt has the earliest Contemporary	
Natural supply of Stone	7	Records	9
Metals and other Minerals	8	Antiquity of Egyptian History	9
Records of the Mode of Work	8	Materials.—Books of Papyrus	10
Representations of Brick-making	8	Testimony of Lepsius	10
Monumental Records in Sculpture,		And of Bünsen	11
Painting, and Writing	8	Different value of the Monuments	12

CHAPTER III.

EPOCHS OF EGYPTIAN HISTORY.

	PAGE		PAGE
It begins with the Pyramids	13	The Shepherd Kings and the Middle Monarchy	15
Records of traditional history	13	The Kingdoms of Lower Egypt	15
HERODOTUS of Halicarnassus	13	The Ethiopian Conquest	15
Plan and Spirit of his Work	14	The New Saïte Kingdom	16
Diodorus Siculus	14	The Persian Conquest	16
MANETHO's Egyptian History	14	Dynasty of the Ptolemies	16
His *List of Dynasties and Kings*	14, 15	Egypt a Roman Province	16
The old Memphian Monarchy	15		

CHAPTER IV.

THE OLD MEMPHIAN MONARCHY—THE PYRAMID KINGS.

	PAGE		PAGE
Fabulous Antiquity of the Monarchy	18	Necropolis of Memphis	20
Rule of Gods and Demigods	18	The Pyramids, Tombs of Kings	21
MENES the first mortal king	18	Approach to the Pyramids	21
First Dynasty—Thinite	18	Their artistic purpose	21
Second Dynasty—Thinite	19	The Pyramids of *Jizeh*	22
Third Dynasty—Memphian	19	Construction of the Pyramids	22
Traditions of Laws and Civilization	19	The *Great Pyramid*, of CHEOPS	23
Capital established at Memphis	19	Hieroglyphics of its Builders	24
The Site gained from the River	19	The *Second Pyramid*, of CEPHREN	25
Names and Titles of MEMPHIS	20	The *Third Pyramid*, of MYCERINUS	25
Its Remains at Mitrabenny	20	His Coffin and Mummy	25

CHAPTER V.

LIFE UNDER THE OLD MONARCHY.

	PAGE		PAGE
The Pyramids themselves silent	26	Stories about the early Kings	30
Traditions of their Building	27	Evidences of a religious conflict	30
Evidences of advanced Civilization	27	Antagonism of Upper and Lower Egypt	30
Pictures of Daily Life in the Tombs	27	*Fourth Dynasty—Memphian*	30
Features, Clothing, and Ornaments	27	*Fifth Dynasty—Elephantine*	30
Social State depicted	28	*Sixth Dynasty—Memphian*	30
Agricultural and Pastoral Operations	28	King PHIOPS I.—*Pepi-Mairé*	30
Out-door and In-door Amusements	28	Commerce by way of the Red Sea	31
Domestic Animals—*No Horses*	29	PHIOPS II.—*Pepi-Neferkera*	31
Excellent Style of Art	29	The time of ABRAHAM	31
No Soldiers in these pictures	29	Queen NITOCRIS—*Neïtakri*	31
Wars in the Sinaitic Peninsula	29	*Seventh and Eighth Dynasties—Memphian*	31
Sudden perfection of the Civilization and Art of Egypt	29		

CHAPTER VI.

THE MIDDLE MONARCHY.

	PAGE		PAGE
Contemporary Dynasties in Manetho	32	*Eleventh Dynasty—Theban*	33
Rivalry of Upper and Lower Egypt	32	*Twelfth Dynasty—Theban*	33
Dynasties IX.-XIV.	33	Rise of the Theban Monarchy	33
Ninth and Tenth Dynasties—Heracleopolitan or Hermonthite?	33	The SESORTASENS and AMENEMES	34
The ENENTEFS and MANDOPTS	33	Conquests in Ethiopia	34
		And in Arabia	34

	PAGE		PAGE
A deified SESORTASEN	34	Sepulchres at *Beni-hassan*	37
Works in Middle Egypt	35	Life under the Middle Monarchy	37
Labyrinth and Lake of Mœris	33	Record of an Egyptian Noble	37
Purpose of the Lake	35	Soldiers and Slaves conspicuous	38
Changes of the Inundation	35	Group of Jebusites, mistaken for the	
The Palace of AMENEMES III.	36	Family of Jacob	38

CHAPTER VII.

THE SHEPHERD KINGS.—ADMINISTRATION OF JOSEPH.

	PAGE		PAGE
Fragment of Manetho's History	39	Religion of the Shepherds	42
Invasion of the *Shepherds*	39	Their destruction of Monuments	42
Their King SALATIS (or SAITES)	39	Internal Divisions of Egypt	42
Memphis their capital	39	*Thirteenth Dynasty—Theban*	43
Their fortress of *Avaris*	40	Vassals to the Hyksos	43
Their name of HYKSOS	40	Age of JOSEPH	43
Their Expulsion to Syria	40	Revolt of the Thebaïd	44
Their *Semitic* Race	41	TIAAKEN—KAMES—AAHMES	44
Time of their Invasion	41	Siege of Avaris	44
Avaris = Tanis = Zoan	41	Expulsion of the Shepherds	45
Importance of its position	42	Mistakes about *Jerusalem*	45
The "Field of Zoan"	42	Shemites in the Delta	45

CHAPTER VIII.

THE NEW THEBAN MONARCHY.—THE EIGHTEENTH DYNASTY.—EGYPT AT HER CLIMAX.

	PAGE		PAGE
THEBES with its "Hundred Gates"	46	Conquests of THOTHMES III.	51
Origin of the Name	47	His victory at Megiddo	51
Its Situation and Importance	47	Nineveh, Babylon, and Armenia	51
Villages on its Site	48	Monuments at Napata	51
Temples and Palaces of Thebes	49	Slave-hunting Expeditions	51
Necropolis of Thebes	49	Conquests in Arabia and Libya	52
Sculptured and painted Records	49	Maritime Expeditions	52
Extent of Conquests claimed	49	"Numerical Wall" of *Karnak*	52
The Eighteenth Dynasty	50	Scenes of Brick-making	52
Rapid revival under them	50	Obelisks and colossal statues	52
Their Power in Lower Egypt	50	The "Vocal Memnon"	53
Conquests in Ethiopia	50	The "Stranger Kings"	53
In Syria and Mesopotamia	50	Schism of AMENHOTEP IV.	53
Military Route to Asia	50	His capital at *Tel-Amarna*	53
The *Kheta, Rotno,* and *Naharain*	51	Mutilation of Monuments	53

CHAPTER IX.

THE NEW THEBAN MONARCHY.—NINETEENTH DYNASTY.—RAMESES II., THE OPPRESSOR OF THE HEBREWS.

	PAGE		PAGE
Probable Change of Family	54	His colossal statues	58
SETI I. and RAMESES II.	54	Library in the Rameseum	58
Extent of their Dominion	55	His Men of Learning	58
Records of Seti I. at *Karnak*	55	The oldest Fairy Tale	58
The Red Sea Canal begun	55	The *Oppressor of Israel*	58
RAMESES II. MERIAMUN	55	Contemporary Evidence	59
His Wars with the Hittites	55	The cities of *Rameses* and *Pachtum*	59
Bas-reliefs of the Rameseum	56	His connection with Tanis (*Zoan*)	60
Epic Poem of *Pentaour*	56	Slave-hunting and deportations	60
Peace with the Hittite King	56	Oppressive Government	60
Greek Story of SESOSTRIS	56	State of the Peasantry	61
Monuments of Rameses II.	56	The "groans of the soldier"	61

CHAPTER X.

End of the Theban Monarchy.—Dynasty XIX. *continued.*—The Exodus—Dynasty XX.

	PAGE
New Invaders of Egypt	62
Menephtha or Phtha-men, the *Pharaoh of the Exodus*	63
Flies to the Thebaid	63
Victory over the Invaders	63
Scene of the Plagues	63
Passage of the Red Sea	64
New Semitic Invasion	64
Flight and Death of Menephtha	65
Usurping kings at *Chebu*	65
Seti II., son of Menephtha	65
The *Twentieth Dynasty*	65
Monuments of Rameses III.	65
His Victories in Asia	65
The Oldest Sea-fight	65
Line of kings named Rameses	66
A Mesopotamian Story	66
Priestly Line of Her-Hor	66
Alliance with Assyria	67
Seat of Empire changing	67

CHAPTER XI.

The Kingdoms of the Delta, and the Dynasty of the Ethiopians.

B.C.		PAGE
1100 (about).	*Twenty-first Dynasty—Tanite*	68
	Converging Currents of History	68
	A Basis of Chronology	68
	Kingdom of Israel	68
1005.	The Temple of Solomon	68
	His Egyptian Alliance	69
	Twenty-second Dynasty—Bubastite	69
	Sheshonk I., or Shishak	69
	Their Assyrian Origin	70
	The city of *Bubastis*	70
975.	*Jeroboam* a vassal king	71
970.	Subjection of Rehoboam	71
	Recorded at Karnak	71
	Relations to Ethiopia	71
954.	"Zerah the Cushite"	72

B.C.		PAGE
	Twenty-third Dynasty—Tanite	72
	Several petty Kingdoms	72
	Tnephachtus of Sais	72
	Twenty-fourth Dynasty—Saite	72
	Bocchoris the Wise	72
	Twenty-fifth Dynasty—Ethiopian	73
	The Sabacos and Tirhakah	73
	The Kingdom of Napata	73
	Relations of Ethiopia to Egypt	73
	Conflict with Assyria	74
	Retirement of both the Assyrians and Ethiopians	74
670 (about).	Lower Egypt left open to Greek Influence	74

CHAPTER XII.

The Later Saite Monarchy—Psammetichus, Neco, and Psammis.

B.C.		PAGE
	Twenty-sixth Dynasty—Saite	75
664.	Epoch of trustworthy history marked by Herodotus	75
	The so-called *Dodecarchy*	75
	Oracle of the Brazen Cup	75
	Fulfilled by Psammetichus	76
	The Men of Bronze	76
	Psamatik or Psammeticus I.	76
	His foreign mercenaries	76
	He obtains Upper Egypt	76
	Admission of foreign merchants	77
	Sais, the city of *Neith*	77
	The "Feast of Lamps"	77

B.C.		PAGE
	Siege of Azotus (Ashdod)	78
	Secession of the Warriors	78
610.	Neco, or Pharaoh-Necho	79
	His Asiatic Expedition	79
	Battle of Megiddo	79
	Capture of Carchemish	79
605.	Victory of Nebuchadnezzar	79
	Egypt shut out of Asia	79
	Neco's pacific enterprises	79
	His Navy and Docks	79
	The Red Sea Canal	80
	Circumnavigation of Africa	80
594.	Psammatik II., or Psammis	81
	Greek Envoys in Egypt	81
	Chronology of the *Apis-Stelæ*	81

CHAPTER XIII.

The Saïte Monarchy *continued.* Apries and Amasis.

B.C.		PAGE	B.C.		PAGE
588.	Wah-yba-hat, Pharaoh-Hophra, or Apries	82		Battle of Momemphis	84
	His enterprise and arrogance	82		Death of Apries	84
	Expedition to Phoenicia, &c.	83	569.	Babylonian Conquest	81
	Alliance with Zedekiah ..	83		Amasis, or Aahmes II... ..	84
	Vengeance of Nebuchadnez-			A Vassal of Babylon	85
	zar	83		His character and rule	85
	Expedition to Cyrene	83		Treatment of the Oracles ..	86
	Revolt of the Army	83		Business and Pleasure	86
	Amasis saluted king	84		Prosperity of Egypt	87
				Encouragement of Greeks ..	87

CHAPTER XIV.

The Conquest of Egypt by Cambyses. Dominion of the Persians and the Ptolemies—B.C. 527 to B.C. 32.

B.C.		PAGE	B.C.		PAGE
527 or 525.	League with Lydia and Babylon	88		Rebellion of Inarus	93
				Kept up by Amyrtæus ..	93
	Cambyses invades Egypt ..	89	408 (about).	Egypt independent ..	93
	Death of Amasis	89		*Twenty-eighth Dynasty—Saite*	93
	Defeat of Psammenitus ..	90		*Twenty-ninth Dynasty—Men-*	
	Persian and Egyptian skulls	90		*desian*	93
	Capture of Memphis	90		*Thirtieth Dynasty—Saite* ..	93
	Treatment of Psammenitus	90		Their beautiful monuments ..	93
	Cambyses king of Egypt ..	91		Nectanebo II. the last Pha-	
	His zeal against Idolatry ..	91		raoh	94
	Expeditions against Ethiopia	91	353 (about).	Ochus conquers Egypt	94
	And against the Ammonians	92		*Thirty-first Dynasty — Per-*	
	Destruction of the latter ..	92		*sian*	94
	Return of the former	92	332.	Egypt submits to Alex-	
	Cambyses kills the Apis ..	92		ander	94
	His alleged madness .. · ..	93		Foundation of Alexandria ..	94
521.	Darius I. son of Hystaspes	93	323.	Greek Dynasty of the Pto-	
486–4.	Rebellion put down	93		lemies	94
527–414.	*Twenty-seventh Dynasty—*			Adopt Egyptian Customs ..	94
	Persians	93		Monuments—Rosetta Stone	94
458.	Artaxerxes I. Longimanus	93	32.	Ends with Cleopatra	94
			30.	Egypt a Roman Province ..	94

CHAPTER XV.

The Institutions, Religions, and Arts of Egypt.

		PAGE			PAGE
1.	*Ethnic Character of the People*	95	III.	The *King,* of divine race ..	98
	Civilization probably derived from Asia	95		His Privileges and Duties ..	98
				Hereditary Succession.. ..	98
II.	*Classes of the Egyptians* ..	96		The Royal Princes—Moses	98
	All equally well-born	96		Legislative Power	99
	The *Priests* and their *Col-*			Criminal and Civil Laws ..	99
	leges	96	IV.	*Judicial Administration* ..	99
	The *Soldiers*—Two bodies	96–7		Independence of Judges ..	99
	Auxiliaries and Mercenaries	97		Forms of Trial	99
	The other Classes	97		The Court of Thirty	99
	Pictures of their Occupa-			The *Civil Service.*.	99
	tions	97		Corporation of the *Scribes* ..	99
				Different Departments ..	99

	PAGE
Sources of Revenue	99
Nomes and their Governors	99
V. The *Religion* of Egypt ..	99
Triads of Deities	100
Symbols of the gods	100
Animal Worship	100
The Bull *Apis*	100
Worship of *Serapis*	101
The Future State..	101
"Ritual of the Dead".. ..	102
The "Hermetic Books" ..	102

	PAGE
VI. Egyptian *Writing*	102
Hieroglyphic, Hieratic, and	
Demotic or *Enchorial* ..	102
Ideographic Characters ..	103
Phonetic Characters	103
VII. Egyptian *Art*	103
Its Character and Merits ..	103-4
Architecture	104
Sculpture	104
Painting	104

BOOK II.

ASSYRIA AND BABYLON.

CHAPTER XVI.

THE LAND OF THE TWO RIVERS.

Valley of the Euphrates and Tigris	105
Courses of the Rivers..	106
The Land of Mesopotamia	106
The Plain of *Shinar*	107
Assyria :—its various limits	107
Mesopotamia Proper	107
Arabia—*Irak-Arabi*	108
Climate and Productions	108
Present Desolation	109
Elam or Susiana..	109

CHAPTER XVII.

PRIMITIVE KINGDOMS OF MESOPOTAMIA.

Babel and Nimrod	110
Early Brick Buildings	110
City and Tower of Babel	111
Kingdom of Nimrod	111
Fate of the Tower	112
Inscription of Nebuchadnezzar ..	112
Temple at Borsippa	112
Temple Towers or *Ziggurats* ..	112
Materials and Construction	113
Connection with heavenly bodies ..	113
Parallel with the Pyramids	114
Remains of the Towers	114
Old Babylonian Kingdom..	114
Cities and Cemeteries	114
The *Akkad* and *Sumiri*	115
Conquests to the West	115
Dominion in Assyria..	115
The Arabian Conquest	115

CHAPTER XVIII.

MYTHICAL HISTORY OF ASSYRIA.

Scriptural Notices of Nineveh.. ..	116
The Greek Traditions	116
From Persian sources	116
Dramatic colouring	117
Legend of *Ninus*	117
Legend of *Semiramis*	117
Her defeat in India	118
Her great buildings	118
Legend of *Ninyas*	118
Legend of *Sardanapalus*	119
Destruction of Nineveh	119
Descriptions of the City	119
Testimony of *Jonah*	120
Extent of the City	120
Its traditional Site	120
Duration of its Name	120

CHAPTER XIX.

RECENT DISCOVERIES IN ASSYRIA.

A.D.

Mounds in Mesopotamia .. 121
Those opposite *Mosul* 121
Nebbi-Yunus and *Koyunjik*.. 121
Khorsabad or *Sarghun*.. .. 122
Mound of *Nimrud* (Calah) .. 122
Local Tradition of Nimrod.. 122
Kileh-Sherghat (Asshur) .. 122
Fragments of Inscribed bricks,
&c., about the sites 122
1811–21. Mr. Claudius James RICH 122
1817-20. Sir Robert Ker PORTER .. 123
1846. Cuneiform Inscriptions deci-

phered by Sir Henry C.
RAWLINSON 123
1845, &c. Mr. Austen Henry LAY-
ARD 123
1842. Discoveries of M. BOTTA .. 123
1845. The Palace of Sargon 124
1845-7. Discoveries at *Nimrud* .. 124
1849, &c. At *Koyunjik* and *Kileh-
Sherghat* 125
The Kileh-Sherghat Cylinders 125
1857. Epoch of Cuneiform Interpretation 125

CHAPTER XX.

RISE OF THE ASSYRIAN MONARCHY. TO ABOUT B.C. 1100.

B.C.

Two Assyrian Monarchies .. 126
Scenes on the Sculptures .. 126
Annals of the Kings 127
Notices of Older Events .. 127
Readings of Assyrian Names (*note*)
19th cent. (prob.) } Assyria under Babylon 128
13th cent. (prob.) } Gains her independence
and the supremacy in
Mesopotamia 128
12th cent. Names of Four Kings .. 128

B.C.

Capital at *Kileh-Sherghat* .. 128
Mesopotamia Proper subdued 128
1100 (about). TIGLATH-PILESER I... 129
The *Contemporary History*
of Assyria begins with his
Annals.. 129
His Effigy at *Korkhar* 129
Extent of his Conquests .. 129
His mode of warfare 130
His hunting exploits 130
Religious tone of all 130

CHAPTER XXI.

THE OLD ASSYRIAN MONARCHY. FROM ABOUT B.C. 1100. THE GREAT NIMRUD KING, B.C. 886-858.*

The *Nimrud* Sculptures .. 131
Depression of Assyria after
B.C. 1100 132
909-745. Chronological Lists of
Kings 132
Capital at Calah (*Nimrud*) .. 132
Royal Quarter.. 133
The City in its glory 134
Assyrian Palaces 135
N.W. Palace of Nimrud .. 135

The "Standard Inscription" 135
Temple of *Nin* or *Ninip* .. 135
886-58. Effigy of ASSHUR-NASIR-PAL 135
His Titles and Dominions .. 135
His Ten Campaigns 136
His hunts and park 136
The *Nimrud* bas-reliefs .. 136
The Spirit of his Annals .. 136
Cruelty of Assyria.. 137
Despotism self-condemned .. 137

CHAPTER XXII.

CLIMAX AND FALL OF THE OLD ASSYRIAN MONARCHY. ITS RELATIONS WITH SYRIA AND ISRAEL, B.C. 853-745.

858-823. SHALMANESER II. 138
His "Black Obelisk" 139

The Tributary Nations.. .. 139
"Jehu, son of Omri" 140

* Till the accession of the "New Monarchy" the dates are only *approximate*.

xiv CONTENTS.

B.C.		PAGE	B.C.		PAGE
	Wars with Syria	140		Name = Semiramis	141
	"Ahab of Jezreel"	140		Temporary Union of Assyria and Babylon	141
	"Hazael of Damascus"	140		The PUL of Scripture	141
	Invasion of Babylonia	140		*Menahem* his tributary	142
	Rebellion of the king's son	140	781–745.	Three other kings	143
823–10.	SHAMAS-IVA, or SAMSI-HOU	141		Growth of the *Medes*	143
	Wars beyond Mt. Zagrus	141		This period obscure	143
810–781.	IVA-LUSH, or HULIKHUS IV.	141		Independence of Babylon	143
	His wife *Sammuramit*	141	747.	*Era of Nabonassar*	143

CHAPTER XXIII.

THE NEW ASSYRIAN MONARCHY. PART I.—TIGLATH-PILESER II. AND SHALMANESER IV. FROM B.C. 745 TO B.C. 721.

B.C.		PAGE	B.C.		PAGE
	Kings of the New Monarchy	144		Syria, Palestine, and Phœnicia	146
	Chronological Epoch	145		First Captivity of Israel	146
	The "Canon" of Ptolemy	145		Destruction of Damascus	147
	The "Assyrian Canon"	145		Judah becomes tributary	147
	Contemporary Epochs of Greek and Roman History	145		Deportation of Captives	147
745–727.	TIGLATH-PILESER II.	145	727–721.	SHALMANESER IV.	147
	Probably an usurper	145		Rebellion of Hoshea	148
	His Palaces at *Nimrud*	145		His League with Sabaco I.	148
	War with Babylon	145		His Imprisonment	148
	Merodach-Baladan I.	145	723.	Siege of Samaria	148
				Usurpation of Sargon	148

CHAPTER XXIV.

THE NEW ASSYRIAN MONARCHY—*continued*. SARGON. FROM B.C. 721 TO B.C. 704.

B.C.		PAGE	B.C.		PAGE
721.	*Sargon, Sarkin,* or *Saryukin*	149	714.	Also the queen of Arabia	152
	Meaning of the Name	149	710.	Capture of Ashdod	152
	Merodach - Baladan II. at Babylon	149	709.	Defeat of Merodach-Baladan	153
	War with Susiana	150		Sargon king of Babylon	153
	Capture of Samaria	150		Revolt of Babylon	153
	Captivity of Israel	150	706.	Sennacherib in Babylonia	153
	New Settlers at Samaria	150		Reverses of Sargon	153
	Conquest of Hamath	150	704 (Aug.).	He is assassinated	153
	And of Phœnicia	151		His Conquests in Media, &c.	153
	Collision with Egypt	151	708.	Conquest of Cyprus, &c.	154
718.	Battle of *Raphia*	151		His Works at *Nimrud*	154
	"Pharaoh" made tributary	152		His Palace at *Khorsabad*	154
				Transparent Glass	154
				Cylinders of his Annals	154

CHAPTER XXV.

THE NEW ASSYRIAN MONARCHY—*continued*. SENNACHERIB. FROM B.C. 704 TO B.C. 680.

B.C.		PAGE	B.C.		PAGE
704.	Meaning of *Sin-akhi-irib*	155	701.	Conquests in the E. and N.	156
	Concurrence of testimonies	155	700.	His Syrian Campaign	156
	His Palace at *Koyunjik*	156		Power of *Hezekiah*	156
	Cylinders of his Annals	156		Phœnicia, &c., reduced by Sennacherib	156
702.	Conquest of Babylon	156			

B C.		PAGE
700.	Victory at *Attaku* over the Egyptians and Ethiopians	157
	Fenced cities of Judah taken	157
	Siege of Jerusalem	157
	Hezekiah sends tribute	158
	Sennacherib at Lachish	158
	Mission of Rab-shakeh	158
	Sennacherib at Libnah	159
	Destruction of his Army	159
	The Egyptian account	*note*

B.C.		PAGE
699–6.	Reduction of Chaldæa	160
	Victory at *Khaluli* over the Elamites, Babylonians, and Arabians	160
688–0.	New Revolt of Babylonia	160
680.	Murder of Sennacherib	161
	His Titles and Character	161
	Inscription on his Palace	161
	Sculptures in British Museum	161
	Moral of his history	161

CHAPTER XXVI.

THE NEW ASSYRIAN MONARCHY—*continued.* ESAR-HADDON, KING OF ASSYRIA AND BABYLON. FROM B.C. 680 TO B.C. 667.

680.	Meaning of *Asshur-akh-idin*	162 n.
	His conquest of Babylon	162
	Fate of his brothers	162
	Reconquest of W. Provinces	162
	Expedition to Arabia	162
	Cilicia and Cyprus	162
	Spoils used for Palaces	163
	Captivity of Manasseh	163

	Repeopling of Samaria	163
	War in Chaldæa and Elam	164
	Wars in Media, &c.	164
668–7.	Conquest of Egypt	164
	Palaces of Esar-haddon	164
	Peculiarity of Sculptures	164
	Severance of Assyria and Babylonia	165

CHAPTER XXVII.

THE NEW ASSYRIAN MONARCHY—*continued.* ASSHUR-BANI-PAL OR SARDANAPALUS. FROM B.C. 667 TO B.C. 660 OR 647.

667.	Meaning of the Name	166 n.
	Resemblance to the "warlike Sardanapalus"	166
	His Palace at *Koyunjik*	167
	His Public Library	167
	Books of burnt clay	167
667–60.	Annals of the King	167
	Tirhakah, king of Egypt	168
668–7.	Expelled by Esarhaddon	168
	Petty Kings of Egypt	168
	Return of Tirhakah	168
	His expulsion by Asshur-bani-pal	168
	Who takes Thebes	168
	New Revolt of Egypt	169
	Chastised by Asshur-bani-pal	169
	Necho, king at Saïs	169
667–6.	Tirhakah dies at Memphis	169

	Succeeded in Ethiopia and Thebes by his son *Rot-men* or *Urdamané*	169
	Who invades Lower Egypt	169
	Defeated by Asshur-bani-pal	169
	Great sack of Thebes	169
	Prophesied by *Isaiah*	170
	Recorded by *Nahum*	170
	Assyria and Lydia	170
	Wars in Babylonia and Susiana	171
	Scenes on the bas-reliefs	171
	Nineveh "the city of bloods"	171
	Sculptures at *Koyunjik*	171
	Magnificence of this King	172
	Presages of decay	172
	Prophetic image of Assyria as "a cedar in Lebanon"	172

CHAPTER XXVIII.

FALL OF THE ASSYRIAN MONARCHY. FROM B.C. 660 OR 647 TO B.C. 625 OR 606.

	Rapid declension of Assyria	173
	The details wanting	173
	The last known king	174
	Revolt of the Provinces	174
	Rivalry of Babylon	174
	Growth of the Medes	174
	They attack Nineveh	175
	The Scythian Invasion	175
	Final attack on Nineveh	175
	The traditional story	175

	League of Nabopolassar and Cyaxares	175
	Saracus burns himself with Nineveh	175
	Prophetic Descriptions of the Fall of Nineveh	175
	By *Ezekiel*	175
	By *Nahum*	176
	By *Zephaniah*	176
	Question of the Date	176

CHAPTER XXIX.

THE BABYLONIAN OR CHALDÆAN EMPIRE. FROM B.C. 625 TO B.C. 538.
PART I.—THE CONQUESTS OF NEBUCHADNEZZAR.

B.C.		PAGE
	Continuity of the Monarchy at *Babel* and *Babylon*	177
	Vicissitudes of Power	178
625 (Jan. 27).	The New Empire founded by NABOPALASSAR	178
	Its Extent and Limits	178
	Its brief duration	178
	List of the Kings	178
	The name *Chaldæan*	178
	Works of Nabopolassar	179
	State of Babylon	179
	Contest with Egypt	179
606.	Defeat of Neco	179
	Death of Nabopolassar	180
604 (Jan. 21).	Accession of NEBU-CHADNEZZAR	180
	Forms and Meaning of the Name	*note*
	His place in History	180
	Master of Western Asia	180
	Tyre and Judah resist	180
604–5.	*First Captivity* of Judah	180
	DANIEL and his companions	181
602.	Rebellion of *Jehoiakim*	181
597.	Capture of Jerusalem	181
	Rebellion of *Jehoiachin*	181
	Great Captivity of Judah	181
	Zedekiah vassal king	181
	Motives for sparing Jerusalem	181
603.	Dream of the Image	181
597 ?	The fiery furnace	182
	False prophets "roasted"	182
589.	Rebellion of Zedekiah	182
	Siege of Jerusalem	182
	Patriotism of Jeremiah	182
586.	Capture of the City	182
588–575 ?	Siege of Tyre	183
570.	Conquest of Egypt	184

CHAPTER XXX.

THE BABYLONIAN OR CHALDÆAN EMPIRE. FROM B.C. 625 TO B.C. 538.
PART II.—ITS CLIMAX AND FALL.

B.C.		PAGE
	Works of Nebuchadnezzar	185
	Materials and Labour	185
	Wall of Babylon	185
	Palace (the *Kasr*)	185
	Hanging Gardens	186
	Reservoirs and Canals	186
	Quays and Breakwaters	186
	Birs-i-Nimrud at Borsippa	186
	Other Temples, &c.	186
	His Inscriptions	186
	Religious spirit	186
	Three great lessons	186
	His madness (*Lycanthropy*)	187
	The Regent *Rab-Mag*	188
	Recovery and Death	188
	Decline of the Empire	188
561.	EVIL-MERODACH	188
560.	Release of Jehoiachin	188
559.	NERIGLISSAR, the *Rab-Mag* or chief of the Chaldæans	189
	His New Palace	189
556.	LABOROSOARCHOD, a boy	189
	Murdered by the Chaldæans	189
555.	NABONADIUS (*Nabu-nahid*)	189
540 (or earlier).	His son BELSHAZZAR associated in the kingdom	189
	Inscriptions of their Names	189
	The Queen NITOCRIS	189
	Works of Defence	190
	Inscription at Calneh	190
	Alliance with Crœsus	190
539.	CYRUS marches from Ecbatana	190
	Defeats Nabonadius, who flies to Borsippa	190
	Belshazzar in Babylon	190
538.	Capture of the City	190
	Nabonadius surrenders	191
538–6.	DARIUS THE MEDIAN regent at Babylon	191
536.	CYRUS reigns there	191
	Residence of Persian kings	191
	Revolts of Babylon	191
	Decay of the City	191
	Its present desolation	192
	Preservation of the Name	193
	Epoch marked by its Fall	193

BOOK III.

THE MEDO-PERSIAN EMPIRE AND ITS SUBJECT COUNTRIES IN ASIA.

CHAPTER XXXI.

IRAN AND THE PRIMITIVE ARYANS.

	Page		Page
Transfer of Empire from the Semitic to the Aryan Race	194	Migrations to the West	197
Cradle of the Race	195	Primitive Social Condition	197
Table-land of IRAN	195	Manners and Laws	198
Iranians and Indians	195	Patriarchal Constitution	198
Turan and Turanians	195	Primitive Religion	198
Bactria and Sogdiana	196	*Ormazd* and *Ahriman*	198
Traditions of the *Zendavesta*	196	Zoroastrian Religion	198
The *Aryas* and *Yavanas*	197	*Mazdeism* and *Magism*	199
		Further Semitic Corruptions	199

CHAPTER XXXII.

RISE OF THE MEDIAN KINGDOM.

MEDIA and PERSIA	200	Doubtful Traditions	203
Mountains and Desert	201	ARBACES and DEJOCES	203
Media Magna, and Atropatene	201	Revolt from Assyria	203
Persia Proper (or *Persis*)	201	The Median Tribes	203
Climate and Productions	201	The capital, *Ecbatana*	204
Rivers, Lakes, and Cities	202	PHRAORTES killed in attacking Nineveh	204
The Nisæan Horses	202	CYAXARES the real founder of the *Medo-Persian Empire*	204
Turanian Inhabitants	202		
The Aryan Medes	203	Close connection between the "Medes and Persians"	205
Early state of Media	203		
Assyrian Records	203		

CHAPTER XXXIII.

RISE OF THE LYDIAN KINGDOM AND ITS FIRST CONTACT WITH MEDIA.

Progress of the Medes westward	206	Aryan *Phrygians* and *Thracians*	208
Description of ASIA MINOR	207	*Semitic Races* in the South	208
A bridge between Asia and Europe	207	With *Lycians* and *Carians*	208
Movements of peoples to and fro over its surface	207	Hellenic Colonies	208
Civilization and Conquests	207	Origin of the LYDIANS	208
Great mixture of Races	208	*Atyadæ* and *Heraclidæ*	208
Turanian *Cappadocians*	208	The History of Lydia begins with the *Mermnadæ*	208
		List of Lydian Kings	209

B.C.		PAGE	B.C.		PAGE
716.*	Gyges attacks the Greeks	209		Makes peace with Miletus	210
	Consults the Greek Oracles	209		Expels the Cimmerians..	210
	His offerings at Delphi	209	631-606?	Scythian Domination in Asia	211
	Relations with Assyria..	209			
678.	Ardys, son of Gyges	209	610?	War of Media and Lydia	211
	War with Miletus..	209		"Eclipse of Thales"	211
	The Cimmerian Inroad..	209		Boundary fixed at the Halys	211
	Cimmerians and *Scythians*	210		Matrimonial Alliances..	211
629.	Sadyattes, son of Ardys	210	594.	Death of Cyaxares..	211
	New war with Miletus..	210	560.	Death of Alyattes..	211
617.	Alyattes, son of Sadyattes	210		Tomb of Alyattes	211

CHAPTER XXXIV.

Astyages and Cyrus. The Empire passes from Media to Persia. From B.C. 594 to B.C. 558.

B.C.		PAGE	B.C.		PAGE
591-560.	Peace of Western Asia	212		State of the Persians	215
	Alliances between Lydia, Media, Babylon, and Egypt..	212		Their Ten Tribes	215
				The noble *Pasargadæ*	215
560.	Epoch of New Convulsions	213		The royal *Achæmenidæ*	215
594.	Astyages, king of Media..	213		Native kings of Persia..	215
	Sudden decline of the Empire	213		Cambyses, father of Cyrus	216
	Picture drawn by Xenophon	213		Legends about Cyrus	216
	The Median Court..	213	558.	He dethrones Astyages..	216
	Character of Astyages	214		Place of Cyrus in Scripture	217
	Relations with Armenia	214		His real work..	217
	An Armenian Legend	214		Stem of the *Achæmenids*	217

CHAPTER XXXV.

Crœsus and Cyrus—B.C. 560-529. Fall of Lydia and Babylon.

B.C.		PAGE	B.C.		PAGE
560.	Crœsus, king of Lydia..	218		Manners of the Persians	221
	As drawn by Herodotus	219		Their Policy of Conquest	221
	In a Legendary Spirit	219		Preparations of Cyrus	221
	Subdues the Greeks	219	546.	Crœsus passes the Halys	221
	Apologue of Bias	219		Loses two great battles	221
	Warning of Solon	219		Capture of Sardis	222
	Conquests west of the Halys	219		Cyrus and Crœsus..	222
	Resolves to attack Cyrus	219		Subjugation of Ionia, &c.	222
	Crœsus and the Oracles..	220		Further Schemes of Cyrus	222
	Alliances with Egypt, Babylon, and Lacedæmon	220	538.	Conquest of Babylon	222
				Eastern Wars of Cyrus..	222
	Warning of Sandanis	220	529.	His Death and Tomb	222

CHAPTER XXXVI.

Cambyses and the Magian Usurper. From January B.C. 529 to the end of B C 522.

B.C.		PAGE	B.C.		PAGE
529.	Character of Cambyses	223		Cambyses marries his sisters	224
	Family of Cyrus	223		And murders his brother	224
	Cambyses and Smerdis..	224		Testimony of Darius	225
	Their Persian names	(*note*)	527.	Conquest of Egypt..	225

---

* The dates of the Lydian Kings are doubtful, but only within a narrow limit.

B.C.		PAGE	B.C.		PAGE
700.	Submission of Phœnicia	225	522.	Suicide of Cambyses	226
	Flattery of the Courtiers	225		Policy of the Magian	227
	Madness of Cambyses	225		Darius, son of Hystaspes	228
	Religious Revolt of Persia	225		His seven "faithful men"	229
522.	Usurpation of the Magian Gomates (Gaumata), who personates Smerdis	226		They slay the Usurper	229
				Massacre of the Magians	229
				Feast of the Magophonia	229

CHAPTER XXXVII.

CLIMAX OF THE PERSIAN EMPIRE. DARIUS, THE SON OF HYSTASPES. FROM B.C. 521 TO B.C. 486 INCLUSIVE.

		PAGE			PAGE
521 (Jan. 1).	Age of Darius I.	231		The Temple at Jerusalem	235
	Dreamt of by Cyrus	231		Voyage of Scylax	236
	His Achæmenid descent	231		Conquest of India	236
	Marriages of Darius	232		Its Tribute and Soldiers	236
	His Inscription at Behistun	232	508 (about).	Expedition to Scythia	236
	Annals of his first five years	232		Retreat of Darius	237
	Recovery of the Empire	233		The Ionian chiefs	237
	Restoration of Religion	233		Services of Megabazus	237
	Nature of the Rebellions	233	506.	Thrace and Macedonia	238
	Babylon twice taken	234	500.	The Ionian Revolt	238
	Revolt of Media	234	490.	Invasion of Greece	238
	And of other Provinces	234		Battle of Marathon	238
	Of Orœtes in Lydia	235	487.	Revolt of Egypt	238
	Of Aryandes in Egypt	235	486 (Dec. 23).	Death of Darius	238

CHAPTER XXXVIII.

THE DECLINE AND FALL OF THE PERSIAN EMPIRE. XERXES I. TO DARIUS III. FROM B.C. 486 TO B.C. 330.

		PAGE			PAGE
486 (Dec. 23).	Accession of Xerxes I.	239	425 (Dec. 17).	Xerxes II. reigned 45 days	241
	Meaning of the Name	239	424.	Murdered by Sogdianus	241
	He reconquers Egypt	239		Who is killed by Ochus, viz.	241
480.	Invasion of Greece	239		Darius II., Nothus	241
480–479.	Battles of Salamis, Platæa, and Mycalé	239		His wife Parysatis	241
	Revolt of Babylon	240		His sons Arsaces and Cyrus	241
	Its temples plundered	240		Cruelties of Parysatis	241
	The court of Xerxes	240		Continual rebellions	241
	The Book of Esther	240	408 (about).	Loss of Egypt	241
	Cruelties of Amestris	240	405.	Succession of Arsaces as	241
	Murder of Xerxes	240		Artaxerxes II., Mnemon	241
	Exhaustion of the Empire	240	401.	Cyrus the Younger	241
465 (Dec 7).	Artaxerxes I., Longimanus	240		His Attempt and Death	241
	Meaning of the Name	(note)		Xenophon and the 10,000	241
	Murders his brother Darius	240		Relations with Greece	241
	Defeats his brother Hystaspes	240	396–4.	Campaigns of Agesilaus	241
449.	Greek Colonies independent	240	387.	Peace of Antalcidas	241
	Rebellion of Egypt	240		Greek Colonies recovered	241
	Of Megabyzus in Syria	240	380.	Evagoras of Cyprus	242
	Of other Satraps	240		Failure in Egypt	242
	Loyalty of the Caunians	240		Rebellions and Confusion	242
458.	Commission of Ezra	240		Domestic Horrors	242
444.	And of Nehemiah	240		Artaxerxes dies, aged 94	242
				His Character and Biography	242

B.C.		PAGE
359.	Ochus, or Artaxerxes III...	242
	His abilities and cruelty	242
	Murder of royal princes	242
	The eunuch Bagoas	242
	Mentor and Memnon	242
	Revolt of Artabanus	242
	Mentor serves in Egypt	242
	Phœnicia and Cyprus revolt	242
	Reduction of Cyprus	242
	Destruction of Sidon	243
	Mentor serves under Ochus	243
346.	Reconquest of Egypt	243
	Philip threatens Persia	243
338.	Ochus poisoned by Bagoas	243
	Battle of Chæronea	243
	Arses, king of Persia	243
336.	Murdered by Bagoas	243
	Assassination of Philip	243

B.C.		PAGE
336.	Darius III., Codomannus	243
	His beauty and bravery	243
	He puts Bagoas to death	244
334.	Alexander attacks Persia	244
333.	Defeats Darius at Issus	244
331.	And finally at Arbela	244
330.	Murder of Darius	244
	Prophecy of Daniel	244
	End of the Persian Empire	244
	Constitution of the Empire	245
	System of *Satrapies*	245
	Powers of the Satraps	245
	The Military Force	245
	The *Royal Judges*	245
	Assessment of *Tribute*	246
	The *Royal Secretaries*	246
	Position of the Great King	246
	Assassination the only check	247

CHAPTER XXXIX.

The History of Phœnicia. Part I.—To the time of Tyre's Supremacy.

	PAGE
Importance of Phœnicia	248
Its commerce carried Civilisation and *Letters* from the East to the West	248
The strip of Coast	249
Headlands and Harbours	249
Its length and Breadth	249
Rivers of Phœnicia	249
Egyptian and Assyrian Monuments at the *Nahr-el-Kelb*	249
The coast-road and *Climaces*	250
Natural barriers	250
Climate and Productions	250
The chain of Lebanon	251
Its forests and cedars	251
Beasts, fisheries, and mines	252
The Tyrian purple	252
Early Biblical Notices	252
The Phœnician Canaanites	252
Their own native name	252
Immigrants from the East	252
Time of the Migration	253
Their Language Semitic	253
Precedence of Sidon	253
Phœnicians called Sidonians	253
Their other settlements	254

	PAGE
Arca and Orthosia	254
Gebal or Byblus	254
Berytus on the Lycus	255
Aradus and Antaradus	255
Hamath (Epiphania)	255
Kingdom of Hamath	256
Tyre, the island city	256
Palætyrus, or *Sarra*	256
The joint colony of Tripolis	256
Acco (Ptolemais) *Ace*	257
The Egyptian domination	257
14th cent. (about). Contemporary account of Phœnicia under Rameses II	257
State of Sidon and Byblus	258
Colonies and Commerce	259
Decline of power at sea	259
Phœnicia not included in the conquests of Israel	260
Her peaceful policy	260
1300 (about). Sidon taken by the Philistines	260
Supremacy of Tyre	260
Federal Constitution	261
Tyrian navy and army	261
Colonies of Tyre	261

CHAPTER XL.

The History of Phœnicia. Part II.—From the age of David and Hiram to the taking of Tyre by Alexander. About B.C. 1050 to B.C. 332.

	PAGE
List of Tyrian kings	263
1050.* Abibaal, father of Hiram	264
1025. Hiram allied with David	264

	PAGE
Common interests of Phœnicia and Israel	264
Alliance with Solomon	265

---

* These dates are only approximate.

CONTENTS.   xxi

B.C.		PAGE
	Tyrian Manufactures	265
	Hiram's buildings at Tyre ..	265
	Dynastic Troubles..	265
941.	ETHBAAL, father of *Jezebel* ..	266
903.	MATGEN	266
871.	PYGMALION and DIDO	266
	Foundation of *Carthage* ..	266
1100 seq.	Relations with Assyria ..	267
886–745.	Phœnicia tributary to Asshur-nasir-pal and his successors	267
	Objects found at Nimrud ..	267
	Phœnician Weights	267
	Nature of the connection ..	268
824–786.	Thalassocracy of Phœnicia	
745 seq.	New Assyrian Monarchy ..	268
742.	*Hiram II.* of Tyre and *Sibitbaal* of Gebal subject to Tiglath-pileser II.	268
731.	Twenty-three vassal kings ..	268
730.	*Muthon* rebels and submits ..	268
	Loss of Sicily, except three towns	268
726.	*Elulœus*, king of Tyre	268
	He reduces Cyprus	268
720.	Sargon conquers Phœnicia ..	269
715.	Resistance of Tyre	269
	Great naval victory	269
	Her supremacy lost	269
	The Parians take Thasos ..	269
708.	Sargon conquers Cyprus ..	269
	His *stela* at Citium	269
	Phœnicia revolts again.. ..	269
700.	Reconquered by Sennacherib	269
	His *stela* at the *Nahr-el-Kelb*	269
	Ethbaal, vassal king of Tyre	269
680.	Revolt of Phœnicia under *Abdi-Milkut*, king of Sidon	269
	Quelled by Esar-haddon ..	269
667.	Revolt on his death	270
666.	Reduced by Asshur-bani-pal Resistance of Aradus	270
610.	Alliance with Egypt	270
	The fleet serves Neco	270
604.	Submission to Babylon.. ..	270
	Resistance of Tyre..	270
588–75 ?	Siege by Nebuchadnezzar..	270
584.	Prophetic descriptions of Tyre	270
	Occasion of the prophecies ..	271
	Jealousy towards Judah ..	271
	Capture of Old Tyre	272
	Baal a vassal king..	272
	Apries attacks Phœnicia ..	272
	Inscription on the sarcophagus of *Esmunazar*, king of Sidon	273
	Supremacy of Sidon	273
	Revolutions at Tyre	273
563.	*Suffetes* or "Judges"	273
555.	*Meherbaal* vassal to Nabonadius, king of Babylon ..	273
551.	*Hiram III.*, king of Tyre ..	273
531.	*Muthon*, his son	273
529.	Phœnicia submits to Persia ..	273
	Their ships her chief sea force	274
	Refuse to serve Cambyses against Carthage	274
	Friendship with the Jews ..	274
480.	Favour of Xerxes to Sidon ..	274
	Later history under Persia ..	274
	Evagoras takes Tyre	274
350.	Sidon destroyed by Ochus ..	274
333.	Opens her gates to Alexander	275
	Submission of other cities ..	275
333–2.	Siege of Tyre..	275
	Massacre and slavery	275
	Later history of Phœnicia under Seleucidæ, Romans, and Mahometans	275
	Tyre and Sidon flourish ..	276
A.D. 12th cent.	Tyrian *glass* famous	276
	Decline from the Crusades ..	276
	Christian kingdom of Tyre ..	276
	Acre taken by the Saracens ..	276
1291.	Tyre abandoned	276
	Her later desolation	276
	Her present state	276
	Fulfilment of prophecy.. ..	276
	State of Sidon	277
	Phœnician Remains	277
	Sarcophagus of Esmunazar ..	277
	Tripoli, Beyrut, and Acre ..	278
	Notice of CARTHAGE	278
B.C. 146.	Epoch marked by her fall	278

LIST OF ILLUSTRATIONS.

Damascus .. .. FRONTISPIECE.

Alexander the Great as Ammon.. .. .. TITLE-PAGE.

An Assyrian Standard .. .. BACK OF TITLE.

Names of Pharaohs of XIXth Dynasty .. .. Page vii.

	PAGE
Cattle during the Inundation	1
A Funeral Service	6
Scribe at his Writing-table	7
Egyptian Walking-sticks..	12
Plucking Grapes in a Vineyard ..	13
Egyptian Wig	17
Pyramids during the Inundation ..	18
Hieroglyph of Menes..	19
Diagram of Great Pyramid	24
Cooking Geese and Joints	26
Egyptian Tumblers	32
Modes of gathering Corn	38
Asiatic Enemies of Egypt	39
The two Colossi of Thebes	46
The Son of King Rameses with his Charioteer	54
Phalanx of the Kheta and Fortified Town	57
Egyptian War Galley in Action ..	62
Guard with a Lantern	67
An Ethiopian Princess	68
Egyptian Shrine or Ark	75
Egyptian Buffoons	82
Siphons used by the Egyptians ..	87
Bronze Figure of Apis	88
Priests clad in the Leopard's Skin ..	95
The Mesopotamian Plain..	105
Early Assyrian Chariot	109
A Babylonian Tomb..	110
Diagram of a Temple Tower	113
Mugheir Temple	115
Assyrians (Nimrud)..	116
Royal Bracelet (Khorsabad)	120
Mound of Nebbi-Yunus	121
Statue of Shalmaneser II.	126
Arched Drain (Nimrud)	131
Plan of the Mound of Nimrud ..	133
Assyrian Sacred Tree	137
Prisoners presented by the Chief Eunuch	138
Black Obelisk, from Nimrud	139

	PAGE
Captive Women in a Cart..	143
Siege of a City and Captives Impaled..	144
Groom and Horses (Khorsabad) ..	149
Assyrian Temple with Ionic Capitals..	155
King and Attendants (Khorsabad)..	162
Cart drawn by Mules (Koyunjik) ..	165
Dog modelled in Clay (Koyunjik) ..	166
King travelling in a mountainous Country	172
King, Queen, and Attendants (Koyunjik)	173
Priest-Vizier presenting Captives to a King of Babylon..	177
Babylonian Brick with a Cuneiform Inscription	184
The Kasr, or Palace of Nebuchadnezzar	185
Men and Monsters (from a Cylinder)	193
Aryan Physiognomy (Persepolis) ..	194
A Mede or Persian wearing a Collar and Earrings (Persepolis)	199
The Rock of Behistun	200
Sculptures on the Rock	205
Ruins of Sardis	206
Coin of Sardis	211
Persian King on his Throne	212
Staircase of Artaxerxes (Persepolis)	217
Tomb of Cyrus (Pasargadæ)	218
Mound of Susa	223
Ordinary Persian Costume	230
Persian King hunting the Lion ..	231
Ruins of a Massive Gateway (Istakr)	239
Staircase at Persepolis (restored) ..	247
Grand Range of Lebanon..	248
Phœnician Bireme (Koyunjik) ..	262
Palmyra	263
Bronze Lion Weight, from Nimrud	267
Coin of Tyre	278

SMALLER ANCIENT HISTORY.

Cattle during the Inundation.

BOOK I.

EGYPT AND ETHIOPIA.

CHAPTER I.

THE LAND AND ITS RIVER.

EGYPT *is wholly the gift of the Nile.* These words of Herodotus, the "father of history," describe the real limits of the country, as well as the bounty of the river.

The vast belt of sandy desert which stretches across northern Africa and central Asia, from the Atlantic to the eastern shores of Tartary, is severed by the three chasms of the Nile-valley, the Red Sea, and the Persian Gulf.

Geology shows that the first of these was probably once, like the other two, an arm of the sea, from the bottom of which it has been raised, together with the adjoining isthmus of Suez. But, during the course of human history, the country has shewn the same chief features, and there is no ground for the notion that the deposits of the Nile have gradually redeemed its valley from the sea.

The great puzzle of antiquity—" to search out the sources of the Nile"—has been solved, or nearly so, within the last few years. If not its sources, the great reservoirs from which it flows, have been found in the lakes called the Victoria and Albert Nyanza.

From the latter the main stream, or *White River*, issues in 31° 25' E. long. and 2° 45' N. lat.; and flows northward, increased by numerous tributaries, for about 1000 miles to *Khartûm*. Here it receives the *Blue River* (the ancient Astapus), and about 170 miles lower the *Black River* (*Tacazzé* or *Atbarah*, the ancient Astaboras): names derived from the earthy matters which these turbid streams wash down from the highlands of Abyssinia to deposit on the soil of Egypt. The part of Ethiopia enclosed between these tributaries was called the island of MEROË, and was the seat of a great sacerdotal kingdom, connected by kindred and customs with Egypt, over which it once ruled for a short time.

Below its confluence with the *Atbarah*, the Nile completes the second half of its course without receiving a single tributary. Its circuitous passage through the rocky slopes of Nubia is marked by a series of rapids, which the Greeks called *Cataracts*: and the lowest of these, called the *First Cataract* (to those ascending the river), has always formed the proper southern boundary of Egypt. It lies between the islets of Philæ and Elephantine, a little above 24° N. latitude, scarcely more than half a degree outside of the Tropic of Cancer. Hence it happened that a person looking almost, but not quite, perpendicularly down a well, at the noon of the longest day, could see the sun reflected in the water.

From this point the alluvial plain which forms the soil of Egypt, and through which the river flows between high banks of mud, is bordered first by hills of shifting sand, and shut in beyond them by two ranges of mountains, which divide it from the Arabian Desert on the east and the Libyan Desert on the west—regions which the ancients assigned respectively to Arabia and Libya.

These mountains, which attain the height of from 1000 to 1200 feet opposite to Thebes, are of granite along the upper course of the river, and of limestone lower down. The average breadth of the valley is about 7 miles (varying from 2 miles to 10), as far as the Pyramids and Memphis, where the two ranges part to the east and west, opening up that triangular termination to the valley, which the Greeks named from the form of their letter *Delta* (Δ).

On entering this alluvial plain the river branched out into seven mouths, of which only two are now navigable. Their sluggish waters formed marshes, which more than once afforded refuge to native princes from foreign conquest. The coast-line of the Delta is fringed with extensive lakes. Its surface is intersected by numerous canals, dug by the troops of captives whom the kings brought home after their successful foreign wars. The extent of the Delta was about 100 miles from north to south, and 200 miles along the coast.

The valley of the Nile, north of the First Cataract, was the same thing as the land of Egypt. An oracle of Ammon, the chief deity of the land, defined the Egyptians to be the people who dwelt below the Cataracts, and drank of the water of the Nile. On the map it resembles a funnel with a long pipe, or—to use a less homely figure—its own native lotus-flower spreading out from its long stem.

Hence the natural division of the country, in all ages, into *Upper* and *Lower Egypt*. The former is the long narrow valley, shut in by the Arabian and Libyan hills, nearly as far as Memphis: the latter is the Delta. This division is denoted by the *dual form* of the Hebrew name *Mizraim*, that is, "the two Mizrs;" for to this day the Arabs, who now possess the land, call it *Misr*. The old kings of Egypt bore the title of "Lord of the Upper and Lower country," and they wore a double crown called *Pshent*, adorned with the papyrus and lotus, as emblems of Lower and Upper Egypt. Upper Egypt was also called the *Thebaid*, from its capital, Thebes. A certain portion of the country above Memphis was sometimes distinguished by the name of *Middle Egypt*. This region, in which lay the famous *Lake of Mœris*, and the palace of the *Labyrinth*, was also called the *Heptanomis* or *Seven Nomes*. The *Nomes* were the districts (like cantons or counties) into which all Egypt was divided, each containing the land belonging to a city.

This formation of the country gave its people a security and isolation which distinguished them from all other nations. Besides the narrow entrance down the valley from the south, Egypt lay open only on the three sides of the Delta. The coast could, of course, be attacked only by a maritime power; and no great conquering navy grew up for many ages. The eastern and western sides, though undefended by great rivers or mountains, were protected by deserts even harder to be crossed. On the west there was little danger from the Libyan barbarians; and almost all the foreign wars of Egypt, whether as invader or invaded, were waged with the Ethiopians to the south of the Cataract, and the Asiatics to the east of the Delta. In such wars, for a period of from 1000 to 2000 years, she was, with two great exceptions, the aggressor and the conqueror.

This isolation and security gave a singular character of permanence to the people and their institutions. While other lands were constantly changing their inhabitants, the Egyptians remained stationary in the valley where they at first settled, cultivating the arts of agriculture and peace, and retaining the civilization which they were among the first of the peoples to acquire. We shall see, as we proceed, the contrast presented by the revolutions that followed one another in the more open valley of the Tigris and Euphrates, surrounded by the homes of warlike and conquering races.

The country, thus guarded by its rocky ranges and broad deserts, was fertilized and vivified by its beneficent River, like a great life-giving artery, ever pulsating within its narrow limits: for the periodic rise and fall of the Nile, which distinguished it from all the other rivers of the world, gives Egypt its very existence. Other rivers, indeed, overflow and fertilize the surrounding lands, but their capricious inundations often carry desolation to life and property. The Nile alone rises at regular intervals, and spreads over its valley at once a fertilizing deposit and the water without which no agriculture can exist, especially in a hot climate.

We must not stay to entertain our readers with the amusing reasons which the ancients guessed at for the inundation: as—to name but one—that the sun, driven southwards by the northern blasts of winter, dried up the sources of the river, which filled again as he returned northward to his proper course in summer! The true cause is found in the periodic rains which follow the course of the vertical sun within the tropics. Falling on the mountains of Ethiopia, these rains swell the confluents of the Nile, which begins to rise in Egypt after the summer solstice (June 21st). During July the waters mount higher and higher every day. About the middle of August the dams are cut, and the water is allowed to flow out of the canals which lead it to the further limits of the valley. The greatest height is reached in September, and after about a fortnight the water gradually retires to its ordinary bed. During the inundation, the land bears the aspect of a vast lake, out of which the towns—standing on hills or artificial embankments—rise like islands.

When the waters subside, they leave behind a thick black mud, which is superior to the richest manure, and produces extraordinary crops with hardly any cultivation. The ground requires neither plough nor spade to prepare it for the seed, which, after being scattered upon the soil and trodden in by cattle, springs up rapidly under the hot sun of that climate. It was this which made Egypt the granary of the ancient world, from the time of the Jewish patriarchs to the downfall of the Roman Empire, and which still keeps it a great corn-growing country.

But this inundation is subject to variations of degree, which are the more dangerous from the very reliance placed on its regularity. The rise has been always watched with the deepest anxiety, and at various places there were "Nilometers"—stone pillars divided into cubits and palms—to measure its height. An ancient one is

still to be seen at Elephantine; that at Cairo is of the times of the
Caliphs. The rise of " a good Nile " is about 24 feet. If it much
exceeds this, the floods sweep away houses, people, and cattle, and
leave the ground too sodden for the seed. If it falls below 18 feet,
" the lean kine," the years of famine, " eat up the fat kine," the
years of plenty; nay, the wretched peasants have been known to
eat each other. But both these extremes are rare.

The exuberant fertility of the well-watered and ever-virgin soil
secures that surplus of food which at once promotes population,
stimulates the production of luxuries, and gives leisure for the
cultivation of art and science. The labour and forethought required to secure the easy harvest, to store up food to last while
the fields were covered, and to protect their dwellings from the
flood, preserved the Egyptians from the idleness common in fertile
lands. Nay more, the circumstances of the inundation had a direct
tendency to call forth their inventive powers. To calculate the
time of its recurrence required a knowledge of *Astronomy;* and the
Egyptians are said to have first discovered the true length of the
year from the sun's path among the stars. The art of *Geometry*
was needed to restore the landmarks swept away by the inundation. *Engineering* was required to carry the flood to lands beyond
its natural reach, in order to provide for an increase of population.
Canals were dug to conduct the water where it was wanted, and
its course was controlled by sluices, dykes, and similar means. Of
certain other great works of engineering connected with the river,
we shall have to speak in the proper place. *Navigation,* in the
wider sense, was never much cultivated by the Egyptians; but
their river and canals made them boatmen from the earliest times.

Next to an abundant supply of food, social prosperity depends
on easy means of communication. One of the greatest difficulties
with which an infant state has to struggle is the absence of roads;
and till these are made, each part of the community must remain
isolated, and dependent upon itself for the supply of its wants.
But the Egyptians had from the beginning a natural " silent
highway "—broad, level, uninterrupted, and adapted, by a curious
provision of nature, for traffic as well up as down the stream. The
northerly winds from the Mediterranean, which enable vessels to
ascend the river, prevail during three-quarters of the year, and
blow most steadily during the inundation, when the stream is
strongest. These winds were called by the Greeks *Etesian* or
yearly winds.

Even the moral and religious ideas of the Egyptians were in-
fluenced by the river, to which they felt that they owed their very
existence, as well as all the blessings which it redeemed for them

from the devouring desert.   Hence there was ever before their eyes
a struggle between *Life* and *Death*.   The Nile, never growing old,
renewing its life every year, and calling forth nature into a new
and vigorous existence, was the symbol of Life.   The Desert, with
its sombre hues, its unchanging appearance, its deadening and
desolating influence, was the symbol of Death.   By a personification of these contending powers, the Nile, representing Life, became
the Good Power, or *Osiris*; the Desert, representing Death, the Evil
Power, or *Typhon*.

On the margin of the valley, too, the Egyptians buried their
dead, beyond the reach of the inundation.   Preserved by the
climate and by the practice of embalmment, the ever-growing
numbers of the departed seemed to hem in the fleeting generation,
and to keep always before them the idea of death—but of a death
free from corruption, and ready for the renewal of life.   While on
the margin of their valley they were disputing the means of existence with the devouring sand, they were also disputing with
corruption their own persons and immortality.   The present age
seemed only a small moment in time; while the other world
appeared vast, unlimited, and eternal.   Accordingly, this life was
regarded by the Egyptians as only a preparation for a higher and
better state of existence.

A Funeral Service.

Scribe with his inkstand upon the table. One pen is put behind his ear, and he is writing with another.

CHAPTER II.

THE MONUMENTS OF EGYPT, AND THEIR HISTORICAL VALUE.

THE same hope of immortality, which led the Egyp'ians to preserve the bodies of their dead by the process of embalmment impelled them to construct monuments, which are at once the most ancient, the most massive, and the most durable, that the world has ever seen. Those monuments, too, bear the impress of the religious character of the people. All is stately, solemn, and of majestic simplicity, as became the works of those who were building for eternity.

Here again the nature of their country came to their aid. The rocks on either side of the river yielded an unlimited supply of stone, of almost every variety, for the Egyptian workman; while the Nile afforded the ready means of conveying the largest masses from one part of the country to another. In ascending the Nile from the Delta, two parallel courses of *limestone* accompany the traveller for a long distance; and from these were hewn the blocks which were piled up to form the famous pyramids, besides the materials of many other buildings. A little above Thebes began the red *sandstone*, of which most of the Egyptian temples were built. In the neighbourhood of Syene, the particular kind of *granite* appears, to which the name of *syenite* has been given; and on the eastern bank of the river are the granite quarries, from which the obelisks and colossal statues have been hewn. One obelisk still remains there, cut out but never removed from its native rock.

In the mountainous district between the Nile and the Red Sea there is a still greater variety. Here are found quarries of white marble, of porphyry, of basalt, and of the fine green breccia, which is known by the name of *Verde d'Egitto*. The same district was rich in other mineral treasures; in gold, emerald, iron, copper, and lead.

The Egyptians must have possessed *iron* at an early period, since without it they could not have worked the hard rocks of the granite quarries. They found this metal, as well as copper, in the peninsula of Sinai, where we still see the refuse of the mines which were worked under their earliest kings.

Besides the monuments themselves, the Egyptians have left for us the sculptured and painted views of the processes by which they were constructed. Groups of labourers are seen carving and polishing colossal statues, and dragging them on rollers to the vessels in which they were floated down the Nile; whilst inscriptions tell us the number of men employed, and the time taken on the voyage.

Other pictures show the whole process of making the *bricks*, which were largely used in the construction of walls and fortresses, such as the "treasure cities, Pithom and Raamses," which the captive Israelites built for their great oppressor. One striking picture exhibits, not indeed the Israelites themselves, but captives of a kindred race under an earlier Pharaoh, kneading the clay, and moulding it into bricks, which are carried in boxes slung from a yoke across the shoulders. The "taskmasters" either stand over the labourers armed with sticks, or apply the bastinado to a prostrate workman. Even so "the officers of the children of Israel, which Pharaoh's taskmasters had set over them, were beaten, and demanded, Wherefore have ye not fulfilled your task in making bricks?" (*Exodus* v. 14).

All public buildings, temples, palaces, and other monuments—except in the very earliest period—were covered with sculptured reliefs and pictures of the deeds of the sovereigns who erected them, and of religious subjects. Nor is this all: even from the early periods at which the public monuments present blank surfaces, the internal walls of the tombs are adorned with pictures, in which the deceased is made to live over again his life on earth. Besides their inestimable value, as placing the actual life of Egypt before our eyes, these tombs, closed up since their first completion, are even more trustworthy than the public monuments, many of the records of which have been defaced—records which, even when perfect, may have been falsified in the interest of the priestly scribes, or to glorify despotic kings.

Thus far we have spoken of sculptures and pictures; but these are a riddle without some written interpretation. It is our possession of this that has lately given to the history of Egypt the charm of an unveiled mystery. While still a mystery, it had a peculiar attraction, especially from its connection with the earliest records of the Bible. Egypt was already a powerful kingdom when visited by Abraham, a mere wayfarer in the land promised to his children ; and the Exodus, which first made Israel a nation, falls under an advanced period of the Egyptian monarchy. But the reader who looks to his Bible for the history of Egypt will be greatly disappointed. Nothing can be more vivid and more truthful than its scenes of Egyptian life and manners ; but the history, which these touches enliven, is only that of " Israel in Egypt." There is no history of the country itself, and the very identity of the kings is concealed under the common title of Pharaoh.[1] " Egypt, in fact, appears as the instrument of Providence for furthering its eternal purpose, but only as forming the background and contrast to that free spiritual and moral element which was to arise out of Israel " (Bunsen).

But when Moses, in his training as the son of Pharaoh's daughter, was learning in Egypt the writing which he used for the Pentateuch, that art had been employed for centuries to perpetuate the native records. Embedded in the centre of the Great Pyramid, which is older than the time of Abraham, we see not only written characters, preserving the names of the kings who built it, but characters of such a form as to prove that the art was far advanced, and already applied to the commonest uses. The names, which have evidently been painted roughly on the stones while still in the royal quarries—like the " broad arrow " of our own government—are not in that earliest style of picture-writing called " hieroglyphics," but in the freer hand called " cursive." Of these various forms and of the whole system of Egyptian writing, we shall speak among the other arts and sciences of Egypt.

In the tombs of the same age we have a still more striking proof of the advanced state of the art. There we already see the hieroglyphic symbol which denotes " writing "—the *ink-pot* and *reed pen*, with the *palette* on which the scribe spread his thick carbonaceous *ink*, which has lasted to the present day, together with the *paper* on which it was written. For, as if to crown the natural gifts which marked Egypt as the earliest home of civilization, her beneficent river supplied her with the *papyrus* reed,

<hr>

[1] We may as well state, thus early, that this word, so familiar to us from our Bibles, is not a *name*, but a *royal title*. Its exact etymology and meaning are disputed ; the interpretation most generally received explains it as " the son of *Ra* " (*i.e.* the Sun-god).

the Latin name of which gives us our word *paper*, and its Greek name, *byblus*, the word for *book*, perpetuated in our *Bible* (THE BOOK). The stem of the papyrus was split, and its inner membrane spread out into long leaves, about 3 palms in width, and joined with gluten into a long strip, which could be rolled up into a *volume* (Lat. *volumen*, a *roll*), and can still be unrolled without cracking. The writing was from right to left,[2] in the direction of the *length* of the strip, and in lines of convenient length about 6 or 8 inches), arranged in columns, which also succeeded each other from right to left. The whole length of the slip, or—in other words—the size of the volume, was of course governed by the matter to be contained in the book.

These *papyri*—as they are called for the sake of distinction—have been for the most part preserved in the closed tombs and the mummy-cases of the dead. Those placed in libraries above ground —as in the great "Hall of Books," which Rameses II. (the Pharaoh under whom Moses was born) attached to his palace at Thebes— have of course perished. They are for the most part *religious*, as is natural from the places of their deposit; but some are *historical* and *official* documents, of immense value for Egyptian history. Others contain *poems* and *romances*; and among these it is startling to find a *fairy tale*—the oldest in the world—composed for the Pharaoh of the Exodus, when a young prince, by order of his father, the great oppressor of the Israelites.

These books, together with the carved inscriptions with which the monuments are covered, have been well described as "a library of stones and papyri in myriads of volumes." Of the wonderful discovery, by which their unknown characters and language have been deciphered within our own memory, we shall speak in its proper place. Their production, multiplicity, and preservation will be best described in the words of two of the most eminent students of their contents.

Dr. Lepsius, who has published the best collection of the Egyptian monuments, arranged in chronological order, speaks thus:—"An intense desire after posthumous fame and a place in history seems to have been universal in ancient Egypt. This exhibits itself in the incredible multitude of monuments of all descriptions, which have been found in the valley of the Nile. All the principal cities of Egypt were adorned with temples and palaces. Towns of lesser note, and even villages, were always distinguished by one temple at least—oftener more.

"These temples were filled with the statues of gods and kings,

---

[2] The writing engraved on the monuments is also *sometimes* in horizontal lines, either from right to left, or from left to right, but more usually in vertical columns.

generally colossal, and hewn from costly stones. Their walls, also, within and without, were covered with coloured reliefs. To adorn and maintain these public buildings was at once the duty and pride of the kings of Egypt. But even these were rivalled by the more opulent classes of the people in their care for the dead, and in the hewing and decoration of sepulchral chambers. In these things the Egyptians very far surpassed the Greeks and Romans, as well as other known nations of antiquity.

"Still further to enhance to after times the value of these ever-during monuments of ancient Egypt, it was universal with the inhabitants to cover their works of art of every description with hieroglyphics, the purport of which related strictly to the monuments on which they were inscribed. No nation that ever lived on the earth has made so much use of its written system, or applied it to a purpose so strictly historical, as ancient Egypt. There was not a wall, a platform, a pillar, an architrave, a frieze, or even a door-post, in an Egyptian temple, which was not carved, within, without, and on every available surface, with pictures in relief. There is not one of these reliefs that is not history; some of them representing the conquests of foreign nations; others the offerings and devotional exercises of the monarch by whom the temple, or portion of the temple, on which the relief stood, had been constructed. Widely different from the temples of Greece and Rome, on which inscriptions were evidently regarded as unwelcome additions, forming no part of the original architectural design, but, on the contrary, interfering with and marring it—the hieroglyphic writings were absolutely essential and indispensable to the decoration of a perfect Egyptian temple.

"This writing, moreover, was by no means confined to constructions of a public nature, such as temples or tombs, but was also inscribed on objects of art of every other conceivable description. Nothing, even down to the palette of a scribe, the style with which a lady painted her eye-lashes with powdered antimony, or even a walking-stick, was deemed too insignificant to be inscribed with the name of its owner, and a votive dedication of the object itself to his patron divinity. Inscriptions with the names of the artists or owners, so rare on the remains of Greece and Rome, are the universal rule in Egyptian art. There was no colossus too great, and no amulet too small, to be inscribed with the name of its owner, and some account of the occasion on which it was executed."

Of the wonderful preservation of these records for historic use, Baron Bunsen thus speaks:—"No nation of the earth has shown so much zeal and ingenuity, so much method and regularity, in recording the details of private life, as the Egyptians. No country in the world has afforded greater facilities for indulging such a propensity than Egypt, with its limestone and granite, its dry climate, and the protection afforded by its desert against the overpowering force of nature in southern zones. Such a country was adapted, not only for securing its monuments against dilapidation, both above and below ground, for thousands of years, but even for preserving them as perfect as the day they were erected. In the North, rain and frost corrode; in the South, the luxuriant vegetation cracks or obliterates the monuments of time. China has no architecture to bid defiance to thousands of years; Babylon had but bricks; in India the rocks can barely resist the wanton power of nature. Egypt is the monumental land of the earth, as the Egyptians are the monumental people of history. Their *contemporary* records, therefore, are at once the earliest and most certain source of all Egyptian research."

It is to the existence of these contemporary records that Egypt owes her place as the *first country that has a history*; for the records of man's primeval life, in the book of *Genesis*, are not the history of a nation. History treats of the human race as civilized, and as organized into political societies, and it begins only when it can be based upon contemporary records. Hence we must carefully distinguish between those monuments which are contemporary with the events recorded on them, and those which are of a later date. An inscription or sculpture carved in stone is not necessarily more trustworthy than a written book, nor the latter than an oral tradition. Often, indeed, tradition perpetuates truths which formal records have obscured. The sculptured shrines, in which Thothmes III. and Rameses II. (the greatest kings of the most flourishing period of the Theban Monarchy) are represented as adoring a long series of their royal ancestors, and the list of kings in the Turin papyrus, also of the date of Rameses II., are invaluable records of the traditions which had come down to that age about the monarchy; but still their value is vastly below that of the pictures and inscriptions and papyri, which record contemporary events. How far we possess such authorities for the successive periods of Egyptian history, will appear as we proceed.

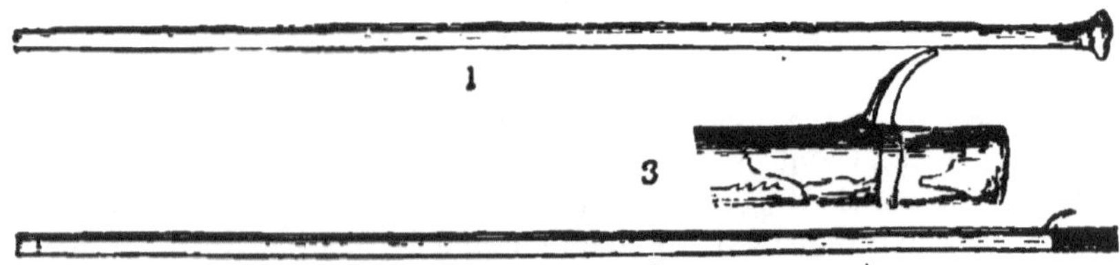

Egyptian Walking-sticks.

Plucking grapes in a vineyard; the vines trained in bowers.

CHAPTER III.

EPOCHS OF EGYPTIAN HISTORY.

THE real history of Egypt, and of the ancient world. begins with her most ancient *Pyramids*. It is not merely that these wonderful structures come forward on the page of history as the oldest works of man—just as their forms rise upon the traveller's sight across the plain of Egypt, exciting never-failing admiration ;—but, just as their real grandeur is only seen on a near approach, so their true historic significance was only revealed when the names of their builders were found inscribed upon them. It is this which justifies Lepsius's description of the most ancient of them all as " the Pyramid of Cheops, *to which the first link of our monumental history is fastened immovably*, not only for Egyptian, but for Universal History."

There is, indeed, a traditional history of Egypt, beginning from a far earlier time, which must not be treated with contempt. All traditions deserve examination by the light of probability and known facts ; but they can only be accepted as *history*, when they may be traced up to contemporaneous sources. Such traditions were preserved by the Egyptian priests, who were the depositaries of all learning, and who imparted to curious travellers just as much of them as they pleased.

Foremost among such travellers, who have left us the result of their enquiries, was HERODOTUS OF HALICARNASSUS, who lived in the middle of the 5th century B.C. The plan on which he related the causes and events of the great wars between Persia and Greece led him to devote a whole book of his history to an account of Egypt, and he visited that country to collect information, which he obtained almost wholly from the priests.

Unable to read their books or the inscriptions on the monuments, he must have often misunderstood them, and must often have been imposed upon. For it was their habit to falsify, or to put a gloss upon, the calamitous events of their history, and they kept back certain kinds of information through religious motives. Indeed, on this point Herodotus himself was very scrupulous, and he tells us that he avoided speaking about the gods, except only their names.

Nor does he give any full and connected account of the history of Egypt. Like a traveller writing home to his friends, he appears to select from his notes what was most interesting and amusing to himself; and his notes—like those of many later travellers—seem often to have got misplaced. Still his truthfulness is as conspicuous as the straightforward simplicity with which he tells his story, not without many a dash of quaint irony. An immense value is added to his testimony by the good faith with which he repeats statements that seemed incredible to himself, but which fuller information has explained. We should have lost many a gem of truth had he acted on any other principle than the following :— "Such as think the tales told by the Egyptians credible, are free to accept them for history. For my own part, I propose to myself, throughout my whole work, *faithfully to record* the traditions of the several nations."

Herodotus gathered most of his information from the priests of Memphis, and of Sais, the city of the Delta most frequented by the Greeks, and his descriptions apply chiefly to Lower Egypt. On the other hand, Diodorus Siculus (the Sicilian), who visited Egypt about 400 years later, records chiefly what he learned at Thebes, and he gives the history mostly of Upper Egypt. He supplies some things omitted by Herodotus, but is far inferior to him in fidelity and good sense.

When Egypt became subject to the Greek dynasty of the *Ptolemies*, those great patrons of learning wished to have her records in the Greek language. Under the second Ptolemy surnamed Philadelphus (B.C. 285–247), a native historian compiled a History of Egypt, in Greek, from the records laid up in the temples. This historian was Manetho, a priest of Sebennytus in the Delta. His 'History' is lost, except a few fragments; but the ancient writers on chronology have preserved his *Lists of Kings*, arranged in Thirty "Dynasties," with the numbers of years that the kings reigned and that the dynasties lasted.

We should only deceive the learner by repeating these lists, as if they were like those of the kings in the History of England. In their early part they are evidently fabulous; and the copyists have corrupted both the names and the numbers. While all the dynasties appear to succeed one another in order, from the First to the Thirtieth, there is good proof that some of them ruled contemporaneously in different parts of Egypt. Manetho registers only the names of kings recognized by the priests; and the monuments prove that he has made many omissions—just as if an English historian were to leave out the Commonwealth and Cromwell. He has also bridged over gaps caused by revolutions and foreign conquests; for it was a maxim of the Egyptian monarchy that " the king never dies," and to every Pharaoh another Pharaoh must immediately succeed.

But all these are only faults in a genuine record of the traditional history of the Egyptian Monarchy. They prevent our accepting the Lists ascribed to Manetho, unless they are confirmed by the monuments; but the Lists remain invaluable as an *index* or *skeleton*, by which to arrange the information gained from all sources.

The Dynasties of Manetho are named (with a very few exceptions) from the cities which were the seat of each. The chief of these were MEMPHIS, in Lower, and THEBES, in Upper Egypt, the capitals of Egypt in the two great epochs of her highest prosperity. From before the time of Abraham till after that of Joseph, the capital was at Memphis; but, during the latter part of this period, the country was subject to a foreign race from Asia—the "Shepherd Kings," who overthrew the native "Old Memphian Monarchy."

Before this, however, a new Kingdom—founded probably on an old one, which threw off the supremacy of Memphis—called the "Middle Monarchy," had gained strength in the Upper country, especially in the part afterwards called "Middle Egypt." Its kings at length expelled the Shepherds, and founded the "New Theban Monarchy," under which Egypt became the first of the great Eastern Empires, and to which belongs the time of Moses and the Exodus.

The decline of this empire gave room for the revival of various kingdoms in Lower Egypt, all of which, as well as that of Thebes, were overwhelmed by a second foreign conquest,—this time from Ethiopia. This age derives peculiar interest from the mention of its kings in Scripture *by their proper names*—no longer as mere *Pharaohs*—as warring with Judah and Assyria. Such are *Shishak*, who conquered Rehoboam; *Zerah the Cushite* (Ethiopian), who was defeated by Asa; and the Ethiopians, *So*—who espoused the cause of the last king of Israel against Assyria—and *Tirhakah*, who came out to fight against Sennacherib. That king's son, Esarbaddon, and his successor, Asshur-bani-pal, reduced Egypt, for a time, to vassalage under Assyria.

When the Assyrian Empire began to wane before the growing power of the Medes, a new Egyptian kingdom, founded by Psammetichus, revived much of the prosperity of the ancient dynasties. Having its capital at *Saïs*, on the western branch of the Nile—the branch chiefly used by voyagers from Greece—this monarchy gave a new character to Egyptian policy by the encouragement of Greek trade and the employment of Greek mercenaries. But this policy gave a fatal blow to the old national spirit, and so made the Persian conquest easier.

This period has a twofold interest, as being the first in which the Greeks wrote the history of Egypt from their own knowledge, and because of its connection with Scripture history. Unlike the shadowy forms of Menes and Mœris, Cheops and Cephrenes, Nitocris and Sesostris,—the Saïte kings, Psammetichus, Necho, Apries, and Amasis, stand out in the pages of Herodotus with a clear historic reality; and two of them appear in Scripture as connected with the last age of the Jewish monarchy—the *Pharaoh-Nechoh* who slew Josiah, deposed Jehoahaz, and was himself defeated by Nebuchadnezzar—and the *Pharaoh-Hophra* (Apries), whose league with Zedekiah provoked a destructive invasion from Babylon.

The conquest of Egypt by Cambyses (B.C. 527 or 525) put an end to the independent Egyptian monarchy, which had lasted (with but two partial interruptions, the Shepherd and Ethiopian conquests) for not less than 1500 or 2000 years—a duration unparalleled in the history of the world. But even within the two centuries of the Persian domination (B.C. 525-332) successful revolts restored Egypt to independence for about a third of the whole period (B.C. 414-353).

Egypt submitted to Alexander in B.C. 332; and, upon his death, the country became subject to the Hellenistic dynasty of the Ptolemies for just three centuries (B.C. 323-30). Its new capital on the Mediterranean—called *Alexandria*, after its founder—became a favoured seat of commerce and of Greek learning and civilization. But the Ptolemies conformed to the national religion and institutions, and inscribed their names in Egyptian characters upon new monuments, which were built in the ancient style.

The last of the Ptolemies was the famous Cleopatra, the power of whose charms, first over Cæsar, and then over Antony, seemed likely to make Egypt the seat of an Eastern Empire, and to raise Alexandria to the rank attained more than three centuries later by Constantinople. But the battle of Actium decided the supremacy of the West, and Egypt became a province of the Roman Empire under Augustus (B.C. 30).

Thus the ancient History of Egypt is divided into the following eight periods:—

I. The *Old Memphian Monarchy.*—Probably about B.C. 2000–1800 or 1750.

II. The *Middle Monarchy* and the *Shepherd Kings.*—Probably about B.C. 1800 or 1750–1500.

III. The *New Theban Monarchy.*—About B.C. 1500–1100.

IV. The *Kingdoms of the Delta*, and the *Ethiopian Conquest.*—About B.C. 1100–660.

V. The *Later Saïte Monarchy.*—B.C. 660 (or very nearly so) to 527 or 525.

VI. The *Persian Domination* (including the recovered independence of the 28th, 29th, and 30th Dynasties).—B.C. 527 or 525 to 332.

VII. The *Greek Dynasty of the Ptolemies.*—B.C. 323–30.

VIII. *Egypt under the Roman Empire,* till the *Arab Conquest.*—B.C. 30 to A.D. 640.

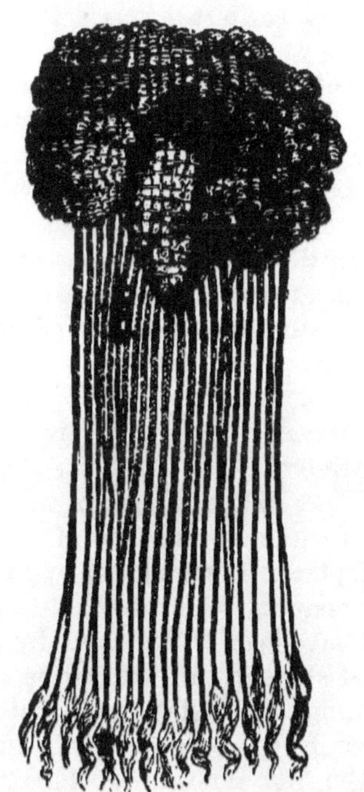

Egyptian Wig (about 2½ feet long).—*Berlin Museum.*

Pyramids during the Inundation.

CHAPTER IV.

THE OLD MEMPHIAN MONARCHY—THE PYRAMID KINGS.

THE traditions of Egypt—like those of Babylonia, China, and most eastern nations—claimed a fabulous antiquity for the nation, and made the gods its earliest kings. Perhaps this indicates a time when the priests were the rulers; or it may have been but a part of the same exalted idea of royal authority which afterwards regarded the kings as gods. The priests told Herodotus that for thousands of years Egypt had gods for its rulers, who dwelt upon the earth with men, one being always supreme above the rest. Manetho prefixes to his thirty dynasties of men one of gods and demigods, who reigned for nearly 25,000 years. This number was probably an imaginary cycle, connected with a system of technical chronology. We shall meet with a similar cycle (but of greater length) in the traditions of Babylonia.

The first man who reigned over Egypt was believed to be *Mna* or *Menai*, in Greek MENES. Some take his name to signify merely *Man*. He was a native of *This*, in Upper Egypt, and head of the *First Dynasty* of *Thinite Kings*. To him was ascribed the foundation of Memphis. He gained the site of the city and the great temple of *Phtha* (Hephæstus or Vulcan) by raising a dyke to force the Nile into a new channel. He was said to have made conquests in Ethiopia, and to have been killed there by a hippopotamus. In aftertimes, these first steps in the foundation of the kingdom were regarded as corruptions of a state of primitive simplicity; and a king, who felt that Egypt was declining, vented his regrets in a curse on Menes as the first innovator. This Tnephachthus, father of Bocchoris, who lived in the 8th century B.C., was the true type of the never-failing generation who "praise the time bygone."

Manetho's *Second Dynasty* is also *Thinite*, and seems to have a close connection with the *Third*, which is *Memphian*. To various kings of these three dynasties are ascribed the first elements of material civilization, science, religion, and legislation. Athothis, the son of Menes, is distinguished (like a king of the Third Dynasty, perhaps the same under another name) by the possession of great medical knowledge, the patronage of letters, and the first use of hewn stones in temple-building. Another king is celebrated as the first author of the sacred books; a third for the introduction of animal-worship, which is thus marked as an innovation; a fourth legalized the succession of women to the crown; and a fifth was a giant.

These traditions indicate the foundation of a civilized state in Egypt before the beginning of recorded history, with the germ of those political and religious institutions which endured for probably not less than 2000 years. They represent that state as having its origin in the valley of Upper Egypt; the narrow limits of which may have been the reason for fixing the capital at the site of Memphis, just where the valley opens out upon the Delta. When Memphis became the capital, the old city of This may have been for a time the seat of a viceroyalty of Upper Egypt, sometimes superseded by the direct rule of the Memphian king. This would account for the connection between the First and Second (*Thinite*) and the Third (*Memphian*) Dynasties.

The ground itself about Memphis bore witness, in historic times, to the preparation it required. The river appears to have divided about 14 miles above the city, and while its chief branch flowed close to the western sand-hills—through which a great part of the water ran to waste—the other branch was only sufficient to convert the Delta into a marsh. The " dyke of Menes " turned the current from the Libyan hills into the middle of the valley, where a bed of clay confined the water to its channel; and Memphis was built on the site thus gained upon the left bank. Herodotus tells us of the care with which the dyke was kept up in his time by the Persians, lest the inundation should burst upon Memphis; but all trace of it has been long since obliterated by the rise of the soil.

These works were real, though the kings to whom they were ascribed have for us only a traditional existence: they may have lived or they may not. The name of MENES is indeed found upon the monuments;[1] but only in a much later age. The carved hiero-

<hr>

[1] We give the hieroglyphic name of Menes as an example of the Egyptian mode of representing royal names within an oval frame or *cartouche*. The three characters stand for *m*, *n*, and *a* or *ai*, and the whole is read MNA or MENAI.

glyphs which make up the *name* on a tablet of Rameses II. (for example) are no more proof of the existence of Menes himself than the five letters which compose it on this printed page. The learner must not accept everything that is found upon a monument, but enquire *when* and *by whom* the record was made. The first records that we can trace to their authors are those, already mentioned, upon the stones of the Great Pyramid, and upon the walls of contemporary tombs.

But the works upon which we find these very records already testify in many ways to the existence of a mighty, wealthy, and highly civilized kingdom. Of that kingdom there can be no doubt that MEMPHIS was the seat, and its position was well fitted for the capital of all Egypt. One of its hieroglyphic titles is "the land of the pyramid;" another is "the abode of Phtha," its patron deity. Its Egyptian name, *Memfi*, *Membe*, or, more fully, *Men-nofre* (*station*, or *place*, *of the good*) is variously interpreted: perhaps it means both "the tomb of the good one (Osiris)," and "the harbour of the blessed," as the place to which the Egyptians were brought for burial.

And, as death rules in the history of the world, the necropolis of Memphis still exists, while the city of the living is only marked by shapeless mounds and the substructions of buildings covering a space of three leagues in circuit. The chief remaining monument is a fallen and mutilated colossus of Rameses II., which once adorned the great temple of the god *Phtha*. This statue, the height of which, when entire, is estimated at above 42 feet, lies prostrate in a trench amidst a grove of palm-trees, which shade the village of *Mitrahenny*, about 10 miles south of Cairo; but this modern capital is on the opposite—the east or right—bank of the river. The site of Memphis is also marked by another colossus of Rameses II., a tablet of the same king, with the title " Lord of the assemblies, like his father Phtha," and a few other statues and fragments of sculpture.

The traveller, who has searched out these few relics of the capital in which the Memphian kings held their state while alive, has only to lift his eyes to see their imperishable tombs standing out on the north-western horizon at the distance of several miles. In the religious philosophy of Egypt – as of most primitive nations—the dayspring of light and life was in the East; the West was the land of darkness and of death, the realm of *Amenti* (the Greek *Hades*). Thither they ferried their embalmed dead, in the boat which symbolized the sacred bark of Osiris, across the lake which was said to have been dug by Menes, to the vast Necropolis, which extended for about 15 miles along the foot-terraces of the Libyan range, from

Jizeh on the north to *Sakkara* on the south. This space contains about 30 tombs of the kings of Memphis, towering over the subterranean sepulchres of their subjects, above whom they had been unapproachably exalted during life.

All who have visited the Pyramids bear the same testimony to the emotions which they excite. We choose the description of Dean Stanley:—" The approach to the Pyramids (by one travelling westward from Cairo and the banks of the Nile) is at first a rich green plain, and then the Desert; that is, they are just at the beginning of the Desert, on a ridge which of itself gives them a lift above the valley of the Nile. It is impossible not to feel a thrill as one finds oneself drawing nearer to the greatest and most ancient monuments in the world, to see them coming out stone by stone into view, and the dark head of the Sphinx peering over the lower sandhills. Yet the usual accounts are correct, which represent this nearer sight as not impressive; their size diminishes, and the clearness with which you see their several stones strips them of their awful and mysterious character.   It is not till you are close under the Great Pyramid, and look up at the huge blocks rising above you into the sky, that the consciousness is forced upon you that this is *the nearest approach to a mountain that the art of man has produced*."

The emotions thus excited in minds of the highest order for nearly forty centuries form the justification of the builders. To those who talk of wasted labour, and calculate the miles of railway cutting and embankment to which the mass of the Great Pyramid is equal, it is enough to answer that that was not an age of railways, as ours is not an age of Pyramids. Each achievement is great in its own kind; and neither need be disparaged except when compared with moral triumphs:—

> " Wisdom alone outbuilds the Pyramids:
> Her monuments shall stand when Egypt's fall."

The dignity and durability required for monuments, which were also temples of deified kings, are secured by their vast solid mass and pyramidal form; but, more than this, the singular adaptation of that form to the country marks them as artistic works of the highest order. Seen over the level plain of Egypt, they have the effect of mountains; as a traveller observes—" they merely supply the otherwise flat-topped landscape with acute hill-points, without offering anything approaching to strongholds for war, or gathering-halls for peace." Like the cathedral spires of the middle ages, they are the landmarks of a vast space, which sets them before the eye in all their sacred dignity. Their huge mass is in harmony with all the objects that surround them, and with the very atmosphere through which they are seen. Hence they could dispense with decoration, which would only have injured their effect; and its absence, not only from the pyramids, but from a neighbouring temple, perhaps bears witness of an age anterior to image-worship.

With a few exceptions,[2] this type of monument is peculiar to the earliest ages of the Egyptian monarchy. The pyramids stand in groups along the western margin of the Nile valley, over a space of nearly 70 miles (30° to 29° N. lat.). Those which may safely be referred to the Necropolis of Memphis reach for about 20 miles, from the ruined pyramid of *Abou-Roash* on the north to the southern-most pyramid of *Dashoor*. The most interesting of all are the three large pyramids of *Jizeh*,[3] which were ascribed by Herodotus to kings whose names have now been found upon them, as well as in neighbouring monuments. They stand *en échelon*[4] on the plat-form of native rock, which raised them, like the rest of the Memphian necropolis, above the reach of the inundation. The north-easternmost is the " First" or " Great Pyramid" of Cheops (*Khufu* or *Shufu*); the next, which is nearly as large, is the " Second Pyramid " of Chephren (*Shafre*); the " Third," which is much smaller, but of choicer materials, is that of Mycerinus (*Menkaré*).

Like all the other pyramids, they have a square base, with its sides facing exactly to the cardinal points, and the entrance is in the northern side. In the beginning of the structure, indeed, the entrance was in the ground itself (usually solid rock), through which was hewn a sloping passage down to a chamber excavated in the rock to form the sepulchre itself. Over the position of this chamber the pyramid was built up of layers of huge blocks, rising above one another in steps: sometimes the central portion was a solid *core*, left when the living rock was cut down to form the base of the pyramid. The huge *steps* from stage to stage were filled in with smaller blocks, and the whole finally covered in to a uniform sloping surface by " casing-stones." A considerable portion of this casing still remains about the upper part of the " Second Pyramid."

By thus adding stage to stage, before the casing was finally put on, the structure could be enlarged to any degree; its base and height being extended together; and, as the " pyramid-kings "[5] prepared their tombs during their lives, the size of each pyramid is

----

[2] The pyramids in the " Island of Meroë," and other parts of Ethiopia, are later imitations of the old type.

[3] They are surrounded by a number of small ones.

[4] This is a military phrase, applied to squares falling back from one another, thus:—

[5] This is not a merely fanciful designation; for these kings are distinguished on the monuments by the addition of a pyramid △ to the hieroglyphics of their names.

thought to bear a proportion to the length of its builder's reign. When the base became so large as to cover the entrance of the subterranean passage, this passage was extended at the same slope through the masonry; and so the entrance was finally at some height above the ground. In the "Third Pyramid" there are two such passages, one above the other, leading down to two subterranean chambers; and there is good reason to believe that these were the respective sepulchres of Mycerinus, the builder of this pyramid, and of Nitocris, a queen of a later age.

In the "Great Pyramid," there is also an *ascending* passage, rising out of the descending passage some distance from the entrance, and ending in a sepulchral chamber in the very heart of the whole mass, in which stands the *sarcophagus* (*i. e.* flesh-consumer), or huge granite coffin, for containing the embalmed body of the king in its splendidly painted and gilded wooden coffin or mummy-case.[6] The sarcophagus must have been placed where it still stands during the progress of the building, and the mummy in its wooden coffin deposited in it afterwards. There is still a third chamber, lower down in the pyramid, approached by a horizontal branch from the ascending passage; and, as two kings—brothers, reigning together—seem to have been concerned in the building of the pyramid, the body of the one may perhaps have been deposited in this chamber by the survivor when the pyramid reached this height.

By a most ingenious contrivance, three huge blocks of stone (which must have been placed in the ascending passage before it was covered in) were let down, after the depositing of the king's body, so as to form a *plug* (or, as it is usually, but less accurately, called, a *portcullis*) to the mouth of the ascending passage. So effectual was this stopper that, when the Caliph Al-Mamoun entered the pyramid in search of hidden treasure (A.D. 830), he had to work round the obstacle by making a passage through the solid masonry of the pyramid; and by this passage all subsequent explorers have entered. Of its three chambers, the topmost, called by explorers the "Kings' Chamber," alone contains a sarcophagus, empty, and without a lid. It is generally supposed that no corpse was ever deposited there; and Herodotus states that Cheops was excluded from this tomb for his impiety and cruelty. But there is an un-

---

[6] The young reader may see in the British Museum numerous examples of *sarco-phagi and mummy-cases*, as well as the mummies themselves, swathed in their bandages. The sarcophagi are of various materials, granite, basalt, and alabaster (a beautiful specimen of the last is in "Sir John Soane's Museum" in Lincoln's Inn Fields). They are usually covered with hieroglyphics, within and without, but that of Cheops, like the pyramid itself, is perfectly plain. The lids of the mummy-cases are carved with the effigies of the deceased, which are also painted on the outmost wrappings of the mummies.

certain story that a mummy *was* taken thence, when the pyramid was entered by El-Mamoun, which the fanatical Arabs of Cairo, mistaking it for an idol, dragged about the streets till it was destroyed.

To conceive of the dimensions and proportions of this oldest and vastest monument of the world, let the reader imagine a pyramid nearly one-third higher than St. Paul's standing on a base somewhat larger than the area of Lincoln's Inn Fields. When complete, its base was a square of 760 English feet = 750 Greek or Egyptian feet = 500 cubits. Its height was 483·66 feet, or about 318 Egyptian cubits. The proportion of the height to the base was obtained by making each edge rise 9 measures (feet or cubits) in height for every 10 measures along the diagonal of the base. If the young reader cuts out of card two such triangles as this, and joins them at their middle lines, C D (so that the vertices D are together and the bases at right angles), and then joins the edges with triangles cut to the proper size, he will have a *model of the exterior of the Great Pyramid*. The "Second" and

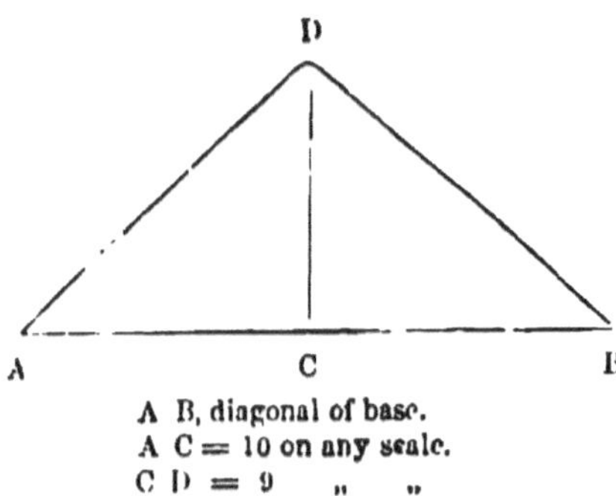

"Third " have the same proportions as the First; their bases are squares respectively of 700 and 350 Egyptian or Greek feet. Some pyramids are steeper; one has two different slopes in the upper and lower parts, and one, called the "Pyramid of Degrees," retains the form of *steps*, not having been filled in to a plane slope by means of casing stones.

The hieroglyphs painted on certain internal stones of the Great Pyramid, and left there by mere accident, are read as KHUFU or SHOFO, and NUM-KHUFU or NU-SHOFO (that is, the *brother of Khufu*). The builder of the Great Pyramid is named CHEOPS by Herodotus, and SUPHIS by Manetho, who gives him as successor another SUPHIS; and these two are the second and third in his "Fourth Dynasty" of Memphian kings. As if to remove all doubt, the Great Pyramid is called in hieroglyphics "the temple of King Khufu." Rightly, then, does Lepsius speak of " the PYRAMID OF CHEOPS, *to which the first link of our monumental history is fastened immovably, not only for Egyptian, but also for Universal History.* . . Nor have I yet found a single cartouche that can be safely assigned to a period previous to the Fourth Dynasty. *The builders of the Great Pyramid seem to assert their right to form the commencement of monumental history,* even if it be clear that they were not the first builders and monumental writers."

The Second Pyramid has no name of a king inscribed upon it; but Herodotus ascribed it to CEPHREN, whom Diodorus calls also CHABRYIS; names that are near enough to *Shafre,* who is mentioned on the tomb of his chief architect with the title, "the great one of the Pyramid," and elsewhere as "he of the Lesser Pyramid." Manetho, too, gives *Sephres* as the second king of the Fifth (Memphian) Dynasty. Belzoni, the great pioneer of modern Egyptian explorers, found in this pyramid an inscription recording a previous entrance by the Caliph Othman (A.D. 1196–7), when the sarcophagus had evidently been rifled.

The evidence as to the builder of the Third Pyramid is still more decisive. The ancients ascribe it unanimously to MYCERINUS, the successor of Cheops and Cephrenes, who stands next to Suphis II. in the Fourth Dynasty of Manetho; and the same name appears in the Fifth Dynasty. When Belzoni entered this pyramid, he found that here also Arab spoilers had been before him. The coffin had been taken from the sarcophagus and broken open. But its fragments had been left behind, with the coffin-lid, inscribed with the name MEN-KA-RE; and in the passage were the relics of a withered body. That mummy, supposed to have been the body of Mencheres himself, is now slowly crumbling to dust in one of the glass-cases of our Museum.[7] The name of *Men-ka-re* is also found in one of the small pyramids grouped about the great ones, and on other monuments. *Khufu, Shafre,* and *Men-ka-re* are all found on the monumental tablets of the time of the 18th and 19th dynasties.

Such results of efforts of the Pyramid Kings to preserve their mortal remains for ever give point to the noble lines of Spenser:—

> " In vain doo earthly Princes, then, in vaine
> Seek with Pyramidës, to heaven aspired,
> Or huge Colosses, built with costly paine,
> Or brazen Pillours, never to be fired,
> Or shrines, made of the mettal most desired,
> To make their memories for ever live:
> For how can mortal immortalitie give?"
>
> *The Ruines of Time,* vv. 407–413.

---

[7] There is, however, another story, that the mummy of Mencheres was destroyed, like those of Cheops and Cephren, and that the shrivelled remains in our Museum are those of an Arab spoiler, who was left behind and perished in the Pyramid.

Cooking Geese and Joints.

CHAPTER V.

LIFE UNDER THE OLD MONARCHY.

WITH the exception of the mere names of *Khufu* and his brother in the Great Pyramid, and of *Men-ka-re* in the Third, the oldest monuments in the world are silent about its history and their own. "These closed and artificial mountains of stone"—says a recent explorer—"say nothing whatever, either by picture or by inscription." [1]

But yet their "silence" is most "expressive." Their very existence confirms the Greek stories of their building by mighty monarchs, who oppressed the people with forced labour for their erection. The labour and skill expended in piling up the 90,000,000 cubic feet of masonry, weighing about 6,316,000 tons, that form the

[1] Herodotus, indeed, tells us that an interpreter read to him an inscription on the reat Pyramid, in Egyptian characters, recording the quantity of radishes, onions, and garlic consumed by the labourers who constructed it, and that the money expended in this way alone was 1200 talents of silver (£30,000). This may have been a mere memorandum scratched upon the casing-stones, the loss of which leaves it doubtful whether they were inscribed with historical records. The silence of Herodotus, and the absence of hieroglyphs from the neighbouring "temple of Shafre," is a strong argument for the negative.

Great Pyramid alone (not to compute the work in the others);—in levelling the rocky platform for a base;—in constructing the huge stone causeway for the conveyance of the limestone blocks from the quarries on the other side of the Nile;—in transporting masses of granite from Syene to form the sarcophagi, the lining of the "Great Gallery," and the casing of the Third Pyramid;—in working this material to the finest polish, and fitting the stones with such nicety that the joints are as fine as writing paper;—all this tells of vast resources, great command of mechanical art, a long period of peaceful security, at home and abroad, and that "unlimited command of naked human strength" which belongs to a despotic monarchy.

The national traditions made the Pyramid age one of impious arrogance, as well as of gross oppression. The priests told Herodotus that "Cheops closed the temples and forbad the Egyptians to sacrifice, compelling them instead to labour, one and all, in his service. A hundred thousand men worked constantly, and were relieved every three months by a fresh gang. It took ten years' oppression of the people to make the causeway for the conveyance of the stones. The Pyramid itself was twenty years in building."

Not the least striking testimony borne by the pyramids is to the long period of previous progress implied in the perfection of their work. The earliest of human works attest the *long established civilization*, of which they are now found to be no solitary monuments. The means of satisfying that admiring curiosity, which they have roused in successive ages and races of beholders, lay all the time sealed up in the private sepulchres at their feet. The tomb of a wealthy Egyptian was also the painted, and in many cases the written, memoir of his life. The subterranean or rock-hewn sepulchre was surmounted by an upper chamber, where funeral feasts were held, and the decoration of which was one occupation of the owner's life. These pictures and hieroglyphics, sealed up for about four thousand years, and now revealed in all their freshness, show us the subjects of the Old Memphian kingdom in the midst of their daily business, banquets, and recreations; as M. Renan says, "we have Egypt caught in the fact."

These pictures give the external features, as the mummies give the anatomical structure, which help us to discern the *race* of the ·old Egyptians ;—*not Negroes*, but intermediate between the Asiatic and African type. Here we see the reddish-brown complexion, the long straight or aquiline nose, the somewhat low forehead, and the full lips, which strike us also in their portrait statues. The shape of the head is hidden by the universal wig, a perfect specimen of which may be seen in the British Museum The *clothing* and *orna-*

ments of the men, women, and servants, are also carefully represented.
The priests are conspicuous by the leopard-skins over their shoulders.

The scenes depicted reveal the *social state* of an aristocracy of
landowners and officials using with harsh oppression the labour of a
servile peasantry and of domestic slaves. The owner of the tomb
is represented as a colossal figure, armed with a stick, and standing
the whole height of the wall, which is divided, in front of him,
into horizontal compartments, in which his servants are busy at
their various occupations. The taskmaster is always present, and
the bastinado at work: not even the cripples are exempt from
labour. They do not, indeed, like our old English " thralls," wear
a collar bearing the owner's name, but over their heads is the more
hopeless inscription :—" Slaves born in the house : on the books of
the house for ever."

Idleness appears to have had no place under the Old Monarchy.
The scenes in which a scribe seems to be taking a census of the
peasants remind us of the law, which Herodotus ascribes to a much
later king, requiring the people of each nome to appear before the
governor once a year, and show their means of livelihood, on pain
of death. The care taken to register every article of property is
conspicuous in all these scenes, and gives another proof of the universal employment of writing. Scribes, tablet and pen in hand,
enter the account of the produce which the overseer presents to his
master ; and the inscriptions record the number, size, and names of
his estates. Everything is done on a scale of vastness and profu-
sion : the droves of oxen are numbered by thousands ; two or three
herds of cows are milked at once—standing in rows above one
another, owing to the painter's ignorance of perspective. Long
trains of servants come in laden with provisions : whole droves of
oxen are slaughtered before the master; and his table is piled up
with slices of bread, pyramids of fruit, joints of meat, and roast
geese—a favourite Egyptian dish.

Pastoral operations are on a larger scale than agricultural. The
seed is sown broad-cast, and beaten in by driving sheep and goats
over the newly inundated land. Reaping is performed with a
sickle; thrashing by driving herds of donkeys about a floor; and
winnowing with spades.

The amusements of the field, hunting, fishing, and fowling, are
eagerly pursued. We see the fowler, in his papyrus boat, approaching the reeds that then fringed the banks of the Nile, to strike the
birds which fly into the clap-nets spread by his servants. The
chief in-door amusements are concerts and the performances of
dancing girls, witnessed by the master and by ladies, who sit on
chairs of an elegant form.

Such furniture is one specimen of the great advance of common handicrafts, the *processes* of which are also exhibited. But the handleless hammers of the carpenters show an age in which human labour was unrelieved by even the simplest machinery. *Glass-blowing* is thought to be one of the arts represented.

A curious feature of these scenes is the number and variety of the domestic animals : donkeys, dogs, apes, antelopes, gazelles, geese, ducks, tame storks, and pigeons ; but others, familiar to a later age of Egypt, are never seen, as fowls, camels, giraffes, elephants, and horses. The absence of the horse is peculiarly interesting, as shewing that we have not yet reached the period of that Pharaoh who made Joseph to ride in the second chariot that he had.

These animal forms are depicted with remarkable fidelity to nature ; and the human figures have a truth of proportion and a freedom of motion in striking contrast to the sacred conventionalism of later times.

While all shews a civilization equal to that of the great age of the 18th Dynasty, the art is even higher. This free style of art is thought to indicate a period when the sacerdotal power was not dominant ; and the inscriptions, which tell us of the social position and offices of these long-buried dead, confirm the view that the country was now governed by the military and not by the priestly class.

At all events, the government was settled, and the peace of the nation was so secure that no soldiers appear upon the monuments, and none of the great men carry arms. Nor were there, properly speaking, any foreign wars; for the hostilities against the Arab tribes, recorded by inscriptions of the Fourth and Fifth Dynasties on the rocks of Sinai, look rather like measures for the protection of the mines wrought by the Memphian kings in that peninsula.

Thus it is that the earliest contemporary records of the world shew us a country at a high pitch of wealth and art under a powerful kingly government ; a spectacle which has filled every student of history with the amazement expressed in the vivid words of M. Renan :—" When we think of this civilization, that it had no known history ; that this art, of which there remain innumerable monuments, had no archaic epoch ; that the Egypt of Cheops and Cephren is superior, in a sense, to all that followed, *we feel dizzy with surprise (on est pris de vertige).*" The solution of this wonder awaits further light ; but there are indications that this civilization came from Asia. At all events, the old view, that the social and political state of Egypt had its cradle in Ethiopia, is now generally rejected.

The doubtful traditions repeated by the Greeks about Cheops, Cephren, and Mycerinus, may be deferred till the learner can read them in the pages of Herodotus, and pursue the criticism which they require. The stories which ascribe impiety to Cheops, and the restoration of religion to Mycerinus, indicate a religious conflict, of which the monuments give some signs. In the newly discovered temple near the Pyramids, which is ascribed to Shafre (Cephren), is a well, containing broken fragments of statues of that king, made of the most costly stones, and evidently flung in by violence. The issue of the conflict seems to have been the establishment of the power of the priests, whose traditions gratefully recorded the piety of Mycerinus.

There was probably a struggle between the religious systems of Upper and Lower Egypt, attendant upon their union into one kingdom. The relations between the two divisions of Egypt under the Old Monarchy, however, are very obscure; and the name of Thebes is never mentioned on the monuments of this age. But it must be always borne in mind that, as the crowns and symbols of Upper and Lower Egypt are distinct upon the monuments from the earliest times, so, through the whole of Egyptian history, there is a marked distinction, and generally an antagonism, between the two divisions of the country.

The great kings of whom we have been speaking form the *Fourth and Fifth Dynasties* of Manetho. The latter Dynasty, of *Elephantine* Kings, some of whose names are the same as the Memphians of the former Dynasty, seems to imply the existence of a vice-royalty of Upper Egypt, with its seat on the Ethiopian frontier.

The transition from the *Fifth* to the *Sixth Dynasty* is marked by a civil commotion, in which the king was killed by his guards. But the splendour of the Memphian monarchy is renewed under Pnios,[2] the second of the Sixth Dynasty. This king, whose Egyptian name was *Pepi-Maire* or *Pepi-Remai*, or, more fully, *Pepi-meri-ra* (that is, "beloved of Ra," the Sun), has left the proof in his numerous monuments that his power embraced all Egypt, from the Delta to Elephantine. It is supposed that the Memphian monarchy was dismembered at the close of the Fifth Dynasty, and that Pepi, being at first King of Upper and Middle Egypt, extended his power over the whole country, and fixed his capital at Memphis.

Most of his monuments are in the Upper country. Besides subduing the Arabs of Sinai (like the kings of the Fourth Dynasty), he warred in Ethiopia, above the Second Cataract, against the *Wa-wa*, a negro people; and against Arabs in the region between Upper Egypt and the Red Sea. In the last quarter, his monument on the road to the port of *Kosseir*—still the highway for travellers

---

[2] This is probably a faulty reading for Pniors, a name which recurs next but one in *Manetho's* list. Perhaps the two kings are the same, and their Egyptian surnames only different titles.

from India to Upper Egypt—appears to indicate a beginning of that commerce by way of the Red Sea, which formed in later ages a great source of wealth to Egypt.

Another Pepi, surnamed Neferkera, may correspond to the second Phiops of Manetho, who assigns him a reign of a full century, wanting only a month. His long rule is confirmed by records of the festivals he celebrated on the completion of different portions of his reign. This example of longevity is the more interesting because, though we are as yet without any certain details of chronology, we cannot be far from the time when Abraham went down into Egypt. The age of the Pyramid builders is too early; and yet the Pharaoh of the time of Abraham was evidently a powerful king of Lower Egypt. The rebuke incurred by the dissimulation of the patriarch would have come well from the venerable Pepi. (See Genesis xii. 18–19.)

The centenarian reign of Phiops is followed, in the list of Manetho, by one of a year only; and then the Sixth Dynasty ends with a queen, the "rosy-checked Nitocris, the most spirited and beautiful woman of her time, who erected the Third Pyramid,³ and reigned six years." Herodotus also mentions her as the one queen, among the 330 kings from Menes to Mœris, whose names were read to him from a papyrus by the priests; and he tells a romantic legend of her courage and her fate. She succeeded her brother, who had been put to death by his subjects; and, having invited the principal murderers to a banquet in the subterranean chamber, she let in the river upon them as they were feasting. Then, to escape the vengeance of their friends, she threw herself into an apartment full of ashes.

The name of this queen appears in the royal list of the "Turin Papyrus" in the form *Neitakri*, that is, "Neith the victorious;"⁴ and we have seen that the old law of Egypt allowed the succession of females to the throne. For the rest, we may infer from the legend of Herodotus about Nitocris, and the one year's reign of her predecessor in Manetho, that the Sixth Dynasty ended amidst convulsions.

And this is confirmed by the shadowy accounts of two more Memphian Dynasties. The *Seventh*, of 70 kings in 70 days, looks like an interregnum of a senate or a priestly college. Of the *Eighth*, of 28 kings in 146 years (or, according to another reading, 5 kings in 100 years), no particulars are given in Manetho or elsewhere.

---

³ That is, she enlarged the pyramid of Mycerinus; comp. Chap. IV.

⁴ *Neith* was a famous Egyptian goddess, corresponding to the Greek *Athena*, and the Latin *Minerva*. She was the patron deity of Saïs, and the name of *Neitakri* occurs again among the princesses of the later Saïte Dynasty. The name of the celebrated Babylonian queen Nitocris was derived, in all probability, from a marriage alliance between the family of Nebuchadnezzar and the Egyptian royal house of Saïs

Tumblers.

CHAPTER VI.

THE MIDDLE MONARCHY.

THERE is little doubt that several of Manetho's Dynasties were
contemporary. The earliest political state of Egypt seems to have
been like that of the neighbouring parts of Asia. A number of
petty kings reigned each over a single city, with its surrounding
territory; and hence originated the *nomes*, into which the country
was divided. The several cities had their own temples and local
worship, which was often in antagonism to that of their neighbours; especially as to the animals held sacred in each place. The
political, and to some extent the religious, union of Egypt is the
change connected with the name of Menes and the great Memphian
kings.

But this union did not extinguish local claims and rivalries,
which were ready to revive at any weakening of the ruling dynasty,
and to rally round new centres of power. Especially was this the
case in the remoter and narrower valley of Upper Egypt, which
often furnished a refuge to the national spirit, when the Delta was
a prey to internal disorder or to foreign conquest. Besides, as
we have seen, there was always a certain degree of antagonism
between the Upper and the Lower country, though the causes of
this demand further light; and the weakness of the one was the
opportunity of the other.

It is probable that the Old Memphian Monarchy fell finally
before the great foreign invasion of which we have presently to
speak—that of the "Shepherd Kings," or Semitic hordes from
Asia. But long before this conquest—whether from the early

irruptions of these hordes, or from whatever other cause—the Old Monarchy began, as we have seen, to show symptoms of decline. Its decay afforded an opportunity for the rise of two new, or revived, kingdoms in Upper Egypt; while another petty kingdom seems to have acquired new power in the marshes of the Delta. These form the 9th and 10th (*Heracleopolitan*), the 11th, 12th, and 13th (*Diospolitan* or *Theban*), and the 14th (*Xoïte*) *Dynasties* of Manetho.

The kingdom of Heracleopolis is so obscure, that some even suppose it to be misnamed, and place its seat at Hermonthis (*Erment*), a very ancient city of Upper Egypt, a little above Thebes. Here are found monuments of kings, whom some refer to the 9th dynasty, others to the 11th; and there is a similar doubt about a series of kings, with the common name of *Enentef*, whose tombs are found at Thebes. Heracleopolis, on the other hand, is in Middle Egypt, and at the mouth of the valley of the *Fyûm*, the great monuments of which belong clearly to the Twelfth (Theban) Dynasty. No light is gained by Manetho's solitary mention of Acuthoës, as the first king of the 9th dynasty, who was "the most atrocious of all who preceded him, did much mischief to the people of all Egypt, and afterwards fell into madness, and was destroyed by a crocodile."

Amidst this obscurity there stands forth one important name, *Mantoftep, Mandopt,* or *Muntotp I.*, probably the founder of the 11*th Dynasty*. The name is derived from *Mandoo* or *Munt*, the patron deity of Hermonthis; but the Dynasty is reckoned by Manetho as of Diospolis, that is, Thebes, which perhaps now first became the capital of Upper Egypt. Mandopt I. was esteemed the original founder of the Theban monarchy; for in the List of Rameses II. his name alone occurs between that of Menes and the kings of the Eighteenth Dynasty. The name of a second Mandopt is found on the road to *Kosseir*, together with that of Amenemhe or Amenemenes I. The latter, who is made by Manetho the last king of the Eleventh Dynasty, may also be regarded as the founder of the *Twelfth*, in which the name alternates with that of *Sesortasen* (or *Osirtasen*).

However great may have been the antiquity of Thebes, as a seat of local power, and as the great sacred city of Upper Egypt,[1] its political importance dates from the *Twelfth Dynasty*. On the earliest of its temples are found the names of Sesortasen I. and his father Amenemes I.; and the monuments of the former at Heliopolis and in the *Fyûm* prove that his power embraced Lower

---

[1] We reserve the account of Thebes for Chapter VIII.

and Middle Egypt. Thebes now became the capital of the reunited monarchy.

The seven great kings of this dynasty are now made out from Manetho and the monuments. They were: *Sesortasen I.*; *Amenemhe II.*; *Sesortasen II.*; *Sesortasen III.*; *Amenemhe III.*; *Amenemhe IV.*; and *Ra-Sebeknofru*, whom Manetho makes a queen (Skemiophris), and others a king.[2] They are alike conspicuous for their conquests and for their works of peace. Pent up, probably, on the side of Lower Egypt by the growing power of the Semitic tribes, they carried their arms into ETHIOPIA, and built the two fortresses of *Semneh* and *Khumneh*, above the Second Cataract. The southern limit of the Egyptian monarchy at this time is marked not only by the inscriptions which record victories over "the vile race of Cush," but also by the interesting fact that the water-gates of both fortresses are on the side of the works *towards Egypt*.

Their wars against the Arabs between Upper Egypt and the Red Sea—and, as some think, even in the peninsula of Arabia itself—are recorded upon monuments on the road to *Kosseir*. Their care for that route indicates the probability of maritime commerce with the Arabian Sea; and the Arabs whom they conquered were of the same race (the *Pount*) who brought to later Theban kings tribute of apes, ivory, ebony, and other products of the south.

Monuments in Ethiopia record the worship of one of the Sesortasens as a god by his successors of the Eighteenth Dynasty; and in this name we seem to have at least *one* original of the great Egyptian conqueror SESOSTRIS, who is celebrated by the Greek writers. The statements of Herodotus—that Sesostris was the only (he should have said the first) Egyptian monarch that ever ruled over Ethiopia, and that his fleets sailed in the Arabian Sea—may have had their first origin from the exploits of the Twelfth Dynasty. But, though the *name* of Sesostris may have been supplied by the *Sesortasens*, the *person* about whom the tradition chiefly centres (so far as it refers to one in particular) is Rameses II. of the 19th Dynasty.[3]

The burial of the last of the Sesortasens in the southernmost of the Memphian Pyramids marks at once the extension of the power

---

[2] We have said above "the great kings;" for neither the Lists of Manetho, nor even the monuments, preserve the names of *all* the kings who reigned in Egypt. The priests registered only the names of kings whom they considered legitimate; and the kings, besides making a *selection* from the long lists of their royal ancestors (as we see in the tablets of Thothmes and Rameses), took pains to obliterate the records of predecessors whom they regarded as usurpers.

[3] See Chapter IX.

of this dynasty to the old capital of Lower Egypt, and the end of the age in which pyramids were used as the sepulchres of the Egyptian kings.[4]

The great works of the Twelfth Dynasty in *Middle Egypt*, however, were far superior to the Pyramids—at least in the estimation of Herodotus. "The Pyramids," says he, "surpass description, and are severally equal to a number of the greatest works of the Greeks ; but the *Labyrinth* surpasses the Pyramids." And again : "Wonderful as is the Labyrinth, the work called the *Lake of Mœris*, which is close by the Labyrinth, is yet more astonishing." The recent discoveries, which have proved the age and uses of these works, confirm the latter judgment at all events ; for the " Lake of Mœris " was a work of hydraulic engineering scarcely second to the "Dyke of Menes," as a means of husbanding the resources provided for Egypt by the Nile.

We have had occasion more than once to mention the great depression now called the *Fyûm*. It lies westward of the Nile in Middle Egypt, and is enclosed on the north and south by ridges of rock. The lowest part of the depression, on the north-west, is occupied by the natural lake called *Birket-el-Kerún*, which has a communication with the Nile. So long as this *natural* sheet of water was taken for the " Lake of Mœris," the description of Herodotus was unintelligible. But the true site of the *artificial* lake has been discovered lately on the limestone plateau between the *Birket-el-Kerûn* and the river, near *Medinet-el-Fyûm*, the ancient Crocodilopolis.[5] It has long formed part of the cultivated plain of the *Fyûm*, which is still irrigated from a small reservoir on the same spot.

But the Lake of Mœris had a far more important purpose than merely to water the *Fyûm*. It was a reservoir for regulating the inundation over a large extent of the Nile valley. In remote ages the hills which border the river-basin approached so near to one another at some points as to dam up the waters of the inundation, till the river forced its way through the rocky barrier. Such a barrier once existed at Silsilis (*Hadjar Selseleh*), some 40 miles below the first cataract. Its effect, in spreading the waters of the inundation over the now barren plains of Nubia, is still seen in

---

[4] It is also the first monument in which we find the use of *brick*, a material which became common under the 18th and 19th dynasties. The pyramid referred to is the southernmost pyramid of *Dashoor*, which is built of brick, but faced with stone. Herodotus mentions a king *Asychis* (a wise legislator), who left a brick pyramid as his distinguishing monument ; but there are several pyramids of this material.

[5] This city was so called from the sacred crocodiles which were kept there in immense numbers ; for the *Fyûm* (or Nomos Arsinoïtes) was the chief seat of the worship of that reptile.

ancient alluvial deposits, and in water-worn rocks at a considerable distance from the river.

To this voice of geology the records of history are added. Inscriptions of the later kings of the Twelfth Dynasty, and of the Thirteenth, on the rocks at *Semneh*, show that the inundation then reached 27 feet above its present height; while, on the other hand, the foundations of buildings on the old deposit, and the caves in the rocks near the Nile, prove that the lower level was permanently established by the time of the Eighteenth Dynasty, which succeeded the Thirteenth in Upper Egypt. The epoch of the rupture of the barrier at Silsilis is thus determined within moderate limits; and the Lake of Mœris was probably constructed at the same period to regulate the inundation, which must have been affected by that catastrophe. There are some who even seek in this great change the explanation of the seven years of plenty and of famine in the time of Joseph.

These marks of time are confirmed by the probability that the Lake of Mœris and the neighbouring *Labyrinth* were works of the same powerful Dynasty. The builder of the latter has left his name upon the edifice, which Herodotus, bewildered as he was led in darkness through its countless halls and corridors, called the *labyrinth*. Those many chambers were ascribed in his time to the Twelve rulers who were said to have governed Egypt for a brief period in a much later age; but Strabo seems nearer the mark in making its 27 halls the palaces of the delegates from the nomes, who held regular meetings there. At all events, the age of the building is fixed by the recent discovery, upon its ruins, of the name of AMENEMHE III., of the Twelfth Dynasty; and, whatever its purpose may have been, it is remarkable as the first example of those great edifices of many chambers, halls, and corridors, partaking of the nature both of temples and palaces, which are the characteristic works of the Theban kings, as the Pyramids are of the Memphian.[6]

Here too we have an instance, too striking to be passed over, of the results of modern research into Egyptian history. The monuments enable us to recover, after more than 3000 years, facts which were forgotten and perverted in the far earlier age of Herodotus,

[6] Not that the Memphian kings had not also their palaces, of which indeed one example has probably come down to us in the newly discovered building near the Pyramids, already mentioned. But their royal abodes have perished, or have been buried beneath the sand, while the Pyramids have survived as the characteristic monuments to which men point—

> " Who boast in mortal things and wondering tell
> Of Babel and *the works of Memphian kings*."

and in the priestly registers copied by Manetho. Mœris, whom the former makes the greatest king after Menes, appears to be simply a name derived from *meri*, the Egyptian word for a *lake*,[7] and Labaris (or Lacheres), whom Manetho asserts to have built the labyrinth for his own tomb, looks like a similar invention of etymology. Thus the monuments have led us to discover, in the kings of the Twelfth Dynasty, the originals of Mœris of the *mere*, and Labaris of the *labyrinth*.

For this age also we have tombs—the sepulchral grottoes of *Beni-hassan*, on the eastern side of the Nile, in Middle Egypt—which reveal a daily life so nearly like that of the Old Monarchy that the details need not be repeated. There is some change in the greater development of agricultural appliances and especially of manufacturing processes. In the words of a recent traveller, "the plough drawn by oxen dispenses with many sheep treading the seed into the soft mud; the cultivation of the vine and the process of wine-making diversify the scenes; flax may be traced through its several stages—men reaping it in the fields, and women weaving its fibres indoors." Some of the inscriptions give curious details of the privileges held by the great nobles; among which the importance attached to *rights of water* is well suited to the age of the Lake Mœris.

One of these nobles, named *Ameni*, has left the record of his life and occupations both painted and written upon his tomb. On one wall we see the fat oxen grazing, and the sheaves of wheat carried in carts of the very model still used by the *fellahs* of Egypt, and threshed out by the feet of oxen. On another is depicted the navigation of the Nile; the building and lading of large ships; the fashioning of elegant furniture from costly woods; and the preparation of garments · in a word, the scenes of busy husbandry and navigation, commerce and handicrafts.

These pictures are interpreted by Ameni himself in a long inscription. As a general, he made a campaign in Ethiopia, and was charged with the protection of the caravans, which transported the gold of *Jebel-Atoky* across the desert to Coptos. As the governor of a province, he recites the praises of his administration : — " All the lands under me were ploughed and sown from north to south. Thanks were given to me on behalf of the royal house for the tribute of fat cattle which I collected. Nothing was ever stolen out of my workshops; *I worked myself, and kept the whole province*

---

[7] We believe this to be the right explanation; but the name may possibly be derived from the title *Maïré* ("beloved of Re") which we have seen borne by a previous king.

at work"—a striking confirmation of the statement, that the law of Egypt punished idleness as a crime. "Never was a child afflicted, never a widow ill-treated by me; never did I disturb the fisherman, or molest the shepherd. Famine never occurred in my time, nor did I let any one hunger in years of short produce. I have given equally to the widow and the married woman; and I have not preferred the great to the small in the judgments I have given."

These sepulchral records confirm the conquests claimed on the monuments of the Twelfth Dynasty, especially in Ethiopia. The *military* element, which was "conspicuous by its absence" from the tombs of Memphis, appears on those of Beni-hassan; and the *negro slaves* attest the forays into Nubia. Nor is this the only case in which the Egyptian artist begins to show his skill in depicting different races. There are strangers from the opposite quarter; whose aquiline features, lighter complexion, and peculiar dress, mark them as immigrants from Arabia and Palestine. Among these a group of 37 *Jebusites*, who had been purchased as slaves from one of their petty kings, are presented by the chief Neofth to Sesortasen II., in the sixth year of his reign, on account of their skill in preparing *stibium*, a black powder produced from antimony, and used profusely throughout ancient Egypt as a cosmetic. This picture was formerly mistaken for Joseph's presentation of Jacob and his family to Pharaoh. The true period of that event will be noticed in the next chapter.

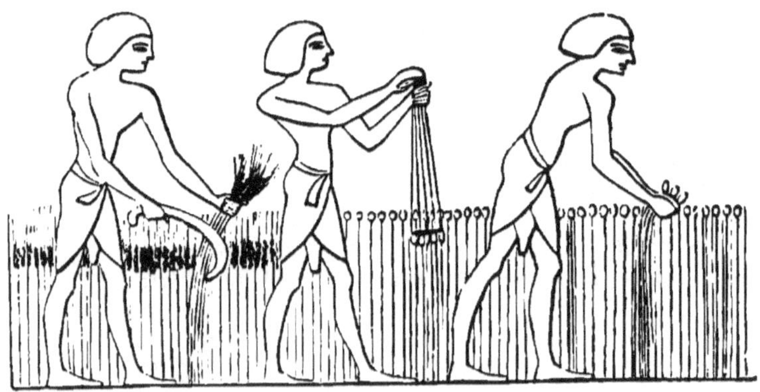

Modes of gathering Corn.

Asiatic Enemies of Egypt.

CHAPTER VII.

THE SHEPHERD KINGS — ADMINISTRATION OF JOSEPH.

THE splendid period of the Twelfth Dynasty was succeeded by the greatest calamity that ever befel the Egypt of the Pharaohs, till the Persian conquest. An account of it forms one of the few fragments which we still possess of the "Egyptian History" of Manetho; but his words are probably garbled in the quotation made by the Jewish historian, Josephus, for a purpose of his own.[1]

"We once had a king named Timæus (or Amintimæus), under whom, from some cause unknown to me, the Deity was unfavourable to us; and there came unexpectedly, *from the eastern parts*, a race *of obscure extraction*, who boldly invaded the country and easily took forcible possession of it *without a battle*. Having subdued those who commanded in it, they proceeded savagely to burn the cities, and *razed the temples of the gods;* inhumanly treating all the natives; murdering some, and carrying the wives and children of others into slavery.

"In the end they also established one of themselves as a king. whose name was SALATIS (*Saïtes* in the *List* of Manetho); and *he took up his abode at Memphis*, exacting tribute from *both the upper and lower country*, and leaving garrisons in the most suitable places.

---

[1] The *italics* in the quotation are intended to draw attention to certain points of importance.

He especially strengthened the parts towards the East, foreseeing that on the part of the *Assyrians, who were then powerful*, there would be a desire to invade the kingdom. Finding therefore in the Sethroïte nome a city very conveniently placed, lying eastward of the Bubastic river, and called from some old religious reason *Avaris* (or Abaris), he built it up, and made it very strong with walls, settling there also a great number of heavy-armed soldiers, to the amount of 240,000 men, for a body-guard. Hither he used to come in the summer season, partly to distribute the rations of corn and pay the troops, partly to exercise them carefully by musters and reviews, in order to inspire fear into foreign nations."

After enumerating the five successors of this first king, he thus proceeds :—" Their whole nation was called HYKSOS, that is, *Shepherd Kings* ; for *Hyk* in the sacred language denotes *king*, and *Sos* is a *shepherd* in the common dialect. The before-named kings," he says, "and their descendants, were masters of Egypt for 511 years "—a period certainly exaggerated.

" After this, Manetho says that a revolt of *the kings of the Thebaïd and the rest of Egypt* took place against the Shepherds, and *a great and prolonged war* was carried on with them. Under a king, whose name was *Misphragmuthosis*,[2] he says that the Shepherds were expelled by that king from the rest of Egypt after a defeat, and shut up in a place having a circuit of 10,000 aruræ.[3] This place was called *Avaris*. Manetho says that the Shepherds surrounded it entirely with a large and strong wall, in order that they might have a secure deposit for all their possessions and all their plunder.

" Thuthmosis, the son of Misphragmuthosis, endeavoured to take the place by siege, attacking the walls with 480,000 men. Despairing of taking it by siege, he made a treaty with them, that they should leave Egypt, and withdraw without injury whithersoever they pleased. In virtue of this agreement, they withdrew from Egypt, with all their families and possessions, to the number of not fewer than 240,000, *and traversed the desert into Syria*. Fearing the power of *the Assyrians, who were at that time masters of Asia*, they *built a city* in that which is now called *Judæa*, which should suffice for so many myriads of men, and called it *Jerusalem*."

In this remarkable quotation the Jewish historian perverts

---

[2] The first part of this name is evidently the prænomen *Mi-phra*, "beloved of Ra": in the second part the name of *Aahmes* (or *Amosis*), who really expelled the Shepherds, seems to be confused with that of his son *Thothmes*.

[3] The *arura* was the square of 100 cubits = 10,000 square cubits. Hence 10,000 aruræ = 100,000,000 square cubits = a square of 10,000 cubits or of 15,000 Egyptian or Greek feet. This would make the city roughly a square of three miles, or nine square miles; or about equal to London from the Tower to Hyde Park, and from Pentonville to Kennington.

Manetho's history of the Shepherd Kings into a false account of the origin of the Hebrew nation. The passage occurs in his controversy with Philo, who had taunted him with the mean origin of the Jewish people; and Josephus catches at the idea of identifying Israel in Egypt with the powerful Hyksos. We have quoted the passage at length, partly to enable every one to see the absurdity of this theory by comparing it with the Scriptural account of the entrance and exodus of the Israelites; and partly because, in the main, it doubtless gives Manetho's own story of the Shepherd Kings.

On the former point, we need only add that, besides the inconsistency of making the famine-stricken family of Jacob a horde of conquering warriors—whose expulsion, when conquered, is a strange substitute (coming from a Jewish patriot!) for the miraculous Exodus—Josephus ignores the 40 years' wandering in the wilderness; and the very mention of *Jerusalem*, which might stagger any reader at first, entirely contradicts his theory; for that city belonged to the *Canaanite Jebusites* for some time after the entrance of Israel into the Holy Land. We shall presently find that the Exodus took place at a much later period of the history of Egypt.

The one sole point of likeness between the Shepherds and the Israelites is this: they were a pastoral people of the same great *Semitic* race. The true interpretation of the name *Hyksos* is probably *Arab sheikhs* or *princes; shaso*, the Egyptian word for *Arab*, being a general term for the Semitic races east of Egypt. In Manetho's list of dynasties, they (or, at least, some of them) are called *Phœnician* Shepherds. From this, and their opposition to the *Assyrians* (a term constantly used for *the people who held power for the time being in Mesopotamia*), we may connect them with the great Semitic migration which was driven westward, at a very early age, by the growth of the earliest Babylonian kingdom. The invasions of nomad hordes, such as that of Egypt by the Shepherds, are generally impelled by a pressure from behind.

There are strong reasons for referring this great Semitic migration to the time of Abraham; and the patriarch's history has some curious points of contact with the Shepherd Dynasty. We are told, in the book of *Numbers* (xiii. 22) that "*Hebron* was built seven years before *Zoan in Egypt*." This singularly precise comparison surely implies some connection between the two cities. Now *Zoan* (the city of the Delta, which the Greeks called *Tanis*) is positively identified with the *Avaris* of the Shepherds, in Egyptian Ha-Awar or Pa-Awar.[4] Hebron, then called *Kirjatharba*, "the city of *Arba*"

<hr>

[4] This name, signifying (like *Zoan* in Hebrew) "the *house of going forth* or *departure*," was probably applied to the city as being the point of departure for caravans on the eastern frontier.

(a name curiously like *Awar*), was originally the city of the giant *Anakim*, a branch of the older population who were conquered by the immigrant-race of the Canaanites.   Is it not then probable that Abraham knew this race as the same which, after founding Hebron, had invaded Egypt and there built Zoan?   In point of time, what we learn of Joseph's connection with Egypt agrees with this reference of Abraham to the beginning of the Shepherd period.

The identification of Tanis with the Shepherd fortress of Avaris has lately been placed beyond doubt by the researches of M. Mariette. He has discovered among its ruins several monuments of the Shepherd Kings, and the remains of the temple of their great god, *Set* or *Soutekh*, another name for the *Baal* of Syria and Phœnicia.   There also was found a tablet of Rameses II., mentioning *Set-aa-pehti Noubti* (the *Saïtes* of Manetho) as having, 400 years before, rebuilt the city and reared the temple of *Set*.   This is invaluable testimony in respect to the *time, place, nationality, and religion* of the Hyksos. It reduces the fabulous length of the Shepherd domination within reasonable limits; for 400 years before·Rameses II. leaves about 200 years for the Shepherd rule, and brings the date of Saïtes to about the 18th century B.C.

The position of this city was admirably suited for the purpose of the invaders.   It lay on the eastern bank of the Tanitic branch of the Nile (the easternmost except one, the Pelusiac), on the margin of a rich plain, "the *field of Zoan*," which stretched about 30 miles to the east.   Though not strictly a border fortress, it lay in the route of an invading army, and at the same time commanded the most fertile part of the Delta.   It is clearly from the national pride, which made the Egyptians hate and affect to despise the Shepherds, that Manetho represents the purpose of this fortress to be solely to keep out the Assyrians, and not to overawe the Egyptians.   It was properly a fortified camp rather than a capital; and Manetho expressly says that the capital of the Shepherds was Memphis.   But the ravages which Memphis suffered from the Shepherds tended to transfer much of its consequence to Tanis, which appears henceforth as one of the most important cities of the Delta.

In his account of the extent and thoroughness of those ravages, Manetho is confirmed by the almost utter obliteration of all the public monuments of the earlier dynasties, to the Twelfth inclusive, excepting the pyramids, the obelisk of Sesortasen I. at Heliopolis, the few remains in the *Fyûm*, and one or two at Thebes.   The whole subject of the relations of the native dynasties to the Hyksos is obscure.[5]

---

[5] The interesting questions about the 13th (*Theban*), the 14th (*Xoïte*), and the 15th, 16th, and 17th Dynasties (which are variously styled, in different versions of Manetho, as *Shepherd* and as *Theban*) are too intricate for discussion in this work.

The easy conquest of Lower Egypt, "without a battle," may be explained by internal divisions, and it is worth notice that Manetho speaks of "those who ruled in it," in the plural. It is probable that the Semitic hordes, which had perhaps for some time been pressing into the Delta, were invited to aid the native princes against the domination of Thebes. A document, describing the calamities of another invasion, in the time of Menephtha (the Pharaoh of the Exodus), has these remarkable expressions :—" Nothing was seen the like of this, even in the time of the *Kings of Lower Egypt, when this land of Egypt was in their power*, and the calamity lasted, at the time when *the Kings of Upper Egypt had not strength to repulse the foreigners*." The latter were of the *Thirteenth (Theban) Dynasty*.

The last phrase shews that Upper Egypt submitted to the invaders, while retaining her own kings as vassals to the Hyksos. The last two of these vassal kings of Thebes are known from the monuments. Their names are *Taaken* and *Kamès;* and the latter assumes the very title of " nourisher of the world" (*Tsaf-en-to*, in Hebrew *Zaphnath*) which Pharaoh conferred on Joseph ; as if either claiming the merit of the policy which he had to administer, or assuming the title in rivalry to the minister of the Shepherd King.

For there is scarcely a doubt that the Pharaoh under whom Joseph lived was one of the later Shepherd Kings. The limits of chronology, reckoned back from the Exodus, agree with the vivid descriptions of the court of Pharaoh in the book of Genesis, and are confirmed by the monuments of the Hyksos.

Those monuments prove how completely the Shepherds became true Pharaohs, without renouncing their own nationality. They set up again the statues of former ages, belonging to the temples overthrown in the first violence of their invasion, carving their own names upon them as dedicators; and they made new statues, in a style of Egyptian art even purer than that of the comtemporary Theban monuments, but with certain features distinctly Semitic. Though they intruded their god, Set or Soutekh, into the Egyptian Pantheon, and built his temple beside the temples of the old gods, they gave the latter the supreme place. They and their followers adopted the manners of their new country, mixed with some Semitic usages.

And this is precisely the state in which the narrative of *Genesis* depicts Egypt under the Pharaoh whom Joseph served. The king and his people are "Egyptians," both in name and customs, and yet they have some characters of a foreign race. Such are their cordial reception of strangers, whom the Egyptians hated and despised ; and the pure despotism of Joseph's Pharaoh, whose will is absolute, and who reduces the Egyptians to serfdom ; whereas the native monarchs were restrained by law, and set a high value on the attachment of their subjects. A Semitic ruler would be much more likely than a native king to make a Hebrew slave his prime minister; and the policy of Joseph would be more easily enforced on a conquered country. Indeed, that policy, by which Pharaoh was made the supreme owner of the land of Egypt, looks like the last stroke in the subjugation of the country, and especially of Upper Egypt.[6]

All these things confirm the express statement made in a fragment of Manetho, that *Joseph was brought into Egypt under the Shepherd King* Aphophis, the *Apepi*, whose monuments are by far the most numerous of this dynasty. And we now learn, from native records, that this was the very king against whom began that "revolt of the kings of the Thebaid and the rest of Egypt," which (Manetho tells us) led to "a great and prolonged war." A papyrus in the British Museum says :—" Now it came to pass that the land of Egypt fell into the hands of enemies; and there was no longer any king at the time when this happened. And it was so that the king *Tiaaken* was only a *hak* (vassal prince) of Upper Egypt. The enemies were in Heliopolis,[7] and their chief *Apepi* in Avaris." Here Apepi received the news of the rebellion of Tiaaken, who refused to worship the god Soutekh, to whom Apepi had built "an everlasting temple."

The ensuing war occupied the remainder of *Tiaaken's* time, the whole of the short reign of his successor, *Kamès*, and the greater part of that of *Aahmes*, who brought it to an end. Manetho says that, after a great defeat, the Shepherds were shut up in Avaris; and we are now able to quote the naval operations against that city from the epitaph of the admiral who conducted them. This officer. who was the namesake of the king, *Aahmes*, speaks thus :—" When I was born in the fortress of Ilithyia [in Upper Egypt], my father was lieutenant of the late king, Tiaaken. . . . . I acted as lieutenant in turn with him on board the vessel named the *Calf*, in the time of the late King Aahmes. I went to the fleet of the north to fight. It was my duty to accompany the sovereign when he mounted his chariot. They were besieging the fortress of Tanis, and I fought on my legs before his majesty. This is what followed on board the vessel named the *Enthronisation of Memphis*. A naval battle was fought on the Water of Tanis (*Lake Menzaleh*). . . . The praise of the king was bestowed on me, and I received a collar

---

[6] A minor, but very striking, point is Pharaoh's use of *chariots*, which are most characteristic of the warlike tribes of Palestine, but entirely absent from the Egyptian monuments before the Eighteenth Dynasty, by which the Shepherds were expelled.

[7] Here is another coincidence with Scripture, which makes Heliopolis the chief sacred city of Egypt at this time; for Joseph marries the daughter of Potipherah, the priest of *On* (Heliopolis). The Shepherds, whose national god personified the Sun, would naturally favour the religious city where the Sun was specially adored.

of gold for my bravery. . . . The (decisive) combat took place at the southern part of the fortress. . . . They took the fortress of Tanis; and I carried off a man and two women, three heads in all, whom his majesty granted me as slaves." This very moderate booty, while it shows the veracity of the narrator, seems to indicate the very partial success of the assault, and confirms the account of Manetho, that the fortress was evacuated under a capitulation.

But what shall we say of the retreat of the Shepherds to *Judæa* and their building of *Jerusalem?* The mystery is easily solved. The Eastern nations have always had sacred cities: and several such are denoted in the Bible and elsewhere by the Semitic name of *Kadesh* or *Kodesh*, which means *Holy.* Thus Jerusalem is, at the present day, called in Arabic *El Khods*, "the Holy;" and there has been a frequent tendency to mistake any city called *Kadesh* for Jerusalem.[8] In this case we cannot doubt that the city meant is *Kadesh* on the Orontes, in Northern Syria, the capital of the *Kheta*, or Hittites, with whom the Theban Kings of the New Monarchy waged many and great wars, which are often recorded on the monuments. These Semitic Hittites, who were worshippers of *Soutekh*, were the descendants of the Hyksos, and the hereditary enemies of Egypt.

It must not be supposed that the whole mass of the Shepherd invaders were driven, with their warriors, from the soil of Egypt. Many were permitted to remain as cultivators of the lands on which they had long been settled, in a condition very similar to that of the Hebrews. The more the condition of ancient Egypt unfolds itself to our researches, the more clearly do we see that the Delta was largely peopled by Semitic races, who formed a nationality distinct from the true Egyptians, and became at last, under the tyrants of the Nineteenth Dynasty, the Poland of the New Monarchy. M. Mariette believes that he has discovered the descendants of some of these Shemites—perhaps of the Hyksos themselves—in the strong-limbed people, with long faces and a grave expression, who live at the present day on the borders of the *Lake Menzaleh*.

One momentous consequence of the Shepherd conquest appears to have been that the expelled Shemites carried back with them into Syria the arts and letters of Egypt, which were thence diffused by the maritime Phœnicians over the opposite shores of Greece. Thus Egypt begins, at this epoch, to come in contact at once with the East and the West, with Asia and with Europe.

[8] In the same way, when Herodotus speaks twice of *Cadytis* in Syria (and in one place as a great city of the "Palestinian Syrians," or "Syrian Philistines"), it has been hastily assumed that he means Jerusalem; whereas, in one passage, it is pretty certainly *Gaza*, and, in the other, very probably the Hittite city of Kadesh on the Orontes, of which more in the following chapters.

The two Colossi of Thebes before the temple built by Amunoph III., with the ruins
of Luxor in the distance, during the inundation.

CHAPTER VIII.

THE NEW THEBAN MONARCHY.

THE EIGHTEENTH DYNASTY — EGYPT AT HER CLIMAX.

WE have now reached the third and culminating epoch of Egypt's
greatness, and the point from which we possess her continuous
monumental history, though often sadly mutilated and interrupted.
The seat of power is transferred to Upper Egypt, and to that
famous city which Homer celebrates as

> " Egyptian THEBES, where countless wealth her palaces adorns,
>   And from whose hundred gates pour forth, from each, two hundred men,
>   With horses and with chariots, 'midst clouds of sand and dust."

The war-chariots of Thebes are still to be seen depicted on the
walls of her palaces; but there are no traces of the gates which
gave her the famous epithet of *Hecatompylos*, the "Hundred-
gated," nor indeed of any city wall. The great cities of Egypt
appear to have been unenclosed; their power of resistance de-
pending on the strength of the separate buildings, and sometimes
on a citadel, like the " White Castle" of Memphis.

Still the " hundred gates" need not be set down as a fable,
though the exact number is, of course, poetical. Pliny describes
Thebes as " a hanging city"—that is, built upon arches—so that
an army could be led forth from beneath it without the knowledge

of the inhabitants; and there may have been near the river line
arched barracks capable of sending forth 10,000 chariots:—

> " Lo! these are they whom, lords of Afric's fates,
> Old Thebes hath poured from all her hundred gates,
> Mother of armies!"

Though the name coincides with that of the Greek city in
Bœotia, it is purely Egyptian. TAPE, compounded of the femi-
nine article T and APE (*head*, or capital, became in the Memphitic
dialect *Thaba*, and in Greek and Latin *Thebæ* or *Thebe*;[1] in English
Thebes. Its sacred name was P-AMEN or AMUN-EI, "the abode
of *Amen* or *Amun*," the great god of Upper Egypt especially.
Hence the Hebrew prophets call it *No-Ammon* (or simply *No*), and
hence also its classical name of *Diospolis the Great*, for the Greeks
regarded the Egyptian *Amun* as their *Jove*, and called him *Zeus
Ammon* (in Latin, *Jupiter Ammon*). As the great seat of this
worship, Thebes had an unknown antiquity; and it is difficult to
settle the question of precedence between it and Memphis, the
sacred city of *Phtha*.

The political consequence of Thebes dates from the kings of the
11th and 12th Dynasties; and under those of the 18th it became
the capital of all Egypt. When Memphis had been ravaged by the
Shepherds, and the Delta lay open to the growing power of the
Asiatic Shemites, Upper Egypt was the securer locality for a
capital, and the site of Thebes was the best in Upper Egypt. In
about 25° 40' N. latitude, the two chains of hills which hem in the
valley of the Nile sweep away on both sides, and return again on
the north, leaving a circular plain of about 10 miles in diameter,
divided almost equally by the river (here about half a mile in
width), and protected by a narrow entrance against a force ascending the Nile. The city, with its necropolis, seems to have once
covered the whole plain.

As a sacred city, Thebes stood to Ethiopia, as well as to Egypt,
in the relation occupied by Rome to medieval Christendom. She
was the sacerdotal capital of all who worshipped Amun, from
Pelusium to Axumé in Abyssinia, and from the Oases of Libya
to the Red Sea. Indeed, as her relations with Ethiopia became
closer, and as Semitic influence increased in the Delta, there was
more than one period in Egyptian history when Upper Egypt and
Ethiopia appear in league against Lower Egypt. The construction
of her temples and palaces, and the vast population of priests and
their attendants, in addition to the presence of the court, must
have attracted to Thebes a multitude of artisans. Her monuments

---

[1] This singular is preferred by some Latin writers to the Greek plural form.

shew the handicrafts for which she was famous, in glass, pottery, and intaglios; and her manufacture of linen was peculiarly important, as the priests were not allowed to wear woollen garments.

Thebes was also the centre of an extensive commerce. An opening in the Arabian hills gave access to the port of Kosseir, on the Red Sea, by a road which, as we have seen, was used as early as the times of the Old Monarchy. On the other side, the city was the best starting-point for the caravan-routes across the desert, to the three chief *Oases* (the Greater, the Lesser, and that of Ammon) and to the interior of Africa. Thus Thebes commanded the trade with India, and with the gold, ivory, and aromatic districts. It is almost needless to add that she held the key to the whole upper valley of the Nile; and, besides all the other products of Ethiopia, several of the Theban kings made great slave-hunting raids into negroland. The mines of the neighbouring limestone hills added to her wealth.

Thus enriched by religion, royalty, manufactures, and trade, Thebes not only flourished under her own great kings of the New Monarchy (Dynasties XVIII. to XX.), but her importance under the later Pharaohs, whether sprung from the Delta or Ethiopia, is attested by their pictures and inscriptions. The first great blow that fell upon her from a foreign conqueror was struck by Nebuchadnezzar; and the Persian invader completed the destruction that the Babylonian had begun. "No-Ammon, that was situate among the rivers, and whose rampart was the sea," sank from its metropolitan splendour to the position of a mere provincial town; and, notwithstanding the spasmodic efforts of the Ptolemies to revive its ancient glory, became at last only the desolate and ruined sepulchre of the empire it had once embodied. It lies to-day, a nest of Arab hovels, amid crumbling columns and drifting sands.

Such was also its state at the time when Egypt fell under the power of Rome. Strabo, writing just at the Christian era, says:—"Vestiges of its magnitude still exist, which extend 80 stadia (8 geographical miles) in length. . . . The spot is at present occupied by villages." Four such villages now mark the four corners of a quadrangle, measuring two miles from north to south, and four from east to west, within which lie the remains of the *monumental* city. This was probably the extent of the royal and sacred quarters of ancient Thebes. East of the Nile are *Karnak* on the north, and *Luxor* (*El-Uqsor*) on the south; while *Kurneh* and *Medinet-Abou* occupy the corresponding sites west of the river. At these four angles are four great temples, and the whole quadrangle appears to have been completed by four connecting avenues lined with sphinxes and other colossal figures.

The great temple of *Karnak* was the work of nearly every age, from Sesortasen I. to the Ptolemies. It is famed above every edifice in the world for its vast " Hall of Columns," built by Seti I. of the 19th Dynasty. This is a perfect forest of sculptured columns, of enormous height and thickness. A moonlight view of the hall is the most weird and impressive scene among all the ruins of antiquity, the Coliseum not excepted. On the opposite side of the river, at *Old Kurneh*, is another palace of Seti, called the *Menephtheion* ; and a mile further to the south is the famous *Memnonium*, now called more properly the *Rameseum*, built by Rameses II., the son of Seti, and the great oppressor of the Hebrews. The *Southern Rameseum*, of Rameses III., at *Medinet-Abou*, and other important monuments, such as the " Vocal Memnon," will be noticed in their historical places.

Further to the west lies the vast *Necropolis*, excavated to a depth of several hundred feet in the Libyan hills, over a length of five miles. The royal sepulchres are not reared aloft like the Memphian pyramids, but hollowed out in a retired valley, called *Biban-el-Melook*, or " Gates of the Kings." The whole western quarter bore the name of *Pathyris* (in Greek *Pathros*), that is, " the Abode of *Athur* (or *Athor*)," the goddess who was believed to receive the sun in her arms as he sank behind the Libyan hills.

Painted and sculptured on the walls of these temples, palaces. and tombs—and inscribed on the obelisks, colossal statues, and other monuments—we have the contemporary records of the Theban kings and of many of their successors. There is a sameness, not only in the painted bas-reliefs, which represent the king— distinguished by his colossal size—driving his chariot over hosts of prostrate enemies, or presenting to his patron god long files of captives strung together ; not only in the grandiloquent language of the hieroglyphics which record the invariably successful wars ; but even the scenes of those wars, the names of the conquered nations, and the description of their tribute, are constantly repeated, proving that the most was made of every expedition, however partial or even doubtful its success.

Many of the names are still imperfectly identified ; and a king often seems to claim the conquests of

<blockquote>" Regions Pharaoh never knew "</blockquote>

on the strength of some tribute, or present, or friendly embassy. A nation may be set down as conquered when only a detachment of its forces fought as the allies of Egypt's enemies—nay, even when it had invaded the soil of Egypt. We shall not follow the annals of these reiterated campaigns, much less enter on the discussions they involve. It will be more interesting and profitable to trace boldly the grand outlines, and to dwell on the few picturesque details of this culminating period of the greatness of the Pharaohs.

The following succession of the chief kings of the *Eighteenth Dynasty* is determined from the monuments:—(1) AAHMES or AMES; (2) AMENHOTEP[2] I.; (3) THOUTMES or THOTHMES I.; (4) THOTHMES II., and the queen-regent, HATASOU; (5) THOTHMES III.; (6) AMENHOTEP II.; (7) THOTHMES IV.; (8) AMENHOTEP III.; (9) AMENHOTEP IV.; (10) HAR-EM-HEBI, the HORUS of Manetho.

Immediately upon the expulsion of the Hyksos, the agriculture, commerce, and art of Egypt reappear in full vigour. The conformity of the strangers to Egyptian manners doubtless fostered the revival, of which the credit is given to their conquerors. *Aahmes* at once set about restoring the temples destroyed by the Hyksos, especially at Thebes and Memphis; and an inscription of his 22nd year, in the quarries of *Jebel Mokattem* (opposite *Cairo*), which he reopened for this purpose, proves his power over Lower Egypt.

From the very beginning of the new period, also, began those conquests, both in Asia and Ethiopia, which form the chief exploits of the Theban kings. Aahmes quelled a revolt in Nubia; and his marriage with an Ethiopian princess, *Nofre-t-ari*, appears to have given his successors a claim to the sovereignty of that country. The same founder of the dynasty, pursuing the Hyksos into their new settlements in Syria, began that long conflict of a thousand years with Western Asia, which made Egypt in turn the mistress and the vassal of Assyria, the successful and conquered enemy of Babylon, and at last a province of Persia.

To understand the nature of these wars, the reader must remember that a great highway between Egypt and the Euphrates lay open along the *maritime plain* of Western Palestine—leaving the heart of the country to the right—thence, striking eastwards through the plain of Esdraëlon, or valley of Megiddo (the scene of two great Egyptian victories), up the valley of the Upper Jordan into that traversed in opposite directions by the Leontes in the south and the Orontes in the north—the region called Cœle-Syria and Hamath, between the two chains of Lebanon. An army could either traverse this whole valley before striking across to the Euphrates and Upper Mesopotamia, or turn off through Anti-Libanus to Damascus, and cross the desert by way of Palmyra.

By taking military possession of the maritime plain (in which the Philistines were not established till a much later time), the kings of Egypt had at once a secure base of operations against the

<hr>

[2] The Greeks made the name *Amenoyhis*, and modern writers often use the convenient abbreviation *Amunoph*.

divided tribes of the Canaanites and the Arabs of the neighbouring Desert, and the gate of entrance into Syria and Mesopotamia. In these regions they came into contact chiefly with the *Kheta*, the *Rotno*, and the land of *Naharain*. The first, who appear to be the same nation as the *Hittites* of Scripture, and—to some extent at least—identical with the *Hyksos*, consolidated a great power in the valley of the Orontes, which became a formidable enemy of Egypt under the 19th Dynasty.

The earliest expeditions of the 18th Dynasty appear to have followed chiefly the more southern route by way of Damascus; and their monuments continually mention the *Rotno*, who appear to be a confederacy of Semitic tribes in Eastern Syria and Northern Mesopotamia. Sir Gardner Wilkinson observes that "the tight dress, the long gloves, the red hair and blue eyes of the *Rotno*, proclaim them to be of a colder climate than Syria, though the jars of bitumen appear to place them in the neighbourhood of the Euphrates or the Tigris. The beauty of their silver, gold, and porcelain vases, at all events, point them out as a people far advanced in luxury and taste."

To what extent this *people* coincide with the *land* called on the monuments *Naharain* is uncertain; but the latter name is evidently the *Naharaim* of Scripture, "the land of the two rivers," or MESOPOTAMIA. The conquests of the Theban kings, in this direction, seem to have embraced the whole of Assyria, which was still occupied by petty states. THOTHMES III., the greatest king of the 18th Dynasty, records that, after gaining a great victory over a Syrian and Hittite confederacy at *Megiddo*, conquering Cœle-Syria, and receiving the submission of the *Rotno*, "he stopped at NINEVEH (*Ninicu*), where he set up a monumental tablet in *Naharaïn*, having enlarged the frontiers of Egypt." He claims BABYLON as belonging to his empire; and in the north he received tribute from the *Remenen*, who are supposed to be the people of ARMENIA, "where heaven rests upon its four pillars."

In the opposite direction the Theban kings effected a complete conquest of Ethiopia, as far south, at least, as the capital city of Napata (*Jebel Berkel*); and the government of the country was committed to a viceroy, probably a prince of the royal family, who bore the title of "the royal son of *Kesh* or *Cush*." Raids were made further south, into negro-land (*Soudan*); and an inscription at *Semneh* mentions the capture of 740 and 1052 "living head" of negroes, many of them children. Another inscription brings the conquests at the two extremities of the empire into vigorous contrast. AMENHOTEP II., having put down an insurrection in Mesopotamia, sends the dead bodies of seven kings to be hung, six under the walls of Thebes, and the seventh at Napata, "that the blacks might see that the king's victories went on for ever, in all lands and all peoples of the world, since he at once held possession of the nations of the south, and chastised the nations of the north."

To these may be added the *Shasou*, or Arabs east of the Delta, and the *Pount*, who are supposed to be people of Arabia Felix; and the *Lebu* or *Rebu*, the Libyans to the west of Egypt, who are also called the people of the *Nine Bows*. It seems, too, that Thothmes III. used the maritime power of the Phœnicians—who appear to have submitted to him on easy terms—to extend his conquests far westward along the north coast of Africa, and even to the opposite shores of the Mediterranean. Cyprus, Crete, the southern isles of the Ægean, the neighbouring shores of Asia Minor and Greece, and perhaps the southern extremity of Italy, are named on his monuments, if correctly interpreted. Egypt, usually a non-maritime power, now seems, for once in her long history, to have been mistress of the Mediterranean.

At all events, it is clear that under the Pharaohs of the Eighteenth Dynasty Egypt became the first of the great Eastern empires. Their monuments give vivid pictures of the nations they subdued and the tribute brought by each. One of these records, inscribed by Thothmes III. on the great temple of which he was the chief builder, is called "The Numerical Wall of Karnak" from its statistics of prisoners and booty. This king was a great builder in *brick*; and it is on one of his monuments that the curious process of brick-making is represented, which tallies so exactly with that described in *Exodus*. "In these pictures," says Dr. Brugsch, "we see the reprisals of Egypt on their Shemite oppressors of the time of the Hyksos. Thousands of Semitic prisoners are represented on the temple walls in the act of carrying water to knead the mortar, forming bricks in wooden frames, spreading them out to dry in the sun, carrying them to the buildings in course of erection, and the like; all this being done under the eye of Egyptian officials, lounging about armed with weighty sticks, while different inscriptions inform us of the special work done by these 'prisoners whom the king has taken, that they might build temples to his gods.'"

Among the means of perpetuating their fame, these kings made great use of *obelisks* and *colossal statues*. Perhaps the most beautiful and exquisitely sculptured of the obelisks are the two in rose-coloured granite at *Karnak*, erected in memory of Thothmes I. by his daughter *Hatasou* (or *Nemt-Amen*), who possessed great power in the reign of her brothers Thothmes II. and Thothmes III., and ruled Egypt as regent during the minority of the latter. The style of the colossi can be partly judged of from the gigantic head and arm of Thothmes III. in the British Museum.

One monument of this class has been a wonder of the world from the time of the Ptolemies to our own day. This is the broken seated colossus of AMENHOTEP III., called by the ancients the "Vocal Memnon," from the sounds which it emitted at sunrise. The Greeks supposed it to represent Memnon, the son of Aurora, whom Homer represents as coming from Ethiopia to the aid of Troy; and the sounds were interpreted as his greeting to the Sun, his father. On the legs of the statue are numerous attestations in Greek and Latin, by visitors in the time of the Roman Empire, who had heard the statue emit a sound like a harp-string, or, as Strabo says, *like a slight blow.* The last statement tends to confirm the explanation of Sir Gardner Wilkinson, who found in the lap of the colossus (where a priest or a servant may have been concealed) a stone which, on being struck with a hammer, gave out a metallic sound, such that the peasants, whom he had placed to listen below, cried out, "You are striking brass." Another traveller reversed the experiment, and himself remained below to hear the sound. "Not at sunrise, but in the glaring noon, the statue emitted a sharp, clear sound, like the ringing of a disc of brass under a sudden concussion. This was produced by a ragged urchin, who, for a few piastres, clambered up the knees of the 'vocal Memnon,' and there *effectually concealing himself from observation,* struck with a hammer a sonorous sound in the lap of the statue."

The latter period of the Eighteenth Dynasty was a time of religious troubles. The native records tell us of a race of "Stranger Kings," whose tombs have been found apart from the other royal sepulchres at Thebes. The chief of these was AMENHOTEP IV., the features of whose statue are decidedly un-Egyptian. He discarded the old gods of Egypt for the direct worship of the Sun, under the Syrian name of *Aten;* changed his own name to *Chou-en-Aten,* that is, "brilliancy of the solar disc;" and set up a new capital, on the ruins of which, at *Tel-Amarna,* he is depicted as presiding over the new worship. There are traces of a violent reaction against the religious innovations of this king. His buildings have been overthrown and his capital at *Tel-Amarna* systematically devastated; and the names of the "Stranger Kings" are effaced from their monuments.

This, indeed, is a process which has been adopted in many other cases, from motives of hatred or of vanity, so that we may apply to the Egyptian monuments what Pope says of the names of *critics* on the 'Temple of Fame':—

> " *Pharaohs* I saw, who other names displace,
> And grave their own with labour in their place:
> Their own, like others, soon their place resigned,
> Or disappeared, and left the first behind."

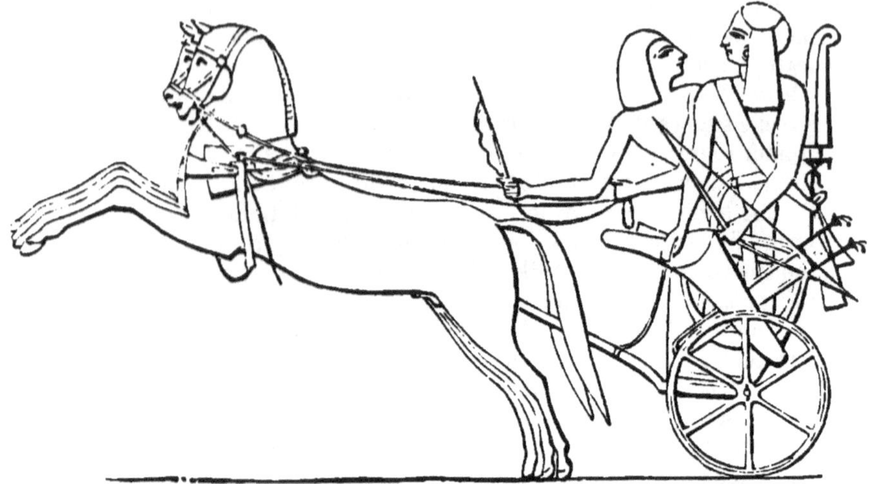

The Son of King Rameses with his Charioteer.

CHAPTER IX.

THE NEW THEBAN MONARCHY.

NINETEENTH DYNASTY — RAMESES II., THE OPPRESSOR OF THE HEBREWS.

MANETHO has not explained what constitutes the change from one *Dynasty* to another; nor can we always suggest a reason for the distinction. But in the second of the great Theban dynasties there appears to have been a real change of family, in which the pure blood of the line of Aahmes was united with a foreign element, and that element the race of the detested Shepherds! The founder of the dynasty in Manetho's list is RHAMSES or RAMESES I., who appears to have belonged to the old line; but its glories begin with the next two kings, SETI I. and his son, RAMESES II.

Inscriptions of the latter state that he was king before his birth, and that his father Seti only governed for him. This is explained by supposing that Seti was not really the son, but the son-in-law, of Rameses I., whose rights were regarded as transmitted direct to his grandson Rameses II., and that the latter was associated in the kingdom from his birth. Hence we may account for the great length of the reign of Rameses II. (66 or 68 years), following upon the 51 or 55 years which Manetho assigns to Seti; and hence also it is that the warlike exploits and great buildings of the father and son are often confounded.

As to the parentage of Seti, we have a curious piece of evidence, besides the foreign features which some trace in his portrait as well as in his son's. A recently discovered inscription at Tanis exhibits Rameses II. as not only restoring the worship of the god *Soutekh* in the ancient capital of the Shepherds, but even calling the founder of their dynasty, *Set-aa-pehti Noubti*, his ancestor. The very name of *Seti*, and the favour which his family showed to Tanis, are circumstances of no small significance.

The splendid monuments of these two rulers, and the fact that the famous Sesostris denoted (if any individual king) Rameses II., have led many to regard their age as the climax of Egyptian glory. But their utmost exploits only defended the empire won by Thothmes III. As a recent writer well observes, "Egypt, so threatening under the Eighteenth Dynasty, becomes now almost always threatened."   Her power, as well as her art, shewed visible symptoms of decline before the death of Rameses II.

Seti I., surnamed *Merenphtha* or *Menephtha*, "beloved of *Phtha*," has left the sculptured and painted records of his exploits, forming what has been called "an epic of war, a *real Setheïd*," on the walls of his "Hall of Columns" at *Karnak*. Covering much the same ground as those of the Eighteenth Dynasty, they prove that the empire then won had to be defended or reconquered on every side, except in Ethiopia. There are no naval victories in the Mediterranean, but the fleets of Seti command the Red Sea; and to him is ascribed the beginning of the canal uniting that sea with the Nile, the continuation of which by his son Rameses is indicated by tablets along its banks.

It seems probable that the work was completed, and used for the Indian commerce of Egypt and Phœnicia. But the experience of to-day proves that vigilance and toil are needed to guard such a canal from choking by the sands of the desert. It fell into disuse, and the enterprise was renewed in vain by Pharaoh-Necho about B.C. 600, and by Darius Hystaspis a century later. The course of the canal, however, may still be traced from the neighbourhood of Heliopolis to the "Bitter Lakes," and thence to the Gulf of Suez. The recent work of M. de Lesseps, opened in 1869, only coincides with the latter section of the ancient canal, proceeding not from the Nile, but in a direct line, north and south, from the Mediterranean to the "Bitter Lakes." *Esto perpetua!*

Rameses II., surnamed Meriamun or Miamun, that is, "beloved of Amun," is first mentioned as distinguished in his father's wars. His own exploits were almost limited to the north of Syria, where he carried on a long war with the *Kheta*, or Hittites, of the valley of the Orontes.

His bas-reliefs on the walls of the *Rameseum* at *Kurneh* (commonly called the *Memnonium*) exhibit interesting details of a siege. The whole system of attack and defence is curiously like what we see on the Assyrian sculptures, and what we read of in Greek and Roman tactics. Here are the scaling-ladder and the *testudo*, with its wicker roof protecting the *terebra* or boring-pike; there the pioneers attack the gates with axes, while the archers clear the wall of its defenders. We see the defeat of the enemy, the dispersion of their chariots, and their leader drowned in attempting to cross the river.

But we have a still more interesting written record of this war. Among the literary treasures of ancient Egypt is a papyrus containing *the most ancient epic in the world*, written by the scribe *Pentaour*, and celebrating in the true vein of heroic hyperbole a personal exploit of Rameses. By the fault of his generals and scouts, the king has fallen into an ambush. Disdaining to fly, and deserted by his followers, he rushes with his charioteer alone into the midst of the enemy, and cuts his way through their 2500 chariots of war. There is a truly Homeric spirit in the vow which the king makes at the moment of extremest peril; in the reproof to his warriors, and the praise of his horses who alone have saved him, in reward whereof they are to be served each day with grain in his palace before the god Ra. After the final victory, we have the king's return to Egypt, and his welcome by *Amun:*—"Health to thee, Rameses, our cherished son. We grant thee terms of years innumerable. Sit for ever on the throne of thy father Amun, and let the barbarians be crushed beneath thy sandals."

The issue of the war scarcely corresponded to this blessing. It continued at intervals from the 5th to the 21st year of Rameses, and ended with a treaty of peace on terms of remarkable equality. This most ancient of treaties has an amusing resemblance to the terms of similar instruments down to the present day—perpetual amity—surrender of deserters—equality of commercial privileges— and so forth. A very interesting article is the provision for the restoration of the worship of *Soutekh* at Tanis, while the Hittite king, *Khetasar*, engages on his part to pay equal honours to the gods of Egypt in his capital.

This seems to have been the last great war of Rameses II.; and when the young student reads the story of Sesostris in Herodotus, he will see how completely it is a poetical exaggeration, based on combining the exploits of several great Egyptian kings.

The long tranquillity of his later years enabled Rameses to achieve those works of architecture and sculpture which stud the whole course of the Nile, from Tanis, in the Delta, to Napata, the

capital of Ethiopia.   There is scarcely a ruin or colossal fragment
that does not bear his name; but he was one of the chief offenders
in the practice of erasing the names of his predecessors to substitute
his own.

His works show the vast proportions of Egyptian art carried to

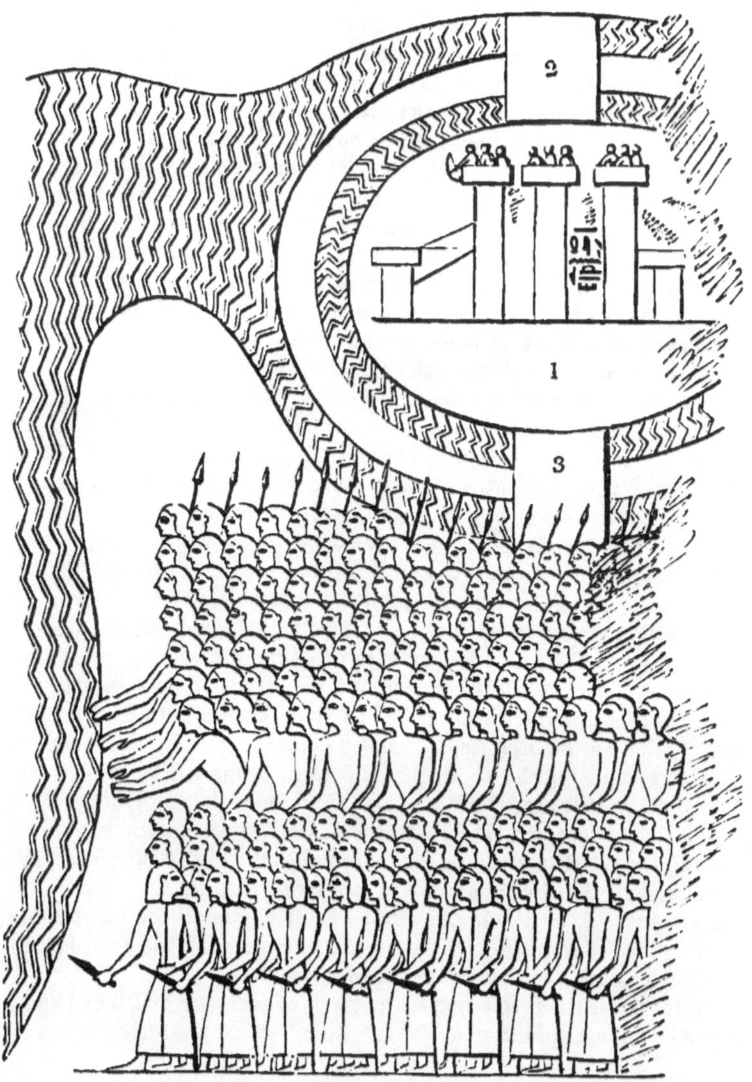

Phalanx of the Kheta, drawn up as a corps de réserve, with the fortified town (1),
surrounded by double ditches, over which are *bridges* (figs. 2 and 3).

their extremest scale, especially in the rock-hewn temples of *Abou-Simbel* in Nubia, with their frontispiece of four seated colossi —the largest in the world—and in his numerous other colossal statues. The most beautiful of these was the image of himself in granite, about 60 feet high, which adorned the court of the Rameseum, and the bust of which was brought to England by Belzoni. Every visitor to the British Museum may admire the features so finely chiselled, though of so huge a size, marked by an expression of dignity, with a quiet smile about the lips characteristic of the self-satisfied despot. As a portrait it carries its own evidence.

Rameses II. was a magnificent patron of letters as well as art. The " sacred library," which Diodorus mentions at Thebes, with the inscription " Dispensary of the Soul," has been discovered in his palace, the *Rameseum* at Karnak. The jambs of the doorway leading from the great hall to a suite of nine small rooms are sculptured with figures of *Thoth*, the great god of letters, and his companion goddess *Saf*—the former with the emblem of *sight*, the latter with that of *hearing*—and with the titles of " Lady of Letters " and " President of the HALL OF BOOKS."

Nine chief men of learning were attached to the person of this king, and at their head was a certain *Kagabu*, as " Master of the Rolls," a man " unrivalled in elegance of style and diction." From the pen of this master, who may have helped to train Moses, the king's adopted grandson, in " all the learning of the Egyptians," we still possess *the oldest fairy tale in the world*, a moral story, resembling that of Joseph and Potiphar's wife, composed for the king's son *Menephtha*, the destined opponent of Moses.

Thus are we drawn on to the great point of interest in the history of Rameses II.; for his identity with the Pharaoh who oppressed the Israelites is now established beyond dispute. If Joseph was the minister of a Shepherd king, it has long been felt that the " *new* king" who " *arose over Egypt*," and " *knew not Joseph*," must denote the Theban monarchy or one of its great kings. The choice lies between the 18th and 19th Dynasty, and there is no evidence that the former were great oppressors. Secure in their conquests abroad, the Thothmeses and Amunophs seem to have cherished the Shemites of the Delta as useful subjects, though they employed some in forced labour, and doubtless exacted from all the full tribute of their fertile lands, for the extreme harshness of the field labour was a feature of the subsequent oppression.[1]

Under the 19th Dynasty new motives of jealousy and fear began to work. The rapid increase of the Israelites on the fertile lands of

---

[1] Exod. i. 14.

Goshen, "the best land of Egypt," was doubtless shared by the other Shemites of the Delta, whose numbers must have been vastly augmented by captives taken in the long wars of the 18th Dynasty, till "the land was filled with them."[2] Then it was that "the new king over Egypt,"[3] finding it necessary to renew the Syrian and Mesopotamian wars, took the alarm at this vast population kindred to his enemies. "And he said unto his people, Behold, the people of the children of Israel *are more and mightier than we: Come on, let us deal wisely with them; lest they multiply, and it come to pass, that, when there falleth out any war, they join also unto our enemies, and fight against us, and get them up out of the land.*"[4]

Terror begets tyranny; and the fear, not only of their actual hostility, but of losing their services as slaves, dictated the means used to keep them under. Employment upon public works is one great resource of a magnificent despot for amusing a disaffected populace if they be free, for coercing them if slaves. "Mortar, bricks, and all manner of service in the field" were the means by which "the Egyptians made the children of Israel *to serve with rigour,* and made *their lives bitter with hard bondage.*"[5] We are told, and here is the decisive point, the very *names* of "the treasure cities which they built for Pharaoh, *Pithom* and *Raamses* (or *Rameses*)";[6] and any doubt of what this means is now cleared up by what we may venture to call the *court news* of that day, and by *official reports* preserved among Egyptian books.

Papyri of the time of Rameses II. give a glowing description of the chain of fortified cities, which the hieroglyphics tell us that *Pherāo* (the *Pharaoh* or King) erected from Pelusium to Heliopolis. The two principal of these bore the names of *Rameses* and *Pachtum,* both situated in the present *Wady-Tumeilat,* near the sweet water canal that joined the Nile with the Red Sea, along the course of which we still find monuments bearing the name of Rameses II. One of these monuments describes the reception of the king *at the city of Rameses* in the tenth year of his reign. As this was eleven years before the end of his Hittite wars, and apparently about the time when the enemy were for a time masters of Palestine and the military road, we can now see a motive for the building of this chain of " treasure cities " or strongholds.

But a still more striking testimony remains. *The very name of the* Hebrews *is officially recorded by their persecutors as the builders of the city of Rameses.* In a papyrus preserved in the museum of Leyden, the scribe *Kautsir* reports to his superior, the scribe *Bakenphtha,* that in compliance with his instructions he has "distributed

<hr>

[2] Exod. i. 7.   [3] Ib. 8.   [4] Ib. 9, 10.   [5] Ib. 13, 14.   [6] Ib. 11.

the rations among the soldiers *and likewise among the* HEBREWS
(*Aberiou* or *Apuru*), *who carry the stones to the great city of King*
RAMESES MIAMUN, *the lover of truth*, and who are under the orders
of the captain of the police soldiers *Ameneman*. I distribute the
food among them monthly, according to the excellent instructions
which my lord has given me." There are also other documents
referring to the people and their serfdom.

This discovery agrees with all the minor circumstances of the
Scripture narrative. The reign of Rameses II. is the only one
which, by its great length, suits the history of Moses. The whole
complexion of the narrative produces the conviction that both he
and his successor were sovereigns who wielded the whole power of
Egypt, when Egypt was at her highest state, and yet who frequently
resided in the Delta, nay in the part of the Delta where the
Hebrews dwelt. This circumstance, at first sight adverse to the
notion of a *Theban* dynasty, turns out (like all difficulties in the way
of truth) a striking confirmation, now that the connection of
Rameses II. and his son Menephtha with TANIS is established.
Nay, as usual when difficulties are removed, we open our eyes to
what we ought to have seen before, and we find that the exact locality had been plainly stated in words we have read again and again,
"*Jehovah did wondrous things in the field of* ZOAN." 7

We have spoken all along of the general oppression of the Shemites
of the Delta as connected with that of the Israelites. The Scripture
narrative is naturally confined to the latter; but it gives some
indication of the wider view in its mention of the vast " mixed multitude " or "great mixture" that " went up also with them " at the
Exodus, and proved a great source of trouble in the Desert.8 But
the mania of Rameses for building could not find an adequate supply of labour in Egypt, even in the myriads of captives that worked
under the stick, bedewing every brick and stone with sweat and
blood. So the system of slave-hunting was carried on to a vaster
extent than ever, and nearly every year we find records of *razzias*
into Soudan, bringing back· thousands of negroes. Rameses II.
appears also to have been the first king of Egypt who practised the
system, afterwards so common with the Assyrian and Babylonian
conquerors, of deporting whole tribes from one part of his dominions
to another, settling negroes in Asia, and Asiatics in Nubia.

His government over his native subjects was harsh and oppressive.
Existing documents prove that he ruled his enormous harem with
a cruelty worthy of the wretch who ordered the male children of
Israel to be murdered; and they give examples of the tyranny that

<hr>

7 Psalm lxxviii. 12, 43.   8 Exod. xii. 38; Numbers xi. 4.

he exercised even over the judges whom the law of Egypt made independent and inviolable. The state of the peasantry is described in a correspondence between *Ameneman*, the chief librarian of Rameses II., and his pupil, the poet *Pentaour*.

"Have you ever figured to yourself what is the life of the peasant who tills the land? Even before he has reaped, the insects destroy a portion of his crop: there are multitudes of rats in the fields: then come the flights of locusts, the beasts that ravage his harvest, the sparrows that settle in flocks upon his sheaves. If he is slow to get in what he has reaped, thieves come and take it from him: so his horse dies with fatigue in dragging the cart. The tax-gatherer arrives at the store-house of the district, having with him officers armed with sticks, and negroes armed with palm-branches. All cry, 'Give us your corn;' and he has no means of repelling their extortions. Then the wretch is seized, bound, and carried off to forced labour at the canals: his wife is bound: his children are stripped of their all. During all this time his neighbours are each at his own work, unable to help, and fearing for their own turn." The Egyptian peasant under " the great " Rameses was no better off than the *fellah* under the Mameluke or Turk.

The " groans of the soldier " form the subject of one of those literary exercises which were composed to exhibit ingenuity in the use of the Egyptian language. The composition is in accentuated parallel verses, not unlike those of the Psalms :—

" When you receive this piece of accentuated prose :
      may you find the work of the writer agreeable!
I wish to depict for you the many troubles : of the infantry officer.
While still young : he is shut up in the barrack.
A cramping coat of mail encloses his body : a helmet falls over his eyes.
The visor is on his eyelids : his head is protected from wounds.
He feels swaddled like a roll of papyrus :
      his movements are hampered in the battle.
Shall I tell you of his expeditions into Syria : his marches to regions far off?
He must carry his water on his shoulder : as asses carry their pack.
His back is bowed like that of a beast of burthen : and his spine is bent.
When he is disordered by unwholesome water : he must return to his night duty.
When he meets the enemy, he is like a bird caught in a snare :
      and his limbs have no strength.
When he returns to Egypt : he is like a block of worm-eaten wood.
If sickness befals him and makes him lie down :
      he is packed on the back of an ass.
His effects are pillaged by thieves : and his servants desert him."

War Galley during an Action.

CHAPTER X.

END OF THE THEBAN MONARCHY.

DYNASTY XIX. *continued* — THE EXODUS — DYNASTY XX.

THAT signal retribution for the tyranny of Rameses II., which fell
upon Egypt under his son, began to work before his own reign
closed. We have already seen that the records of the Nineteenth
Dynasty make no claim to that naval power in the Mediterranean
which had been wielded by Thotmes III. The maritime powers of
Asia Minor and Europe, especially the Tyrrheno-Pelasgians, began,
in their turn, to harass the the coast of Egypt, in league with the
tribes of North Africa, amongst whom the *Mashuash* (the *Maxyes* of
classical geography) are conspicuous on the monuments.

Whenever these enemies ventured on the soil of Egypt, their
attacks were repulsed by Seti I. and Rameses II.; and the prisoners
taken from the warlike Maxyes were enrolled as an auxiliary force,
which afterwards attained great importance, and even gave a race
of kings to Egypt.[1] But in the old age of Rameses they began to
effect settlements in the Delta; and Egypt was handed to his suc-

---

[1] The allusion is to the later Saïte Dynasty, founded by Psammetichus. See
Chapter XII.

cessor with an oppressed multitude of alien slaves in the east, and a powerful enemy in the west, of her richest province.

That successor, the thirteenth son of Rameses, was named MEREN-PHTHA or MENEPHTHA, that is "beloved of Phtha." His name is also read in the inverse order, *Phtha-men*, and he is sometimes called *Seti-Menephtha II.* in contradistinction to his grandfather. He shares with his father the "bad eminence" of being the great oppressor of Israel; and if the one was the haughtiest, the other was the most obstinate, of the Pharaohs. The terrible place which he occupies in history is marked by the voice of the judge of all ;— "for the Scripture saith unto Pharaoh, Even for this very purpose have I raised thee up, that I might show my power in thee, and that my name might be declared throughout all the earth." [2]

This Pharaoh of the Exodus is peculiarly connected with Lower Egypt; and most of his monuments are found at Memphis. That city, however, as well as Heliopolis, was taken by the invaders early in the reign of Menephtha, who fled to the Thebaid. We have had occasion to quote the contemporary document, which describes the calamity as surpassing anything that Egypt had suffered even in times of the Shepherd Kings. At length Mene-phtha despatched an army from Thebes under his father's generals, who defeated the advancing foes at *Paari*, in Middle Egypt. The mass of the invaders was driven out of Egypt; but lands were assigned to some bodies of them in the Delta.

The issue of this campaign would naturally lead Menephtha to return to Lower Egypt, and to hold his court, generally at Mem-phis, but sometimes also at Tanis. The proximity of this city to the land of Goshen, and all the "local colouring" of the story of the plagues and the Exodus, confirm the literal acceptation of the statement of the Psalmist, that "the marvellous things which God did in Egypt" were wrought "*in the field of* ZOAN." There were the river and canals which Moses turned into blood ; the ponds and marshes which sent up frogs and swarms of flies. There were the fat pastures of the cattle which were smitten with disease, and the fertile crops which the hail destroyed; and as we read how

> " the potent rod
> Of Amram's son, in Egypt's evil day,
> Waved round her coasts, called up a pitchy cloud
> Of locusts, warping on the *eastern* wind,
> That o'er the realm of impious Pharaoh hung
> Like night, and darkened all the land of Nile,

we recognize the neighbouring desert on the east as the quarter from which the like plague has repeatedly come upon the Delta.

[2] Exod. ix. 16 ; Rom. ix. 17.

The repeated interviews, not only of Moses and Aaron, but of the elders and overseers of Israel, with the king, and the story of the last night of the conflict, prove that the court was close to the region where the mass of the Israelites resided, and whence they began their Exodus. Nay more, a special reason may be given for the king's presence at Tanis at this precise juncture. Fortified as that city had been by the Shepherds, and favoured as it was by the house of Rameses, what is more probable than its continued use as the station of a frontier militia? The same motives which led the Shepherd Kings to visit it *in the early summer* (as Josephus tells us) would probably bring later kings there at the same season—the very season to which the plagues and the Exodus are fixed.

Here too Pharaoh would find, assembled to his hand, the army with which he pursued the retiring Israelites; and the force of the whole story is enhanced by the knowledge that that army was flushed with the pride of having expelled another host of enemies from Egypt. With what security must the conquerors of the Tyrrhenians, Cretes, and Maxyans, have urged their chariots upon the track of

> " Those flocks and herds, that faint and weary train,
> Red from the scourge, and recent from the chain!"

With what terror must the Israelites have been " sore afraid," and " cried unto the Lord," and called on Moses to lead them back to their " graves in Egypt," when overtaken by such a force! And how must the remembrance of its might have exalted " the honour gotten by Jehovah upon Pharaoh, upon his chariots, and upon his horsemen;" and have swollen the chorus in which Moses and the children of Israel re-echoed the strain of Miriam:—" Sing ye to the Lord, for he hath triumphed gloriously: the horse and his rider hath he thrown into the sea!"

It is, however, a mistake to suppose that Pharaoh himself perished in the Red Sea: the Scripture narrative declares only the destruction of his army. But the state of the country in his later years, and after his death, confirms one striking expression in the Scripture:—" Knowest thou not yet that Egypt is destroyed?" Menephtha survived to suffer a third great disaster in the invasion of a new body of Shemites, the descendants or kindred of the Hyksos, who re-occupied the lands left vacant by the Israelites, and before whom the king fled again to the Thebaid.[3] There he was buried in one of the most splendid of the royal tombs at Thebes. It is not

---

[3] We learn this from another important fragment quoted from Manetho by Josephus, and again obscured (like the story of the Shepherd Kings) by an attempt (this time on the part of his antagonist Philo) to wrest it into a connection with the Exodus.

surprising that we find on his monuments no mention of the Exodus of Israel, any more than of the two great invasions before which he fled. The monuments are always either silent about Egypt's great defeats, or pervert them into victories; nor is it the custom of any nation to make monumental records of its own disgrace.

The death of Menephtha was followed by the usurpation of a branch of the royal family at *Chev* (Aphroditopolis) in the *Fyûm*, who recovered most of Egypt from the invaders. But Seti II., the son of Menephtha, whom his father had sent for safety into Ethiopia, regained the crown, and was the last king of the 19th Dynasty.

The troubles amidst which that dynasty drew to its end account for Egypt's not interfering with Israel's conquest of Canaan, which she regarded as her own territory. But she had not lost her empire in Mesopotamia and Syria, as long as she kept her hold on the route through the maritime plain of Palestine; and this was the very portion of the Promised Land which Joshua was not strong enough to attack.

The *Twentieth Dynasty*—the last of the three which composed the New Theban Monarchy—claimed descent from Rameses II.; and all its kings, except the first, adopted his name as an appellation of royalty, like that of *Cæsar*. Conspicuous among them is Rameses III., whose exploits threw a dying lustre over the last years in which Egypt had an empire. The painted bas-reliefs, in which his campaigns are depicted on the walls of "the southern *Rameseum*" at *Medinet Abou*, are among the finest remains of Egyptian art, and contain the most animated pictures of battle-scenes, marches, and sieges.

Their chief subjects are the victories over the Hittites and Mesopotamians, by which Rameses III. recovered the empire of Egypt in Western Asia; and the great sea-fight in which he defeated the navies of the West off the Phœnician coast. The inscriptions appended to the pictures give examples of a royal style, which is worth comparing with modern *bulletins*. The following passage shows, by the way, that these vaunted victories were essentially defensive. "The king starts for the country of *Tsahi* (Cœle-Syria), like an image of the god Month, to trample under foot *the nations that have violated his frontiers*. His soldiers are like bulls charging flocks of sheep, his horses like hawks in a flock of small birds." The decisive victory in the valley of the Orontes is thus announced. "I have blotted out these nations and their country, as if they had never been."

The king's naval victory over the combined fleet of the chief maritime nations of the Mediterranean is a subject perfectly unique on the Egyptian monuments. Its date goes back to at least the

13th century B.C., five or six hundred years before the great sea-fight between the Corinthians and Corcyreans, which the Greek historians name as the first on record. Its scene is off the "Tower of Rameses," a fort erected on the spot where the king had already defeated an army disembarked by the allies. The ships of Rameses, ornamented with a lion's head upon each prow, have shut in the enemy's fleet between themselves and the lofty shore, whence the soldiers, commanded by the king himself, hurl showers of missiles. In a long inscription, Rameses vaunts the prowess of his soldiers, and especially his own: as for his enemies, "they will reap no more harvests in this world; the time of their soul is counted in eternity."

The bas-reliefs of *Medinet Abou* exhibit other campaigns of Rameses in Asia and Africa, and an inscription records the tribute brought to him by the people of the south and other regions;—vessels of gold and silver, bags of gold-dust, objects made of various metals, lapis-lazuli, and all sorts of precious stones. The vast subterranean tomb of Rameses III. is one of the finest in the *Biban-el-Molook*, or "Gates of the Kings," at Thebes.

The long line of succeeding kings of the same name presents little worthy of notice, except a curious story engraved on a tablet at Thebes. Rameses XII., in passing through Mesopotamia to collect his tribute, was captivated by the beauty of a chief's daughter, and married her. Some years afterwards, the chieftain came to Thebes, to ask the services of one of the king's physicians for his younger daughter, who was possessed by an evil spirit. The spirit proved stronger than the physician; and eleven years later the father made another journey to Thebes, to seek more effectual aid from the gods of Egypt. The king granted him the use of the ark of the god *Chons*, and the desired cure was wrought. But the Mesopotamian prince was unwilling to part with so potent a talisman; till, after three years and three quarters, seeing in a dream the god fly back to Egypt in the form of a golden hawk, he returned the ark to Rameses. While this story shows Mesopotamia as still subject to Egypt, it proves how loose was the bond of vassalage.

In fact, we have now reached the period when the Assyrian monarchy was gaining power beyond the Euphrates, though not yet strong enough to pass that boundary. Nearer home, the Philistines had barred the military road to Asia, and for a time obtained the mastery which Egypt had once held in Canaan. While Egypt was thus thrown back upon her natural limits, the crown was usurped by the high-priest of Amun at Thebes, whose name was HER-HOR, that is, "the supreme Horus;" and, after some vicissitudes, the line of Rameses was supplanted by a sacerdotal monarchy.

The monuments preserve some interesting records of this priestly line, who also appear as the heads of the military class by the title of " Commander of the Soldiers " (or " Archers "). In the temple of Chons, the founder is invested by his patron deity, Horus, with the *white cap*, and by the goddess Nebti with the *red cap*, the symbols of dominion over Upper and Lower Egypt. To establish his power at home, the new ruler gave up all claim to dominion in Asia, as the price of an alliance with the king now reigning at Nineveh.

This alliance must have added strength to the Semitic element which had long gained a firm footing on the Nile. Asia now revenged herself for her subjection to the Theban kings by inroads upon that exclusive nationality which was the great bond of Egypt's strength. Semitic words had appeared in her language, foreign gods in her inaccessible sanctuaries. Thebes yielded her place as capital to the city which had been the stronghold of the Shepherds. Assyrian names become common among the kings of the next three dynasties, one of which we shall find to have been purely Assyrian. The seat of empire is departing from the Nile to the Tigris and Euphrates: but a conflict of five or six centuries has still to be decided before Egypt succumbs to Asia.

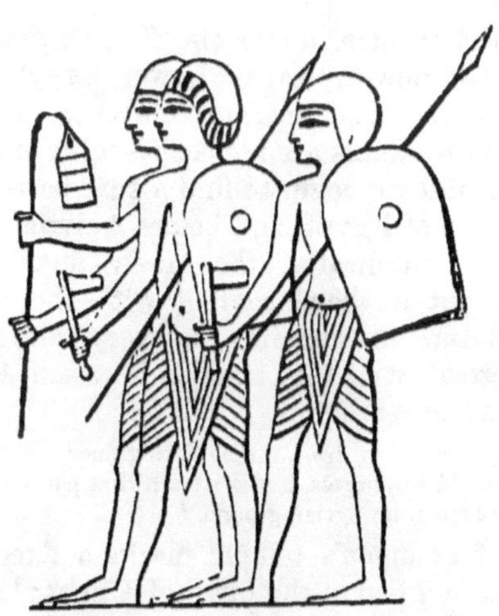

Guard with a Lantern—*Tel Amarna.*

An Ethiopian Princess.

CHAPTER XI.

THE KINGDOMS OF THE DELTA; AND THE DYNASTY OF ETHIOPIANS.

THE transfer of the sceptre, under the *Twenty-first Dynasty*, from Thebes to TANIS, the new capital of Lower Egypt, forms an epoch of great importance. The separate currents of the Egyptian, Assyrian, and Jewish annals are now converging into the stream of universal history; and we begin to find a sure basis of chronology.

During the decline of Egypt, and before Assyrian conquests were carried west of the Euphrates, the newly founded kingdom of Israel had fought out its hard conflict with the Philistines; and David, having subdued his enemies on every side, left to his son a *real empire*—the greatest at this time in Western Asia—occupying the region promised to Abraham

> " from the bordering flood
> Of old Euphrates, to the stream that parts
> Egypt from Syrian ground."

The building of Solomon's temple marks a fixed epoch in chronology, the *millennium* before the birth of Christ;[1] and that king's

[1] The received chronology gives B.C. 1015 for the accession of Solomon, B.C. 1012 for his beginning to build the Temple, and B.C. 1005 for his completion; and all

name, " the peaceful," expressed not only the state of his own kingdom, but the relations of the monarchies from the Tigris to the
Nile.   The friendship of the priest-kings of the line of Horus for
Assyria was evidently continued by the *Twenty-first Dynasty ;* and
one of the later kings of this dynasty was, in all probability, the
Pharaoh with whom Solomon made affinity, and married his
daughter.[2]

The position of Egypt in regard to Asia is indicated by the statement that Pharaoh gave as his daughter's dowry the site of *Gezar*,
between *Jaffa* and Jerusalem, which he had taken from the Canaanites and destroyed.   Thus the hold of Egypt upon the great
military road into Asia, newly recovered from the Philistines, seems
to have been renounced for the sake of the alliance with Solomon,
who himself occupied it by fortifying the newly ceded city.

Not only was the power of Israel thus interposed between Egypt
and her former enemies and subjects in Asia, but the commerce
between them helped to increase the wealth of Solomon.   He carried on a trade with Egypt in linen yarn, and in horses and chariots : not only importing the latter for his own use, but selling
them to the kings of the Hittites and of Syria.   Great indeed was
the change from the time when the Theban kings fought against
the chariots of the Hittites and their Syrian allies to that when
these nations were supplied with chariots from Egypt through the
medium of a great commercial empire founded by a people who
were once her slaves !

For the rest, we know little of the *Twenty-first (Tanite) Dynasty*,
to which Manetho assigns seven kings in 130 years; a period extending from about B.C. 1100 to about the end of Solomon's reign, B.C. 975
of the received chronology.   From the resemblance of the last three
names in Manetho's list of this dynasty to those of the   priest-kings"
found upon the monuments, it is thought that the sacerdotal line of
Her-Hor may have been united by marriage with the royal house
of Tanis.   This adoption of the claims of a monarchy in Lower
Egypt, together with their Assyrian alliance, would confirm their
power against the legitimate princes of Thebes.

At all events we now know that such a union of the two lines
was effected in the *Twenty-second (Bubastite) Dynasty*, which stands
forth in the full light of the Egyptian monuments and of Jewish
history.   Its first king, Sheshonk I. (*Shishak*), is at once *the first
Pharaoh who is mentioned in Scripture by his personal name*, and

chronologers agree to these dates within a variation of less than 20 years. The
birth of Christ falls at B.C. 4 of the technical era; but there are some reasons for
preferring B.C. 5 or 6.

    [2] 1 Kings iii. 1; vii. 8; ix. 24.

the first on whose monuments are read the name of the Jewish kingdom.
The researches of M. Mariette have recovered, from the *Apis-stelæ*
and the *Serapeum* at Memphis, the true order and origin of this
dynasty, and accounted for the distinctly Assyrian names which
are borne by all of them but one. They were a military dynasty,
sprung (like the modern Mamelukes) from the king's body-guard.
An officer bearing the same name as a famous Assyrian king of a later
age, *Sargon* (in Egyptian *Osorchon*), who was posted at Bubastis,
being already allied by marriage to the royal sacerdotal line of *Her-
Hor*, appears to have married the daughter of the last king of the
Twenty-first Dynasty. Their son SHESHONK, having been adopted
by his grandfather, became at first regent and afterwards king.

Thus the capital was again changed — but only for this one
dynasty—from Tanis to *Bubastis*, the sacred city of the goddess
Bast or *Pasht*, the goddess of fire. Her animal symbol was the
cat; and the sacred cats were brought for burial to Bubastis. Her
statues have the head of a lion. The Greeks identified her with
Artemis, and resorted much to her oracle.

The city was so ancient, that Manetho mentions it as the scene
of a destructive earthquake under the first king of the Second
Dynasty. It stood raised above the reach of the inundation by a
high embankment, on the Pelusiac or easternmost branch of the
Nile, where the lofty mounds of *Tel-Basta* ("the Hill of Pasht")
look down upon the ruins of the great temple of the goddess in
the low site described by Herodotus.[3] Here (besides the name of
Osorchon I. of the 22nd Dynasty) that of *Rameses II.* adds another
witness to his care for the sanctuaries of the Delta.

Herodotus, who saw the city at the height of its prosperity, gives
a pleasant description of the annual festival of *Bubastis*—the
greatest in all Egypt — to which as many as 700,000 men and
women came from all quarters in boats, amidst the noise of pipes
and castanets, singing and clapping of hands, and contests of rude
raillery with the villagers along the banks. More *grape-wine*, he
says (for *barley-wine* also was largely made in Egypt), was consumed
at this festival than in all the rest of the year besides.

The accession of the Bubastite Dynasty took place just when the
disaffection of Israel, under the burthen of Solomon's magnificence,
furnished the new and warlike king of Egypt with an opportunity
to revive her claims of sovereignty over Palestine.[4] SHISHAK (SHE-

---

[3] We have here an interesting example of the way in which a city of the Delta
was gradually raised by the process of embankment around the original site marked
by its old temple. In other times and countries sacred buildings give way to
embankments and cuttings.

[4] A fuller account of the events of Scripture History, to which we have now
frequently alluded, will be found in our text books on that subject. But it is as

shonk I.) is expressly mentioned as the Pharaoh who received the fugitive Jeroboam, and sent him back at the invitation of the ten tribes. The clear inference, that he returned to reign *as a vassal of Egypt*, is put beyond all doubt by his setting up the worship of Egyptian idols at his two frontier cities—*Dan* and *Bethel*—which were both ancient sanctuaries. The golden calves of Jeroboam, like that of Aaron, were images of the god Apis.

In accordance with Egypt's wonted policy—to avoid needless interference with kings whom she regarded as vassals—Rehoboam might have remained unmolested at Jerusalem. But when he placed garrisons in the cities of Southern Judah and even of the maritime plain, Shishak treated him as a rebel. At the head of an army resistless from its numbers, he reduced the frontier fortresses, entered Jerusalem and plundered the temple, and received the unreserved submission of the king and princes (B.C. 971). It was as *the vassal of Egypt* that Rehoboam "strengthened himself in Jerusalem and reigned"; and, among the conquered cities depicted on the splendid bas-relief of Sheshonk at *Karnak*, there is a shield inscribed JEHOUADA-MALEK, with the hieroglyphic sign for "land." The identification is equally clear, whether we read the phrase, with some, "*the Land of the King of Judah*," or, with others, "*Judah the royal (city) of the land.*"

In this bas-relief, which vies in scale and in the number of the conquests recorded with the proudest monuments of the Theban dynasty, the ruler of Assyrian race assumes the favourite title of those kings: he is *Miamun Sheshonk*, "Sheshonk beloved of Amun." [5] The place of the picture, at Thebes, the signs of the *lotus* and *papyrus*, the shields referring to Ethiopia and Libya, and the composition of the vast army which Shishak led into Judah [6]—unite to prove him master of Upper as well as Lower Egypt, with the adjacent regions to the east and west and at least a part of Ethiopia.

But the relations of the latter country to Egypt become obscure as we approach the period when the Ethiopian kings began to turn

well to remind the young student at this point that the rivalry of the Ten Tribes against Judah, which reached its climax in the secession of the kingdom of Israel, had existed from the elevation of David to the throne.

[5] We may here notice a distinction between the use of a title as a *prænomen* and its incorporation with the king's name. Rameses III. and Sheshonk, as well as some other kings, adopt *Miamun* as a mere prænomen: but the only king who uses it as his *real name* is *Rameses II. Miamun*. The immense variety in the forms of royal titles may be imagined from the fact that the name of the great Thothmes III. is found in *thirty* different forms.

[6] 2 Chron. xii. 2. It included *Lubim* (Lybians), *Cushites* (Ethiopians), and *Sukkiim*, who appear to be the Troglodytæ (*cave-dwellers*) on the W. shore of the Red Sea, who were famed as slingers.

the tables upon their former masters; and when Upper Egypt appears often suspended between the rival powers. In "Zerah the Cushite," who invaded Judah about 30 years later, and was signally defeated by Asa, some see an Ethiopian conqueror of Egypt, named *Azerch-Amen;* while others take him to be Osorchon I., the son and successor of Sheshonk.

Recent discoveries prove that the Ethiopian kings of Napata were at this time pressing upon Egypt, encouraged by a party in Thebes, and seizing the opportunity of divisions in the Delta. One result of those divisions appears to have been the re-establishment of *Tanis* as the capital under the *Twenty-third Dynasty*, the Semitic character of which may be inferred from the names of kings identical with those of the 22nd.

But while Manetho only registers the recognized dynasties, we learn from other sources that several cities set up rival kings. The prophet Isaiah, who lived at this time, seems to point to these divisions as one cause of the ruin coming upon Egypt:—"The princess of *Zoan* (Tanis) have become fools, the princes of *Noph* (Memphis) are deceived;"[7] and three *Memphian* kings of this age have been discovered from the inscriptions in the *Serapeum*. *Saïs*, too, which ultimately became the capital of the last independent kingdom of Egypt, had already its own kings. How these divisions prepared the way for the conquest of Egypt by Ethiopia is now made clear by a *stela* at Napata (*Jebel Berkel*), which was at this time the Ethiopian capital.

It appears from this monument that Lower and Middle Egypt were divided among *thirteen* petty states, when the Ethiopian king, *Piankh*, marched from Napata; and, having been welcomed at Thebes as a deliverer, took Memphis by force, and gained several battles against the princes of the Delta. Several of these were military adventurers of the Libyan race, and five only are called *kings*. The most powerful were *Osorchon* and *Pet-se-Pasht*, both of whom are named by Manetho in the 23rd Tanite Dynasty, and *Tafnekht*, of Saïs. The last-named king is called Tnephachthus by Diodorus Siculus, who ascribes to him that curse upon Menes which has been mentioned above (page 18).

Bokenranf, the son of Tnephachthus—whom the Greeks call Bocchoris the Wise, and celebrate as a lawgiver—stands alone in the List of Manetho as forming the *Twenty-fourth (Saïte) Dynasty*. Whether he was placed in this rank by driving out the Ethiopian invader, or whether he reigned as his vassal, is a question which

---

[7] Isaiah xix. 13. The precedence of Tanis above Memphis at this time seems to be indicated both by the *order* of the names, and especially by verse 11, where "the princes of Zoan" are "the wise counsellors of Pharaoh."

the silence of the monuments gives us no means of deciding. If
the latter was his real position, we may account for the statement
that he was burnt alive by Sabaco, the Ethiopian, as the punishment of his rebellion. At all events, he succumbed to that conqueror, and Egypt fell under the dominion of Ethiopia.

The *Twenty-fifth Dynasty*, of *Ethiopians*, consists of three kings :
—*Shabaka* or *Sebek*, in Greek SABACO I. ; *Sabatak* (surnamed *Meriamun*), in Greek SEBICHUS, SEVECHUS, or SABACO II., who is probably
the priest-king, SETHOS, of Herodotus ; and *Tarhaka*, the TARKUS
or TARACUS of Manetho (in Strabo TEARCO), and the *Tirhakah* of
Scripture. These kings are singularly interesting from their appearance in Jewish history, their antagonism to the New Assyrian
monarchy when at the height of its power, and the accounts given
of them by Herodotus. But all these points, as well as their relations to the native Egyptian princes, involve discussions quite unsuited to our elementary work, and on which the Egyptian and,
still more, the Assyrian monuments are continually throwing new
light. We must be content to give the results thus far gained in
their broadest and simplest form.

Nor must we enter into the discussion upon the origin, the seat,
and the extent of the monarchy of *Cush* or Ethiopia. We have
seen that the capital of these kings was at Napata (now *Jebel-
Berkel*), a little below the Fourth Cataract. The power of the
great Theban kings had extended to this city ; and there (from
causes which are disputed) a monarchy grew up, kindred to theirs
in race, language, religion, civilization, arts, and institutions, but
more completely under the power of the priests.[8]

"Both the historical and prophetic books of the Jews"—says
Mr. Kenrick—"afford evidence of their military power. They
bear a part in the invasions of Palestine ; they are joined by Isaiah
with the Egyptians when he endeavours to dissuade his countrymen from relying on their aid to resist Assyria. In the 87th
Psalm, Ethiopia is mentioned, along with Egypt, Babylon, Tyre,
and Philistia, as one of the most illustrious nations. Throughout
the prophetic writings the Ethiopians are very generally conjoined
with Egypt, so as to shew that the union between them was so

---

[8] Some ascribe the foundation of this kingdom to the sacerdota' line of *Her-Hor*,
when driven from Thebes by *Sheshonk's* conquest of Upper Egypt : others trace its
origin to *Meroë*. The *known period* of the great Ethiopian kingdom of *Meroë* only
begins in the age of the Ptolemies ; but there is evidence enough of the high antiquity of Meroë. In the Assyrian inscriptions of this age Ethiopia is denoted both
by *Kuusu* (or *Kuusi*), that is, *Cush*, and by *Miluhi* or *Meluhi*, that is, *Meroë* ; but the
latter, like the former, may be a general name of the country. In the interesting
account given of Meroë by Herodotus, there is much that may probably refer to
Napata, which he does not mention.

close that their foreign policy was usually the same. We are not therefore to consider the subjugation of Egypt by the Ethiopians as if they had fallen under the dominion of a horde of Arabs or Scythians. The dynasty was changed, but the order of government appears to have suffered little change. No difference of religion or manners embittered the animosity of the two nations. They had been connected by royal intermarriages : and to the inhabitants of Upper Egypt the Ethiopians would seem hardly so foreign as the inhabitants of Saïs." So true is the last remark that, in the history of this dynasty, the internal conflict seems to be not so much between Egypt and Ethiopia, as that of Ethiopia and Thebes—the common worshippers of Ammon and adherents to the old institutions—against the principalities of the Delta, where the population was largely mingled with Semites and Libyans, and where foreign gods had long been worshipped.

Hence, in the conflict with Assyria, to which this warlike dynasty was impelled for the possession of Egypt's old supremacy in Palestine, they seldom appear at the head of a united nation. The events of that conflict can only be understood in the light of Assyrian history.[9] For the present it will suffice to say that after many vicissitudes of conquest and reconquest, extending over about half a century, the Assyrian and Ethiopian both retired, the one from exhaustion, probably caused by the decline of his power, the other before the combined disaffection of the princes of the Delta.

Thus Egypt now presents the aspect of a stage from which the chief actors have just withdrawn ; and, after a last scene of confusion, the curtain rises again amidst the full light of well-known history. The strength of the old priestly party has retired to the Thebaid and Ethiopia, leaving Lower Egypt free to act under the influence of ideas derived from intercourse with Europe. Whether those influences can imbue her with the spirit of Western civilization, or whether she is shorn of her own peculiar strength, is the experiment wrought out in the last stage of the history of the Pharaohs.

[9] For the story of this conflict, as told in the Annals of the Assyrian Kings. see Book II., Chaps. XXIV.–XXVII.

Shrine, or Ark.

CHAPTER XII.

THE LATER SAÏTE MONARCHY — PSAMMETICHUS, NECO, AND PSAMMIS.

"In what follows"—says Herodotus at this point—"I have the authority, not of the Egyptians only, but of others also who agree with them." His picturesque story of the accession of the *Twenty-sixth Dynasty*, of *Saïte Kings*,—whether true in fact or not—illustrates the means by which the rulers of that time contrived to have the voice of the *oracles* on their side.

After the departure of the Ethiopian, he says, the government of Egypt was shared by twelve princes, who were united to each other by intermarriages and oaths. They had made these engagements the more binding, as an oracle had predicted that "the one of them who should pour a libation from *a cup of bronze* in the temple of Phtha would become monarch of the whole land of Egypt."

Now the Twelve were wont to worship together in all the chief temples; and they had thus met in the temple of Phtha, when the high-priest, by some *accident*, brought out only *eleven* golden goblets for the libations of the kings. The one who stood last, named PSAMMETICHUS, forthwith took off his helmet of *bronze*, stretched it out to receive the liquor, and so made his libation. His colleagues remembered the oracle, and banished him to the marshes. Meditating on revenge, he sent to the oracle of Buto, the most truth-telling of all in Egypt;[1] and the oracle replied that "Vengeance would come *from the sea*, when *brazen men* should appear."

Psammetichus did not believe that brazen men would rise out of the sea. But, shortly afterwards, certain Carian and Ionian pirates, being driven by stress of weather to Egypt, disembarked in their brazen armour. A terrified native carried the news to Psammetichus that *brazen men had come from the sea*, and were plundering the plain. He now believed the oracle, and engaged the strangers in his service. By their aid, and that of the Egyptians who sided with him, he vanquished the Eleven, and made himself king of Egypt.

This PSAMMETICHUS, or, in Egyptian, PSAMATIK I., was the son of *Nechao* or *Neco*, who had been set up as king at Saïs by the Assyrians, and had been put to death by Sabaco or Tirhakah. The son, who then saved his life by flight, found the means of regaining his kingdom, amidst the divisions of the Delta, by the aid of foreign mercenaries. A marriage alliance with the royal house of Ethiopia, which had reigned till now in Upper Egypt, seems to have given him that part of the country.[2] Thus the whole of Egypt was once more re-united under the *Twenty-sixth Dynasty*, of *Saïs*, which governed the land for nearly a century and a half, till its conquest by Cambyses.

With this dynasty began a new policy, quite in accordance with the acquisition of the crown by the aid of foreign adventurers. Psammetichus kept on foot a large body of mercenaries, Greeks and Carians, as well as Arabians. He assigned to his Greek soldiers two "camps"—as the abodes of foreign settlers were called—on the two banks of the Pelusiac river, evidently as a garrison for the eastern frontier. "From the date of the original settlement of these persons in Egypt," says Herodotus, "we Greeks, through our intercourse with them, have acquired an accurate

---

[1] The ancients ascribed different degrees of truthfulness to their inspired oracles, just as they ascribed various qualities of knowledge and power to their gods. This will appear more fully in the story of Crœsus. (See Chap. XXXV.)

[2] The Ethiopian princess whom Psammetichus married was *Shap-en-ap* (or *Tape-sutapes*), the daughter of *Piankh II.* and *Ameniritis* (or *Amunotis*), the sister of *Shabaka*. The mother was a woman of high intelligence, who had several times been regent of Upper Egypt under the Ethiopian Dynasty.

knowledge of the several events in Egyptian history, from the time of Psammetichus' downwards; but before his time no foreigners had ever taken up their residence in that land."

The new commercial policy of Psammetichus is thus described by Diodorus :—" He received with hospitality the strangers who came to visit Egypt.   He loved Greece so much that he caused his children to be taught its language.[3] He was the first of the Egyptian kings who opened to other nations *emporia* for their merchandize, and gave security to voyagers; for his predecessors had rendered Egypt inaccessible to foreigners, by putting some to death, and condemning others to slavery."

The site of the new capital was specially suited for this policy. *Saïs* was situated about 40 miles from the sea, on the right bank of the Canopic or westernmost branch of the Nile. By that branch lay the direct route of the Greeks into Egypt; and on it (a little below Saïs) stood Naucratis, which was assigned for their abode. The great embankment, which raised Saïs above the inundation, made it conspicuous to voyagers ascending the river; and its site is still marked by the great mounds to the north of *Sa-el-Hagar* (*Sa of the Stone*), the village near which preserves the old Egyptian name of *Ssa*. The epithet is derived from the broken blocks of stone which are the sole ruins of the ancient city.

Saïs had a special attraction for the Athenians from the identification of its patron goddess, *Neith*, with their own *Athena:* their civic hero, Cecrops, was said to be a native of Saïs; and the Egyptian priests invented many stories to make the connection closer. Pythagoras, Solon, and Herodotus, all resorted to Saïs, to learn the sacred traditions.   The great historian has left a minute description of the Temple of Neith, with its tombs of the Saïte kings, and an account of what must have been the most beautiful of the yearly festivals of Egypt.   " At Saïs, when the assembly takes place for the sacrifices, there is one night on which the inhabitants all burn a multitude of lights around their houses in the open air. They use lamps, which are flat saucers filled with a mixture of oil and salt, on the top of which the wick floats.   These burn the whole night, and give to the festival the name of the *Feast of Lamps*. The Egyptians who are absent from the festival observe the night of the sacrifice, no less than the rest, by a general lighting of lamps; so that the illumination is not confined to the city of Saïs, but extends over the whole of Egypt."

[3] We learn from Herodotus that Psammetichus made systematic provision for the use of Greek (doubtless chiefly as the medium of commercial intercourse), by entrusting Egyptian children to the care of his Greek soldiers. The children thus instructed became the parents of the entire class of " interpreters " in Egypt.

With the aid of his foreign mercenaries, and of the Phœnician sailors, Psammetichus aspired to recover the empire of Western Asia, where the power of Assyria was tending to its decline. But his enterprise was stopped on the very threshold by the resistance of the Philistine city of Azotus (*Ashdod*), the key to the great military route, which he only took after a siege of twenty-nine years, the longest, says Herodotus, of any city that we know.

This city, formerly the great stronghold of the Philistines [4] (its name means "strong") had been taken by the *Tartan* or Commander-in-chief of Sargon, and was probably still held by an Assyrian garrison. But the siege may also have been prolonged by a fatal disaster which now befel the military strength of Egypt.[5]

In his invasion of Palestine, Psammetichus gave his mercenaries the post of honour on the right wing. The native military class, already jealous of the favours heaped upon the Greeks, now deserted in a body, to the number of 200,000 or 240,000, and marched away to Ethiopia. Herodotus tells us that Psammetichus pursued and overtook them; but his entreaties that they would return were insolently repelled.

It is now known, from a curious Greek inscription at *Abou-simbel*, that the king himself did not follow the deserters higher than Elephantine, but the pursuit was continued by his Greek soldiers, who, on their return, left this record of their adventure.[6] The Egyptian warriors were welcomed by the King of Ethiopia, which may now be regarded as the refuge of the institutions of "Old Egypt." He gave them the lands of certain Ethiopians with whom he was at feud; and they were known in the time of Herodotus by the Greek name of *Automoli*, "deserters," as well as by the native name of *Asmach*, "those on the left hand," *i. e.* "the men of the left wing." [7]

Thus was the old stock of Egyptian exclusiveness proved to be incapable of receiving the new graft of Hellenism. But yet the concurrence of great personal ability in the Saïte kings with the entire revolution which now took place in Western Asia gave

---

[4] 1 Sam. v. 2.

[5] There are different versions of the following story. We follow that which appears the most consistent.

[6] The name of the leader of the force, "*Psamatichus*, the son of Theocles"—the latter a pure Greek name, the former the same as that of the king—and also the name of *Amasis* in the inscription—indicate that these foreigners (like Joseph) received Egyptian names of honour. The king's name also occurs in the inscription as *Psamatichus*, which is nearer to the Egyptian *Psamatik* than the common form, which is that used by Herodotus.

[7] Later Greek geographers mention an Ethiopian tribe called *Euonomitæ*, the Greek equivalent of Asmach.

Egypt a last brilliant century, from the fall of Nineveh, in B.C. 625 or B.C. 606, to her own conquest by Persia, in B.C. 527 or 525. Having made and lost two great strokes for the recovery of Asiatic Empire, and paid the penalty of a disastrous invasion, she was permitted, as the nominal vassal of Babylon, to enjoy the material fruits of the policy of the Saïte kings. But, the moment she was forced to defend herself, she betrayed the loss of her native strength.

After a reign of 54 years,[8] Psammetichus was succeeded by his son NEKU or NECHAO, the NECOS of Herodotus, and the PHARAOH-NECHO of Scripture. This enterprising king—proved such by his deeds both at home and abroad—found the gate of Asia opened by the capture of Ashdod. The Median conqueror, Cyaxares, and the new king of Babylon, Nabopolassar, were fully engaged in the wars attendant upon the end of the Assyrian Empire.[9] Neco set out to seize Carchemish, the key of the Euphrates, crushing on his way the rash resistance of Josiah in the valley of Megiddo, the scene where Thothmes III. had gained an equally decisive victory. Having reached the goal of his expedition, he left a garrison at Carchemish to hold the passage of the Euphrates, and returned home through Cœle-Syria, where he arranged the affairs of Judah.

This recovery of the boundary of the Euphrates was but a dying gleam of military glory for the Saïte Pharaohs. The empire of south-western Asia was destined for NEBUCHADNEZZAR. Just before his father's death (B.C. 605) that prince crushed the Egyptian army at Carchemish; marched on to Jerusalem and received the submission of Neco's vassal king, Jehoiakim; and at one blow stripped Egypt of all power in Asia. In the emphatic words of Scripture— " The king of Egypt came not again any more out of his land; for the king of Babylon had taken, from the river of Egypt unto the river Euphrates, all that pertained to the king of Egypt." [10]

The death of his father in this campaign recalled Nebuchadnezzar from the further pursuit of Neco, who may very probably have sent the usual tokens of submission. At all events the king of Egypt turned his whole attention to works of internal improvement; and, while Nebuchadnezzar was dealing with the stubborn resistance of Jerusalem and Tyre, Neco appears to have secured the commerce of Western Asia. He maintained fleets both in the Mediterranean and the Erythræan Seas;[11] and his docks on the Red Sea.

---

[8] Probably from B.C. 664 to B.C. 610.

[9] The events which are here merely indicated are related in Book II., Chapter XXIX. For the details of the resistance and death of Josiah, and the deposition of Jehoahaz and the elevation of Jehoiakim by Neco, the reader is referred to the ' Smaller Scripture History,' chap. xvi.   [10] 2 Kings xxiv. 7.

[11] The latter is a general term for what we now call the *Red Sea* (the *Arabian Gulf* of Herodotus) and the sea between the shores of Africa, Arabia, and India.

for the latter fleet, were visible in the time of Herodotus. His attempt to re-open the Red Sea Canal of Seti and Rameses cost the lives of 120,000 of his subjects, and proved at last abortive. The story that he desisted on account of an oracle, which warned him that he was labouring for the barbarians, seems to mark at once the growth of foreign commerce and the obstructive power of the old Egyptian party.

Foiled in this attempt to connect the commerce of the two seas —for his object was as clearly *commercial* as that achieved by M. de Lesseps in A.D. 1869—Neco boldly tried to anticipate the discovery made by Vasco de Gama, in A.D. 1497. Whether his fleet really circumnavigated Africa, is an argument which the young reader can better pursue at a future time. We tell the story as it is told by Herodotus, who heard it in Egypt, about 150 years after the voyage. Speaking of the anomalous division of the three continents of Libya (Africa), Asia, and Europe, he says (iv. 42) :—

"As for Libya, we know it to be washed on all sides by the sea, except where it is attached to Asia. This discovery was first made by Necos, the Egyptian king, who, on desisting from the canal which he had begun between the Nile and the Arabian Gulf, sent to sea a number of ships manned by Phœnicians, with orders to make for the Pillars of Hercules,[12] and return to Egypt through them, and by the Mediterranean.

"The Phœnicians took their departure from Egypt by way of the Erythræan Sea, and so sailed into the Southern Ocean. When autumn came, they went ashore, wherever they might happen to be, and, having sown a tract of land with corn, waited till the grain was fit to cut.[13] Having reaped it, they again set sail; and thus it came to pass that two whole years went by, and it was not till the third year that they doubled the Pillars of Hercules, and made good their voyage home.

"On their return, they declared—*I, for my part, do not believe them, but perhaps others may*[14]—that, in sailing round Libya, *they had the sun upon their right hand*. In this way Libya was first discovered." Apart from the arguments from which we here abstain, it is difficult to reject *the simple fact asserted*, that the fleet

12 The rocks of Gibraltar and Ceuta at the Straits of Gibraltar.

13 This would require about three months in that climate.

14 The two-fold argument from *astronomy* and the force of *evidence repeated faithfully by an incredulous witness* is one of the many matters which, throughout this work, we leave the teacher to explain, rather than encumber our elementary text-book with discussion on the one hand, or leave out essential matter on the other. We have often aimed at stimulating enquiry for the teacher to satisfy, thus benefiting both the pupil and himself. In the case before us, the argument abstained from here will be found in our 'Student's Manual of Ancient History,' Chap. viii. p. 148, where we would call attention to a caution in note 45.

which started from the Gulf of Suez made its appearance at the mouth of the Nile.   Neco reigned 16 years.[15]

Of his son and successor, Psamatik II., whom Manetho calls Psammuthis, and Herodotus Psammis, the latter tells a curious story, illustrating the growing intercourse of Egypt with Greece, and the respect of the Greeks for Egyptian wisdom.[16]   In the reign of Psammis, ambassadors from Elis arrived in Egypt, boasting that their arrangements for the conduct of the Olympic games were the best and fairest that could be devised, and fancying that not even the Egyptians, *who surpassed all other nations in wisdom*, could add anything to their perfection.   When these persons reached Egypt, and explained the reason of their visit, the king summoned an assembly of all the wisest of the Egyptians.   They met, and the Eleans, having given them a full account of all their rules and regulations with respect to the contests, said that they had come to Egypt for the express purpose of learning whether the Egyptians could improve the fairness of their regulations in any particular.

" The Egyptians considered awhile, and then made made enquiry, ' If they allowed their own citizens to enter the lists?'   The Eleans answered, 'That the lists were open to all Greeks, whether they belonged to Elis or to any other state.'   Hereupon the Egyptians observed, ' That if this were so, they departed from justice very widely, since it was impossible but that they would favour their own countrymen, and deal unfairly by foreigners.   If therefore they really wished to manage the games with fairness, and if this was the object of their coming to Egypt, they advised them to confine the contests to strangers, and allow no native of Elis to be a candidate.'"

Herodotus adds that Psammis reigned only 6 years ; and died immediately after an attack on Ethiopia.[17]   His otherwise insignificant reign affords an interesting example of the way in which the monuments enable us to settle questions of chronology.   From one of the tablets (*Apis-stelæ*) in the Apis-sepulchre at Memphis, we learn that an Apis born in the 16th year of Neco, and consecrated in the 1st year of Psammetichus II., died in the 12th year of his son Apries, aged 17 years, 6 months, and 5 days.   As it appears to have been the custom of the Egyptians, like the Orientals in general, to reckon the civil years in which a king was born and died as belonging to his reign, we see that this calculation agrees with the length assigned by Herodotus to the reigns both of Neco and Psammis.   If the former died in B.C. 594, the latter reigned to B.C. 589 or 588.

---

[15] Probably B.C. 610-594.   This is the number assigned by Manetho, and his 16th year is on the monuments.   [16] Herod. ii. 160.

[17] The name of Psamatik II. frequently occurs at Syene, together with those of Psamatik I. and Amasis.

Egyptian Buffoons.

CHAPTER XIII.

THE SAÏTE MONARCHY, *continued*—APRIES AND AMASIS.

THE name of the fourth king of the Saïte Dynasty is read on the monuments as WAH-PRA-HAT, that is, "the Sun enlarges his heart." He is the PHARAOH-HOPHRA of Scripture,[1] the VAPHRIS of Manetho, and the APRIES of Herodotus, who accounted him the most prosperous of all the kings that ever ruled over Egypt, with the exception of his great-grandfather, Psammetichus I.[2] In him was revived the martial enterprise of his grandfather, Neco; but to that temper he added an arrogance which proved his ruin. It is this Pharaoh whom the prophet Ezekiel describes as "the great crocodile that lieth in the midst of his rivers, which hath said, My river is mine own, and I have made it for myself;" and Herodotus tells us that "Apries believed that there was not a god who could cast him from his eminence, so firmly did he think he had established himself in his kingdom."

---

[1] Jerem. xliv. 30.

[2] Herod. ii. 161. Here, as also in his account of the unexampled prosperity of Egypt under Amasis, it would seem that Herodotus, having once fixed his limit for the trustworthy history of Egypt at the accession of Psammetichus, tacitly ignores all the older traditions of the priests. He could not have meant to imply, for example, that these Saïte kings were more prosperous than Sesostris if he had really believed his own story of Sesostris.

The story of his fall, as related by Herodotus, is a manifest attempt of the priests to gloss over a national disgrace. That Egypt was really conquered by Nebuchadnezzar, and reduced to a vassal kingdom, is a truth now recovered from the Scripture and Josephus. The military and naval expeditions of Apries against Sidon, Tyre, and Cyprus, were evidently part of the same venture for the recovery of Western Asia, which led him to support the rebellion of Zedekiah, king of Judah. By marching an army into Palestine, he caused the Chaldæans to raise the siege of Jerusalem. But when Nebuchadnezzar thus turned to meet him, Apries retreated back to Egypt, and the only further help he gave the Jews was to receive the remnant who took refuge in Egypt after the fall of Jerusalem and the murder of the Jewish governor set up by Nebuchadnezzar (B.C. 586).[3]

The vivid language of the Hebrew prophets describes the signal vengeance taken by Nebuchadnezzar upon Egypt and her king.[4] But it is difficult to fix the precise order of the events, and to fit into its place that expedition against Cyrene, which Herodotus makes the occasion of the fall of Apries.

The long low line of the Libyan coast west of Egypt is broken, just opposite to Greece, by the high ground which juts out in a bold sweep before you reach the Great Syrtis; forming terraces protected from the sands of the Sahara on the south, and looking over the Mediterranean to the north. Here, in one of the fairest regions of the earth, the Lacedæmonians had founded the colony of Cyrene in B.C. 630.

The natives, displaced by the rapid growth of the colony, sought the protection of Apries, who levied a vast army of *Egyptians*, and sent them against Cyrene. This reappearance of the warrior class is easily accounted for by the fact, expressly stated by Herodotus, that the deserters from Psammetichus left their children behind in Egypt. Apries may have been glad to send them on a distant and dangerous expedition to the West, rather than employ them in the critical war in Asia, or trust them for the defence of the kingdom against Nebuchadnezzar. If so, the distrust was mutual; and they vented upon the king their mortification at a severe defeat inflicted on them by the Greeks. "They believed he had wished a vast number of them to be slain, that he might reign the more securely over the rest of the Egyptians."

Returning in open revolt to Egypt, and being joined by the friends of the slain, they were met by an envoy of the king, who bore the name of the founder of the Eighteenth Dynasty, *Aahmes*, or,

---

[3] For the details, see the 'Scripture History.'
[4] Jerem. xliii., xliv., xlvi.; Ezek. xxix.-xxxii.

in Greek, *Amasis*. As he was haranguing the mutineers, a soldier, coming behind him, placed a crown upon his helmet, and proclaimed him king. Amasis, not displeased, led the army against Apries, and when a second envoy, Patarbemis, was sent to bring him alive to the king, he replied, after an insulting jest, that "Apries would have no reason to complain of him on the score of delay; he would shortly come himself to the king, *and bring others with him.*"

When Apries saw Patarbemis returning without Amasis, he fell into a paroxysm of rage, and, not giving himself time for reflection, commanded his nose and ears to be cut off. This outrage drove those Egyptians who had remained loyal to join the rebels; and the king was left at Saïs with his 30,000 Greek and Carian mercenaries. He led them out to meet the vastly superior numbers of Amasis at Momemphis (on the edge of the desert); and, being utterly defeated, he was brought back a prisoner to the palace at Saïs. Amasis treated him kindly at first; but, yielding to the remonstrances of the Egyptians, he gave Apries into their hands. "Then," says Herodotus, "the Egyptians took him and strangled him; but, having done so, they buried him in the sepulchre of his fathers."

Such was the story told to Herodotus by the Egyptian priests; but Josephus has preserved the distinct statement of the Babylonian historian, Berosus, that *Egypt was conquered by Nebuchadnezzar*, who put Apries to death, and set up a vassal king in his room. It is uncertain whether Nebuchadnezzar seized the opportunity afforded by the disastrous campaign against Cyrene and the civil war between Apries and Amasis, or whether the Babylonian invasion was the cause of the disaffection of the Egyptians towards Apries. But the desolation of the whole country, "from Migdol to Syene and the border of Ethiopia;" the spoliation of the shrine of Amun in Thebes and of all the gods of Egypt; the shameful captivity of a large part of the people; the fate of Pharaoh-Hophra, "given into the hand of his enemies, and into the hand of them that seek his life;" and the restoration of Egypt "as the basest of the kingdoms"— that is, a subject and tributary state—never more to "exalt itself to rule over the nations:"—all these calamities are described in some of the most vivid pictures of Hebrew prophecy.[5] Manetho assigns 16 years to Apries, Herodotus 25; but the difference only affects the beginning of his reign, which ended about B.C. 570-69.

The reign of AMASIS (or AAHMES II.) is set in its true light by the fact (though it was unknown to Herodotus) that this king

was *the vassal of Babylon*, and by our knowledge of the freedom
which the great Asiatic monarchs left to their obedient vassals.
Accepting his position, he applied himself to foster that material
prosperity which too often consoles a rich country for the loss of
liberty.

His origin and temper alike fitted him for this part. An humble
birth and a doubtful title made the protection of a superior lord
not unwelcome. His place in the Saïte Dynasty was confirmed by
his marriage with *Ankhs-en-Ranofrehet*, the daughter of Psammetichus II.;[6] and he adopted the title of *Neit-se*, "son of Neith." The
respect of his subjects was won by his genial and elastic spirit.
combined with singular good sense, and a regular and just government. Of these qualities Herodotus gives some amusing illustrations.

"He belonged to the nome (or canton) of Saïs, being a native of
the town called Siouph. At first his subjects looked down on him,
and held him in small esteem, because he had been a mere private
person, and of a house of no great distinction; but, after a time,
Amasis succeeded in reconciling them to his rule, not by severity,
but by cleverness. Among his other splendour, he had a golden foot-
pan, in which his guests and himself were wont upon occasion to
wash their feet. This vessel he caused to be broken in pieces, and
made of the gold an image of one of the gods, which he set up in
the most public place in the whole city; upon which the Egyptians
flocked to the image, and worshipped it with the utmost reverence.
Amasis, finding this was so, called an assembly and opened the
matter to them, explaining how the image had been made of the
foot-pan, wherein they had been wont formerly to wash their feet
and to put all manner of filth, yet now it was greatly reverenced.
'And truly,' he went on to say, 'it had gone with him as with the
foot-pan. If he was a private person formerly, yet now he had
come to be their king. And so he bade them honour and reverence
him.' Such was the mode in which he won over the Egyptians,
and brought them to be content to do him service."[7]

The covert satire on the sacred image itself was characteristic of
an Egyptian imbued with Greek ideas; and of this spirit Herodotus
gives another curious example. "It is said that Amasis, while he
was a private man, had tastes for drinking and jesting, and was
averse to engaging in any serious employment. He lived in con-

---

[6] The granite sarcophagus of this queen, covered inside and outside with hieroglyphics, is one of the most elaborate specimens of this class of objects. Some make
her the daughter of a king, PSAMMETICHUS III., whose name is found on some monuments at Thebes, but whose place in the dynasty—whether before, after, or contemporary with Apries—is very doubtful.   [7] Herod. ii. 172.

stant feasts and revelries, and, whenever his means failed him, he roamed about and robbed people. On such occasions the persons from whom he had stolen would bring him, if he denied the charge, before the nearest oracle. Sometimes the oracle would pronounce him guilty of the theft, at other times it would acquit him.

" When afterwards he came to be king, he neglected the temples of such gods as had declared that he was not a thief, and neither contributed to their adornment nor frequented them for sacrifice; since he regarded them as utterly worthless, and their oracles as wholly false; but the gods who had detected his guilt he considered to be true gods, whose oracles did not deceive; and these he honoured greatly."[8] His contemporary, Crœsus, king of Lydia, shewed the like spirit of mingled superstition and scepticism in dealing with the oracles of Greece.

Amasis carried his love of pleasure to the throne; but he did not permit it to interfere with business, nor his business with his pleasure. Herodotus gives us the following picture of his daily life. " From early dawn to the time of the ' full market ' (about (9 A.M.) he sedulously transacted all the business that was brought before him: during the remainder of the day, he drank and joked with his guests, passing the time in witty and sometimes scarcely seemly conversation. It grieved his friends that he should thus demean himself, and accordingly some of them chid him on the subject, saying to him—' O king, thou dost but ill guard thy royal dignity whilst thou allowest thyself in such levities. Thou shouldest sit in state upon a stately throne, and busy thyself with affairs the whole day long. So would the Egyptians feel that a great man rules them, and thou wouldest be better spoken of. But now thou conductest thyself in no kingly fashion.'

" Amasis answered them thus—' Bowmen bend their bows when they wish to shoot; unbrace them when the shooting is over. Were they kept always strung, they would break, and fail the archer in time of need. So it is with men. If they give themselves constantly to serious work, and never indulge awhile in pastime or sport, they lose their senses, and become mad or moody. Knowing this, I divide my life between pastime and business.'"[9] Such is the antiquity of a proverb not new to some readers of this book

" neque semper arcum
Tendit Apollo."

Under such a government, and with its irrepressible fertility, Egypt rapidly recovered from its late devastation. Herodotus reports the saying " that the reign of Amasis was the most prosperous

[8] Herod. ii. 174.   [9] Ibid. 173.

time that Egypt ever saw—the river was more liberal to the land,
and the land brought forth more abundantly for the service of man,
than had ever been known before, while the number of inhabited
cities was not less than 20,000."[10] The foreign and commercial policy
of the Saïtes was carried out most fully by Amasis. Besides a permanent abode at the port of Naucratis, below Saïs, the king granted
the Greeks sites for their temples, and himself contributed money
and works of art to the sanctuaries of Greece. He even married a
Greek, Ladice, the daughter of a noble of Cyrene.

This high prosperity and Greek influence are both attested by
the monuments of the Saïte age, private as well as public, which
have a grace and refinement unsurpassed in Egyptian art. But
the foreign relations of Amasis, and the consciousness of the power
attained during his long reign of forty-four years, tempted him
to a war which brings the history of independent Egypt to a
disastrous end.

[10] Herod. ii. 177.

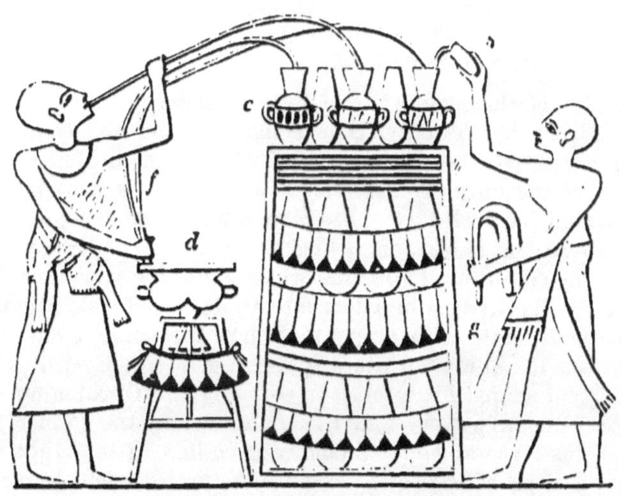

Siphons used by the Egyptians—*Thebes*. .

Bronze Figure of Apis.

CHAPTER XIV.

THE CONQUEST OF EGYPT BY CAMBYSES — DOMINION OF THE PERSIANS AND THE PTOLEMIES.   FROM B.C. 527 TO B.C. 32.

OUR idea of the magnitude of Egypt's history is aided by remembering that her Twenty-sixth Dynasty alone was contemporary with *five* Asiatic empires, three of which rose and fell within the period of the Saïte kings.   It was after the accession of Psammetichus that Nineveh succumbed to Media and Babylon ; and Amasis was already on the throne when the Persians under Cyrus over·threw the empire of Media, and when, about the same time, Crœsus converted the Lydian kingdom into an empire of Asia Minor.

We shall relate in its proper place how the ambition and jealousy of Crœsus led him to measure his strength with Cyrus.   Babylon and Egypt shared his interest in stopping the threatening growth of the Persian power ; and the claim which the former had on Amasis as a vassal would probably have had little weight but for his own hope of recovering some of Egypt's ancient empire.   He had already used the fleet founded by Neco to take Cyprus, which was a dependency of Phœnicia, and to reduce it to tribute.   Now he joined the league of kings, whom the precipitancy of Crœsus and the rapid advance of Cyrus left no time to fulfil their engagements before Sardis fell.   But his earnestness in the cause was proved (according to Xenophon) by the despatch of an army of 120,000 men to attack the Persians in Assyria ; and this force was admitted by Cyrus to a capitulation at Larissa on the Tigris.

The prudent Amasis would doubtless use this occasion to conciliate the conqueror, to whose aid we find him sending one of the famous eye-doctors of Egypt. But the aggressive spirit of Persian conquest was not likely to be content with the nominal sovereignty and the tribute, which satisfied Assyria and Babylon. "The moment Lydia was subdued, Cyrus," says Herodotus, "wished to war in person against Babylon, the Bactrians, the Sacæ (Asiatic Scythians), and *Egypt*. He had accomplished three parts of this scheme, when, carrying his arms into Central Asia beyond the subjugated Scythians, he fell in battle against the Massagetæ (B.C. 529).

His son CAMBYSES, coming to the throne full of youthful energy and with no small military capacity, saw the fourth part of his father's scheme lying before him as a golden opportunity; and he found himself with special means of ensuring success. The recent conquest of the Ionians and Æolians of Asia Minor armed him with a Greek force to oppose to the mercenaries of Amasis; and the Phœnicians, who appear to have submitted to Cambyses himself as subject allies, provided a fleet stronger than that of Egypt. A treaty with the chief sheikh of the desert, which reaches from Gaza to the eastern frontier of the Delta, secured the safe passage of his army through the Bedouin tribes of that region, and the means of transporting water on the backs of camels.

It is hardly worth while to repeat the various pretexts, which Herodotus had heard, for an attack which was its own motive. Enough, Cambyses fixed a quarrel upon Amasis; but this king died on the very eve of the invasion, after a reign of 44 years, "during all which time," says Herodotus, "no great misfortune had befallen him."[1] His son, PSAMMENITUS, had to meet the enemy under the disadvantage of a new reign, and, as usual, at such a crisis, with the discouragement of a prodigy. Rain fell at Thebes; an unusual event, indeed, but not, as Herodotus says, unexampled.

The new king lay with his army at the Pelusiac mouth of the Nile—the extreme eastern point of the Delta—to await Cambyses. When the armies were encamped face to face, the Greeks of the Egyptian party gave a horrid pledge of animosity to their countrymen of the other side. Among the advisers and aiders of Cambyses was Phanes, a Greek deserter from Amasis. "This man," says Herodotus, "had left sons in Egypt. The mercenaries took these, and, leading them to the camp, displayed them before the eyes of their father; after which they brought out a bowl, and, placing it in the space between the two hosts, they led the sons of Phanes one by one to the vessel, and slew them over it. When the last

[1] As to the date of the invasion (which is the cardinal point of the chronology of this period) the best authorities differ by two years, B.C. 527 or B.C. 525.

was dead, water and wine were poured into the bowl, and all the soldiers tasted of the blood, and so they went to the battle. Stubborn was the fight which followed, and it was not till vast numbers had been slain upon both sides that the Egyptians turned and fled." [2]

The historian adds a curious fact in physiology, which he himself observed on the field of battle. The Persian skulls were so weak that a pebble broke a hole in them; but the Egyptian skulls were hardly broken with a big stone. The latter statement is confirmed by the modern traveller, Sir Gardner Wilkinson:— " The thickness of the Egyptian skulls is observable in the mummies; and those of the modern Egyptians fortunately possess the same property of hardness, to judge from the blows they bear from the Turks, and in their combats among themselves."

The defeated Egyptians fled behind the walls of Memphis. What had become of their fleet we are not told; but the Phœnician navy of Cambyses had evidently the command of the sea and river. After a massacre, perpetrated by the Egyptians in senseless desperation, on the crew of the ship which carried up a herald to summon the city, Memphis was besieged, and in due time surrendered. This conquest of Lower Egypt was followed by the submission of the Libyans on the west, and of the Greeks of Cyrene and Barca.

The scene in which Herodotus represents the king of Egypt as hearing the insulting triumph of Cambyses with a mixture of constancy under the doom of his own princes and nobles and of sympathy for an old comrade reduced to ask alms of the soldiers, which excited the conqueror's pity, is too much in the vein of Greek sentiment to be repeated as history. The like legends adorn the tale of the fall of Crœsus, who is now seen at the side of Cambyses shedding tears over his new companion in misfortune.[3]

In both cases, the kind treatment of the conquered king was in the true spirit of Persian policy, as Herodotus himself observes:— " Cambyses allowed Psammenitus to live with him, and gave him no more harsh treatment; nay, could he have kept from intermeddling with affairs, he might have recovered Egypt and ruled it as governor. For the Persian wont is to treat the sons of kings with honour, and even to give their fathers' kingdoms to the sons of such as revolt from them:"—of which he adds examples from the history of Egypt itself under the Persians.[4] It was not till Psammenitus was discovered stirring up revolt in Egypt, that he was forced to put himself to death by drinking bull's blood.

<hr>

[2] Herod. iii. 1. [3] Compare Book III., Chapter XXXV.
[4] See below, p. 93.

The kind treatment of the king is a sign of the conduct which Cambyses at first pursued towards the country. In the monuments we find him paying honour to the gods of Egypt, and enrolling himself among her kings by the title of " *Cambat* (or *Cambosh*) [5] king of Upper and Lower Egypt." Memphis was left under the government of its own magistrates.

The story told by Herodotus—that, on proceeding from Memphis to Saïs, Cambyses had the newly buried corpse of Amasis taken from the sepulchre, treated with every indignity, and finally burnt— is mixed up with another which the historian himself rejects ; and, as he himself confesses, it makes Cambyses outrage that very religion which was the motive of his zeal against Egyptian idolatry. For it was a prime tenet of the Zoroastrian faith that the sacred element of fire must not be polluted by burning the dead. The stories of the Egyptian priests against Cambyses are coloured by their intense hatred for their conqueror—a hatred passing that borne to the Shepherds. Even the cruelties which unquestionably marked the latter part of his rule in Egypt may have been exaggerated to support their theory of his judicial madness.

Those cruelties do not seem to have begun till, returning from an unsuccessful expedition to Ethiopia, and further embittered by the loss of an entire army which he had sent to subdue the Ammonians, he found the Egyptians exulting over his discomfiture, and at the beginning of an open revolt.

The policy which Cambyses inherited from his father being one of conquest for its own sake, we do not need the marvellous legends —which may be read at the proper time in Herodotus—to account for his following the steps of the Sesortasens and Amunophs up the Nile. The exact situation of the " long-lived Ethiopians," and the point which he reached, before famine drove his soldiers to cannibalism and compelled him to retreat, are alike uncertain. It seems probable that *Meroë* was the goal of the expedition ; and that the fatal turning point was about *Wady Omgat*, in latitude 22° N., where the sands become quite barren.[6]

The " by" expedition, which was detached from this " main," had a spot of great interest for its object. The term *Oasis*—which is now familiar in our common language for those *islands* in the *sea of sand* where a stream of water bursts out, and gives life to some herbage and palm-trees before it is again lost in the desert—is of

---

[5] His own Persian name was *Kabujiya;* and the *m* is a mere euphonic insertion.

[6] To understand the relative positions of the parts of Ethiopia which we have had to mention throughout this book, the reader should refer to the description of the course of the Nile in Chap. I. and also to a good map. *History should always be read with maps.*

Egyptian origin,[7] and was first applied to the fertile spots which break the vast expanse of the Libyan Desert, west of Egypt.

Three of these were of considerable size: the *Lesser Oasis*, west of Middle Egypt; the *Greater Oasis*, or *Oasis* simply, with a city of the same name (now *El Khargeh*), west of Upper Egypt, and seven days' journey from Abydos and from Thebes; and, much farther west, and in a more northerly position than either of these two, the *Oasis of Ammon*, which the ancients called simply *Ammon*, *Ammonium*, or, from its people, the *Ammonitæ*.[8]

Here, amidst the Libyan natives, a ruling tribe, kindred to the Ethiopians above Egypt, established a sanctuary of *Amun*, with the most famous of his oracles, by which Alexander was afterwards saluted as his son. Considerable remains of the temple are still seen at *Siwah*, which lies in 29° 12′ N. latitude and 26° 17′ E. long., at about 12 days' journey from *Cairo*, and the same from Memphis.

It was, however, from Thebes, on his way to Ethiopia, that Cambyses—eager to prove the ascendancy of Ormuzd above Amun—detached a force of 50,000 men, with orders to burn the temple and to bring back the Ammonians as captives. They were traced as far as the Greater Oasis; and no more was heard of them, except a story told by the Ammonians:—"that the Persians set forth from Oasis across the sand, and had reached about half-way between that place and themselves, when, as they were at their mid-day meal, a wind arose from the south, strong and deadly, bringing with it vast columns of whirling sand, which entirely covered up the troops, and caused them wholly to disappear."[9] Their fate was more probably caused by the *Simoom* or by thirst.

At the moment when Cambyses returned to Memphis after these terrible disasters, all the Egyptians had put on holiday attire, and begun feasting and rejoicing, to celebrate the discovery of a new Apis.[10] Scorning this explanation of what seemed a triumph over his own reverses, Cambyses put the Egyptian magistrates of Memphis to death; and, bidding the priests bring Apis into his presence, he drew his dagger, but, missing his mark, only stabbed the animal in the thigh. Then he laughed and said to the priests, "Oh! blockheads, and think ye that gods become like this, of flesh and

---

[7] The word has been preserved in the Coptic *Ouahé*, signifying "an inhabited place;" the Greek form is *Auasis* as well as *Oasis*. For an account of the physical formation of the Oases, and of what was known of them by the ancients, see Dr. Smith's *Classical Dictionary*.

[8] By one of those strange courses which words are apt to follow, this name, derived from the god *Amun*, is preserved in the chemical substance *ammonia*, the *sal-ammoniac* (*chloride of ammonium*), from which it is obtained, being found in large quantities about the spot.

[9] Herod. iii. 26.　　　　　[10] See Chapter XV.

blood and sensible to steel? A fit god, indeed, for Egyptians, such an one!" The priests were scourged; the rejoicings were stopped on pain of death; and the Apis, dying of his wound, was buried by the priests in secret.

From that moment the Egyptians believed that Cambyses was smitten with the madness for which some find more natural causes, and which others disbelieve.[11] After all allowance for the exaggerations of hatred, it seems clear that he treated the Egyptians, and the sacred objects of their reverence, with an excess of cruelty and insult. But if his ferocity was insane, there was "method in his madness." Herodotus, who repeats the story of the priests, has incidentally mentioned the detection of Psammenitus in stirring up a revolt; and religious festivals were often seized as the opportunities for insurrection. There is little doubt that the stern measures of Cambyses crushed an incipient revolt; and Egypt remained quiet from his departure to near the end of his successor's reign.

That successor, DARIUS I., the son of Hystaspes, pursued the mild policy of Persia to an obedient province. His visit to Egypt is commemorated in hieroglyphics on several monuments, and his name is found on the *Apis-stelæ*. The rebellion which broke out in the last year of his reign (B.C. 486) was put down in the second year of Xerxes (B.C. 484). The Persian kings, from CAMBYSES to DARIUS II. NOTHUS (B.C. 527 or 525 to 414) are enrolled in the Lists of Manetho as the *Twenty-seventh Dynasty;* and their names are recorded on the monuments with the honorary titles of the old Pharaohs.

Under ARTAXERXES I. LONGIMANUS, a formidable rebellion was begun by INARUS, the son of a Psammetichus, with aid from the Athenians (B.C. 458). Though it was quelled by a vast army, and its leader was crucified in violation of a promise of pardon, the embers of revolt were kept alive by his confederate AMYRTÆUS, who had escaped to the isle of Elbo, in the marshes; and the Persian king endeavoured to conciliate the Egyptians by appointing as satraps Pausiris, the son of Amyrtæus, and Thannyris, the son of Inarus.

At length, in the tenth year of Darius Nothus, Amyrtæus succeeded in restoring the independence of Egypt; and his reign forms the *Twenty-eighth (Saïte) Dynasty of Manetho.*[12] His successors of the *Twenty-ninth (Mendesian)* and *Thirtieth (Saïte) Dynasties* reigned for about half a century (B.C. 408 or 405 to 353); but the intricate details of their history are not worth pursuing. They ruled Egypt with great prosperity, and left beautiful monuments of art, in the

[11] See below, Chapter XXXVI.
[12] About B.C. 414-408; but the dates are doubtful.

remains of which our Museum is rich.[13] They resisted all the attacks of Persia, till the last king, NECTANEBO II., lost heart at the advance of the immense army of Artaxerxes Ochus, and fled up the river to Pelusium (about B.C. 353). Thus ignominiously ended the long line of the Pharaohs, after a duration perhaps of 24 centuries, and almost certainly equal to the 22 succeeding centuries of Egypt's subjection to foreign rulers.

The restored Persians, who form the *Thirty-first Dynasty* of Manetho (Ochus, Arses, and Darius Codomannus), fell, in the short space of twenty years, before the Macedonian conqueror, to whom Egypt submitted in B.C. 332. The far-sighted policy of Alexander gave Egypt what she most wanted, a port on the Mediterranean itself. *Alexandria*, which is to this day the commercial capital of Egypt, commanded the chief trade between the Mediterranean and the East.

The Greek Dynasty of the *Ptolemies*, who obtained the throne of Egypt on the death of Alexander (B.C. 323), conformed to the religion and fostered the traditional art of Egypt. Many splendid monuments, which were formerly referred as a matter of course to the Pharaohs, are now found from their inscriptions to belong to the Ptolemies; and the inscription on the famous *Rosetta Stone*, which has given the key to hieroglyphic writing, is a decree of the priests at Memphis in honour of Ptolemy V. Epiphanes (about B.C. 200). At the same time these kings made Alexandria a splendid seat of Greek learning, and collected there the largest library in the world.

At length family dissensions tempted a recourse to the arbitration of Rome (B.C. 164); and the independence of the Ptolemies was henceforth only nominal. CLEOPATRA, the last of their race, and the captivator of Cæsar and of Antony, seemed almost to have regained more than the Eastern empire of the Pharaohs, when the battle of Actium made Octavian the master of the world; and Egypt became a Roman province (B.C. 30). That battle was the decisive turning-point of the victory of European progress over the despotic spirit and the barbarian immobility of the East.

<hr>

[13] Among these is the splendid sarcophagus of *Nakhtnebo*, or NECTANEBO I. formerly called the sarcophagus of Alexander the Greek.

Priests clad in the Leopard's Skin.

CHAPTER XV.

THE INSTITUTIONS, RELIGION, AND ARTS OF EGYPT.

I. To which family of mankind the ancient Egyptians belonged; whence they came to the valley of the Nile; and what was their social state at the period of their entrance into the land, are questions still open to a discussion which lies beyond the limits of this work. According to the opinions now commonly received, they were of that Asiatic race which is called *Hamitic*, a name denoting at once a swarthy (not negro-black) complexion and a supposed descent from Ham. The native name of the country, *Khem*, "black," or "brown," is in fact identical with that of the patriarch;[1] and *Mizraim*, the Semitic name of Egypt, is that of the second son of Ham, in Genesis x, where his eldest son, *Cush*, represents the Ethiopians, who were akin to the Egyptians.

Few writers of authority now hold the opinion that the course of civilization was down the Nile. In the earliest known state of Egypt, we find it with the same monarchical and priestly institutions, and the same taste for massive buildings, which mark the

---

[1] Our form *Ham* conceals the strong initial guttural of the Hebrew.

race of Ham upon the Euphrates. The temple-towers of Babylonia, "the land of Shinar," have a near affinity with the pyramids of Egypt.[2] We have seen, too, that the earliest state of Egypt, as seen in the pyramids, and in the tombs of the same age, reveals an orderly society and a civilization, of which the origin is unknown.

II. The Egyptians were divided into distinct *classes*, which are usually confounded with *castes*. There was not that restriction to one profession, and prohibition of intermarriage, which mark the true system of *caste*, as in India; but still professions were usually hereditary. The nobility of an Egyptian consisted in his high functions; and high birth is never put forward in the laudatory epitaphs. Except the royal race, which claimed a descent from the gods, all Egyptians were equally well born. Still there was a marked line between the privileged classes, who had a share, and the people, who had none, in the offices of government and religion. As a French writer well states the case:—"Priests, warriors, judges, architects, chiefs of districts and provinces, are nearly the only ranks and classes that appear in the inscriptions. We do not find the labourer, the agriculturist, the artist, or the physician, receiving those funereal honours which consist in the representation of the deceased as offering to the gods and praying for their protection in another world."

The two privileged classes or orders were the *priests* and *warriors;* who, with the king, owned the whole soil of Egypt. The Priests ranked first; and their office was strictly hereditary. For each deity there was a high-priest, at the head of a numerous hierarchy of priests, scribes, and attendants of all sorts. Those of the chief temples formed *sacerdotal colleges*, the most famous of which were at Memphis, Heliopolis, and Thebes. They kept the annals, civil as well as religious, and were the depositaries of all that mass of learning which formed "the wisdom of the Egyptians." To their service in the temples was added a course of minute ritual observances. They shaved the head and body every other day, washed in cold water twice a day and twice each night, and wore robes of linen and shoes of papyrus, wool and leather being forbidden them. Besides the rent of their lands, they received daily rations of cooked food, and contributions of oxen, sheep, and wine: fish they might not eat. They were exempt from taxation; and their lands alone were free from the quit-rent, or double tithe (of one fifth of the produce) to the king, which the policy of Joseph imposed on all the land of Egpyt.[3]

The Soldiers were the second class. Their profession also was hereditary, and they practised no other trade. They lived upon

<hr>

[2] Comp. Chapter XVII.   [3] Gen. xlvii. 22.

the produce of their lands, the cultivation of which appears to have occupied their leisure. They were divided into two bodies, the *Hermotybians* and *Calasirians*,[4] each of which furnished 1000 men yearly for the king's body-guard, who received special pay and rations. Their peculiar arms, clothing, and ensigns are seen on the monuments, which also exhibit a great variety of battle-scenes. Foreign auxiliaries appear in the earlier times of the monarchy, but in a thoroughly subordinate position. We have seen how the reliance of Psammetichus on his Greek and Carian mercenaries broke up this system, and ultimately left Egypt an easy prey to Persia.

The rest of the people comprised, speaking generally, the classes of *shepherds or herdsmen, agriculturists,* and *artisans:* in fact these three make up, with the priests and soldiers, the five classes named by Diodorus. Herodotus enumerates *seven classes;* those below the priests and soldiers being the *herdsmen, swineherds, tradesmen, interpreters,* and *steersmen* or *pilots.* The last three doubtless rose into the position of regular classes (as we have seen in the case of the interpreters) from the commercial development of Egypt under the Saïte kings; and the unclean *swineherds,* who were social out-casts, like the *pariahs* of India, had perhaps been separated from the general class of herdsmen. We must not place the latter on the same level of degradation. The statement, that " every shepherd was an *abomination* (that is, an object of religious abhorrence) to the Egyptians " applies probably to the pastoral races of the Delta, not so much on account of their occupation as of their kindred to the detested Hyksos.[5]

The class of *artisans* is best described by the pictures on the monuments and in the tombs, in which, after thousands of years, we see the old Egyptians engaged in all the operations of agriculture, gardening, hunting, and boating; in the manufactures of glass, pottery, metal-work, and textile fabrics; in the handicrafts of shoe-making and carpentry, masonry and building, polishing pillars and colossal statues ; in the occupations of shopkeepers, public weighers and notaries, fowlers, fishermen, brickmakers, and common labourers; besides other scenes too many to enumerate.[6]

---

[4] These are the Greek forms of their names used by Herodotus : the latter appears on the monuments in the form *klashr,* with the figure of an *archer:* the archers being a very important part of the Egyptian infantry.

[5] As to the *agriculturists* there are some interesting questions, the discussion of which is hardly suited to the present work.

[6] The detailed description of these scenes is quite beyond our limits, and would require innumerable illustrations. Both are amply given in Sir Gardner Wilkinson's ' Popular Account of the Ancient Egyptians,' 2 vols. crown 8vo. The same remark will apply to the whole mass of interesting details concerning the daily life, manners

III. At the head of the state was the KING, who was exalted immeasurably above the highest of his subjects by the real practical belief not only in his divine descent, but in his being the representative of deity upon earth. "The king is the image of *Ra* (the Sun god) among men"—says an inscription; and the sublime title of PHARAOH, "Son of Ra,"[7] was prefixed to the name of every king in an oval surmounted by a crowned hawk, the symbol of Ra. The divine and regal emblems are so interchanged upon the monuments, the images of the god and king are so associated, that it is often difficult to say which is which: and the king is even seen in the act of worshipping his own image. After death, the long line of kings are worshipped by their successors, as we have seen in several cases.

But even from this dignity of the king's nature arose one class of restrictions on his power. The divine Pharaoh must observe in his own life an order worthy of a god; and of this the priests were the interpreters. His occupations were arranged for every hour of the day; his food and the quantity of his wine, his exercises and his pleasures, were all prescribed by a ceremonial contained in one of the books of Hermes (or *Thoth*).[8] He was diligently instructed by the scribes in the moral precepts, and in the histories of eminent and virtuous men, contained in the sacred books. He was bound to use his power according to the law; and, on the other hand, a solemn formula, daily pronounced by the priest, exempted the king from all accusation, and fixed the injury and penalty on those who had been his ministers and who had taught him wrong. The statement of some writers, that the deceased king was subjected to a judgment by the people, who granted or denied him the funeral honours, is now believed to be a mistake.

The succession to the crown was hereditary; and the princes of the royal blood were distinguished by appropriate titles and insignia. As the king was at once priest and soldier, so the princes were initiated into the learning of the priests, and they followed the military profession. We can hardly doubt therefore, that Moses, besides the training for his legislative work which he received from the Egyptian scribes, learned, as a commander in the Egyptian armies, how to manage the vast camp in the wilderness. And, whether the marvellous tales which Josephus tells of his military exploits be true or false, we have a higher testimony to the fact

and customs, banquets, and amusements, dress, houses, furniture, implements, arms, and so forth, which can only be properly studied with the whole apparatus of illustrative pictures spread before the eye and commented upon in detail.

[7] This is the interpretation usually accepted; but other etymologies are given; such as *Per-ao*, "exalted house."　　　　　　　[8] On these books see below, p. 102.

that, besides being "learned (which is good old English for *in-structed*) in all the wisdom of the Egyptians," Moses was also "mighty in words and *deeds*" (Acts vii. 22).

The ceremonies of election, spoken of by some late writers, seem to have been merely formal; the people, as at modern coronations, welcoming the new king by their acclamations. In the case of a real or formal election, owing to a dynastic revolution or the failure of the royal line, the new king must be either a priest or a soldier; and, if the latter, he was admitted to the sacerdotal order, and initiated in the hidden wisdom of the priests. In the narrative of *Exodus* there are signs of a *Royal Council*.

Legislative Power seems to have been vested in the king; and several kings of Egypt had the reputation of wise legislators. The Greeks regarded the laws of Egypt as the expression of the highest wisdom; and their influence is clearly traced in those of Moses. The general fairness of the *criminal code* is seen in the details given by Diodorus; but we know little of the *civil law*.

IV. Egypt enjoyed the blessing of a *judicial administration* independent of the crown; but, in a case affecting the court, we know one instance in which a tyrannical king punished the judges for passing what he deemed too mild a sentence. This case, which was that of a conspiracy in the harem of Rameses II., is recorded in a papyrus. The only other extant record of a trial is that of a band of thieves, who had carried on a systematic pillage of the Theban tombs, under Rameses IV. All trials were conducted in writing, and with very solemn forms. The judges were probably of the priestly order. There was a supreme court of *Thirty*; ten members being sent from each of the three cities—probably from the priestly colleges—of Memphis, Heliopolis, and Thebes.

The *Administration* was conducted by an army of officials, belonging to the great corporation of the Scribes, a branch of the sacerdotal order. Their official orders and reports are among the most interesting of the existing papyri. The chief departments were those of *public works, war,* and *finance*. Taxes were collected in kind,—for coined money seems to have been unknown to the Egyptians—the three divisions of *arable lands, marshes,* and *canals* paying their dues in *corn, cattle, fish*. Each *nome* (or canton) had a governor, whom the Greeks call *Nomarch*, and under him were local magistrates called *Toparchs*.

V. The great bond of the Egyptian society was its *Religion*: a full exposition of which would be too abstruse for this work. Its foundation was an original faith in the unity of God, perverted into polytheism by the impersonation of His attributes. Many of the deities were local; others were common to all Egypt.

The great gods were arranged in *triads*, consisting of *father, mother,* and *son.* The chief of these were that of Thebes, headed by *Amun* the inconceivable deity, and the supreme god of Egypt: that of Memphis, headed by *Phtha,* the all-working principle of *fire,* who perhaps at one time held the same rank: that of Hermonthis, headed by *Month,* the brilliancy of the *Sun:* and that of *Osiris, Isis,* and *Horus,* the most popular deities of all Egypt.

In the *symbols* always attached to the several gods—as the *ram* for *Amun,* the *bull* for *Phtha,* the *hawk for Ra*[9] and *Month,* the *ibis* for Osiris, the sacred beetle for *Kheper*[10] (the creator), and many others—we may probably trace the origin of that *animalworship,* which has always seemed the most surprising feature of the Egyptian religion. We cannot enter into details of the immense variety of beasts, birds, fishes, reptiles, and insects, which were adorned in the strange spirit which

> " With monstrous shapes and sorceries abused
> Fanatic Egypt and her priests, to seek
> Their wandering gods disguised in brutish forms
> Rather than human."

The worship of many animals was purely local, and (as in the case of the crocodile) creatures consecrated in one nome were hunted down in the next. The *hawk* and *ibis* were reverenced throughout all Egypt, as the symbols of *Ra* and *Osiris;* and their slaughter, however involuntary, was always punished with death. The cat (the symbol of *Pasht*) was held in like honour in the Delta; and, under one of the la-t Ptolemies, when the fate of Egypt hung on the friendship or anger of Rome, the king himself could not save a Roman soldier, who had killed a cat, from the enraged people. Diodorus relates this as an eye witness.

It was only in three cases that the sacred animal was believed to be the actual *incarnation* of a deity. These were the bull *Apis,* worshipped at Memphis, as the incarnation of *Phtha ;* the bull *Mneris,* at Heliopolis, the incarnation of Osiris; and the *goat,* at Mendes, the incarnation of *Khem.* The most revered was *Apis,* in Egyptian *Hapi,* who was revealed by certain marks : his colour was black, with a white triangular spot on the forehead, a half-

---

[9] *Ra*—whose name constantly enters into the royal titles (as in *Pha-ra-oh, Ra-meses,* &c.), and is combined in that of the great god of Thebes, *Amun-ra*—represents the *Sun in his meridian splendour : Month,* the *piercing power* of his beams. Hence the Pharaoh is described (as we have seen) as going forth to war like an image of *Ra,* and like *Month* to pierce his enemies.

[10] This explains the motive for sculpturing the gigantic *scarabæus* (sacred beetle), which is so conspicuous in the Egyptian gallery of our Museum, as well as the small *scarabæi,* which were worn as ornaments and kept as amulets, and which have been found in great numbers.

moon upon the back, and a swelling in the shape of a *scarabæus* on the tongue. He was kept in great pomp, in a splendid building, and it was esteemed the highest honour to be one of his ministering priests. When he died, all Egypt went into mourning ; and when a new Apis was manifested, the land gave itself up to festivity and joy. The dead Apises were embalmed (as was usual with the sacred animals), and buried in the vast subterranean sepulchre, the discovery of which, by M. Mariette, has yielded the most important results for Egyptian history and chronology. The soul of the deceased Apis was supposed to become assimilated, in the lower world, to one of the manifestations of *Osiris*, and was worshipped as *Osir-hapi*. This name was corrupted by the Greeks into that of a new and famous deity, *Serapis*, whose worship became the great religious bond between the old Egyptians and the Greek settlers under the Ptolemies.

The whole worship of *Osiris* was connected with the doctrine, always firmly held in Egypt, of the *immortality of the soul*, and *a future state of rewards and punishments*. Hence the practice of *embalmment*, which was accompanied with mystic formularies for the preservation of the vital germ in the uncorrupted body. The future life and resurrection are often depicted on the coffins by symbols connected with *the course of the Sun*, especially through the lower world. During this journey it was under the care of Osiris, who had himself performed the same pilgrimage after passing through the sufferings of humanity upon earth.

We also see upon the coffins the *judgment of the dead* represented under the figure of weighing the souls [11] (*psychostasy*). This awful ceremony is conducted by Osiris and his forty-four assessors in the "hall of the two-fold justice." The balances are held by Horus and Anubis. A figure, or sometimes the heart, of the deceased is placed in one scale, to be weighed against an image of *Thoth*, the god of justice, in the other, and the same deity registers the result.

The reprobate is condemned to annihilation. He is beheaded by Horus, or by *Smou* (another form of *Set*), on the *nemma* or infernal scaffold, and devoured by a monster with the head of a hippopotamus. But, before his annihilation, he is subjected to a long course of torments, and returns to act as an evil genius upon earth, where his abode is in the bodies of unclean animals. The justified, after expiating his venial sins by a long series of ordeals, labours, and conflicts with monsters, in *Ker-neter*, the Egyptian *Hades*, shares the bliss of *Osiris* the "good being" (Ounnofre), and is finally identified with that deity.

The exposition of this doctrine, and all the rites and ordeals con-

[11] Comp. Dan. v. 27 : "Thou art weighed in the balances, and art found wanting."

nected with it, are contained in the great religious book, which is
the most important of the remains of Egyptian literature. This
work, which was gradually compiled, from the earliest to the latest
age of the monarchy, is usually entitled the *Ritual of the Dead*, but
more properly the *Book of Manifestation to the Light;* and it may
be called the *Egyptian Bible.* Incidentally to its main subject, it
supplies a code of Egyptian morals, in the declarations made by the
Soul before its judges of the sins it has abstained from and the
good deeds it has done. Among the latter we read, " I have given
food to the hungry; I have given the thirsty to drink; I have
furnished clothing to the naked."

This work is the chief of the *Hermetic Books*, which the priests
ascribed to the first or celestial *Thoth*, the *Hermes Trismegistus* of
the Greeks, a personification of the divine intelligence. His earthly
counterpart, the *Second Thoth*, was esteemed the author of all
the social institutions of the land. It was he that organized the
Egyptian nation; established religion and regulated worship;
taught men all the sciences—astronomy, geometry, arithmetic,
weights and measures, language, writing, and the fine arts; in a
word, all the elements of civilization. He was the institutor and
personification of the priesthood, who were the custodians of all this
learning; but to discuss its nature, extent, and limits, lies beyond
the scope of our present work.

VI. We have already seen that the *letters*, which embodied this
learning, were by no means the exclusive accomplishment of the
priests, as might be inferred from the Greek name of *hieroglyphics,*
" sacred carvings," and *hieratic* or " priestly" characters. The
difference between these two forms of writing was just that between
our " uncial," or regularly-formed " capital " letters and the
" cursive" or freer characters used in ordinary writing : and so we
commonly find the former in carved inscriptions, the latter in the
papyri.[12] There was no *secret* about either character, as the Greeks
supposed, simply because they could not read them, just as an
ordinary Englishman cannot read Greek or Hebrew, any more than
he can Egyptian or Assyrian. The sculptured monuments were
for universal information : the *papyri* for all who had the opportunity of reading them. The error is carried on in the name of
demotic, "popular," or *enchorial*, "of the country," given by the

---

[12] It is a common mistake to suppose that the more regular forms were older than
the freer. Probably this would be the case in the very first origin of writing; but,
in practice, the most ancient Egyptian characters known,—those forming the names
of *Khufu* and *Nu-Khufu* in the Great Pyramid,—are *cursive* or *hieratic.* And for a
a very good reason : they are not monumental inscriptions, but *quarry-marks,*
roughly painted by the workmen with a brush. In short, the difference is one of
material and *purpose,* rather than of age.

Greeks to a third form, more abbreviated than the hieratic, which came into use about the 7th century, B.C., for civil documents in the vulgar language.[13] The inscription of the Rosetta stone is written in *hieroglyphics* and in *enchorial* letters, with a Greek translation.

Another common mistake is to suppose that *hieroglyphics* are mere *picture-writing*: if they were, they could be read by all mankind, each in his own tongue, like the riddle called a *rebus*. The characters (like all writing most probably) are *pictorial in their origin*, and a mere glance at an inscribed Egyptian monument shows us how much they retain of pictorial element.

Sometimes, indeed, they are *purely pictorial*, or in the next stage of *well-known conventional symbols*: as ⟨figure⟩ for *man*, ⟨figure⟩ for *ox*, ⊙ for *sun*, ⌒ for *moon*: and such pictures are also used *symbolically*, as ⊙ for *day*, ⌒ for *month*, (∘ ∘) (a pair of eyes) for *seeing*; and in more *enigmatic* applications. These characters are called *ideographic*.

But far more generally the characters are *phonetic*; that is, they represent not *things* or *actions* but *sounds*, namely the *letters* and *syllables* of words. So when we trace our own alphabet to its origin, we find our A to be but another form of ⟨figure⟩, the *head of an ox* put for the *ox*, in Hebrew and Phœnician *Aleph*—the character standing for the *initial letter* of the word, and then for the same sound (*a*) in all words. So much may suffice for a first idea of the subject: to pursue it in detail, and to trace the history of the discovery, by which these unknown letters were deciphered and the unknown language that they preserve was translated, belongs to a more advanced stage of the reader's studies. By far the greater part of Egyptian writing can now be read and understood.

VII. In *Art*, as in history and learning, Egypt takes precedence of all nations in point of time; and, in point of merit, it is an ignorant taste which pronounces her monuments uncouth. In majestic grandeur she has no rival: the delicate beauty of her best *colossi* is but partially concealed by their vast size and their attitudes of repose; and it has been said by no mean judge, "Give motion to these rocks, and Greek art would be surpassed."

[13] We may *roughly* illustrate the matter for those of our readers who have learnt Greek, and who know anything of Greek MSS. and old editions of Greek books, by comparing the *hieroglyphics* to the *uncial* letters used in very old MSS.; the *hieratic* to the characters of the later MSS., and our ordinary printed books; and the *enchorial* to the old fashioned editions full of abbreviations.

Egyptian art has that one supreme merit, which is most wanting
to our modern works, *reality* of meaning. Its source, its object, its
inspiring motive, was religion. Its purpose was monumental. Its
prevailing characters are stability, repose, dignity, and grandeur;
but not without a peculiar grace.

In *Architecture*, the builders took little care for the abodes of the
living, and lavished toil and skill on the tombs of the dead and the
temples of the gods. The great palaces of the Theban kings, indeed,
were the ostentatious works of despots; but these also partook of
the character of temples. All these edifices look like the work
of men who, believing in the immortality of the soul and of the
body too, sought to give eternity to matter. Their endurance for
periods reaching up to 4000 years is the result, not so much of their
materials, as of their form and structure. As Egyptian art begins
with the pyramids, so the whole series of its works is marked by a
pyramidal form, a width of base, and a breadth great in proportion
to the height: all elements of imperishable stability.

Sculpture is generally subordinate to architecture; and even
statues which stand alone have usually a sort of pilaster down the
back. Its spirit is *symbolism*, rather than the direct imitation of
nature, and an attitude of *repose*, expressive of religious peace.
Details are suppressed, not from ignorance or want of skill, but for
the sake of simple majesty. The conventional rules, which affected
all ancient sculpture (till they were thrown off by the Greeks), had
less influence in the earliest than in later ages. When detail is
appropriate, as in figures of animals, the execution is often perfect;
and the great works of the best age, carved from the most intract-
able of stones, evince the highest technical skill, as well as untold
labour.

Painting was almost confined to the colouring of bas-reliefs and
to the decoration of buildings; but, among examples of the latter
use, it had considerable scope in the scenes of daily life depicted on
the walls of tombs. The figures are often well drawn, but generally
in profile, and with complete ignorance of perspective: scarcely
any colours are used but white, black, red, blue, yellow, and green;
and these are laid on in simple patches, as a child colours a print.
On the wrappings of the mummies the Egyptians painted effigies
of the deceased, and the coffins were lined with painted hieroglyphics. We have a few pictures on panels of wood; and the *Ritual
of the Dead* is illustrated with vignettes drawn by the pen with
a freedom, firmness, and purity, not far short of the Greek painted
vases.

The Mesopotamian Plain.

BOOK II.

ASSYRIA AND BABYLON.

CHAPTER XVI.

THE LAND OF THE TWO RIVERS.

"RIVERS are at first the highways of civilization, and it spreads spontaneously over fertile plains." The principle, thus happily expressed by a French historian, leads us to seek in the region watered by the Euphrates and the Tigris, the second centre of primeval civilization. We say the *second*, because the existing records of Egypt take precedence in point of time; though, from the notices in Scripture, it is most probable that political societies were organized, and cities built, on the Euphrates earlier than on the Nile. In both regions, the arts of raising vast edifices, and of expressing thought by writing, are found at so early a period, as the possession of races probably kindred, that the question whether they sprang up in Egypt or Babylonia is still undecided.

The earliest geographical record in existence—the second chapter of *Genesis*—distinguishes two of the four rivers of Eden by the names which they bear to the present day. The Hebrew name *Hiddekel*, "the lively," equally with the Assyrian *Tiggar* or *Tigra* "an arrow," described the swift course of the Tigris, "which goeth forth *eastward*" through its upper valley, along the foot of Mount Niphates, in Armenia, before it turns south "into Assyria" (Genesis ii. 14), by the chain of Zagrus (the mountains of *Kurdistan* and *Luristan*). Its direct course along the foot of that chain, and onward to the Persian Gulf, is so rapid as to admit only of local navigation in small vessels.

"The fourth river is EUPHRATES" (Gen. ii. 14), a name supposed to mean "good and abounding;" and the essential part of which is seen in the Hebrew and the modern *Frat*. As the mightiest river of western Asia, it is called "the great river, the river Euphrates" (Gen. xv. 18), and often simply "the river." This divinely appointed limit of the promised land was often the boundary between great empires; so that it is well named by Milton,—

> "The bordering flood
> Of old Euphrates."

Its upper course—from where the united waters of two mountain streams, which flow westward through Armenia, break through the chain of Niphates—divides Armenia from Asia Minor; and its middle and lower course, winding sluggishly through the eastern margin of the great Desert of Syria and Arabia, forms a natural boundary between the countries beyond that Desert, to the West, and the region encircled by the river, to the East, till it unites with the Tigris.

This region is known in ancient geography by the general name of MESOPOTAMIA, which has the same sense in Greek as the *Naharaim* or *Naharain*,[1] which we find in the Hebrew Bible and in the Assyrian and Egyptian inscriptions, "the land of the two rivers." But there are divisions, both physical and political, which it is of the utmost consequence to understand, before we can follow with any clearness the history of Assyria and Babylonia.

Though Mesopotamia may be described generally as a plain, in contrast with the mountains of Armenia on the north and Zagrus on the east, it is not all level like the flats of Holland and our fens. The southern part only is a nearly level plain, formed by the

---

[1] These are simply dual forms of *nahar*, "river," a word common to the various Semitic languages.

alluvial deposits of the two rivers, which gain upon the head of the Persian Gulf at the rate of a mile in from 30 to 70 years. The upper limit of this flat—extending nearly along the 34th parallel of North latitude, from *Hit* on the Euphrates to *Samara* on the Tigris—is distinctly marked by a sudden descent from the undulating country above, which slopes down from the mountains. The alluvial plain to the south of this boundary was the Land of *Shinar*,[2] Babylonia or Lower Mesopotamia; to the north, the undulating country of Upper Mesopotamia was also called Assyria, in the widest sense.[3]

Properly, however, the name of ASSYRIA—the land of *Asshur* [4]—belongs to the region east of the Tigris, between the river and the chain of Zagrus; its surface varying from the foot-hills of that chain to the plain along the river. In the narrowest sense, it was the triangle formed by the Tigris and the *Great Zab*—the *Aturia* [5] of classical geography—within which lay Nineveh, and two others of the four great Assyrian capitals. But Assyria Proper also included the adjacent region to the south-east, between the *Great* and the *Lesser Zab* (the Adiabene of classical geography), and at least part of that between the *Lesser Zab* and the *Dijaleh* (Gyndes). Though thus lying chiefly on the left bank of the Tigris, Assyria included also the right bank to an indefinite extent, towards the Euphrates and its great tributary, the Chaboras (*Khabour*).

The country lying west of the last-named river, and encircled by the great sweep of the Euphrates, formed the comparatively high undulating region of Padan-Aram (the "upland field" or "pasture ground"), in which lay Haran, the resting-place of Abram, and the abode of Nahor, Bethuel, and Laban. The Mesopotamia Proper of classical geography included this country, together with the plains along the left bank of the Euphrates, as far as the alluvial flat. This whole region still bears the name of *El-Jezireh*, "the Island," in the language of the Arabs, who, like the sands of their own desert, have in all ages pressed beyond the middle and lower

---

[2] This word, like *Sennaar*, probably signifies "two rivers."

[3] The Greek historians, who regarded Assyria and Babylonia politically as the same empire, with its seat first at Nineveh and afterwards at Babylon, include both countries under the name of Assyria; but the geographical distinction should be carefully observed.

[4] In the Semitic dialects, both of the Assyrian records and the Bible, *Asshur* is the name alike of the country, of its chief deity, and of one of its capital cities (*Kileh Sherghat*), as well as of the second son of Shem, who represents the Assyrian nation in the ethnic table of *Genesis* (x. 22).

[5] This is the same word as *Asshur* and *Assyria*: the sh, ss, and t being mere dialectic variations. By a similar variety the Phœnician *Tsur* became in Greek *Tyrus*, and gave its name to *Syria*. We point this out the rather, in order to show the distinction between *Assyria* and *Syria*, which the Greeks confounded.

Euphrates. Xenophon describes the march of the younger Cyrus, along the *left* bank of the middle Euphrates, as lying *through Arabia;* and, at the present day, the district below *El-Jezireh*, where the rivers approach nearest to each other,—the very heart of ancient Babylonia—bears the name of *Irak-Arabi*.

Lying beneath a sub-tropical sun, on the margin of, and partly within, the " rainless zone," the whole of Mesopotamia is richly productive, wherever water is abundant; but its absence leaves deserts of sand, gravel, and, in the alluvial plain, of parched clay. The upper undulating plains form a beautiful pasture-ground, enamelled with flowers during the spring and early summer, but afterwards burnt up except along the rivers. The northern and eastern parts of Assyria, watered by the tributaries of the Tigris, and rising over the foot-hills of Zagrus to its wooded heights, were rich in grass and timber. The lower plains, in the interior of *El-Jezireh*, are now, through the neglect of irrigation, a complete desert, generally sandy and sometimes salt, affording only the unprofitable plants to which such a soil is congenial.

The hot and rainless alluvium of Babylonia was of surpassing fertility when irrigated by the canals which intersected its whole surface. It is the only country where wheat is known to be indigenous, and it is said to have yielded two crops yearly, with an increase of two or even three hundred-fold, besides an after-pasture for cattle.

The date-palm, which now marks a few green islands in the arid plain, once covered its whole surface, to the shores of the Persian Gulf, with a forest of verdure. This wonderful tree furnished the people with bread, wine, vinegar, honey, porridge, and ropes; with a fuel equal to charcoal, and with a means of fattening cattle and sheep; besides supplying timber for wooden houses, and for the roofs, linings, and partitions of the brick buildings. A Persian poem celebrated the 360 uses of the palm.

Now mark the contrast between Babylonia under Nebuchadnezzar and the Persians, and Irak-Arabi under the Turks. The most fertile of countries, in the time of Herodotus, is now almost a complete desert. The soil is a sandy clay, encumbered with the rubbish of ruined towns and canals. To use the words of the best recent explorer of the region :—" The wants of a teeming population were supplied by a rich soil, not less bountiful than that on the banks of the Egyptian Nile. Like islands from a golden sea of waving corn, stood frequent groves of palm-trees and pleasant gardens, affording to the idler or traveller their grateful and highly valued shade. Crowds of passengers hurried along the dusty road to and from the busy city. The land was rich in corn and wine. How changed is

the aspect of that region in the present day!   Long lines of mounds,
it is true, mark the courses of those main arteries which formerly
diffused life and vegetation along their banks; but their channels
are now bereft of moisture and choked with drifted sand; the
smaller offshoots are wholly effaced. All that remains of that
ancient civilization—that 'glory of kingdoms,' 'the praise of the
whole earth '—is recognizable in the numerous mouldering heaps of
brick rubbish which overspread the surface of the plain. Instead
of the luxuriant fields, the groves and gardens, nothing now meets
the eye but an arid waste—the dense population of the former times
has vanished, and no man dwells there." [6]

The soil is still rich, but more than half the country is left dry
and waste from the want of a proper system of irrigation; while the
remaining half is to a great extent covered with marshes owing to
the same neglect.   Thus the prophecies, which to an ignorant reader
might seem contradictory, are literally fulfilled:—" A drought is
upon the waters, and they are dried up,"—" The sea is come upon
Babylon; she is covered with the multitude of the waves thereof"
(Jerem. l. 38; li. 42). She is made " a possession for the bittern,
and pools of water:" she is " wholly desolate " (Isaiah xiv. 23)—
" the hindermost of the nations, a wilderness, a dry land, and a
desert " (Jer. l. 12).

The alluvial plain, however, did not belong entirely to Babylonia.
On the eastern side of the Tigris and the Persian Gulf, as far south
as the Persian highlands, the land of *Elam*, or Susiana, extended
up to the chain of Zagrus, which divided it from Media. The
Elamites or Susianians play a most important part in the whole
history of Babylonia. Their chief city Susa (the *Shushan* of
Scripture) afterwards a capital of the Persian Empire, lay in the
alluvial plain.

[6] Leftus, ' Chaldæa, and Susiana,' pp. 14, 15.

Early Assyrian Chariot.

A Babylonian Tomb.

CHAPTER XVII.

PRIMITIVE KINGDOMS OF MESOPOTAMIA.

THE names of *Babel*[1] and of *Nimrod* still cling, in local tradition, to
the spot marked by Scripture as the site of the first city built after
the Deluge, and of the first monarchy founded on the earth.   The
same land which first attracted men to settle and to cultivate the
arts of civilization, by its abundant supply of food and the means
of intercourse provided by its rivers, furnished them also with the
easiest materials for building.

That their houses were formed of the straight tall trunks and
broad fronds of the palm-tree, is a fact attested by the type of their
domestic architecture.   The more permanent materials required for
city walls, towers of defence, and temples, might appear at first
sight to have been wanting in a land as destitute of stone as is the
London clay.   But, in both cases, the same resource was at hand in
an unlimited supply of plastic earth; and brick had, in the infancy
of art, one advantage over stone, in saving the labour of quarrying
and working.   The torrid sun of Babylonia hardened the masses of
moulded clay into bricks fit for many uses.   Where greater strength

---

[1] *Babylon* is only the Greek form of *Babel.*

and resistance to weather were wanted, the bricks were burnt like ours. The mud formed by mixing the clay-dust with water formed a mortar which hardened like the walls themselves; but a far stronger cement was furnished by the bitumen or asphalt, which springs up in many parts of the plain. The abundance of this substance, in one of the most remarkable ruins, gives it the name of *Mugheir*, the "mother of bitumen."

It is in the light of these facts that we should view the first record of the movements of men after the Deluge:—"And it came to pass, as they journeyed from the east (or eastwards), that they found a plain in the land of *Shinar;* and they dwelt there. And they said one to another, Go to, let us make *brick*, and *burn them thoroughly*. And they had brick for stone, and *slime*[2] had they for mortar. And they said, Go to, let us build, us a *city* and a *tower*, whose top may reach unto heaven; and let us *make us a name*, lest we be scattered abroad upon the face of the whole earth " (Gen. xi. 2-4). This language expresses plainly the design of building a city of defence and a temple, as a rallying point to stay the dispersion of mankind, and as the seat of a universal empire. Hence it is reasonable to connect the building of the city of Babel with the power of Nimrod, the son of Cush, " who first was a *mighty one* on the earth," . . . "and the beginning of his *kingdom* was *Babel*, and Erech, and Accad, and Calneh, in the *land of Shinar*" (Gen. x. 8-10). There is nothing to shew that Nimrod was the leader of, or even contemporary with, the Babel builders; but we have here clearly *the first kingdom upon record;* and there is good ground to believe that this " mighty hunter " was the earliest type of those hateful despots and conquerors who make men their prey.

The divine rebuke, which ever awaits such schemes of empire, was seen in the confusion of speech which gave the city and tower the name of *Babel*.[3]

> " Divided thence, through every age,
> Thy rebels, Lord, their warfare wage,
> And hoarse and jarring all
> Mount up their heaven-assailing cries
> To thy bright watchmen in the skies
> From Babel's shattered wall."

"So they left off to build the city." But the place remained con-

---

[2] Commentators are divided as to whether this means mud or asphalt. Both are found as mortar in the existing ruins.

[3] Gen. xi. 5-9. Observe the direct reference to the *design* in the latter part of ver. 6. Another etymology of *Babel* is the "Gate (or House) of Il or El," the name of the supreme god in Babylonian, like *El* and *Elohim* in Hebrew. There can be no doubt that the "tower" was also a temple. A double significance of proper names is not unfrequent.

secrated to the genius of despotism, and the historic Babylon rose close to, if not precisely on, the same spot.

Tradition has added various legends to the silence of Scripture about the fate of the Tower. But we know, from other cases, the process of decay through which such an edifice would pass when neglected, without any miraculous agency for its destruction. And that very process is faithfully described in a recently deciphered inscription of Nebuchadnezzar, which describes his restoration of the temple at Borsippa, near Babylon, the ruins of which are now called *Birs-Nimrud*, "the Mound of Nimrod." He says, " A former king had built it (they reckon 42 ages), *but he did not complete its head*. SINCE A REMOTE TIME PEOPLE HAD ABANDONED IT, WITHOUT ORDER EXPRESSING THEIR WORDS. Since that time the earthquake and the thunder had dispersed its sun-dried clay : the bricks of the casing had been split; and the earth of the interior had been scattered in heaps."

The idea suggested by these words, that this very edifice may have been the original tower of Babel, is somewhat confirmed by facts tending to show that Borsippa was the old citadel of Babylon, though seven miles distant from the historical city. It was the sacred seat of the Chaldæan priests ; its name signifies a fortress, and it was the refuge of the last king of Babylon, when his capital was taken and his son Belshazzar slain by the Persians.

Without attempting to decide this question, we cite the inscription of Nebuchadnezzar as evidence of the type of the towers (called *ziggurats*) built after the model of the Tower of Babel, the ruins of which now form mounds scattered over the plain of Babylonia and Susiana. The tradition which has always regarded them as *temples* is confirmed by the inscriptions on their ruins ; but they may also have served, like later church-towers (and especially the " round towers " of Ireland), for purposes of defence. The Temple of Belus at Borsippa, described by Herodotus, is the very edifice celebrated in the inscription of Nebuchadnezzar as the " House of the Seven Lights of the Earth."

This title is connected with the *form* still traceable in this and other ruins, in Assyria as well as Babylonia. The structure was pyramidal, though not strictly a pyramid. The building rose above its platform of crude brick by stages, each smaller than that below, like a series of huge steps ; one stage for each of the heavenly bodies ; the summit being crowned with a chapel of the god to whom the temple was specially dedicated.[4] Each stage was sacred to one

[4] In the *Birs-Nimrud*, the three lower stages are each 26 feet high, the four upper 15 feet, the total height, including the chapel, being 153¼ feet The stages

of the "Seven Lights," in the order of the system believed in till the time of Copernicus; and each was distinguished by an appropriate colour. (See the Diagram.) The chapel or shrine on the summit was richly decorated with colours, metals, and costly stones, both within and without.

The body of the edifice was a solid mass of crude (or sun-dried) bricks, enclosed in a casing of burnt brick, as we learn both from the existing ruins and from Nebuchadnezzar's inscription:—" I undertook to build porticoes around the crude brick masses and the casing of burnt bricks." In some of the earliest extant examples the lowest storey is supported by buttresses of burnt brick, and the remains of gateways and staircases are still visible. The number of storeys is frequently less than seven; *two*, besides the chapel, appears to have been a very ancient type.

Some of the oldest towers are built entirely of crude brick, bonded together by thick layers of mats, made from the reeds which abounded in the marshes of Chaldæa, steeped in bitumen, which projected (or, at least, now project) beyond the surface, so as to form not only a bond but a protection from the weather. This structure is seen in the chief ruin at *Warka* (probably the ancient Erech), which is hence called *Bowariyeh* (" reed mats"), where the mound looks like a natural hill with strata of dark hard rock in a softer material.

Thus, in Babylonia, as in Egypt, the earliest monuments of civilization are towering edifices designed for sacred uses, and suited by their pyramidal form to give resting-places for the eye as it looks over a vast level unbroken by nature. It is worth while to compare the two types. The Babylonian temple tower might be formed into a pyramid by filling up its angles; and we know that the Egyptian pyramid was built in steps, which were afterwards filled up. The " Pyramid of Degrees" is formed in steps, though many and small compared with the Babylonian towers. In the latter the stages were used to reach the culminating shrine, and probably for astronomical observations; but the Pyramid, once complete, seems to have re-

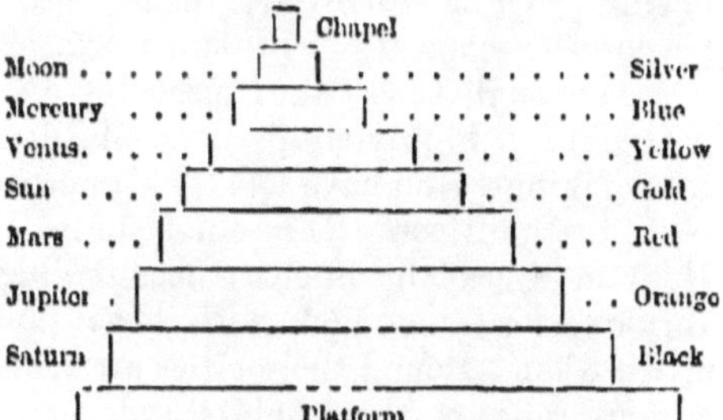

diminish by 12 feet in the length of the side, the lowest being a square of 272 feet, and the summit a square of 20 feet. The annexed diagram, representing the S.E. elevation, is drawn to scale.

mained a mere monument, and we have no evidence that it was put to any further use.

The Egyptian pyramids are nearly always on a square base; the base of the Babylonian towers is often oblong, but in the *Birs-Nimrud* it is square. In two other respects there is a striking contrast. Both forms are carefully adjusted to the cardinal points—a common evidence of astronomical knowledge; but in the Egyptian pyramids it is the *four sides*—in the Babylonian towers the *four corners*—that look to the four quarters of the heavens. Nor in the latter is each stage placed centrally over the one below. For example, in the *Birs Nimrud*, the side of each stage diminishes by 42 feet, the recess or step being 21 feet wide equally on the S.E and N.W. sides; but on the N.E., which may be considered the front. it is 30 feet, and on the S.W. only 12 feet, so that the centre of the summit is not over the centre of the base. In regarding both forms as examples of that passion for massive buildings, which some ascribe to the race of Ham. these differences are not to be overlooked.

More striking than all, in lasting results, is the difference of material. It has taken 4000 years for the forces of nature and the wantonness of man to strip the pyramids of their mere surface, and they have attracted the enquiries of every age ; but the brick towers of Babylonia have long since crumbled into shapeless mounds, about which there have only flitted vague traditions of Babel and of Nimrod. But the very process of decay, by which portions of the upper storeys have fallen over the rest, has preserved what lay beneath the rude surface which presented no attraction for the spoiler. And now these mounds, like the nobler monuments of Egypt, are revealing the story of a civilization of like antiquity.

Nebuchadnezzar tells us that "he put the inscription of his name" in parts of the temple which he restored ; and in the ruins of other edifices we now read the names of kings who are supposed to have reigned in Babylonia 15 or 16 centuries before Nebuchadnezzar. These discoveries, which are still under discussion, lie beyond the scope of our present work.

It is enough to say that, probably about the age of the Hebrew patriarchs, a highly civilized people lived in Babylonia under the rule of kings, who have left their names on the temples which they built to the Moon (their chief deity) and the other "Lights of Heaven," especially in cities near the head of the Persian Gulf, the very quarter from which native traditions trace the source of their civilization. Round those cities are vast burying-places, containing curious relics of their habits and their arts, and, among the rest. the engraved cylinders which they used for signets.

Among the ruins of their cities it is supposed that, besides Babel, the *Erech* and *Calneh*, which belonged to the kingdom of Nimrod, have been identified; while his *Accad* seems to have been the primitive name of the lower part of Babylonia, which was afterwards called Chaldæa.   It is thought that the people of Akkad were conquered by the *Sumiri*, a foreign race from the land to the east of Babylonia, whose dominion is represented by the reign of Nimrod.   From the midst of our imperfect knowledge there emerge names not unlike those of the Elamite Chedorlaomer, and signs of conquests towards the west, like his over Sodom and its allies.

Still clearer are the indications of the extension of this early Babylonian kingdom up the Tigris and over Assyria, corresponding to the statement that Nimrod, or the power which he founded, "went forth out of that land into Asshur and built Nineveh," &c. (Gen. x. 11, 12).   About the 19th century, B.C., it appears from the evidence of inscriptions that a king of Babylon built a temple at Asshur (*Kileh Sherghat*), one of the Assyrian capitals.

About this time, too, a Semitic dynasty had been established in Babylonia; and henceforth the Semitic race was dominant both in Upper and Lower Mesopotamia.   Berosus, the native historian of Babylon (about B.C. 250), represents this early Babylonian or "Chaldean" monarchy as overthrown by the Arabians about B.C. 1500, but who these Arabians were is quite uncertain.   The fall of the kingdom appears to have coincided with the climax of the Egyptian empire under the kings of the 18th Dynasty, who are said even to claim Babylon among their conquests in Mesopotamia.

Mugheir Temple.

Assyrians (*Nimrud*).

CHAPTER XVIII.

MYTHICAL HISTORY OF ASSYRIA.

FROM the brief notice of Nimrod in the book of *Genesis*, it may be inferred that the primitive kingdom of Babel was soon extended into Assyria, and that NINEVEH and its three associated cities were little inferior in antiquity to Babylon and the cities of Chaldæa. But henceforth, except in Balaam's prophecy of her conquests, Assyria does not appear in Scripture history till the mission of Jonah to Nineveh, and till the empire comes in contact with Israel in the eighth century B.C. The only *literary* records of her early condition are the romantic legends of the Greek writers, which passed for history till the wonderful discoveries, which have been made among her ruined palaces in our own time, revealed her own authentic records.

The Greeks use the name of *Assyria*, politically, for the whole series of kingdoms and empires which succeeded one another in the valley of the Tigris and Euphrates, from a mythical antiquity to the time of Cyrus. Without attempting a regular history, they strung together the legends, which they learnt from Persian poets and romancers, into a form suited to amuse their countrymen and to illustrate their political ideas. Knowing nothing of the primitive Babylonian kingdoms, they placed Nineveh at the head of those Asiatic empires, their whole interest in which was centred on the ultimate conflict between Persia and themselves—between Asiatic despotism and European liberty.   This is the key-note struck by Herodotus at the beginning of his history.

From this point of view the history of Assyria is dressed up like a drama, in which the chief persons are the king who founds, and the more heroic queen who extends the empire; their luxurious but politic son, who impresses upon it the type of an Oriental despotism, such as Herodotus and Ctesias saw in Persia; and the last king, on whom falls the long-contracted Nemesis of tyranny and luxury, but whose degeneracy is redeemed by some last flashes of heroic spirit, and his end raised to tragic dignity by his self-sacrifice of fire.

NINUS, the son of Belus, the Greek hero-eponymus of Nineveh,[1] represents (if any Assyrian personage) the god *Ninip* (Saturn). The frequent occurrence of *Ninip* or *Nin*, as an element in the names of Assyrian kings, has suggested the identification of Ninus with some of those kings, whose real exploits may, in fact, have contributed something to his legendary story.   But no such identification has any historical value.   The conquests ascribed to Ninus are not a bad summary of the spread of the Assyrian empire, though their extent is exaggerated, evidently in order to make that empire conterminous with the Persian.

The first exploit of Ninus is the conquest of Babylon'a, which had been overrun by the Arabs.   Next he marches against Armenia, whose king submits to him as a subject ally.   The resistance of the King of Media is punished with crucifixion; and, in the course of seventeen years, Ninus made himself master of all the lands from the Indus to the Tanaïs (*Don*) and the Mediterranean Sea.   He now rebuilt Nineveh, and called it after his own name; and, by attracting foreigners as well as natives to his capital, he made it the greatest and most flourishing city of the world.

It was in the course of a war against Bactria that SEMIRAMIS attracted his attention.   She was the daughter of the great goddess of Ascalon, Derceto, who had exposed this fruit of her love for a mortal youth to perish.   But, being saved and brought up by a shepherd, she became the wife of the governor of Syria, and went with him to the Bactrian war, where, disguised as a soldier, she scaled the wall of the capital.   Ninus rewarded her courage by taking her to wife, and after his death she became sole queen.

In emulation of her husband's creation of Nineveh, Semiramis built a new capital in Babylonia; and the legend ascribes to her the walls and bridges, quays and gates, temples, fortresses, and

---

[1] *Ninus* is the Greek form of the name *Nineveh*, as the Hebrew is read with the vowel points or *Ninuë* without them (*Nineví* in the LXX.).   The Assyrian form is *Ninua*.

reservoirs of Babylon, which belong chiefly to Nebuchadnezzar and his successors.[2] The rock-built city and palace at *Van*, the inscriptions on whose ruins still preserve the memory of a race of Armenian kings, are called hers; as, in short, was nearly every great work in every part of Asia. Her edifices found their limit only at the bounds of the habitable world on the frontiers of Scythia, and there, a Greek writer says, Alexander saw her own records of her deeds in the following inscription :—

" Nature gave me the form of a woman, but my deeds have equalled those of the bravest men. I ruled over the empire of Ninus, which on the east touches the river Indus, on the north the Scythians and the Sogdians. Before me no Assyrian beheld the seas : I looked upon four so remote that none had reached them. I forced rivers to flow where I wished, and I only wished it in places where they were useful. I made the barren soil fruitful, by watering it with my rivers. I raised impregnable fortresses; I pierced roads across impracticable rocks. My chariots have rollen on roads where the wild beasts had found no path. And, in the midst of all my labours, I found time for pleasure and for love."

These great works occupied the later years of Semiramis, after her career had found in India at once a check and a rebuke. Having conquered Egypt and a great part of Ethiopia, she coveted the wealth which lay on her opposite frontier. The king of India, informed of her preparations, sent her a letter of defiance, reproaching her with her debaucheries, and threatening her with crucifixion. His elephants gave him the victory, and Semiramis only escaped with the loss of two-thirds of her army.

At last she heard that her son, Ninyas, was plotting against her. Instead of punishing his treason, she resigned the crown to him ; and, after commanding all the governors to obey their new king, she flew away in the form of a dove, and was worshipped as a goddess. This mythical apotheosis is consistent with her whole story. She is the ideal of a female demigod, according to the Oriental standard, which is reproduced in Astarte, Derceto, and Dido. The truth is that Ninus, the warrior and founder, Semiramis, the conqueror and builder, and their son Ninyas, the politic and self-indulgent ruler, represent on earth the supreme *triad* of the Babylonian and Assyrian religion.

The whole legend is of Babylonian origin ; but its Persian colouring is clearest in the character of NINYAS. He is the very pattern of the later Achæmenid kings ; withdrawn like a god from

---

[2] In this part of the legend the *name* of Semiramis seems to have been derived from a real Assyrian queen, *Sammuramit*, who was especially connected with Babylon, in the 8th century. (See below, Chapter XXII.)

the eyes of his subjects amidst the pleasures of his palace, but yet securing their obedience by profound policy. He kept on foot an immense army, which was levied annually from all the provinces, over each of which he set a governor devoted to his person. This army was assembled at Nineveh, and was renewed at the end of every year; so that no close relations could be formed between the soldiers and their officers, and military plots were hard to concoct.

This system continued under all his successors, down to SARDANAPALUS; and even this degenerate sovereign has a divine prototype in the androgynous deity Sandon, and a sort of apotheosis in the manner of his death. When Arbaces, the satrap of Media, and Belesys, the chief of the Chaldæan priests of Babylon, march against him in rebellion, he suddenly takes the field, and performs prodigies of valour before he is defeated. He holds out in Nineveh for two years, trusting to an oracle, which had assured his safety till the Tigris should become his foe. But when an inundation washes down the river wall of the city, he perceives that his hour has come, and resigns himself to fate. He collects all his treasures, with his wives and concubines, on a vast funeral pile; ascending which, and setting fire to it with his own hand, he perishes in the conflagration of his palace. How far this agrees with the real fall of Nineveh will be seen as we proceed.[3]

The final destruction of Nineveh took place either in 625 B.C., or certainly not later than 606 B.C.; and the ruins must soon have fallen into the state of shapeless mounds, in which they exist at present. It was not till nearly 200 years later that the Greeks began their enquiries into Assyrian history, when the city had long since been literally buried. Herodotus, who well knew the *name* of the capital of Assyria, attempts no further description of Nineveh than that it *formerly* stood upon the Tigris, nor are later writers agreed as to which bank it stood on.

The particulars given by less trustworthy authors may have been drawn from tradition, imagination, or analogy, especially from the ruins of Babylon. Thus Nineveh is described as larger than Babylon, its form being an oblong quadrangle, of about 17 miles by 10, enclosed by walls 100 feet high, and thick enough to allow three chariots to pass each other upon their top; with 1500 towers, 200 feet in height. In fact the walls of Assyrian cities were earthen

---

[3] In the case of Sardanapalus, as of Semiramis, the *name* is derived from history. There are several kings whose names are composed on the type *Asshur-*✳*-pal;* where *Asshur* is the chief god, *pal,* " a son," and the middle element is a word of various forms, with the root meaning of " to protect." Some modern writers call all these kings, among whom are some great conquerors, *Sardanapalus;* and the Greek legend knows of a warrior Sardanapalus, distinct from the king who perished with his capital.

enbankments of great height, and therefore necessarily of enormous thickness.

The authentic testimony of the prophet Jonah tells us that "Nineveh was an exceeding great city, of three days' journey;" and that this means *in length* seems proved by what follows, "Jonah began to enter into the city a day's journey" (Jonah iii. 3, 4). Its description as "Nineveh, that great city, wherein are more than six score thousand souls that cannot discern between their right hand and their left hand, and also much cattle"—if these 120,000 mean children—implies a total population of 600,000. The mention of "cattle" calls to mind the vast extent of open space always included in an eastern city; and the ruins of the Assyrian cities prove how large a part of the ground within the walls was occupied by the royal palaces and by the temples. Nor is it unlikely that the Hebrew prophet, like the chief modern explorer of the site, may have included under the name of *Nineveh* the royal city of Calah, which stood on the eastern bank of the Tigris, 17 miles south of the true Nineveh, to which it may have been united by suburban villages.

For ages after the city perished, the name survived at and near its site, and a *Nineve* is still mentioned under the Roman empire. In the mounds which skirt the east bank of the Tigris, for miles above its confluence with the *Great Zab*, the Greeks and Romans saw the tombs of Semiramis and Sardanapalus; and the tradition which ultimately prevailed fixed Nineveh on its true site at the mounds opposite *Mosul*, one of which (probably the oldest part of the city) bears the name of "the prophet Jonah" (*Nebbi-Yunus*). Arabian and other Oriental writers, from the 7th to the 15th century, speak of *Ninawi* or *Ninue* on the left bank, opposite to Mosul on the right. The discoveries reserved in those mounds for the 18th century are now to be unfolded.

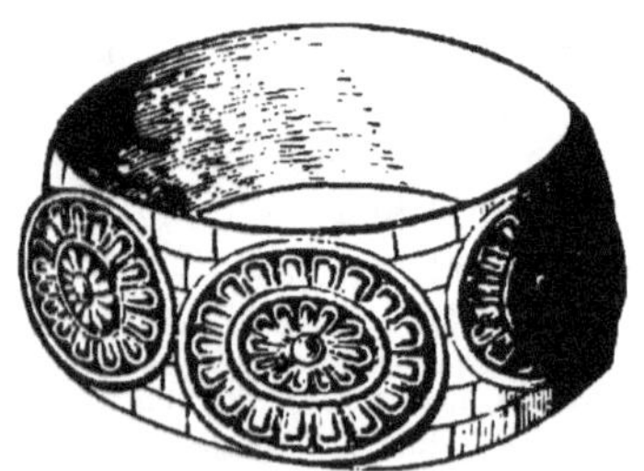

Royal Bracelet (*Khorsabad*).

Mound of *Nebbi-Yunus, i.e.* the *Prophet Jonah.*   See p. 41.

CHAPTER XIX.

RECENT DISCOVERIES IN ASSYRIA.

THE whole surface of Upper Mesopotamia is dotted here and there with mounds, or small hills, which are now known to contain the ruins of Assyrian cities.   In the angle formed by the Tigris and the Great Zab, and chiefly on the left bank of the former river, some such mounds had long attracted special notice from their conspicuous forms, and from their connection with the traditional site of Nineveh. That site is determined, as we have seen, on the left bank of the Tigris, opposite to the village of *Mosul,* where, besides the mound of *Nebbi Yunus,* that of *Koyunjik* is now known to cover the ruins of Sennacherib's palace.

Nearly 10 miles further to the North, and about the same distance from the Tigris, its little tributary, the *Khosru*, washes the foot of the mound called *Khorsabad*, that is, "the abode of Khosru." But these later Persian names had not succeeded, down to the time when the dynasty itself succumbed to the Mohammedans (A.D. 652), in obliterating the name of *Sarghun*, whereby faithful tradition had preserved, for nearly 14 centuries, the name of the builder SARGON. the father of Sennacherib.

About 17 miles South of the spot named as the site of Nineveh, or 30 miles along the course of the Tigris, and 5 or 6 above its confluence with the Great Zab, is another mound, smaller in extent than the ruins of Nineveh, but made strikingly conspicuous by the pyramid or cone, which towers high above its surface, and which attracted the notice of Xenophon in his famous retreat (Xen. *Anab.* iii. 4 § 9). Inscriptions mark the ruins as those of *Calah* or *Calach;* and the mound contains the palaces of some of the greatest Assyrian kings. Not only does the mound bear the name of *Nimrud*, but Mr. Layard was informed by an Arab sheikh that "the palace was built by ATHUR, the lieutenant of Nimrod:"—that very Nimrod, "out of whose land went forth Asshur, and builded Nineveh and *Calah*" (Gen. xi. 11). Such is the tenacity of local tradition.

These three royal residences lie all within the limits of the ancient Aturia. Some 40 miles below *Nimrud*, and just above the mouth of the *Little Zab*, but on the opposite, or *right*, bank of the Tigris, is another mound of equal magnitude, at *Kileh-Sherghat*. These ruins have been explored far less completely than those of *Koyunjik*, *Khorsabad*, and *Nimrud;* but they are peculiarly interesting as those of a city which bore the name of *Asshur* (or, as some read it, *Ellasar*), as having yielded the oldest native records of Assyrian history, and, as having been the earliest residence of the known rulers of Assyria.[1]

Ancient writers speak of tablets, as standing or lying about these mounds, inscribed with "Chaldaic" characters; and, in modern times, among other objects occasionally turned up, were bricks, and fragments of baked clay in the form of tablets and cylinders, stamped with a writing which was called "cuneiform" or "arrow-headed," from the shape of the elementary strokes. The first real explorer was MR. CLAUDIUS JAMES RICH, the East India Company's resident

---

[1] We purposely avoid saying that this was the original *capital*. That rank was probably always held by Nineveh; but various causes may have placed the royal *residence* elsewhere. Kings residing at Calah (*Nimrud*) speak, in their annals, of Nineveh, as if it were the capital, and Sennacherib expressly tells us that he *restored* Nineveh as his royal city.

at *Bagdad*,[2] who, between 1811 and his death in 1821, did all in his power to examine the sites of Babylon and Nineveh, and called special attention to the mound of *Koyunjik*, where fragments of sculpture and pottery had frequently been discovered. But no attempt was made to excavate the mounds; and all the inscribed bricks and fragments gathered by Mr. Rich from the neighbourhoods of *Hillah* (Babylon), *Nimrud*, and *Mosul*, were exhibited at the British Museum in a case scarcely three feet square.

The travels of Sir Robert Ker Porter, in 1817–1820, added a few interesting objects from Babylonia; and among them, what is supposed to have been the *signet-cylinder* of the earliest known king of the primitive Babylonian Monarchy. But the great service rendered by this traveller was in making better known the inscribed monuments of the Persian Achæmenid kings, Darius, Xerxes, and the rest. The long records found on them in the cuneiform character, and in three different dialects, laid the foundation for the vast discovery of their meaning. The work begun by the German Grotefend, in deciphering the elements of the *Persian* cuneiform inscriptions, was virtually completed by Colonel, now Sir Henry Rawlinson just in time for its application to the mass of Assyrian literature, then beginning to be disinterred from the mounds. Colonel Rawlinson published his translation of the great historical inscription of Darius, the son of Hystaspes, at *Behistun*, in 1846, the very year in which Mr. Austen Henry Layard was in the midst of his discoveries at *Nimrud*.

This great explorer, to whom chiefly belongs the honour of the resurrection of ancient Assyria from her buried cities, had long fixed his eager hopes on the mount of *Nimrud*. But first. at his suggestion, M. Botta, the French Consul at *Mosul*, began to excavate the mound of *Koyunjik*, in 1842. Discouraged by the scantiness of his first gleanings from what proved afterwards the richest harvest, M. Botta turned his attention to the mound of *Khorsabad*, and there he discovered an Assyrian edifice, "the first, probably, which had been exposed to the view of man since the fall of the Assyrian empire."

The impression made by this first discovery ought not to be obliterated in the flood of knowledge since acquired. In the words of Mr. Layard :—"He (M. Botta) soon found that he had opened a chamber, which was connected with others, and constructed of

---

[2] The young reader should remember that this city, so well known to him in the stories of "the good Haroun El-Raschid," is, as a capital, the nearest modern representative of Babylon. It stands on the *Tigris*, about 60 miles north of the spot where Babylon stood on the Euphrates.

slabs of gypsum,[3] covered with sculptured representations of battles, sieges, and similar events. His wonder may easily be imagined. A new history had been suddenly opened upon him—the records of an unknown people were before him. He was equally at a loss to account for the age and the nature of the monument. The art shewn in the sculptures—the dresses of the figures—their arms, and the objects which accompanied them—were all new to him, and afforded no clue to the epoch of the erection of the edifice, and to the people who were its founders.

" Numerous inscriptions were cut between the bas-reliefs, and evidently contained the explanation of the events thus recorded in sculpture. The nature of these inscriptions afforded, at least, evidence that the building was of a period preceding the conquest of Alexander; for it was generally admitted that, after the subjugation of the west of Asia by the Macedonians, the cuneiform writing ceased to be employed. But too little was then known of this character to enable M. Botta to draw any inference from the peculiar arrangement of the wedges, which distinguishes the varieties used in different countries.

" However, it was evident that the monument pertained to a very ancient and very civilized people; and it was natural, from its position, to refer it to the inhabitants of Nineveh, a city which, although *it could not have occupied a site so distant from the Tigris*, must have been in the vicinity of the place." When the inscriptions were afterwards deciphered, they proved the edifice to be a palace built by Sargon, the father of Sennacherib, with a surrounding town, as a new country residence in the neighbourhood of Nineveh. The rich treasure of sculptures obtained from it now adorns the Museum of the Louvre.

The uncovering of Sargon's palace at *Khorsabad* was completed in 1845; and it was in the same year that Mr. Layard was enabled, chiefly by the liberality of Sir Stratford Canning (Lord Stratford de Redclyffe), to begin his great excavations at *Nimrud*. In the broken slumbers of the night before the work, the fancies of his " excited brain " were strangely prophetic:—" Visions of palaces underground, of gigantic monsters, of sculptured figures, floated before me. After forming plan after plan for removing the earth, and extricating these treasures, I fancied myself wandering in a maze of chambers from which I could find no outlet. Then

<hr>

[3] The native form of the stone better known as " plaster of Paris " (sulphate of lime), which abounds in Assyria, as well as its finer form of *alabaster*. These two are the usual materials of the sculptured slabs which line the inner walls of the palaces; some, however, are of limestone.

again, all was reburied, and I was standing on the grass-covered
mound."   Even the last words were fulfilled to the letter; for the
only means of preserving from immediate decay the remains that
could not be removed, was to replace the earth over them.   Hence,
in quitting the scene of his work, the explorer says:—"We look
around, in vain, for any traces of the wonderful remains we have
just seen, and are half inclined to believe that we have dreamed
a dream, or have been listening to some tale of Eastern romance.
Some who may hereafter tread on the spot where the grass again
grows over the ruins of the Assyrian palaces may indeed suspect
that we have been relating a vision."   The sculptures and inscriptions transported by Mr. Layard to our Museum would form
a perfect reply to any such doubter.[4]

During this expedition of 1845–1847, Mr. Layard began discoveries at *Koyunjik* and at *Kileh Sherghat*, which were afterwards
followed up by himself and others.   Of the brilliant results obtained
at *Koyunjik*, as well as those at *Nimrud*, we have presently to speak ;
but *Kileh-Sherghat* yielded what may be called the first key to the
authentic history of Assyria in three clay cylinders, inscribed with
the earliest contemporary annals that we possess of any Assyrian
king.   By this time the progress made in deciphering the cuneiform
inscriptions, already gathered from Assyria, had attracted such
attention, that the Council of the Royal Asiatic Society proposed
these cylinders as a test of the new science.   England, Ireland, and
France, divide the honour of the result, in which Sir Henry
Rawlinson, Dr. Hincks, and M. Oppert, without communicating with
each other, sent in versions of the inscription, of which such critics
as Dean Milman and Mr. Grote certified, that "the coincidences
between the translations, both as to the general sense and verbal
rendering, was very remarkable."

From this date (1857) we became possessed at once of a vast mass
of Assyrian literature, and of the power of reading the characters
and language, both hitherto unknown, in which it is written.
Those, however, who set the highest value on what is already
gained, have the keenest sense of how much still remains to be
done, both in discovery and interpretation, before we can be said
to possess the native and contemporary materials for a complete
history of Assyria.

---

[4] We wish we had space for the whole of Mr. Layard's final survey of his work at
Nimrud.   Once for all we refer our readers to the latest and most interesting
accounts of his own and subsequent discoveries in the two small volumes entitled
'Nineveh and its Remains' and 'Nineveh and Babylon,' both "Abridged by the
Author from his larger works," London, 1867. Such a subject as this can only be
properly studied in the light of the original process of discovery.

Statue of Shalmaneser II. (From *Kileh-Sherghat.*) See p. 141.

CHAPTER XX.

RISE OF THE ASSYRIAN MONARCHY. TO ABOUT B.C. 1100.

THE history of Assyria is divided into the two periods of the *Old or Upper Monarchy*, and the *New or Lower Monarchy.* The latter consists of those kings whose names are familiar to us in Scripture History, and whose relations to Egypt, as well as to Syria, are of peculiar importance. For our knowledge of the former we are dependent on their own annals, with the illustrations of their deeds and modes of life which are seen "in living sculpture on the walls" of the British and French Museums, and in a number of objects— arms, furniture, utensils, glass bottles, carvings, engraved gems, weights, seals, and so forth, gathered from the ruins.

Besides their value in the history of art, the vivid scenes of these sculptures exhibit the self-drawn portrait of the great Asiatic despotism, which was denounced—we can now see how deservedly— by the Hebrew prophets. The written annals supply the reading to these pictures, and reveal the growth of the power which was destined to lead Israel into captivity, and to humble Egypt; but which was rebuked by the faith of Hezekiah, and succumbed to

Media and Babylon. But the details have but few points of interest. Each king in turn, and the same king year after year, boasts of the power given him by Asshur to subdue enemies who are often again and again the same. For it was one character of the Assyrian power, to be ever needing to repeat its conquests.

These annals are, in their way, eminently religious. This is a character of the Oriental mind: and despots have always thought to enhance their own honour in honouring the gods of whom they were the vicegerents upon earth. This spirit is seen in the very names of the kings (as well as of other persons); and some understanding of those names will give greater precision and interest to our idea of the persons who bore them. Like those significant names, with which we are familiar in the Bible,[1] the Assyrian names usually form *sentences*, in which the name of *Asshur* is an element as prevalent as *Jeho* or *Jah* (for *Jehovah*) and *El* (*God*) in Hebrew, or *Theo* (*God*) in Greek names. Abundant examples will occur as we proceed.[2]

In beginning to construct a brief outline of Assyrian history from these records, we must recal the important distinction between *native* and *contemporary* documents; for our earliest facts are gathered from the statements of later kings. The oldest known of the Assyrian documents is that found on the famous *Kileh-Sherghat* cylinders, which are the annals of a king named Tiglath-pileser I.[3] He mentions his restoration of a temple at *Kileh-Sherghat*, which had been built 701 years before by the son of a *Babylonian* king. Now another record, by Sennacherib, mentions his own recovery of certain idols which had been taken from this same Tiglath-pileser, and carried away to Babylon, 418 years before, by a king named

---

[1] The young reader should bear in mind that the Assyrians were of the same great Semitic race as the Hebrews, and their languages were cognate dialects of the same stock. It is chiefly by aid of this resemblance that the language of the Assyrian inscriptions has been made out.

[2] We may here, once for all, explain a constant difficulty in the reading of the royal names. The distinction between *ideographic* and *phonetic* signs, in writing, has been stated in connection with the Egyptian hieroglyphics. The cuneiform characters were also originally pictorial, and the elements of the proper names are generally *ideographic*, and their *phonetic* value is often very doubtful. But this only affects the *form of the name*, not the *identity of the person*, or the *reality of the deeds recorded* in his annals, and exhibited in his sculptures;—just as well known events in our own history are not brought into doubt by saying that " *Lackland* signed Magna Carta," or " *Longshanks* conquered Wales."

[3] The *number* is added to distinguish him from the *Tiglath-pileser* of Scripture, who was the founder of the Lower Dynasty. The Assyrian name, *Tiglathi-pal-zira*, means " worship-(to the)son of-*Zira*" probably (*our Lord*) : and it is equivalent to another royal name, *Tiglathi-Nin*, for the god *Ninip* or *Nin* is called *Pal-zira*.

Merodach-idin-akhi.[4]   Assuming that each record is trustworthy,
—and the *exact* numbers used shew at least a definite tradition—
let us see what results we get.

First, as to chronology.   The date of Sennacherib is well known ;
and his conquest of Babylon was in B.C. 702.   Adding 418 years,
we get B.C. 1120 for the war between Tiglath-pileser I. and Merodach-idin-akhi.   At what time in his reign Tiglath-pileser restored
the temple, we cannot tell ; but, adding the 701 years to B.C. 1120,
we get 1821 B.C. as the approximate date of its first erection.

Here, then, is at least some evidence for concluding that, in the
19th century, B.C., Assyria was governed by a Babylonian viceroy,
residing at *Kileh-Sherghat* as the capital ; and the fact of such
a viceroyalty is believed to be confirmed by old Babylonian inscriptions at the same place.   Next, about the end of the 12th century
B.C., we find Assyria independent and (as we know from his own
annals) a conquering power under Tiglath-pileser I. ; but Babylon
is also independent of Assyria, under a king, who inflicts a disgrace
on the rival power.   The royal residence of the Assyrian king is
now at Asshur (*Kileh-Sherghat*); and this position of the capital,
comparatively low down upon the Tigris, is consistent with the
former subjection to Babylonia and the present need for defence
against her.

The inscribed bricks of that city bear the names of certain kings,
stamped by themselves upon their buildings, and forming the oldest
contemporary royal inscriptions of Assyria.   They are headed by
Bel-lush. whose great-grandson, *Shalmaneser I.*, is named in the
chief inscription at *Nimrud* as the founder of the city of Calah
on that site.   He also began the career of Assyrian conquest on the
side of Armenia, which was continued by his son, *Tiglathi-Nin.*

The reign of the latter seems to mark the important epoch of the
transfer of supremacy in Mesopotamia from Babylon to Assyria ;
for Sennacherib relates his own recovery of a signet-ring left at
Babylon by this king, which bore the inscription, "Tiglathi-Nin,
son of Shalmaneser, king of Assyria, and conqueror of *Kar-Dunis*"
(i.e. *Babylonia*).   The inscription also places him 600 years before
Sennacherib, that is, just at 1300 B.C.[5]

For the 13th century we have scarcely any information : the 12th
may be nearly filled up by the four kings whom Tiglath-pileser I.
names as his predecessors.   This was the age when Egypt finally
lost her empire over the divided tribes of Mesopotamia Proper, and
the .kingdom of Israel established a barrier between her and
Assyria.   Accordingly, when the contemporary history of Assyria

---

4 That is, " Merodach-has given brothers."
5 If the 600 years be taken as a round number, the date might be some years lower.

begins with the *Kileh-Sherghat* cylinders, we find Tiglath-pileser I. extending his power over the *Naïri*, that is, the Mesopotamians beyond the *Khabour*, and driving them and their Hittite allies as far as the *Upper Sea*, that is, the Mediterranean.

He carried his arms north and north-east into the mountains of Niphates and Zagrus; and, at *Korkhar*, near the eastern source of the Tigris, the living rock is sculptured with a figure of the king in bas-relief, and an inscription which identifies it as his work. This is the oldest known specimen of Assyrian sculpture. Near it are two tablets with the effigies of later kings, *Asshur-nasir-pal* and his son *Shalmaneser II.*; and it was in consequence of a mention, in the records of the latter king at Nimrud, of the tablet set up by him beside his father's on the Upper Tigris, that these sculptures were sought for and discovered:—a striking evidence of the truth of cuneiform interpretation.

Respecting Babylon the annals of Tiglath-pileser I. are silent; but a valuable tablet in the British Museum, containing a large portion of the parallel history of Assyria and Babylonia,[6] mentions two invasions of the latter country by Tiglath-pileser, who ravaged the land and took Babylon itself. But the capture of his idols by Merodach-adan-akhi[7] bears witness to a serious reverse, inflicted probably on his retreat. We may suppose that these idols had been carried with the army (like the ark of God against the Philistines) as a security for victory. The fact, that such sacred trophies were not recovered till 400 years later, by Sennacherib, is significant of the continued strength of Babylon. While the monuments of successive Assyrian kings testify of their repeated efforts to subdue her, she still remained their most powerful neighbour. More light will be thrown on the relations of the two kingdoms as we proceed.

On his return down the Euphrates, the tablet states that Tiglath-pileser took several cities of the *Tsukhi* (the *Shuhites* of the Bible), an expedition against whom is recorded in his own annals. He "smote them at one blow," crossing the river on inflated skins,[8] and returning laden with plunder. This account sets in their true light a large part of the so-called conquests of the Assyrians—predatory excursions on a vast scale, to strike terror into hostile tribes, and to carry off slaves and booty to enhance the monarch's state at home. Succeeding kings were constantly under the necessity of chastising these Arabs on the Middle Euphrates.

The Annals of Tiglath-pileser I. embrace his first five years, the conquests of which are summed up as follows:—" Thus fell into my

---

[6] The date of this tablet is at least as late as Shalmaneser II. (B.C. 860–825).
[7] See above.
[8] This mode of passing a river is seen on the Assyrian sculptures.

hands altogether, between the commencement of my reign and my fifth year, forty-two countries, with their kings, from the banks of the river Zabto the banks of the river Euphrates, the country of the *Khatti* (Hittites), and the upper ocean of the setting sun. I brought them under one government; I took hostages from them, and I imposed on them tributes and offerings." While the last words shew the nature of the supremacy established over the states tributary to Assyria, her kingdom—now first fully established within the natural boundaries of Mesopotamia, exclusive of Babylon —is strictly confined to those limits.[9]

The king's mode of warfare is fully described by himself. Rivers are crossed on skins, cities burnt, lands laid waste, a vast booty in cattle and treasure carried off; and, as for the people—" The ranks of their warriors, fighting in the battle, were beaten down as if by the tempest. Their carcases covered the valleys and the tops of the mountains. I cut off their heads. Of the battlements of their cities I made heaps, like mounds of earth.[10] Their moveables, their wealth and their valuables, I plundered to a countless amount. Six thousand of their common soldiers, who fled before my servants and accepted my yoke, I took and gave over to the men of my own territory as slaves."

The king glories equally in his exploits in hunting:—" In the country of the Hittites, he boasts of having slain four wild bulls, strong and fierce, with his arrows; while, in the neighbourhood of Haran, on the banks of the Khabour, he had killed ten large wild buffaloes, and taken four alive. These captured animals he had carried with him on his return to Asshur, his capital city, together with the horns and skins of the slain beasts. The *lions*, which he had destroyed in his various journeys, he estimates at 920! All these successes he ascribes to the powerful protection of Nin and Nergal,"[11] deities who correspond nearly to Hercules and Mars. This religious spirit runs through the whole document. In a sense even more literal than the proper force of the Hebrew expletive, the Assyrian kings verified the proverb about their reputed founder. " even as Nimrod, the mighty hunter before the Lord."

---

[9] The vague boast of conquests as far as the Mediterranean seems to be founded on the defeat of the *Khatti* or *Hittites*, who extended to the mouth of the Orontes. As we have observed about the conquests of the Egyptians, a victory over an enemy from a distance is often enrolled in terms which might imply a conquest of their country.   [10] Comp. Isaiah xxv. 2: Micah i. 6

[11] Rawlinson, ' Five Monarchies,' vol. ii. pp. 317, 318.

Arched Drain (North-West Palace, Nimrud).

CHAPTER XXI.

THE OLD ASSYRIAN MONARCHY.

FROM ABOUT B.C. 1100.

THE GREAT NIMRUD KING. B.C. 886–858.

THE deeds of war and hunting, described in the oldest annals of the Assyrian kings, are vividly illustrated by that earliest series of their sculptured slabs, which has been transferred from the walls of the palace at *Nimrud* to those of our Museum.[1] But above two

[1] No reader of this book, who is at any time within reach of the British Museum, should fail to inspect these sculptures. The slabs from *Nimrud* are placed in a gallery devoted to them, with the smaller objects in cases in the middle of the room.

centuries divide the author of the annals from the king to whom
the sculptures belong ; and this period is almost a blank. It was
during this interval that the wars of David and the splendid
government of Solomon established a real *Empire of Israel* up to
the Euphrates itself, and that Rezon founded the Syrian kingdom
of Damascus, which maintained a long conflict against Assyria
before the final triumph of the latter. The weakness and division
of Israel, after Solomon, turned to the gain, not of Assyria but of
Egypt, under Shishak and the 22nd dynasty ; and the striking
signs, which now appear, of relations between Egypt and Assyria,
denote alliance rather than rivalry. All this points to a period of
depression in the Assyrian empire ; but hidden records may exist
to fill up the gap.

When the darkness begins to disperse, we find ourselves on a new
and firm basis both of *time* and *place*. As to the former, we know
that, from a very remote antiquity, the Babylonians and Assyrians
had an exact system of chronology, based upon astronomical calculation. The annals of the Assyrian kings are carefully dated by
the names of certain officers for each year (hence called *eponymi*),
like the Athenian archons and the Roman consuls. But we can
only fix these names to the proper year of our own reckoning when
we have a series complete for several years, and definite marks to
determine one or more points in the series. To explain how this is
effected lies beyond our present scope ; but the result is that we
have a tolerably complete dated list of the Assyrian kings from
B.C. 909 to B.C. 747 or 745.[2]

Next, as to the *place*: the residence of the Assyrian kings has
now been moved 40 miles up the Tigris, to the angle formed by its
confluence with the Great Zab, where the famous mound of *Nimrud*
is proved by inscriptions to cover the ruins of CALAH. But, as we
have already seen that this city was founded some four centuries
earlier by Shalmaneser I., so now we find the kings of Calah con-
tinuing to care for, and even to rebuild, their old capital at Asshur,
and they also mention Nineveh, in the widest sense of which name,
indeed, Calah may have been included. Even after Sennacherib

<hr>

[2] We may explain here, once for all, that we *generally* follow the *dates* of Sir
Henry and Professor Rawlinson, and the *numbers* assigned by them to kings of the
same name (such as the Tiglath-pilesers and Shalmanesers). In both respects,
M. Oppert and the other leading French authorities follow a different system.
As neither can claim to be at all complete, till further materials are discovered, it
seems best, in an English text-book, to preserve general consistency with the chief
English authorities, except where better results seem to have been certainly arrived
at by the French school. The points of difference are almost all of really little importance in comparison with the truly valuable historical results on which all interpreters are agreed

restored Nineveh and built his palace at the spot now called *Koyunjik*, we find his son Esar-haddon adding another palace to those at Calah. So little is it correct to say that there was a continuous movement of the capital up the Tigris, from *Kileh-Sherghat* to the site opposite *Mosul*.

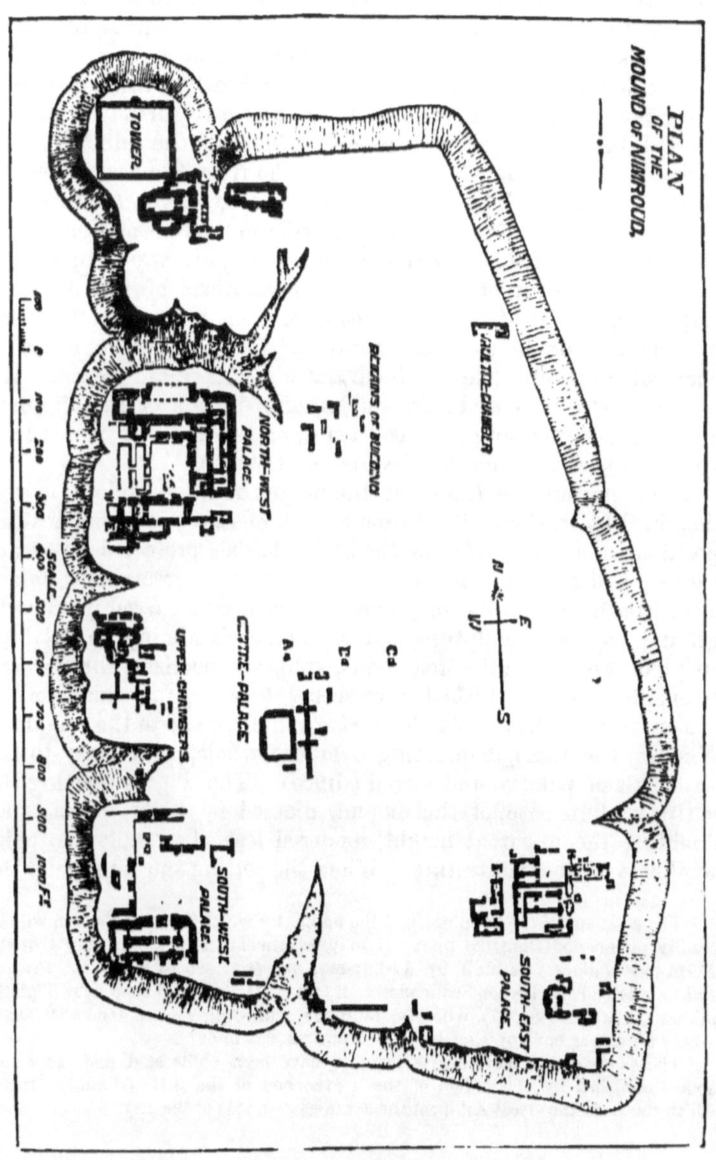

In all the royal cities on the Tigris, the royal quarter lay along the river bank, having a prospect over the open country to the west, and raised above the city by a lofty mound of earth, which was supported and enclosed by massive walls. At *Nimrud*, the mound —composed partly of rubbish and partly of layers of crude bricks, and cased with solid stone masonry—was raised 40 feet above the level of the plain, its top forming a somewhat irregular oblong of 560 yards in length, and from 350 to 450 in breadth.

On this platform of 60 acres, extending nearly a third of a mile along the river, no less than four palaces have already been discovered, besides the remains of some others of the edifices which probably covered the whole mound.[3] The river front was crowned at its northern end by the famous tower or *ziggurat*, which has attracted the attention of all travellers from the time of Xenophon : at its base, and seemingly connected with it, are two temples. It is very significant of the unknown revolutions of the Assyrian empire, that some of these edifices have been built upon the ruins of others, while in some the action of fire is shewn in heaps of charcoal and split and calcined slabs. The plain beneath the mound is strewn with bricks and other remnants of the city over an irregular quadrangle of 1000 acres, on two sides of which may still be traced the remains of walls and towers.[4]

The appearance of Calah, at the height of its splendour, is well imagined by Professor Rawlinson :—" Here, in a strong and healthy position, on a low spur from the *Jebel Maklub*, protected on either side by a deep river, the new capital grew to greatness. Palace after palace rose on its lofty platform, rich with carved woodwork, gilding, painting, sculpture, and enamel, each aiming to outshine its predecessors ; while stone lions, sphinxes, obelisks, shrines, and temple-towers embellished the scene, breaking its monotonous sameness by variety. The lofty *ziggurat* attached to the temple of *Nin* (or Hercules), dominating over the whole, gave unity to the vast mass of palatial and sacred edifices. The Tigris, skirting the entire western base of the mound, glassed it in its waves, and, doubling the apparent height, rendered less observable the chief weakness of the architecture. When the setting sun lighted up the

---

[3] The positions of the buildings, and the names by which they are known, will be readily understood from the plan. It may be convenient to say at once that the *North-west Palace* was built by Asshur-nasir-pal (B.C. 886 to 858) ; the *Central Palace* was built by his son Shalmaneser II. (B.C. 858 to 823), and rebuilt by Tiglath-pileser II. (B.C. 745 to 727), who also built the *South-East Palace*: and the *North-West Palace* was built by Esar-haddon (about B.C. 680 to 667).

[4] The south and west ramparts seem to have been obliterated, and the whole area diminished by the action of the Tigris, and of the little tributary stream which ran from the Great Zab past the south-eastern side of the city.

whole with the gorgeous rays seen only under an Eastern sky, Calah must have seemed, to the traveller who beheld it for the first time, like a vision from fairy land."

The visitor, ambassador, or suppliant, after ascending the platform from the city by a flight of lofty steps, passed between the huge winged lions or bulls with human heads, which flanked the portal, into a great open court, surrounded by long narrow galleries and smaller chambers, all covered in and kept cool by the exclusion of light.   The walls of the chief rooms were lined, to the height of about 9 feet, by the sculptured slabs.

The oldest of these palaces (that on the N.W.), which was Mr. Layard's first discovery, was the work of a great king, whose name is most probably read as Asshur-nasir-pal[5] (B.C. 886 to 858). His deeds are related at length in the inscriptions found among the ruins.   The chief of these is called, from its frequent repetition, "the Standard Inscription of Nimrud."   The slabs which line one of the smaller chambers of the palace are entirely devoted to it, and it appears both on the pavement of the same room, and on a huge paving slab at the entrance of one of the temples.   Nay, such were the pains taken to perpetuate these records, that, when the paving-stones were raised, the same inscription was found cut with equal care on their *under* sides, and a sharp impression of it was left on the asphalt in which the stones were bedded.

On one side of the entrance to the temple of Nin, which has the threshold thus inscribed, is an arched recess containing an effigy of the king in low relief, with divine emblems over his head, and an altar in front, proving that the Assyrian kings claimed divine honours.   Across the middle of the figure, as is usual in such effigies, there runs another inscription, recording the building of the palace, the king's titles, and the extent of his dominions:[6]— " Asshur-nasir-pal, the great king, the powerful king, king of hosts, king of Assyria; the son of *Tiglath-pileser*, the great king, the powerful king, king of hosts, king of Assyria: the son of *Iva-lush*, the great king, the powerful king, king of Assyria.   He possessed the countries from the banks of the Tigris to Lebanon; he subjected to his power the great seas, and all the lands from the rising to the setting of the sun."

---

[5] The authorities are much divided about the *form* of the middle element, but all agree that the name signifies "Asshur-protects-(his or my) son."   Mr. Layard and others call him *Sardanapalus;* but the attempt to distinguish him by this well-known name tends to the confusion of his identity.

[6] We have had occasion to mention above a similar effigy of this king, as set up beside that of Tiglath-pileser I. near the eastern source of the Tigris.   This *stela* (a thick tablet with an arched head) is now in the British Museum.

This comprehensive claim is more definitely explained by his narrative—in the Standard Inscription—of the ten campaigns made by him in his first six years. Their general correspondence with those of Tiglath-pileser I. shows that the dominion of Assyria in Mesopotamia itself had to be reconquered, and the boundary along the Euphrates recovered. In the mountains of Armenia and Kurdistan, he claims to have penetrated to a region " never approached by the kings, his fathers:" but this phrase is too often repeated by the Assyrian kings to be accepted literally. His furthest expedition was through Lebanon and the valley of the Orontes to the shore of the Mediterranean, where he received the submission of the chief cities of Phœnicia. From Lebanon he brought home timber for his new palace; and the beautifully-polished grain of the cedar thus used is to be seen at this day in our Museum. He records his exploits in hunting as minutely as his feats of war; and he had a park stocked with wild animals (like the " paradise" of the younger Cyrus, mentioned by Xenophon), the supply of which was kept up by tributes and presents from subject peoples and kings.

Both sets of exploits are illustrated by the wonderful series of bas-reliefs brought by Mr. Layard from the N. W. palace of Nimrud and the adjacent temples ; wonderful for their artistic execution, their minute details, their vivid reality ; most wonderful for their living picture of the spirit of an Oriental despotism. The king, with the emblem of the supreme deity often hovering above him, rides down his foes, bends his bow against their battlements, or receives their abject submission, which he rewards with torture and death. No detail is spared of the carnage of the battle-field or the cruelties inflicted on the prisoners. In one place headless corpses, or convulsed wretches pierced with spears and arrows, are floated down the stream (for most of the battle scenes and sieges are upon the banks of a river) ; in another, the scribes are counting the heads as they are laid before the king.

These pictures do but faithfully reflect the spirit of his annals. In his first campaign a captive chief of the *Kirkhi*, on the Upper Tigris, was carried to Arbela, and there flayed and hung up on the town wall. In the second a rebellious city of the Euphrates was given up to plunder, and some of the ringleaders were burnt, others crucified, and the rest mutilated of their ears and noses. The king's own words are needed to do justice to his treatment of another revolted city :—" Their men, young and old, I took prisoners. Of some I cut off the feet and hands ; of others I cut off the noses, ears, and lips ; of the young men's ears I made a heap ; of the old men's heads I built a minaret. I exposed their heads as a trophy in front of their city. The male children and the female children

I burnt in the flames. The city I destroyed and consumed and burnt with fire."

Such boasts, illustrated by such pictures, reveal the self-confessed character of the Assyrian empire ; and, if the first feeling excited by these monuments is admiration at the recovery of a lost chapter in the history of nations, the next is a renewed sympathy with the prophets who denounced such an empire, and a confirmation of that hatred of all despotism, which is one of the best lessons taught by history

Assyrian Sacred Tree (from Nimrud).

Prisoners presented by the Chief Eunuch.

CHAPTER XXII.

CLIMAX AND FALL OF THE OLD ASSYRIAN MONARCHY. ITS RELATIONS WITH SYRIA AND ISRAEL. B.C. 858–745.

THE full establishment of the OLD ASSYRIAN EMPIRE, beyond the boundaries of Mesopotamia, was effected by Asshur-nasir-pal and his son SHALMANESER II., who had the longest reign of any Assyrian King (B.C. 858–823). He finished the great pyramid or *ziggurat* at *Nimrud*, which was begun by his father; and he built a new palace in the centre of the platform. It was from the ruins of this palace that Mr. Layard obtained the *Obelisk*, in black marble, which is one of the most precious monuments of Assyria.[1] It may be called an illustrated history of the twenty-seven campaigns of this monarch, who is often called "The Black-Obelisk King."

The twenty bas-reliefs on this monument represent the king receiving the tribute of five nations. Besides metal in various forms, goblets, drapery, and elephant's tusks, carried by attendants, we see a great variety of animals, including some quite foreign to

---

[1] The cut shows the form of the obelisk, and the way in which it is sculptured and inscribed on all the four faces. It is a fair type of the Assyrian obelisks, which differ from the Egyptian by their much smaller size, and by terminating in steps (or *gradines*) instead of a pointed top (or *pyramidion*). The Black obelisk is about 7 feet high, and 22 inches wide on the broader side of the base. The fragments of two somewhat larger obelisks in white stone, ascribed to the preceding king, are also in the British Museum. The largest was from 15 to 20 feet high. The splendid obelisk of the Egyptian queen Hatason, in rose granite, is 90 feet high.

Mesopotamia—the two-humped camel of Bactria, the elephant, and the rhinoceros. But any hasty inferences as to the wide extent of the Assyrian empire are corrected by the inscribed names of the five

Black Obelisk, from Nimrud.

nations, who belong to the mountains of Armenia and Kurdistan, the middle Euphrates, the valley of the Orontes, and the land of *Israel*. For the prostrate figure in the highest row [2] is explained as *Yahua*,

[2] See vignette on p. 138.

son of Khumri, that is, " Jehu, son of Omri," [3] a patronymic derived from the founder of Samaria, which is named in later inscriptions as *Beth-Khumri*, " the house of Omri."

Nor is this the only mention of Israel by this king. In the annals of his campaigns we find no less than five directed against the Syrians of Damascus. In the last two of these, the name of the Syrian king is *Khazail* (Hazael); and hence we can infer that the name read doubtfully in the first three means Ben-hadad.[4] Now, in the ninth year of Shalmaneser, we find a great confederacy formed by the king of Damascus,[5] with the kings of Hamath, of the Hittites, and of the Phœnicians, making war on the Assyrian, doubtless to check his progress westward. The forces of the several allies are carefully enumerated, and among them 10,000 men and 20 chariots are sent by "AHAB of Jezreel." [6] The allies were defeated in a great battle, and in another five years later; which shews the length and obstinacy of the war: but no new territory, or even tribute, is yet claimed by the Assyrian.

Three years later, Shalmaneser collected his forces for a decisive blow, and led 102,000 men across the Euphrates. The allies were put to flight, and the confederacy dissolved. The Scripture narrative of Ben-hadad's murder by Hazael, as he lay in his tent sick and depressed after such a blow, is strikingly confirmed by the Assyrian account: for it is against " Khazail of Damascus" that Shalmaneser pursues his advantage in the following year, and defeats him in the passes of Antilibanus. After another three years he returns to plunder the Syrian cities, apparently unresisted; and receives the tribute of Tyre, Sidon, and Byblus. All this explains the submission of Jehu; which is not mentioned in the chronicles of Israel, as the kingdom was not actually invaded.

A disputed succession and civil war in Babylonia gave Shalmaneser an opportunity to overrun the land as far as the Persian Gulf.

" The power of his army," he says, " struck terror as far as the sea;" but there is no proof of any real conquest. Besides his own campaigns, 23 in all, three or four were conducted by one of his lieutenants, whose exploits are, of course, regarded as the king's; and the result is an amusing mixture of the first and third persons

---

[3] The *J* of *Jehu* is in Hebrew a *Y*, and the *O* of *Omri* is preceded by a consonant, which the Assyrians represent, in some other cases, by *Kh*.

[4] For the history of these Syrian kings, and their relations to Israel, see the ' Smaller Scripture History,' Chap. xiv.

[5] This must be the Benhadad of 1 Kings xx.

[6] This mention of Ahab, which forms the earliest notice of Israel in the Assyrian records, is said to be repeated on the monolith effigy, which Shalmaneser set up at *Korkhar*, on the eastern Tigris, beside those of his father and of Tiglath-pileser I. (See above, p. 129.)

in his annals.[7] A monolith statue in black basalt, representing Shalmaneser II. seated on a throne covered with inscriptions, was found at *Kileh-Sherghat*.[8] We may infer his care for the old capital of Asshur, which we know that his father restored.

The annals of Shalmaneser II. break off five years before his death, at a time when, as we learn from his successor, he was virtually dethroned by the rebellion of his eldest son. The revolt was put down by a younger son, Shamas-Iva or Samsi-Hor, who succeeded his father, and reigned for 13 years (b.c. 823–810). We now find the Assyrian arms carried beyond Zagrus into Media; and this king's victories in Babylonia may have contributed to the union of the two crowns of Mesopotamia under his son and successor, Iva-Lush or Hulikhus IV. (b.c. 810–781).[9]

The union was probably effected by the marriage of Iva-lush to the Babylonian princess, Sammuramit, in whose name we recognize that of the mythical Semiramis.

Among the most curious relics of Assyrian art in our Museum is a pair of statues of Nebo, found in a temple of the god, dedicated by this king, at *Nimrud*. An inscription across the middle of each figure records that they were dedicated to Nebo by the governor of Calah, as a votive offering for the life of " my lord, Iva-lush, and of my lady, Sammuramit." From this, the sole mention of a queen consort, or indeed of any princess, in the Assyrian annals, we may safely infer that Sammuramit had a royal dignity in her own right. It seems probable that she was a Babylonian princess, whom Iva-lush married, in order to legitimatize his acts of sovereignty in Babylonia. This king and queen have been called " the Ferdinand and Isabella of Mesopotamia."

It is interesting to find Iva-lush not only sacrificing to the special gods of Babylonia in the chief cities of that land, but styling himself the king " *to whose son* " (not to himself) " Asshur, the chief of the gods has granted the kingdom of Babylon ; " as if that son derived his title from his mother. The result seems, however, to have been not the lasting union of the two crowns, but the establishment on the throne of Babylon of a rival branch of the royal family, which was ready to claim, if it did not actually overturn, the kingdom of Assyria itself.

These probabilities throw light on the chief, indeed the only serious difficulty, in connecting the Assyrian records with Scripture history. The first contact of Assyria with Israel, *mentioned in the Bible*, is in the reign of Menahem,[10] when " Pul, the king of

---

[7] The same thing occurs in the 'Behistun Inscription' of the Persian Darius I.

[8] It is in the British Museum. See Vignette to Chapter XX.

[9] This name is also read as *Vul-lush* and as *Phalukha*.

[10] b.c. 772–761 of the received chronology; but this is some 20 years too high according to the Assyrian chronology.

Assyria, came up against the land; and Menahem gave Pul 1000 talents of silver, &c.;" and, content with this tribute, "the king of Assyria turned back, and stayed not there in the land" (2 Kings xv. 19, 20). On the first discovery of the Assyrian records, *Pul* or *Phul* seemed to correspond exactly to Iva-lush IV., whose name is also read *Vul-lush* and *Phalukha*.[11] For this king's annals tell us of conquests made by him beyond the Euphrates, in Syria, Phœnicia, Edom, and Palestine, to the "sea of the setting sun;" and, among the cities taken by him, he names Damascus and "the house of Omri" (*Beth-Khumri*), that is Samaria.

But one condition of the advance of knowledge—of which no real lover of truth complains—is the unsettlement, not only of old opinions, but of new and neat conclusions, by newer discoveries. So, in this case, the settlement of the chronology has raised the following difficulty:—The name of *Menahem*, who only reigned *ten years*, occurs as a tributary in the annals of Tiglath-pileser II., whose accession is dated in B.C. 746 or 745, *thirty-five years* later than the death of Iva-lush IV. in B.C. 781. In this interval, the lately discovered Assyrian "Canon," places three kings; thereby upsetting the opinion formerly held, that Iva-lush IV. was the last king of the old monarchy, and the immediate predecessor of Tiglath-pileser II. A not improbable solution is, that the *Pul* of Scripture was really a king of the line established by Iva-lush and Sammuramit at Babylon; who claimed the title, and, perhaps, exercised the power, of king of Assyria, in consequence of the growing weakness of the old dynasty. For the kingdom now begins to show decisive symptoms of decline; and, if we could establish the not improbable opinion, that Iva-lush IV. was the king to whom Jonah preached repentance, the "forty days" left by the prophet to Nineveh might correspond to the interval of about forty years before the fall of the Old Monarchy.[12]

Of the three kings, whose reigns fill up this interva', the first, *Shalmaneser III.*, maintained the warlike character of Assyria by

11 The Hebrew form *Pul* or *Phul* is evidently an abbreviation; for there is no Assyrian royal name of only one element; and it is very like the first syllable of *Vul-lush*. There is a similar abbreviation in the name *Shalman* for *Shalmaneser* (Hosea x. 14). The LXX. give the name as Φαλώχ, which is identical with the form *Phalukha* read by some on the statues of Nebo.

12 Jonah iii. 4. The point is too interesting not to be mentioned here; but this work is unsuited for its discussion. To the obvious objection that "the men of Nineveh repented at the preaching of Jonah," and "God repented of the evil that he had said that he would do unto them; and *he did it not*" (Jonah iii. 10)—there is a twofold answer. (1). The respite may have consisted in the 40 *years* granted in place of the 40 *days* of the warning; for Jonah evidently expected to see his prophecy immediately fulfilled (Jonah iv. 1–3); or (2), in the *mitigation* of the crisis prepared by the faults of the old dynasty, and in the period of greater prosperity under the new monarchy.

expeditions, chiefly against Armenia and Syria, in each of his ten years (B.C. 781-771).   But his successor, *Asshur-danin-il* (B.C. 771-753), passed 9 of his 18 years quietly at home; and the last *Asshur-Lush* or *Asshur-likhus* (B.C. 753-745), spent only 2 years, out of 8, in a war against the mountaineers of Zagrus.

Whether this was a defensive war against the growing power of the MEDES, whose name has already appeared in the victories of preceding kings;—and whether there may be any real foundation for the story told by Ctesias, of the fall of Nineveh and Sardanapalus before the combined attack of the Median Arbaces and the Babylonian Belesys;—are questions, the solution of which is perhaps hidden, with the annals of these kings, under the mound of *Nebbi-Yunus*.   And there, too, may lie buried their palaces, the want of which has been taken as a proof of the decline of their power.   For that traditional site of the true Nineveh seems to have been the residence of the last kings of the Old Monarchy.[14]

At present, the story of Ctesias is unconfirmed, either by the Assyrian annals or by the early history of the Medes; and Herodotus knows of but one destruction of Nineveh.   But the chronology of Babylon is supposed by some to mark the establishment, or at least the full recognition, of her native monarchy, at the ERA OF NABONASSAR (B.C. 747).   All this is thought to indicate a revolution, in which the old Assyrian Monarchy came to an end. At all events, when the darkness clears away, we find a new king, who was clearly a usurper, reigning at Calah, and founding a new Assyrian empire; by the side of which a powerful Babylonian kingdom stands in declared hostility.

[14] Iva-lush IV. is the earliest king whose bricks have been found at *Nebbi-Yunus*. The exploration of that mound has been prevented hitherto by the fanatical opposition of the Arabs to any disturbance of the chapel of the prophet, which crowns its summit.

Captive Women in a Cart (from Nimrud).

Siege of a City and Captives impaled.

CHAPTER XXIII.

THE NEW ASSYRIAN MONARCHY.

PART I. TIGLATH-PILESER II. AND SHALMANESER IV.

FROM B.C. 745 TO B.C. 721.

THE NEW or LOWER ASSYRIAN EMPIRE was governed by seven kings
in its duration of 120 or 139 years (B.C. 745–625 or 606).[1] In the
first five we recognise the well-known Scriptural names of *Tiglath-*

---

[1] Professor Rawlinson and other English authorities place the destruction of
Nineveh at B.C. 625; but the date cannot be regarded as finally settled. The
French school, headed by M. Oppert, adhere to the older opinion in favour of B.C. 606;
and M. Oppert places the event under an *eighth* or even *ninth* king, with a name
resembling *Sardanapalus.*

pileser, Shalmaneser, Sargon, Sennacherib, and *Esar-haddon.* The name of the sixth, *Asshur-bani-pal,* comes nearest, of all we have yet met with, to the legendary SARDANAPALUS ; but his character is that of the "warrior Sardanapalus" of the Greeks, and the fall of Nineveh takes place only under his son *Asshur-emid-ilin,* if not under still another king. With this last exception, we are at length free from serious doubts about their names, their order of succession, the lengths and principal events of their reigns ; while, as to some of them (the celebrated Sennacherib, for instance), our chief embarrassment is caused by the abundance of their records.

We have also reached a sure chronological epoch. The "Canon" of the famous astronomer Ptolemy, founded on the Babylonian records, in conjunction with the "Assyrian Canon," places certain dates beyond dispute. The modern authorities are all agreed in fixing the new foundation of the empire by Tiglath-pileser within a year or two of the "Era of Nabonassar" (B.C. 747). This epoch is just six years later than that commonly accepted for the foundation of Rome (B.C. 753); and one generation after the chronology of Greece becomes fixed by the first Olympic victory (B.C. 776). The brightest and last age of the Assyrian empire coincides with the infancy of Greek and Roman civilization.

TIGLATH-PILESER II. (B.C. 745–727) is clearly marked as the head of a new dynasty, and probably as of obscure origin, by the omission of all mention of his father's name in his inscriptions. As king of Assyria, he speaks in general terms of "the kings his fathers," and of "the palaces of his fathers" at Calah. There he restored the central edifice of Shalmaneser II., and built a new palace at the S. E. angle of the *Nimrud* platform. Calah appears to have been the royal residence till the time of Sargon.

Owing to the destruction of his palaces by Esar-haddon, the records of Tiglath-pileser have come down to us in mere fragments : but enough remains to show that he was engaged in constant wars for the re-establishment of the empire. His first enterprise was against Babylonia, the new strength of which seems to have been already divided by the claims of rival princes. The Assyrian king names several of these, whom he defeated in the upper country ; while, in the maritime region of Chaldæa, he received the submission of *Merodach-Baladan,* the son of *Yakin,* whose capital was *Bit-Yakin,* "the house of Yakin." This was probably the father of the more celebrated "Merodach-Baladan, the son of Baladan" (2 Kings xx. 12; Isaiah xxxix. 1), the champion of Babylonian independence.

Thus secured against the rival kingdom, Tiglath-pileser proceeded to reconquer Syria and Palestine—countries which were already regarded as tributaries of Assyria. His annals relate a series of campaigns—apparently from his fourth year to his eighth—in which he reduced Damascus, Samaria, and Tyre (whose kings are mentioned by the familiar names of Rezin, Menahem, and Hiram), as well as the Arabs on the frontier of Egypt, who were governed by a queen named Khahiba. These conquests did not reach Judæa, Philistia, or Idumæa.

His second attack on the kingdom of Israel may have been provoked by the usurpation of Pekah, and his murder of Menahem's son, Pekahiah, the vassal of Assyria. It was on this occasion that Tiglath-pileser began the captivities of Israel, by carrying away to Assyria the people of Gilead, and a part of the northern Galileans (2 Kings xv. 25-29). By this stroke "the tribes of Zabulon and Naphthali" in Galilee of the Gentiles"[2] were but "lightly afflicted," in comparison with the "more grievous affliction" (Isaiah ix. 1) brought upon them by the league of Pekah, king of Israel, with Rezin, king of Syria, against Ahaz, the new king of Judah.[3]

Some have thought that the kings of Judah had already made a formal acknowledgment of the supremacy of Assyria. At all events, his present peril drove Ahaz to the feet of Tiglath-pileser, with the full admission of vassalage—"I am thy *servant* and thy *son*"—backed by a tribute from the treasures of the temple. This appeal brought down upon Syria and Israel that devastating war which showed the full force of the prophetic description. "Thou, Asshur, art the rod of mine anger, and the staff in mine hand is their indignation" (Isaiah x. 5). The same prophet describes the horrors of the ensuing conquest in the sublimest strains of poetry: "For every battle of the warrior is with confused noise and garments rolled in blood; but this shall be with burning and fuel of fire" (Isaiah ix. 5). "Through the wrath of the Lord of Hosts is the land darkened, and the people shall be as the fuel of the fire; no man shall spare his brother . . . they shall eat every man the flesh of his own arm. For all this his anger is not turned away, but his hand is stretched out still."[4]

Syria first felt the fury of her old enemy. Rezin was defeated and put to death—doubtless by one of those cruel executions which we see in the Assyrian monuments inflicted on rebellious kings (2 Kings xvi. 9). The annals of Tiglath-pileser inform us of a second victory over the son of Rezin, after which Damascus was

---

[2] Northern Galilee deserved this appellation through the idolatry with which its people were infected by their Phœnician neighbours.

[3] Isaiah vii. 6; 2 Kings xvi. 1-2; 2 Chron. xxviii. 1-27. The details of the war belong to Scripture history.　　　[4] Isaiah ix. 19-21. See the whole prophecy.

taken and destroyed.   The other nations mentioned as submitting
to him correspond closely with those enumerated by Isaiah and
Amos as sharing the disasters of Syria and Israel.   He chastised
the Arabs of the peninsula of Sinai, and received the submission
of the kings of Tyre, Gaza, and Ascalon, and of the people of
Aradus, the Moabites, the Ammonites, and the Idumæans (comp.
Amos i. ii).

Nor did Judah fare much better.   The king, at whose entreaty
the war had been made, was summoned to Damascus, to pay homage
to his too powerful helper; and, to satisfy his exactions, "Ahaz
made Judah naked, and Tiglath-pilneser distressed him, but
strengthened him not" (2 Chron. xxviii. 20, 21).   The annals of
the Assyrian king record his receipt of tribute from a king of
Judah whom he calls *Yahu-Khazi*, which seems to stand for
Jehoahaz.   There are other reasons for believing that this was the
full form of the name of Ahaz.

It was in these campaigns against Syria and Israel that Tiglath-
pileser set the example of that far-sighted but cruel policy, which
aimed to eradicate the feeling of local patriotism, by transporting
conquered peoples in mass to distant parts of his empire.   The
Syrians of Damascus were removed to *Kir*, the very place whence
the prophet Amos traces their original migration (2 Kings xvi. 9;
Amos i. 5, ix. 7).   The whole Israelite population east of the
Jordan were carried to Mesopotamia Proper, upon and west of
the *Khabour*, and settled (among other places) in *Haran*, the very
country from which Abraham had come to Palestine.

These campaigns appear, from the Assyrian Canon, to have been
made in the years 734, 733, and 732 B.C.

Shalmaneser IV. (B.C. 727–721), who is familiar to us in Scripture
as the destroyer of the kingdom of Samaria, has no place in the
Assyrian Canon, nor has his name been found on any monuments.[5]
In connection with the fall of the kingdom of Israel, his reign is
memorable for the first collision between Assyria and Egypt.

Great changes occurred about the time of his accession in the
three western kingdoms.   At Samaria—for to its territory the kingdom of Israel was now reduced—the usurper Pekah had been
murdered by *Hoshea*, who appears to have had at least the virtue of
devotion to his country's falling cause[6] (B.C. 730 or 729).   In his

---

[5] His name may have been erased from his monuments by Sargon, who usurped
his throne.   For the like reason, there is great difficulty in distinguishing between
the acts of the two kings.   They are evidently confounded by Menander, the historian followed by Josephus.   The name signifies "Shalman is a protector;" the
second element being the same as in the Hebrew "Eben-ezer."

[6] 2 Kings xvii. 2.   See further respecting his character in the 'Smaller Scripture
History.'

third year the crown of Judah passed from the infamous[7] idolater Ahaz to the godly and patriotic Hezekiah, who was twenty-five years old (B.C. 726–5). His great religious reform embraced not only his own kingdom, but all that was left of Israel in the north; and, as usual, the fresh spirit of religion rekindled the flame of patriotism. In Egypt, the petty kingdoms of the Delta, which seem to have maintained friendly relations with Assyria, were yielding to the supremacy of the warlike monarchy of Ethiopia.

In such an empire as Assyria—composed of tributary states united by no organic constitution—a change of reign is frequently the signal for revolt. That Hoshea had thus used the opportunity of Shalmaneser's accession, appears from the record at the beginning of his reign, that "Against him came up Shalmaneser king of Assyria; and Hoshea became his servant, and gave him tribute" (2 Kings xviii. 3). It was probably in this first campaign that one of his cities was treated in the true Assyrian fashion;—"As Shalman spoiled Beth-arbel in the day of battle: *the mother was dashed to pieces upon her children*" (Hosea x. 14).

The tribute continued to be paid "year by year," till Hoshea took courage to withhold it, in reliance on a league with Egypt. "And the king of Assyria found conspiracy in Hoshea: for he had sent messengers to So (*Sua, Shave,* or *Shabe,* that is Sabaco I.), king of Egypt, and brought no present to the king of Assyria, as (he had done) year by year" (2 Kings xvii. 4). But, before his ally could march to his support, "the king of Assyria shut him up, and bound him in prison" (2 Kings xvii. 4). In the highly poetic language of the prophet his namesake, "As for Samaria, her king is cut off as the foam upon the face of the water" (Hosea x. 7).

Her own fate was soon accomplished by a new invasion, in which "the king of Assyria came up throughout all the land," and laid siege to Samaria, in the 4th year of Hezekiah and the 7th of Hoshea (B.C. 723). The city was besieged for three years, till the 6th of Hezekiah and the 9th of Hoshea, when it was taken (2 Kings xvii. 5; xviii. 9, 10)—Josephus adds, by storm. But it seems that Shalmaneser did not live to complete the conquest. He appears to have died during the last year of the siege, leaving only an infant son, who was set aside by the Tartan or general-in-chief. After governing for three years in the name of the infant, about whose further fate there is a significant silence, this officer reigned in his assumed name of Sargon; but his annals are evidently dated from the death of Shalmaneser in B.C. 721, which was also the year in which Samaria was taken.

<hr>

[7] This epithet is not used at random; for the memory of Ahaz was stamped by the Jews with infamy (2 Chron. xxviii. 27).

Groom and Horses (*Khorsabad*)

CHAPTER XXIV.

THE NEW ASSYRIAN MONARCHY (*continued*).

SARGON.   FROM B.C. 721 TO B.C. 704.

THE name of SARGON (B.C. 721–704)—or, in the more exact Assyrian form, *Sargin*, *Sarkin*, or *Sar-yukin*—has a sense which explains its assumption by an usurper—"the king (is) established." The one solitary mention of him in Scripture, and that but incidentally in a prophecy (Isaiah xx. 1), had brought his very existence into doubt, till the discovery of his annals in his magnificent palace at *Khorsabad*, revealed him as one of the most splendid kings and most successful warriors of Assyria.

He came to the throne, as he tells us, in the same year that *Merodach-Baladan* became king of Babylon;[1] and this not only fixes his date, but attests the independence of Upper Babylonia.

---

[1] The Canon of Ptolemy fixes the accession of Merodach-Baladan to March B.C. 721. The name of this famous king of Babylon signifies "Merodach has given a son."

But the lower country, or Chaldæa, had been reduced by Tiglath-pileser II.; and here we at once find Sargon warring with Susiana, a power which is henceforth a second thorn in the side of Assyria. His annals open with the words, "This is what I have done from the beginning of my reign to my fifteenth campaign.[2] I defeated in the plains of Chaldæa *Khumbanigas*, king of Elam."

He next proceeded to finish the war in Palestine:—"I besieged, took, and occupied the city of Samaria, and carried away 27,280 persons who dwelt in it. I changed the former establishments of the country, and set over them my lieutenants." The conquered Israelites were removed, partly to join their brethren of the former captivity "in Halah and Habor by the river of Gozan" (the Khabour), and partly in the far remoter "cities of the Medes" (2 Kings xvii. 6; xviii. 11); and, in accordance with this, we find from Sargon's annals that he was the first Assyrian who made real conquests in Media.

The new settlers planted in the vacant lands were drawn "from Babylon, and from Cuthah, and from Ava, and from Hamath, and from Sepharvaim,"[3] which are all, except Hamath (in the north of Coelesyria), cities of Upper Babylonia; and here again we find that Sargon was the first king, at least of the new monarchy, who conquered Babylonia. The colonists from Hamath were doubtless removed after Sargon's second campaign, in which he devastated that country, and flayed its king *Yahubid*, who had headed a formidable rebellion of Syria. In the sculptures from *Koyunjik* we see the same cruelty inflicted by Asshur-bani-pal on the rebel kings of Susiana.[4]

We now approach that most interesting period, at which the relations between Egypt and Assyria are mixed up with the history of Hezekiah's reign and with the allusions of the Jewish prophets; and on this period the annals of Sargon and his successors throw a flood of new light. We have seen that, just when Egypt declined under the 19th, 20th, and 21st dynasties, and Assyria began to rise, the empire of David and Solomon interposed a great power between them. The new energy of the line of Shishak won back for Egypt

---

[2] The Annals embrace 15 years out of the king's 17.

[3] 2 Kings xvii. 24 ; comp. ver. 30, where their gods are named. This colonization is usually confounded (as in the date given in the margin of our Bible) with that afterwards made by Esar-haddon from Lower Babylonia and Susiana. The careful reader of Ezra iv. will see the distinction. The conquests of Sargon in Media and Babylonia were later in his reign; but the process of deportation was of course gradual.

[4] The way in which the victims are bound by their outstretched arms and legs to pegs driven into the earth, seems to prove, what some have doubted, that they were *flayed alive*. We have seen above that, in such cases, the body, or the skin, was fixed to the walls of the rebellious city.

the supremacy in Palestine, while the Assyrians were occupied in consolidating their dominion in Mesopotamia and on its northern and eastern borders.   The power of such kings as Asa, Jehoshaphat, and Ahab, as well as the kingdom of Damascus, restored the barrier of independent states, which still remained effective, in spite of the successes gained by Assyria over Benhadad and Ahab, Hazael, and Jehu.

We have, indeed, very decisive proofs of mutual influence between Egypt and Assyria, under the Tanite and Bubastite Dynasties and the great kings of Calah.   Assyrian names abound, and Assyrian rites are practised in Egypt, while numerous objects of Egyptian art have been found in the *Nimrud* palaces of this age.[5]   All this evidence tends to show friendly relations; and there is no proof of any hostile collision between the two empires down to the close of the old Assyrian monarchy.

But just when a new and warlike government was set up in Assyria, the equally warlike kings of Ethiopia were establishing their supremacy in Egypt, and now began the period " when Egypt with Assyria strove "—not only " in wealth and luxury "—but in war for the supremacy of Western Asia.   The fall of Damascus and Samaria brought the two powers face to face, and Sargon took up the challenge given by Sabaco's league with Hoshea.

Gaza, the key to the great military road, still belonged to Egypt; and Sargon, marching down the maritime plain (probably to attack the city) was met by a great army under " *Hanun*, king of Gaza, and *Sab'e* (Sabaco I.), *Sultan*[6] of Egypt."   A decisive battle ensued at Raphia (in Assyrian *Rapih*, now *Refah*), between Gaza and Rhinocorura (the frontier town of Egypt), and a day's march from both.   On the same battle-field, just 500 years later, Ptolemy Philopator avenged on Antiochus the Great the victory recorded by Sargon, in words which might have been the model of Cæsar's " *Veni! vidi! vici!* "—" They came into my presence : I routed them."   Hanun was taken prisoner, but *Sab'e* " disappeared "—a statement which perhaps illustrates the account of Herodotus, that Sabaco retired from Egypt back to Ethiopia.   The battle of Raphia is fixed to Sargon's third year, B.C. 718–7.

To this campaign, also, may be referred the reduction of Phœnicia and the unsuccessful attack upon Tyre, which Josephus ascribes to Shalmaneser (see Chap. XL.)

---

[5] It is very important to bear in mind that the way in which the N.W. palace of *Nimrud* was buried under its own ruins, *before* the kings of the New Monarchy built their palaces on the same platform, excludes all doubt as to the antiquity of these relics.

[6] This curious title is read differently by different authorities, who are agreed, however, that it denotes some high officer, but not a king.

After an interval of some four years, occupied with wars to the north and east of Assyria, Sargon mentions some conquests in Arabia, and adds, "I imposed tribute on *Pharaoh* (*Pir'u*) *of Egypt*" (evidently a different person from the sultan *Sab'é*) "on Tsamsi, queen of Arabia, on Ithamar the Sabæan, in gold, spices, and camels." (B.C. 714–713.)

Three years later he records that war against Ashdod, in connection with which occurs the solitary mention of his name in Scripture. The mission of the "Tartan" or generalissimo (Isaiah xx. 1), which preceded the king's own campaign, appears from the annals to have had the object of installing a new king, *Akhimit*, in place of his rebel brother *Azur*. But "the people of Syria, always prone to sedition, wearied of the rule of *Akhimit*, and set up *Yaman*." The king now marched in person to avenge the insult. "In the fury of my heart I did not divide my forces nor did I lessen my baggage; I marched upon Ashdod with my warriors, who followed close upon the print of my sandals."

At his approach Yaman fled "beyond Egypt, on the side of Ethiopia." Sargon besieged and took Ashdod, and carried away the king's gods, his wife, his sons and daughters, his treasures and goods, and the inhabitants of his country. These were replaced by captives taken in Sargon's eastern wars, under an Assyrian lieutenant, and not, as usual with subject states, under a vassal king. "I treated them as Assyrians. They were not again guilty of impiety.' We can now understand the obstinate resistance which Ashdod offered to Psammetichus.[7] This war was in Sargon's 11th year (B.C. 711–710).

Content with the full establishment of his power in the maritime plain, and with the surrender of Yaman by the king of Ethiopia, Sargon made no further attack on Egypt and Judah.[8] It must be remembered, in all these transactions, that the latter kingdom did not lie, like Israel, in the way of an army marching from Asia towards Egypt. All that was required was the payment of the tribute, which Hezekiah probably did not yet feel himself strong enough to refuse. That the party at Jerusalem, which always leant to Egypt, was meditating some movement at the beginning of the war with Ashdod, is plain from Isaiah's prophecy against "Egypt their expectation and Ethiopia their glory . . . whither

---

[7] See Chapter XII., p. 78.

[8] The prophecy (Isaiah xx.) of the shameful captivity of Egypt and Ethiopia, from which some infer an invasion by Sargon, was fulfilled, as we shall see, under his third successor. The attack on Judah, recorded in 2 Kings xviii. 13, and Isaiah xxxvi. 1, though dated in the 14th year of Hezekiah (B.C. 713-712), is clearly the great campaign of Sennacherib (who is expressly named), in B.C. 700. The error in the date can be explained with great probability. (See next Chapter.)

they fled for help, to be delivered from the king of Assyria" (Isaiah
xx. 5, 6).   Just at this crisis Hezekiah was seized with that mortal
illness from which he was miraculously raised up.[9]   His recovery
is connected with a new movement against the Assyrian domination at the very seat of its power.

We have seen that Merodach-Baladan became king of Babylonia
at the same time that Sargon seized the Assyrian crown.   When
he had reigned twelve years (B.C. 710–9), this "king of Chaldæa,"
says Sargon, "called to his aid *Khumbanigas*, king of Elam, and
raised against me all the nomad tribes"—the Aramæans of *Irak-
Araby*, who were constantly rebelling against Assyria.   To induce
the king of Judah to join the league was doubtless the object
of the embassy which Merodach-Baladan sent to Jerusalem, on the
pretext of congratulating Hezekiah, and enquiring of the wonder
done in the land.[10]   Hezekiah's ostentatious display of his resources
to the ambassadors of Babylon called forth the prophecy of Isaiah,
that this—and not Assyria—was the power to which Judah was
destined to succumb, though not in his days.   This rebuke would
probably deter the Jewish king from any overt act in concert with
Merodach-Baladan.

Sargon marched against Babylon with all his forces, and Merodach-Baladan was defeated and taken prisoner at his hereditary
stronghold of *Bit-Yakin* or *Dur-Yakin*, in Chaldæa.   Sargon spared
his life, but assumed his kingdom, and he is enrolled in the Canon
as king of Babylon by the name of Arceanus (B.C. 709).   But,
before his death, Babylonia again revolted, and after a season of
anarchy Merodach-Baladan recovered the throne.   This disaster
would, of course, not be mentioned in Sargon's annals; the cessation of which in B.C. 706, two years before his death, is perhaps
another sign of the reverses of his later years.   One of those literary
fragments, which serve to correct formal annals, is a report from
Sennacherib to his father of his failure to put down the Babylonian
revolt.   These reverses may have provoked the conspiracy by which
Sargon was assassinated in August B.C. 704.

Besides the leading events now related, his annals speak of
victories over, and tribute received from, a king of Elam, who had
his capital at Susa; the mountaineers of Zagrus, and, beyond that

[9] Isaiah xxxviii.; 2 Kings xx. 20.   This narrative is clearly misplaced.   The
date of Hezekiah's sickness is absolutely determined by the addition of 15 years to
his life; for the promise, "I will add unto thy days fifteen years," can only mean,
"Thou shalt live fifteen years longer."   Now his reign lasted 29 years, and therefore
his illness was in his 14th year (B.C. 713–712).

[10] 2 Kings xx.; Isaiah xxxix.   The backward movement of the sun on the dial
of Ahaz would naturally excite the curiosity of a people so addicted to astronomy
as the Babylonians.

chain, the *Medes* and (some think) the Persians or Parthians; the Armenians, the Albanians, the Syrians of Commagene, the people of the Taurus and of Cilicia, and the islanders of Cyprus. From this island—which he calls *Iatnan,* and places at *seven days' voyage* in the middle of the sea of the setting sun!—he boasts of receiving an embassy of submission at Babylon (B.C. 708). The fact of his sending an expedition thither is confirmed by a monument found in the island, bearing the effigy and titles of Sargon. This success was perhaps the ground for the vague boast of his annals:—"Arbiter of combats, I traversed the sea of Jamnia like a fish. I annexed Koui and Tyre." Rabshakeh does not name Tyre among the recent conquests of Assyria of which he boasts in his address to the Jews (2 Kings xviii. 33, 34).

This king, whose very existence was till lately doubted, was the first whose monuments were discovered, when his palace at *Khorsabad* revealed itself to the researches of M. Botta in 1842. (See Chap. XIX.) It is from the walls of that palace, and from the tablets and cylinders found in its ruins, that Sargon's annals have been obtained. At the beginning of his reign his residence was at Calah (*Nimrud*), where two inscriptions record his repairs of the north-west palace—that of *Asshur-nasir-pal.* One of these mentions the name of *Judah.* He also rebuilt the walls of Nineveh; but it was his ambition to replace that capital by a new city and royal residence, which the inscriptions at *Khorsabad* prove to have been entirely his work. We have his own account of the site which he chose, amidst rills of water at the foot of the "Musri hills" (*Jebel Maklonb*), 10 miles N.N.E. of Nineveh; of his purpose in building the city which he called "Hisr-Sargina" (also *Bit-Sargina* and *Dur-Sargina,* *i.e.* the *house* or fort of Sargon); and of the materials, construction, ornaments, furniture, and treasures of the "palace of incomparable splendour" which he erected in this city "for the abode of his royalty." The fidelity of tradition preserved the builder's name for centuries after his work had become a shapeless mound; for an Arab geographer calls that mound "the old ruined city of *Sarghun.*" It is well worth notice that the *earliest known specimen of transparent glass* is a small vase inscribed with the name of Sargon, found in the ruins of *Nimrud,* and now in the British Museum.

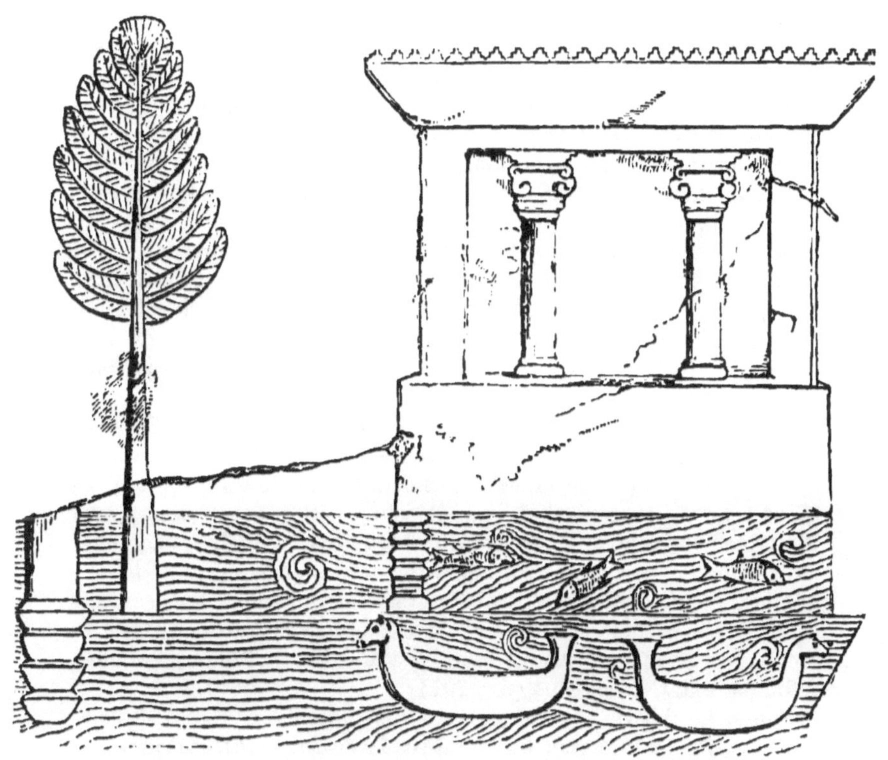

Assyrian Temple, with Ionic Capitals.

CHAPTER XXV.

THE NEW ASSYRIAN MONARCHY (*continued*).

SENNACHERIB.   FROM B.C. 704 TO B.C. 680.

In the reign of SENNACHERIB [1] we have the most valuable results of
the recent Assyrian discoveries.   The names recovered from the
monuments of Egypt and Assyria are, for the most part, either
strange to history, or they are variously read.   But here is a name
familiar to our childhood, from its occurrence in one of the most
striking scenes of Jewish history; preserved by the first Greek

[1] In Assyrian, *Sin-akhi-irib*, i. e. " *Sin* (the Moon-God) has multiplied my
brethren."   This name is one of the few about the *phonetic* value of which there is
no doubt; and it was the first made out in the cuneiform inscriptions.   It occurs in
Herodotus (ii. 141) as *Sanacharib* (Σαναχάριβος.)

historian in connection with the same event; and now plainly deciphered in the king's own inscriptions.

His palace at *Koyunjik*, perhaps the grandest of all those yet found, was the first discovered on the site of Nineveh itself, and the one from which our Museum possesses the richest gleanings, even exceeding those from the N.W. palace at *Nimrud*. He has left us his own records in the longest of Assyrian annals; inscribed partly on his palace walls and on the colossal bulls of its façade and porch, and partly (besides other cylinders, tablets, and fragments) on one of the most remarkable of ancient documents. The visitor to the British Museum may see a fair type of one form of the *baked-clay books* of Assyria in this prism, called the "Taylor Cylinder." Its six faces are inscribed with 480 lines of very minute writing, recording the annals of all but the last 3 years of Sennacherib's 24 years' reign.

The disasters of Sargon's later years had reduced his son's inheritance to little more than Assyria Proper. Babylonia was in open revolt; and Sennacherib did not attempt its conquest till the third year of his reign. His annals open with a great victory over Merodach-Baladan and his Elamite allies; after which Sennacherib took Babylon, and set up a vassal king named *Bel-ipni* (the Belibus of the Canon). Merodach-Baladan once more escaped with his life (B.C. 702). In his second campaign Sennacherib was engaged in reconquering the countries to the East and North, Media, Armenia, Albania, and Commagene (B.C. 701).

Sennacherib's third campaign, in his fourth year (B.C. 701–700), includes that celebrated war against Hezekiah, which brings his annals into contact with Scripture history. The confirmation of, and the new light thrown upon, the sacred narrative, and on its connection with the history of Egypt and of Assyria, is one of the most striking results of cuneiform discoveries.

During the troubles of Sargon's later years, Hezekiah had not only thrown off the yoke of Assyria, but had extended the power of Judah to the maritime plain, where "he smote the Philistines, even unto Gaza and the borders thereof" (2 Kings xviii. 7, 8). The people of one of the cities subject to Assyria in that region, called *Migron*, which some suppose to be *Ekron*, had expelled their king *Padi*, who was "inspired with friendship and zeal for Assyria," and given him up to "Hezekiah, king of Judah." [2]

After reducing the chief cities of Phœnicia, and receiving tribute from those of Philistia, and from Ammon, Moab, and Edom, Sennacherib marched to chastise Migron. But the rebels "had called to their aid the kings of Egypt and the archers, the

---

[2] The words quoted are from the annals of Sennacherib.

chariots and horses of the king of Ethiopia, an innumerable host."
Over these forces the Assyrian gained a great victory at *Altaku* (the
Eltekeh of Scripture), which left him at liberty to wreak his vengeance, as far as he was permitted, on Hezekiah. The knowledge of
this victory gives a new meaning to the taunt, which we presently
find the envoys of Sennacherib addressing to Hezekiah,—" Behold,
thou trustest upon the staff of *this bruised reed*, even upon Egypt,
&c. : so is Pharaoh king of Egypt unto all that trust in him : "—and
the figure itself becomes doubly significant, when we find a *bent
reed* prefixed to the name of the king on the Egyptian monuments.

"Sennacherib, king of Assyria came and entered into Judah,
and encamped against all the fenced cities of Judah, and took
them." [3]　Compare these words with the king's own annals. After
telling us that "Hezekiah, king of Judah," gave up Padi, but "*did
not submit himself*," Sennacherib goes on to mention the capture of
"44 walled cities, and an infinite number of towns, by the force of
fire, massacres, battles, and besieging towers," with the captivity
of 200,150 persons, and innumerable cattle. "As for him, I shut
him up in Jerusalem, the city of his power, like a bird in a cage.
I built towers round the city to hem him in, and raised banks
of earth against the gates to prevent escape. Those who came
out of the great gate were seized and made prisoners." On the
Assyrian bas-reliefs we see pictures of sieges, with towers and
mounds, and *prisoners impaled* in sight of the defenders. Hezekiah
was stripped of his territory; and the towns taken from him were
given to the vassal kings of Ashdod, Migron, and Gaza. How completely the devastation of the country and the investment of the
city suspended the tillage of the land, is seen from the sign of
deliverance given by the prophet Isaiah (2 Kings xix. 29).

Turning to the book of *Chronicles*, we find a full record of the
vigorous preparations for defence made by Hezekiah, " when he
saw that Sennacherib was come, and that his face was to war against
Jerusalem " (2 Chron. xxxii. 2). Best of all was the share which
he infused into the people of his own faith in the God, who, when
raising him up from his deathbed fourteen years before, had
promised to deliver both him and the city out of the hand of
the king of Assyria (2 Kings xx. 6). His words, recorded by the
Jewish chronicler (2 Chron. xxxii. 6-8), form a striking contrast
with the boast of Sennacherib,—" Then the immense fear of my
majesty terrified this Hezekiah, king of Judah."

---

[3] 2 Chron. xxxii. 1 ; 2 Kings xxviii. 13 ; Isaiah x. xxvi. 1. The erroneous date of
" the 14th year of Hezekiah," which has crept into the two latter passages (but not
the first) is really that of Hezekiah's illness, which was in the 14th year before the
invasion: hence perhaps the confusion. The supposition of *two invasions* of Judæa
by Sennacherib is quite gratuitous.

But, before the deliverance was accomplished, Hezekiah had to submit to loss and humiliation ; "there was wrath upon him, and upon Judah and Jerusalem . . . . for the pride of his heart" in his time of prosperity (2 Chron. xxxii. 25, 26, 31).   His pious patriotism did save the city from destruction and the people from captivity ; but at the cost of a nominal submission, as well as a heavy ransom. Here, again, let us place the Scripture story and the Assyrian annals side by side.   Sennacherib says that "Hezekiah dismissed the garrison which he had assembled for the defence of Jerusalem.   He sent after me to Nineveh, the city of my sovereignty, 30 talents of gold and 800 talents of silver," and a vast quantity of other gifts, by "an ambassador to present his tribute and offer his submission." In the book of Kings we read, " And Hezekiah, king of Judah, sent to the king of Assyria to Lachish, saying, I have offended ; return from me ; that which thou puttest upon me I will bear.   And the king of Assyria appointed unto Hezekiah 300 talents of silver and 30 talents of gold, &c."[4]

The mention of Lachish, as the head-quarters of Sennacherib, is confirmed by the statement, that he himself "laid siege against Lachish, and all his power with him."[5]   He seems to have reckoned on the submission of Jerusalem, without interrupting his own operations on the frontier towards Egypt.   The investment of the city appears to have been formed by the " great host" detached under his chief general (*Tartan*), his chief eunuch (*Rab-saris*), and his chief cupbearer (*Rab-shakeh*).   And now that Hezekiah was stripped of his wealth and strength, these officers received a new commission to follow up exactions by extinction.

It is needless to recite that memorable address, in which they defy the helpless king, and invite the people to accept a complete transplantation, recommending it by the pictures, which despots and their admirers are fond of drawing, of the material blessings attendant on political servitude (2 Kings xviii. 17–xx. 7 ; 2 Chron. xxxii. 9–16 ; Isaiah xxxvi. 2–xxxvii. 7).   The tone of this address so strikingly resembles the Assyrian annals, as to leave little doubt that at least the king's own message was couched (as on the next occasion) in a letter, of which we have the substance.   The opening,

---

[4] 2 Kings xviii. 14-16.   The mention of *Lachish* in the one passage, and of *Nineveh* in the other, is one of those minor variations which confirm testimony better than literal agreement.   The treasures and slaves sent by Hezekiah to the king's head-quarters would naturally be sent on by him to Nineveh.   Returning to his capital, after the destruction of his army—perhaps even outstripping the convoy in his headlong flight – he would display these trophies of his campaign as proudly as if they were the signs of victory, and so he records them in his annals.

[5] 2 Chron. xxxii. 9.   Lachish was a frontier city of Judah, on the edge of the maritime plain, remarkable for its strong position.   (See Joshua ix.)

" Thus saith the great king, the king of Assyria," repeats a constant title; and the boast of the power of his gods over those of the conquered peoples agrees with the frequent statement, that " the immense fear of Asshur fell upon the nations."   The piety of Hezekiah obtained the promise that Jehovah would accept the challenge; and no answer was given to the envoys.

Meanwhile Sennacherib had advanced to the place where that promise was fulfilled; *not before Jerusalem*, but on the frontier of the land of Judah towards Egypt. " So Rabshakeh returned, and found the king of Assyria warring against *Libnah*; for he had heard that *he was departed from Lachish*. And when he heard say of Tirhakah, king of Ethiopia, Behold he is come out to fight against thee, he sent messengers to Hezekiah." [6]   This new message, which was accompanied by a letter of open defiance to the God of Israel, called forth the final promise of the destruction of the Assyrian and the salvation of Jerusalem.

On the same night, and (as it seems) before the arrival of the warlike Ethiopian, " the angel of the Lord went out, and smote in the camp of the Assyrians 185,000. So Sennacherib returned with shame of face to his own land." [7]

The Scripture narrative,—having no more concern with him, except to mark that he never returned again, and that Judah was finally and perfectly delivered from Assyria [8] — passes on to the mention of his death; which did not occur till 20 years later. His annals are continued for nearly the whole of that time; and the young reader may naturally ask—after all this wonderful agreement with Scripture—what light those annals throw upon the catastrophe before Libnah. The answer is, *None!* any more than the monu-

---

[6] 2 Kings xix. 8, 9; Isaiah xxxvi. 8, 9. *Libnah* is supposed to be the city of that name near Lachish (Josh. x. 31 ; xv. 42); but a great authority (M. Oppert) attempts to prove that it is only a Hebrew rendering of *Pelusium*, the frontier city of Egypt, where Herodotus places the catastrophe of the Assyrian army. The advance from Lachish (the *capture* of which is very doubtful) seems to have been in order to crush that " *bruised reed*, Pharaoh, king of Egypt," before the arrival of his Ethiopian ally.

[7] 2 Kings xix. 35, 36; 2 Chron. xxxii. 21; Isaiah xxxvii. 36, 37. The Scripture account of the catastrophe is remarkably confirmed by the story which the Egyptian priests told Herodotus (ii. 141)—though in such a form as to give the honour to their own gods—how the host of the Assyrian *Sanacharib*, in its camp before Pelusium, was rendered helpless by an army of field mice, which devoured their bowstrings, quivers, and thongs of their shields; and so they fell an easy prey to the troop of traders and artisans, who had been called out by Sethos (probably Sabaco II.) king of Egypt, when the warriors had deserted him. This desertion may perhaps be explained by the flight of the warriors to Upper Egypt, where they were rallied by Tirhakah. Byron's splendid ode is too well known to need quotation.

[8] Observe the strong expressions to this effect in 2 Kings xix. 33, and Isaiah xlv. 25.

ments of Egypt record the overthrow of Pharaoh's host in the Red Sea. But yet, *not quite none:* for there is a strange significance in their silence about the whole campaign, after the partial submission of Hezekiah. Even the siege of Lachish is not mentioned in the king's annals; though it formed the subject of a great bas-relief in his palace at *Koyunjik* (now in our Museum), with the inscription, "Sennacherib, the mighty king, king of the country of Assyria, sitting on the throne of judgment before the city of *Lakhisha*. I give permission for its slaughter." But the silence, both of his own annals and of Scripture, respecting the *capture* of Lachish, seems to expose the emptiness of the boast.

All that the Assyrians knew, probably, of the result of the campaign, was that the great victories over Phœnicia and Syria, Egypt and Judah, of which their monarch boasted and showed the spoils, had been purchased by a loss of life which new levies would replace. Sennacherib kept his conquests in Phœnicia, and used them with new effect in his Babylonian wars. For, in the year after the Jewish campaign, Merodach-Baladan was once more, and now finally, defeated in Chaldæa; and, when his adherents took refuge in Susiana, Sennacherib pursued them with a fleet built on the Tigris, after Phœnician models, and manned with sailors from Tyre and Sidon. This movement decided the campaign (B.C. 699–96).

But the war was renewed year after year, till the combined forces of the Elamites, the Babylonians, and the Arabs of the middle Euphrates, took the offensive, and advanced to *Khaluli* on the Tigris. There, after a long and bloody battle, they were defeated through the treachery of the Elymæan general, whom Sennacherib had bribed. The king thus exults over a second victory as decisive as that of Altaku: "On the sodden battle-field the arms and armour floated in the blood of the enemies as in a river, for the war-chariots, bearing down men and horses, had crushed their bleeding bodies and limbs. I heaped up the bodies of their soldiers as trophies, and cut off their extremities. I mutilated those whom I took alive, like stalks of straw, and for punishment I cut off their hands." And such scenes as these are remorselessly depicted on his sculptures.

That Babylon again threw off the yoke of Assyria, may be inferred from the *Canon's* marking an *interregnum* from B.C. 688 to the accession of Esar-haddon in B.C. 680. Sennacherib's own annals mention three successful revolts during this period; and, though he boasts of the capture and sack of Babylon (about B.C. 683), the silence of his last three years bears witness to disorder and probable disaster. Such are the periods chosen by conspirators, especially in the royal family, for attempts on the king's life. It may have been after some great defeat (though twenty years after the catastrophe in Palestine) that, "as Sennacherib was worshipping in the house of Nisroch his god, Adrammelech and Sharezer his sons smote him with the sword, and they escaped into the land of Armenia. And Esar-haddon his son reigned in his stead." B.C. 380. (2 Kings xix. 37; Isaiah xxxvii. 38).

Such was the end of this mighty king, who stands forth in Scripture history as the worst type of an Oriental despot, but who describes himself as "The great king, the powerful king, the king of nations, the king of Assyria, the king of the four regions, the diligent ruler, the favourite of the great gods, the observer of sworn faith, the guardian of the law, the embellisher of public buildings, the noble hero, the strong warrior, the first of kings, the punisher of unbelievers, the destroyer of wicked men." Some of these titles are illustrated by the remains of the palace which he built at Nineveh. On its sculptured slabs, disinterred from the mound of *Koyunjik*, and now in our Museum, we see, among other scenes of slaughter in war, and of cruelty in the name of justice, the executioners with their pincers tearing out the tongues of wretches, above whose heads it is written that they were blasphemers of the gods. The palace itself, which surpassed in splendour those of *Nimrud* and *Khorsabad*, formed part of a grand scheme for the restoration of Nineveh. An inscription of Sennacherib says, "I have raised again all the edifices of Nineveh my royal city, I have reconstructed its old streets, and have widened those which were too narrow. I have made the whole town a city shining like the sun."

Another inscription, on the walls of this "palace of alabaster and cedar," affords a rich example of that *irony* which history is ever casting over the utterances of men about the future: "This palace will grow old and fall in ruins in the lapse of time. Let my successor raise up its ruins; let him restore the lines which contain the writing of my name. Let him renovate the paintings, and clean the bas-reliefs, and replace them on the walls. Then will Asshur and Ishtar hear his prayer. But whoever should deface the writing of my name, may Asshur, the great god, the father of the gods, treat him as a rebel; may he take away his sceptre and his throne, may he break his sword!" Two generations only passed away before the palace and Nineveh were buried under their own ruins. Twenty-five centuries later the bas-reliefs were "cleaned and replaced on the walls" of our Museum, and "the writing of his name" and his annals were deciphered, to confirm a free people, who inherit the faith against which he warred, in our belief of the sacred records, and our abhorrence of all despotism.

King and Attendants (*Khorsabad*).

CHAPTER XXVI.

THE NEW ASSYRIAN MONARCHY (*continued*).

ESAR-HADDON, KING OF ASSYRIA AND BABYLON.   FROM B.C. 680 TO B.C. 667.

THE Scripture narrative of Sennacherib's death concludes—"And ESAR-HADDON his son reigned in his stead." [1]   This king, the fourth son of Sennacherib, seems to have been already established on the throne of Babylon, having just reconquered it for his father.   He probably used the forces of that kingdom, first to compel his traitor brothers to fly to Armenia, and next to resist the attempt of the elder to regain the crown.   Adram-melech, leading into Assyria an army of mercenaries, levied probably in Armenia, was taken prisoner and put to death.   Esar-haddon is the only Assyrian king who ruled over Babylon during his whole reign (B.C. 680–667).

This authority over united Mesopotamia set him at liberty to recover the western provinces which had been lost during his father's later years.   In his first campaign he conquered Phœnicia, Syria, the Edomites, and certain Arabian tribes, and he seems to have led an army through a portion of the great desert of Arabia. To the north-west he carried his arms as far as Cilicia, and across the sea to Cyprus.

As the spoil of these expeditions (especially that taken from

---

[1] 2 Kings xix. 37, Isaiah xxxvii. 38; and in Ezra iv. 2, we have "Esarhaddon, king of Assur." It is convenient to write the king's name in this familiar manner, though the first syllable should be *Assur* or *Asshur*. The Greek of the Canon, *Asaridinus* ('Ασαριδινος) is nearer to the Assyrian form *Asshur-akh-idin*, "Asshur give a brother."

Phœnicia), he gives an interesting enumeration of the materials obtained for the decoration of his palaces—gold, silver, precious stones, amber, seal-skins, sandal-wood, and ebony, stuffs dyed with purple and blue—the use of which in their palaces, also, is mentioned by Sargon and Sennacherib. For his palace at Nineveh, which he describes as a splendid edifice, erected on the site of a former palace of his predecessors, [2] similar materials were furnished as the tribute of twenty-two kings, chiefly of Syria, Cyprus, and Phœnicia, and in this list we read the name of "*Minasi*, king of Judah."

Now, turning to the Scripture history, we find that *Manasseh* succeeded his father Hezekiah three years after the great deliverance from Sennacherib (B.C. 697). He was then twelve years old, and he had reigned seventeen years at the accession of Esar-haddon in B.C. 680. His minority doubtless encouraged the reactionary party in Judah to those idolatries, cruelties, and vices of all kinds, in which he himself soon took the lead; and to these he appears to have added some rash defiance of Assyria. "Wherefore the Lord brought upon them the captains of the host of the king of Assyria, which took Manasseh among the thorns, and bound him with fetters, and carried him *to Babylon*" (2 Chron. xxxiii. 11).

Not *to Nineveh*, as any fabricator would have said. For the truth of the history, and the genuineness of the record, are attested by the fact, that Esar-haddon was not merely the only Assyrian king who reigned at Babylon, but he frequently resided there. Bricks inscribed with his name still bear witness to the palace that he built at Babylon. These "undesigned coincidences" between Scripture and secular history are multiplied with every addition to our knowledge of the ancient records of the East.

The captivity of Manasseh seems naturally to belong Esar-haddon's western campaign (B.C. 679 or 678); [3] and his restoration is as naturally connected with the king's renewal of the wars with Egypt. The policy of maintaining a barrier in Palestine against the rival kingdom is also to be traced in the measures of Esar-haddon for repeopling the territory of Samaria. The colonies from Hamath and Upper Babylonia, planted there by Sargon, had not prospered; and

---

[2] This edifice is the more interesting from its being on the traditional site of the true Nineveh, and under the mound of *Nebbi-Yunus* (*i. e.* "the prophet Jonah"), the exploration of which has been hindered hitherto by the fanatical opposition of the Arabs to any disturbance of the prophet's chapel on its summit.

[3] This agrees, within two or three years, with the Jewish tradition which places the event in the 22nd year of Manasseh. The duration of the captivity is not mentioned, but it does not seem to have been long. The 30th year of Manasseh was the last of Esar-haddon (B.C. 668-7); and his reign lasted 55 years, to B.C. 643-2.

wild beasts had so multiplied in their desolate lands as to attack
the people themselves (1 Kings xvii. 25). A successful war against
a renewed league of Lower Babylonia and Susiana gave Esar-
haddon the opportunity of strengthening the population with new
settlers from those regions, "Susanchites" (from Susa), Elamites,
and others (Ezra iv). This mixture of races, who engrafted on
their heathen worship a superstitious service of Jehovah, formed
that Samaritan people so hostile to and hated by the restored Jews.

The religious establishment, which the Assyrian king gave "to
teach them the manner of the god of the land," is curiously illustrated by another incident of Esar-haddon's western campaigns.
The Assyrians—as we see constantly in their annals, as well as in
the speech of Rabshakeh—acknowledged the gods of other countries,
and that the more in order to vaunt the power of Asshur over them
all. It was in this spirit that, when Esar-haddon conquered the
Arabs, he took away their idols, *inscribed on them the praises of
Asshur*, and then returned them to their owners. Such are the
vagaries of polytheism.

Like his predecessors, Esar-haddon was engaged in wars with
the Arabs on the Euphrates, and the mountaineers of Armenia and
Zagros. Beyond the latter range, he seems to have penetrated
further into Media than any of his predecessors. But he is most
distinguished from them as being the first Assyrian king who
invaded Egypt; and he is the only one who bears the proud title,
repeated on several of his monuments, "King of Egypt and
Ethiopia"—"King of the kings of Egypt, and conqueror of
Ethiopia." The campaign by which he won these titles, probably
at the end of his reign, is not recorded in his own annals but in his
son's, under whose reign the whole story will best be told.

Esar-haddon rivalled his father and grandfather as a builder,
having reared, as he tells us, three palaces and above thirty temples,
or, as some read, fortresses. We have mentioned his palaces at
Nineveh and Babylon; the third was the south-west edifice on the
mound of Calah (*Nimrud*). This palace, which was never finished,
is remarkable for two things. The slabs which line its walls have
been torn down from the palaces of former kings, chiefly from
the central and south-east palaces of Tiglath-pileser on the same
platform. Not, however, that Esar-haddon decorated his walls with
his predecessor's *sculptures;* the art of Assyria was too real for this.
The sculptured faces *are turned inwards against the walls of sun-
dried bricks*, and their backs are smoothed preparatory to being
carved with the king's own deeds. Of such sculptures as had been
completed, many were found split to fragments or calcined to lime-
dust by a fierce conflagration that had destroyed the building.

Among these were some *sphinxes*, which bear witness to Esar-haddon's Egyptian conquests.

Near the close of Esar-haddon's reign, the union between Assyria and Babylonia appears to have been again severed by the appointment of two of his sons to succeed him on the thrones of Nineveh and Babylon. His successor in Assyria is only known to us from his monuments and annals; but these furnish some of the most valuable results of the recent Assyrian discoveries.

Cart drawn by Mules (*Koyunjik*).

Dog modelled in clay, from the Palace of Asshur-bani-pal (*Koyunjik*).

CHAPTER XXVII.

THE NEW ASSYRIAN MONARCHY (*continued*).

ASSHUR-BANI-PAL OR SARDANAPALUS. FROM B.C. 667 TO B.C. 660 OR 647.

THE resemblance of the name of ASSHUR-BANI-PAL,[1] the son of Esar-haddon, to SARDANAPALUS is the more striking from its occurrence near the end of the monarchy. But, if the classical story borrowed the *name* from him, it must have been as "the warlike Sardanapalus," instead of the effeminate prince who perished with Nineveh. For his annals and monuments reveal him as one of the greatest conquerors and most magnificent monarchs of the whole Assyrian empire, and he surpassed all his predecessors in the true glory of a systematic care for the literature of his country.

At this king's palace at Nineveh (*Koyunjik*) Mr. Layard made the

---

[1] This name, which signifies "Asshur create a son," comes nearer to *Sardana-palus* than any before it in the whole list. Still the Greek form may have been borrowed from others of the many names of which *Asshur* is the first element, and *pal* the third and last. Hence some modern writers call all the kings, who bear names of this form, *Sardanapalus;* but this is a sacrifice of accuracy to the mere semblance of a known name.

following discovery :—" The doorway guarded by the fish-gods led into two small chambers opening into each other, and once panelled with bas-reliefs, the greater part of which have been destroyed. . . . To the height of a foot or more from the floor they were entirely filled with them (*i.e. books of burnt clay*), some entire, but the greater part broken into fragments. They were of different sizes ; the largest tablets were flat, and measured about 9 inches by 6½ inches ; the smaller were slightly convex, and some were not more than an inch long, with but one or two lines of writing. The cuneiform characters on most of them were singularly sharp and well-defined, but so minute in some instances as to be almost illegible without a magnifying glass. They had been impressed by an instrument on the moist clay, which had been afterwards baked."

We may venture to call this not only a *Royal* but a *Public Library;* for one of the most important books found in it bears the following inscription :—" Palace of Asshur-bani-pal, king of the world, king of Assyria, to whom the god Nebo and the goddess Tasmit (the god and goddess of knowledge) have given the ears to hear and opened the eyes to see what is the true foundation of government. They revealed to the kings, my predecessors, this cuneiform writing, the manifestation of the god Nebo, the god of supreme intelligence : I wrote it upon tablets, *I signed and arranged them*, and I placed them in my palace *for the instruction of my subjects.*"

Hence we learn that this library was no mere " Chamber of Records," for preserving the annals of the kingdom. It was a collection of all the learning of Assyria, sacred, secular, and scientific : and the key to the difficulties, which even the Assyrians found in their own language and writing, was provided in an elaborate series of grammatical works. As the king implies in the words, " I signed and arranged them," the several tablets were marked, paged, and placed in cases. But the confusion caused by the destroyers of the palace has unhappily been increased in their transport to our Museum ; and the utmost ingenuity has been required to put together the hundred fragments of the Annals of Asshur-bani-pal. Fortunately those fragments belong to four different copies, besides pieces of others, which not only aid the arrangement but supply interesting variations.

The annals, thus partially restored, are among the most precious of the cuneiform discoveries. They contain a full account of the Egyptian wars of Asshur-bani-pal, and throw a flood of new light on the state of Egypt at the time of the Ethiopian dynasty, as well as on some passages of Scripture. These annals embrace the first seven years, which some suppose to be the whole, of the reign of Asshur-bani-pal (B.C. 667–660.)[2]

The king's first campaign was made in Egypt, to avenge the breach of a treaty, by which *Tirhakah*, having been conquered by Esar-haddon, engaged to confine himself to "his own country."[3] That "king of Ethiopia," of Sennacherib's time, now appears as "king of Egypt and Ethiopia," and accordingly his accession at Memphis is said to be fixed by an "Apis-stela," at B.C. 693. Esar-haddon "did not deprive him of his sovereignty," but expelled him from Lower, and, at all events, a part of Upper Egypt. He left the country under the kings of the several cities, to the number of twenty or more,[4] and beside them he placed Assyrian officers. The mention of these petty kingdoms goes far to dispel the Egyptian darkness which has hitherto preceded the accession of Psammetichus, whose father Necho is found as king of Memphis as well as Saïs, and at the head of the confederacy. Thus the link is supplied between the foundation of the Saïte dynasty by Bocchoris and its revival by Psammetichus.[5]

This gain is great; but, beyond it, we have a full account of the relations of the Egyptian princes to Assyria and Ethiopia, and even of the motives which made them submit alternately to either empire. The death of Esar-haddon would naturally be the signal for Tirhakah's return, and the petty kings sided with him. Enthroned again at Memphis, he treated the officers and adherents of Assyria with a severity which summoned Asshur-bani-pal to call out his whole force to take vengeance for the insult.

Tirhakah, marching out of Memphis to meet him, was defeated at a place called *Karbanit*, and fled in his ships to Thebes, "the city of his empire." Thence he resumed his flight into Ethiopia on the approach of Asshur-bani-pal, who, after a difficult march of forty days, took Thebes with a great slaughter. Returning to Lower Egypt, he defeated the confederate kings, and then restored them to their thrones, but placed Egypt "under a new government." Having strengthened the garrisons and fortifications of the cities, he returned to Nineveh, laden with "a great booty and splendid spoils."

His departure left the vassal kings in a position which he very

---

[2] The general opinion is that Asshur-bani-pal reigned to B.C. 647; but one of the highest authorities (M. Oppert) assigns the 13 years from B.C. 660 to B.C. 647 to a brother of Asshur-bani-pal, named *Tiglath-pileser*.

[3] That is, either Ethiopia alone, or Ethiopia and Upper Egypt; for the latter is now usually under the Ethiopians, with their capital at Thebes.

[4] Twenty are mentioned, by their full names and those of their cities, as submitting to Asshur-bani-pal; but there may of course have been others.

[5] Compare Chapter XII.

frankly explains, while charging them with spontaneous rebellion. "They said among themselves, Tirhakah will never renounce his designs on Egypt; it is him we have to fear." So they sent ambassadors to make a treaty of peace and friendship with the king of Ethiopia, promising not to desert him any more. They also tried to corrupt the Assyrian army; but the officers discovered their plots, intercepted their messengers, and bound the kings in fetters. Asshur-bani-pal came back in person to exact vengeance. Memphis, Saïs, Mendes, Tanis, and the other rebel cities, were taken and their people massacred: "I left not one," boasts the conqueror. The captive kings appear to have been carried to Nineveh.

After a short time Necho was sent back to his throne at Saïs, to hold Lower Egypt, as an Assyrian vassal, against Tirhakah. Here there is, unfortunately, a gap in the annals; but we have other evidence that Tirhakah once more took Memphis (probably putting Necho to death), and there we find him recognised as king, in the last year of a reign which is reckoned as of twenty-six years (about B.C. 693 to 667 or 666).

He was succeeded in Ethiopia by his son (or step-son), who is called on the monuments at Napata[6] *Rout-Amen* or *Rot-men*, whose name becomes *Urda-mané* in Assyrian. This king would not consent to renounce his inheritance in Egypt, where the petty princes seem to have seized the opportunity of Tirhakah's death to declare against Ethiopia. After recovering the Thebaïd (if he did not possess it already) he invaded Lower Egypt.

The Assyrian annals are resumed with an allusion to the death of Tirhakah and to this invasion. Urdamané was totally defeated by Asshur-bani-pal, and "escaped alone to Thebes, the city of his royalty."[7] As before, the Assyrians occupied forty days in the pursuit "through difficult roads;" and, like Tirhakah, Urdamané fled at their approach to Ethiopia.

Thebes was now taken for the second time, and suffered far more terribly than before. "They took possession of the whole city, and *sacked it to its foundations* . . . they treated it as a captured city. They carried into captivity men, male and female, great and small;" besides a spoil "not to be computed by the accountants" which "they brought safe to Nineveh, and they kissed my feet."

This record reveals, for the first time, the full meaning of two striking passages of Hebrew prophecy. At the time of Sargon's war against Ashdod, Isaiah had given the Egyptian party at Jerusalem a sign and warning that "they should be afraid of

---

[6] The reader should remember that Napata was the capital of the Ethiopian kingdom. See Chapter XI.

[7] Observe this sign of the possession of Upper Egypt by the king of Ethiopia.

Ethiopia their expectation, and of Egypt their glory." As the prophet " walked naked and barefoot for three years, so," he says, " shall the king of Assyria lead away the Egyptians prisoners, and the Ethiopians captives, young and old, to the shame of Egypt." (Isaiah xx).

More striking still is the language, not of prophecy only but of history, in which Nahum denounces on " Nineveh, the city of bloods," the very fate she had inflicted upon Thebes : " Art thou better than populous *No*, that was situate among the rivers " (on both sides of the Nile), " that had the waters round about her, whose rampart was the sea, and her wall was from the sea? Ethiopia and Egypt were her strength, and it was infinite; *Put* and *Lubim* were thy helpers." (That is, the Arabians and Libyans on the two borders of Egypt joined the Assyrians against Thebes.) " Yet was she carried away, she went into captivity: her young children also were dashed in pieces at the top of all the streets: and they cast lots for her honourable men, and all her great men were bound in chains." [8]

After this great success the Assyrians appear to have left Egypt to her native kings, under a vassalage which the rapid decline of Assyria soon rendered only nominal. Then began the new era of Egyptian prosperity under the great Saïte kings.[9]

The storm, which was destined soon to bring upon Nineveh the fate prophesied by Nahum, was already gathering in Media; where, as well as in Armenia, we find the old wars still continued, and new victories of course claimed. In other quarters Asshur-bani-pal well maintains the character of a great conqueror. In Cilicia the people showed (but with very doubtful accuracy) the tomb and statue of " the warlike Sardanapalus, who built Tarsus and Anchialus in one day." [10] If a passage in his annals is rightly read, he was the first (and only) Assyrian king who crossed the Taurus, and had some relations with the great Lydian monarchy: " Gyges, king of Lydia, a country on the sea coast, a remote place,

---

[8] Nahum iii. 8–10. This passage is distinctly *historical*, and not only prophetic. There can be no doubt that *No* is here the contraction of *No-Amen*, the name of Thebes as sacred to *Amun*. It is evidently impossible to refer either passage primarily to the invasion of Egypt by Nebuchadnezzar, who was not a king of Assyria, and who lived after the fall of Nineveh, which is here prophesied by Nahum. Nor is there any other Assyrian invasion of Egypt to which the prophecies can allude.   [9] See Chapter XII.

[10] The conquest of Cilicia and foundation of Tarsus are also ascribed to Sennacherib; but we cannot here discuss the relations of Cilicia to Assyria, any more than the very interesting question, whether the cuneiform inscriptions were understood in the later Greek and Roman periods. We know that the characters were not *used* after the time of Alexander

of which the kings my ancestors had never even heard the name,
learned in a dream the fame of my empire, and the same day sent
officers to my presence to perform homage on his behalf."

His campaigns in Babylonia and Susiana—the intricate events
of which we cannot stay to explain—attract our special notice by
the scenes on the bas-reliefs which he added to Sennacherib's palace
at Nineveh.[11] On one slab we see the capture of a city at the
confluence of two rivers, probably Susa, which the annals record to
have been taken, with the express mention of its position on the
Hulai (Eulæus).[12] On another, deeds of cruelty are as vividly
depicted as they are plainly described in the annals:—" Temin-
Umman (the king of Susiana) was taken prisoner, decapitated, and
his head exposed over one of the gates of Nineveh. A son of
Temin-Umman was executed with his father:" and the sculptures
show a prisoner brought to execution with the head of another
hung about his neck. "Several grandees of Merodach-baladan
suffered mutilation; a Chaldæan prince, and another chief, had
their tongues torn out by the roots; two of Temin-Umman's principal officers were chained and flayed:" and there are both operations before our eyes, in the alabaster which has perpetuated them
for twenty-five centuries. On the other slabs we see the scourgers
in attendance upon the king, carrying their whips in their girdles,
and the executioner striking a bound prisoner with his fist before
he puts him to death. Well might the prophet call Nineveh " the
city of bloods."

The like pictures of war, and of what his annals boast as *justice*,
were repeated, side by side with a great variety of hunting scenes,
on the walls of another palace, which Asshur-bani-pal built at
Nineveh (*Koyunjik*), within a few hundred yards of his grandfather's. This palace is remarkable for the beauty of its elaborate
ornaments and for the new style of its sculptures. The scenes
both of battle and of hunting excel all previous bas-reliefs in the
variety, grace, and freedom of the figures. But in simple dignity
they fall as far short of those of Asshur-nasir-pal, as the *spirit* of
the sport—in which the lions are *let out of cages*—is below that
monarch's famous lion hunt.[13] Among them is the only strictly
domestic scene yet known in Assyrian art—and one only too sig-

<hr>

[11] These sculptures are among the most interesting in the " Koyunjik Gallery "
of the British Museum. The scenes are depicted with wonderful reality and fulness.

[12] Comp. Daniel viii. 1 : " I was at *Shushan*, in the province of Elam, by the river
of *Ulai*."

[13] See Chap. XXI. The tablet referred to is perhaps the gem of the *Nimrud* collection. The sculptures of Asshur-bani-pal are exhibited, for the present, in the
basement of the British Museum (1870).

nificant—a banquet at which the king reclines on his couch, with
the queen *sitting at his feet.*   (Vignette to Chap. XXVIII.)

This sole picture of royal luxury among the Assyrian monuments,
as well as the lazier and more ostentatious mode of hunting, have
a tinge of the Greek Sardanapalus, and prepare us for the catastrophe which is now at hand.   Meanwhile these scenes of power
and magnificence, added to the conquests recorded in the king's
annals, prove how well, and at how late a period of its history, the
empire realised the figure under which Ezekiel afterwards described
it : " Behold, the Assyrian was a cedar in Lebanon, fair of branches,
and with a shadowing shroud, and of a high stature; and his top
was among the thick boughs. *The waters*[14] *nourished him* . . . .
Therefore his height was exalted above all the trees of the field,
and his boughs were multiplied, and his branches became long
because of the multitude of waters, when he shot forth.   All the
fowls of heaven made their nests in his boughs, and under his
branches did all the beasts of the field bring forth their young,
and under his shadow dwelt all great nations.   Thus was he fair in
his greatness, in the length of his branches: for his root was by
great waters.   The cedars in the garden of God could not hide
him : the fir trees were not like his boughs, and the chesnut trees
were not like his branches; nor any tree in the garden of God
was like unto him in his beauty. I have made him fair by the multitude of his branches : so that all the trees of Eden, that were in
the garden of God, envied him " (Ezek. xxxi. 3–9.)   We shall now
see how well the prophet's remaining words describe the fate of
this splendid plant.

[14] This means the tributary nations; but the figure is doubtless founded on the
rivers which watered the land.

King travelling in a mountainous country. (From an obelisk in the British Museum.)

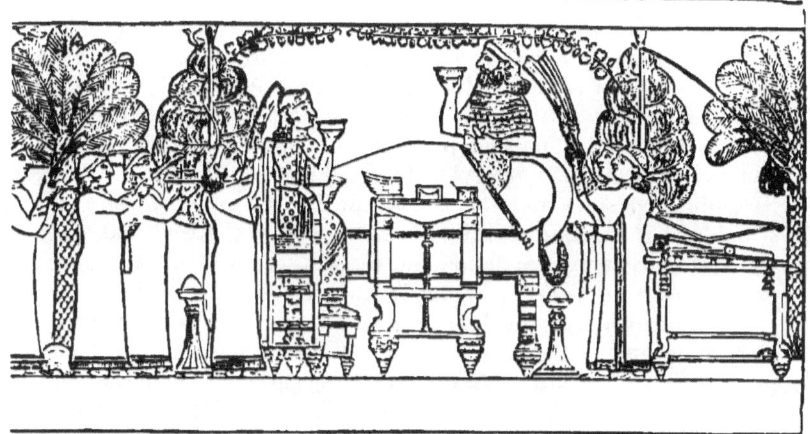

King, Queen, and Attendants (*Koyunjik*).

CHAPTER XXVIII.

THE FALL OF THE ASSYRIAN MONARCHY.

FROM B.C. 660 OR 647 TO B.C. 625 OR 606.

THE length of Asshur-bani-pal's reign is, as we have said, a disputed point; and all the ingenuity of chronologers has not yet fixed the exact epoch of the fall of Nineveh.[1]   But the later date assigned to its fall is only 54 years, and the earlier only 35, after the close of this splendid king's annals at B.C. 660. So rapid a declension is not surprising in the East; and it is paralleled in the other Mesopotamian kingdom. The Babylonian Empire ran its whole course in 88 years,[2] and its descent from its climax under Nebuchadnezzar was completed in 24.[3] Instability was a constitutional element of these great Oriental despotisms.[4]

But the vivid picture of the fall of Babylon, which is preserved by the historians of Cyrus, and especially in the book of Daniel, is totally wanting for Nineveh; and the catastrophe itself seems to have destroyed the monumental records of the events that led

[1] See the end of this chapter.

[2] Reckoning from the epoch of Nabopolassar's accession in the *Canon*, B.C. 625, to the taking of Babylon by Cyrus, B.C. 538.   [3] B.C. 561–538.

[4] The Persian empire owed its duration of nearly 230 years (B.C. 558–330) to its far more perfect organization, to say nothing of the *race* of the ruling people. But it collapsed at once before Alexander; and might have yielded sooner (as the Younger Cyrus all but proved) to any equally vigorous assault.

to it. Of the king who is supposed to have succeeded Asshur-bani-pal, we have only a few inscribed bricks, and an effigy with a genealogical inscription. These fragments identify him as the builder of the South-eastern palace on the *Nimrud* mound, over the ruins of a former edifice.[5] His name is doubtfully read as *Asshur-emit-ilin* or *Asshur-idililan;* and the remains of his palace bear witness to the decline and probably the sudden cessation of the monarchy, by its inferior style, its small and misshapen chambers, its unfinished state, and its unsculptured walls. Nor is the catastrophe itself without a witness in the heaps of charcoal and other signs of devouring fire found among the ruins of all the royal palaces, alike at *Nimrud, Koyunjik,* and *Khorsabad.*

Some incidents of the fate of Nineveh are preserved for us by Herodotus, and in a fragment or two of less known authors; and the causes of the fall of Assyria may be gathered from the very nature of her empire. The conquered tribes and kingdoms, including all the discordant tongues and races of Western Asia, were for the most part left to be governed by their own rulers, as vassals of the Assyrian king. He only required the acknowledgement of subjection, and the payment of tribute. When these were withheld, the rebellion was punished with ferocious cruelty; and the people, who were thus subject to worse treatment than foreign enemies, could feel no attachment to their master. Every Assyrian king boasts of the fear inspired by his majesty: not one thanks Asshur for the willing loyalty of his subjects.

While all the provinces were thus—to use Sargon's words—"ever prone to revolt," there were some which maintained a certain independence on the very borders of the seat of empire. The rival kingdom of Babylon was a perpetual thorn in the side of her neighbour; and on the rare occasions when she was really subdued, the Chaldæans and Elamites were ever ready to renew the contest in their marshes. Almost every Assyrian king had to fight again and again with the Aramæans on the middle Euphrates, and with the mountaineers of Armenia and Zagrus. And, beyond the latter range, the victories claimed over the Medes may often but attest their increasing pressure on the eastern frontier.

The great nation, which was destined to hand over the empire of Asia from the Semitic to the Aryan race, seems to have been reinforced by new immigrants from the East, just at the time when the luxury and weakness of Asshur-bani-pal's successor suspended those military expeditions, by which alone the empire was held

---

[5] Observe the proof that Calah was a royal residence to the very end of the monarchy.

together. "Though their internal state was still flourishing,"—
Herodotus tells us—"the Assyrians of Nineveh stood alone, being
deserted by their allies," when Phraortes the Mede attacked them,
but perished with the greater part of his army.[6] His son Cyaxares,
retiring behind the range of Zagrus, organized the Median tribes
into a well trained army, and made great conquests in the highlands
to the north-west. He then returned to attack Nineveh and avenge
his father. He had gained a battle and laid siege to the city, when
a horde of Scythians (the nomads of Central Asia) attacked and
defeated him, and stripped the Medes of the dominion they had
gained in Asia.

" The Scythians held the dominion of Western Asia for 28 years,
till they were expelled by Cyaxares; when the Medes recovered
their former power and took Nineveh." In this final attack, as we
learn from other writers, they were aided by the Babylonians, as
well as by a new revolt of the Chaldæans and Susianians. For
these must be the host of barbarians, that is, mixed tribes, who
came up (we are told) against Assyria *from the sea.* On hearing of
their approach, the king, Saracus, sent against them his general
Nabopolassar, who at once turned traitor to his falling master.
Having made a league with the Medes, and betrothed his son
Nebuchadnezzar to their king's daughter, he led the Babylonians
against Nineveh. When Saracus was informed of all this, he burnt
himself with his palace, like Sardanapalus in the story of the first
fall of Nineveh. Whether true in fact or not, this fate has a pre-
cedent in Jewish history :—"And it came to pass, when Zimri saw
that the city (of Tirzah) was taken, that he went into the palace of
the king's house, and burnt the king's house over him with fire,
and died" (1 Kings xvi. 18).

Such are the fragments of the story of the fall of Assyria and
Nineveh; and we know not how much of it is trustworthy. But
history has a truth not quite bound up in bare facts; and the real
nature of an event may be clear, when its details are obscure. The
fall of Nineveh is painted for us in the vivid imagery, and the
plainer language, of Hebrew prophecy, which indeed is partly
history. EZEKIEL, writing after the event, tells us how " the
multitude of waters," which denote the tributary states, not only
withdrew their nourishment from that "cedar of Lebanon, the
Assyrian," but swelled up to help in his destruction, when he
"stood alone" to undergo the sentence—" I have delivered him into
the hand of the mighty one of the heathen: in dealing he shall

[6] Respecting the rise of Media, and what is told us of her early kings, see below,
Chapter XXXII.

deal with him. . . . . And strangers, the terrible of the nations, have cut him off and have left him : upon the mountains and in all the valleys his branches are fallen, and his boughs are broken by all the rivers of the land; and all the people of the earth are gone down from his shadow and have left him." [7]

Nahum, in his warning of Nineveh by the fate she had herself inflicted upon Thebes,[8] gives a prophetic description, but in the true spirit of history, of the easy capture of the fortresses and the siege of the city itself:—" All thy strongholds shall be like fig-trees with the first ripe figs : if they be shaken, they shall even fall into the mouth of the eater. Behold, thy people in the midst of thee are women : the gates of thy land shall be set wide open unto thine enemies : the fire shall devour thy bars. There shall the fire devour thee; the sword shall cut thee off'" (Nahum iii.).

The utter and final nature of the destruction is pointed by Zephaniah in words rendered doubly emphatic by the recent discoveries beneath the mounds, among which nomad tribes have pitched their tents, and wild beasts and birds have made their haunts, for five-and-twenty centuries:—" He will stretch out his hand against the north, and destroy Assyria; and will make Nineveh a desolation, and dry like a wilderness. And flocks shall lie down in the midst of her, all the beasts of the nations: both the cormorant and the bittern shall lodge in the upper lintels of it; their voice shall sing in the windows; desolation shall be in the thresholds : for he shall uncover the cedar work. *This is the rejoicing city that dwelt carelessly*, that said in her heart, *I am, and there is none beside me :* how is she become a desolation, a place for beasts to lie down in! Every one that passeth by her shall hiss, and wag his hand" (Zeph. ii. 13-15).

The precise epoch of the fall of Nineveh is an unsettled question ; but the choice seems to lie between the two dates of B.C. 625 and B.C. 606. The former, at which the *Canon* fixes the accession of Nabopolassar *at Babylon*, is adopted by some of the best recent authorities: but others, of equal weight, concur with the older writers in fixing the first attack of Cyaxares on Nineveh at B.C. 625, and the capture and destruction of the city at B.C. 606. Of course, we cannot expect to find the records of the city's fall amidst its ruins; but much information concerning the latest Assyrian kings may lie hidden there, especially beneath the unexplored mound named after the prophet Jonah (*Nebbi-Yunus*).

---

[7] Ezekiel xxxi. The quotations given are only meant to direct attention to the prophecies, each of which should be read as a whole.

[8] See above, Chapter XXVII.

Priest-Vizier presenting Captives to a King.

CHAPTER XXIX.

THE BABYLONIAN OR CHALDÆAN EMPIRE.
FROM B.C. 625 TO B.C. 538.

PART I.—THE CONQUESTS OF NEBUCHADNEZZAR.

THE imperial power of the Semitic race, which ruled for so many
centuries in Mesopotamia, had its first seat at Babel and its last at
Babylon.   Kings, more or less powerful, appear to have reigned there

from Nimrod to Belshazzar. At first, as we have seen, they were masters of Assyria; and, during the space of about 1000 years,[1] in which the order of supremacy was reversed, Babylon was the most powerful of the kingdoms that bordered upon Assyria and were called her subjects. Sometimes the two crowns appear to have been united by matrimonial alliances, as under *Sammuramit* and her husband. Sometimes Babylon shook off the Assyrian yoke; and the brief independence won by Nabonassar, and again by Merodach-baladan, gave a foretaste of the empire secured by Nabopolassar. With the accession of the last named king, on Jan. 27, B.C. 625, begins the history of Babylon *as an Empire*.

We must here guard against the mistake, that Babylon succeeded to the empire of Assyria. After the fall of Nineveh, all that had been most properly *Assyrian*—the districts on the upper and middle Tigris—fell to the share of the Medes. What Babylon gained was the independence of her own country, enlarged by a union with Susiana, and that part of the Assyrian empire which lay along and to the west of the Euphrates. This division marks the new part she had to play in Western Asia. Separated from the regions of Zagrus and Armenia, on which the Assyrians had only kept their hold by incessant wars, she was at liberty to seek expansion towards the West.

Thus Babylon was brought into conflict with Judæa and Egypt; and the place she holds in history, as the predestined destroyer of Jerusalem, forms a striking contrast to the brief duration of her empire. Its whole course was run in 88 years (B.C. 625–538), and half of that time (43 years) is filled by the reign of Nebuchadnezzar. In him centres the whole interest of the story, except the fall of Babylon; and it has been well said that "but for Nebuchadnezzar, the Babylonians would have had no place in history." Of the seven kings of the dynasty, three (the 3rd, 4th, and 5th) are of the slightest possible importance, their united reigns only just reaching six years. The list is as follows:—

		Years.	B.C.
1. Nabopolassar		21	625–604
2. Nebuchadnezzar		43	604–561
3. Evil-Merodach		2	561–559
4. Neriglissar		3–4	559–556
5. Laborosoarchod		(9 m.)	556–555
6. Nabonadius		17	555–538
7. Belshazzar, associated with his father towards the end of his reign.			

Berosus and the classical writers call the dynasty *Chaldæan;* and, in the contemporary Jewish history and prophecy, this name

---

[1] That is, speaking roughly, from the 16th to the 6th century, B.C.

is regularly applied to the kings, their country, and their armies; and particularly to the sacred caste, who were at once the ministers of religion and the masters of all the learning of Babylonia. We have purposely avoided, in this work, the difficulties connected with this famous name. It will be enough to say that its antiquity in Lower Mesopotamia is attested by the annals of the Assyrian kings, as early as the 9th century B.C. The Chaldæan dynasty probably belonged to the ancient race who had long been dominant in Babylonia, and claimed to represent the old native monarchy.

Whatever may be the true date of the fall of Nineveh, that of the accession of NABOPOLASSAR[2] is fixed by Ptolemy's astronomical Canon to the 27th of January, B.C. 625. Except his alliance with the Medes against Assyria,[3] we know no details of his reign till just upon its close. The "Standard Inscription" of Nebuchadnezzar, describing his great works for the restoration of Babylon, tells us that those works were begun by his father. From the account of its previous state we may conclude that the city, which Isaiah had described in the time of Sennacherib as "the glory of kingdoms, the beauty of the Chaldees' excellency" (Isa. xiii. 19, xiv. 14), had been neglected during the troubles of the later times of Assyria.

As the result of those troubles, also, Egypt again came forward to dispute with Babylon the empire of Western Asia as far as the Euphrates. We have seen how Neco, the enterprising son of the founder of the Saïte dynasty, advanced to "the bordering flood," and seized Carchemish, the key to the passage of the river (B.C. 608).[4] Within three or four years after his triumphant return to Egypt, the garrison of Carchemish was utterly routed by Nebuchadnezzar, who followed up this decisive blow by the capture of Jerusalem (B.C. 605).

Egypt was thus finally thrown back within her natural limits. "And the king of Egypt came not any more out of his land: for the king of Babylon had taken from the river of Egypt unto the river Euphrates all that pertained to the king of Egypt." The true spirit of this last conflict between Egypt and Mesopotamia for the dominion of Western Asia is best seen in Jeremiah's grand prophecy, delivered when the Egyptian army was still at Carchemish, of "the sacrifice that the Lord God of hosts had in the north country by the river Euphrates," and of the devastating invasion

---

[2] The name, *Nabu-pal-uzur*, signifies "Nebo, protect (thy or my) son."

[3] His supposed aid to Cyaxares in the Lydian war will be noticed in the proper place, Chapter XXXII.

[4] 2 Kings xxiii. 30, xxiv. 7; 2 Chron. xxxv. 20, xxxvi. 7. In the former passage it is said that "Pharaoh-Nechoh went up against the king of *Assyria*;" which is a strong argument for the later date of the fall of Nineveh.

which Nebuchadrezzar was to bring, at a later period upon Memphis (*Noph*), Thebes (*No*), and the land and king of Egypt (Jerem. xlvi.).

On the present occasion, NEBUCHADNEZZAR [7] was recalled from the frontier of Egypt by the news of his father's death; and he hastened back across the desert with a small escort, to receive the crown from the chief of the Chaldæan priests, who had acted as regent in his absence. The *Canon* dates his accession from the 21st of January, B.C. 604.

No despot, ancient or modern, fills so grand a place on the page of history; and yet none has left so little information about himself. We have his inscriptions concerning his great buildings; but his annals have not been disinterred from the ruins of Babylon, like those of the Assyrian kings from Nineveh. For the true lessons of his history, their place is more than supplied by the sacred writings. No long and boastful details of countries overrun and subjected to tribute, of cities stormed and razed, and prisoners and spoil carried away to Babylon, would have had half the value of the brief record of the part he played as the instrument of Providence in the captivity of the Jews, and of the dramatic pictures in the book of Daniel of his humiliation before the God of the conquered people; while all the poetry to which history has given birth is surpassed by the sublime prophecies of the fate reserved for proud Babylon and her mighty king.

The Babylonian empire was created at one stroke by the victory of Carchemish. But, within the region west of the Euphrates, there remained two powers, almost contemptible in magnitude, but yet mighty. the one in its commercial wealth and colonial empire, the other in its exclusive spirit of religious patriotism. TYRE, now at the height of her prosperity, drew the rest of Phœnicia into resistance; and JUDÆA, which religious declension and political weakness had left helpless before the conqueror, assumed the courage of despair just as she had lost the strength of religious patriotism.

The successive steps of that destruction, to which the crimes of her princes give the character of just retribution, are related in the Scripture history. It is enough here to point them out. First, in Nebuchadnezzar's advance after the victory of Carchemish, the resistance of Jehoiakim, whom Neco had set upon the throne, caused the first capture of Jerusalem and the *First Captivity of*

---

[5] The form *Nebuchadrezzar*, which we find in Jeremiah and Ezekiel, comes nearer to the Babylonian *Nabu-kudurri-uzur*, which signifies probably (for the middle element is of somewhat doubtful meaning) "Nebo, protect my race." The usual form in the Greek and Latin writers is *Nabuchodonosor*. Our chief information about him, besides what Scripture supplies, is furnished by the writers who seem to have preserved some of the statements of the Chaldæan historian Berosus.

Judah. In the train of booty and prisoners that slowly followed the new king to Babylon, were some of the vessels of the temple, and certain chosen youths of the royal and princely families, including DANIEL and his three companions (B.C. 605).[6]

Three years later, Jehoiakim rebelled, in the vain hope of aid from Neco, who "came not any more out of his land" (B.C. 602). But, for some unknown reason, it was not till B.C. 598 that Nebuchadnezzar marched against Judæa and Tyre, with the aid (according to one historian) of a large Median force. Jerusalem was taken for the second time. Jehoiakim was put to death, and "his dead body cast out in the day to the heat, and in the night to the frost" (B.C. 597) (Jerem. xxii. 18, 19 ; xxxvi. 30 .

The example was lost upon his son Jehoiachin or Jeconiah ; who had scarcely been set upon the throne by Nebuchadnezzar, than he was drawn into rebellion by his mother and the princes of Judah. Jerusalem was again invested ; and Jehoiachin, going out to make his submission to Nebuchadnezzar, was deposed and taken captive, after a reign of 100 days. With him were carried away to Babylon all the princes and warriors—the whole strength of the nation— with all the treasures of the temple. "None remained, save the poorest sort of the people of the land;" and over them Nebuchadnezzar set up as king Zedekiah, the youngest son of Josiah, binding him to fidelity by a solemn oath. This, the *Great Captivity of Judah*, took place in the 8th year of Nebuchadnezzar (B.C. 597).[7]

The conqueror's forbearance, in not utterly destroying the city after this third rebellion, is unexampled in the history of Eastern despots. The motive for desiring its continuance, referred to by the prophet Ezekiel—"that by keeping of his covenant it might stand "—may be found in those wonderful revelations, recorded in the book of Daniel, which surround the great figure of Nebuchadnezzar with a light reflected from a source above all earthly splendour.

It was as early as the second year of his reign (B.C. 603), soon after his return from his first conquests beyond the Euphrates, that the young king dreamed the dream in which he saw the colossal image of the empires of the world, with himself for its golden head.

6 Observe that the date in Daniel i. 1, 2, is that of Nebuchadnezzar's *advance upon Jerusalem*, in the year before his accession, though he is very naturally styled *king*. Hence the *three years* of Daniel's probation (ver. 5) expire in the *second* year of Nebuchadnezzar, B.C. 603 (Dan. i. 18, ii. 1, 13).

7 2 Kings xxiv. 13–16 ; 2 Chron. xxxvi. 10–13 ; Ezek. xvii. 13, 14. Among the captives were the prophet Ezekiel and the grandfather of Mordecai. For chronology, it is important to observe that the dates of Ezekiel are reckoned from this epoch.

dashed to pieces by a heavenly power. Confessing as he did in that power the God of the youth who interpreted his dream, it is not wonderful that he should have spared the sacred city of that God. A similar feeling urged Titus to untiring efforts to save the temple; and, in both cases, it was the obstinacy of the Jews that frustrated the forbearance of their heathen conquerors. They would not even take warning from the fate of the false prophets "whom the king of Babylon roasted in the fire" (Jerem. xxix. 22, 23); though the heathen king could learn his second lesson from the deliverance of Shadrach, Meshech, and Abednego, from the like fate.[8]

A gleam of hope from Egypt, on the accession of the rash and arrogant Pharaoh-Hophra (Apries)[9] led Zedekiah to rebel against Nebuchadnezzar, "in sending his ambassadors to Egypt, that they might give him horses and much people"—cavalry and infantry. (Ezek. xvii. 15). Nebuchadnezzar took the field with all the forces of his empire, "all the kingdoms of the earth of his dominion" (Jerem. xxxiv. 1). Like Sennacherib 110 years before, he first overran the country, and took all the fortified cities, except Lachish and Azekah; and then laid siege to Jerusalem on the 10th day of the 10th month in the 9th year of Zedekiah (the 10th of Thebet, about Dec. 20, B.C. 589).[10]

As Isaiah before, so now Jeremiah was prophesying within the beleaguered city; but the simple fact that he was persecuted and imprisoned proved her ripe for the fate which he was commissioned to denounce. Still his message was tempered with the promise of future restoration; not in words only but by deeds. His public purchase of a field at his native village of Anathoth was the occasion of his great prophecy of the return from the captivity. It is full time that the praise lavished on the like act of the Roman, who bought for its full value the ground on which Hannibal had pitched his camp before Rome, should be paid to the patriotism inspired by religion (Jerem. xxxii. foll.; comp. Liv. xxxvi. 11).

The details of the siege, which lasted two years and a half, and of the capture of the city, on the 9th day of the 4th month of the 11th year of Zedekiah and the 19th of Nebuchadnezzar,[11] belong to

---

[8] Daniel iii. It is not unreasonable to suppose that the golden image (of Nebo, Bel, or Merodach), doubtless made from the spoils of conquest, was set up to commemorate the victory of the king's patron deity over the God of Judah at the time of the Great Captivity; and that the rebuke was suited to the impious triumph.

[9] See Chapter XIII.

[10] 2 Kings xxv. 1; Jerem. xxxix. 1, lii. 1. The exactness with which the dates are given through the whole story, both by the years of Nebuchadnezzar and of the Jewish kings, enables us to determine the chronology precisely, with the aid of the Canon.   [11] The 9th of Thammuz, about the 26th June, B.C. 586.

Scripture history. A temporary relief had been afforded, when Pharaoh-Hophra advanced and caused the Chaldæans to raise the siege; but he retreated when Nebuchadnezzar turned to meet him. The vengeance due for this act, and for the shelter given to the Jews who fled to Egypt after the murder of Gedaliah, was postponed for the reduction of Ammon, Moab, and Edom, who now felt the cruelties which they had exulted at seeing Judah suffer.[12]

The next great exploit of Nebuchadnezzar was the siege of Tyre, which lasted 13 years. Some suppose that the siege was formed at the same time that he marched against Jehoiachin; others, that it was begun about the same time as the final investment of Jerusalem (B.C. 589).[13] A remarkable prophecy of Ezekiel, delivered in B.C. 571, describes the extraordinary labour and the poor results of this siege, for which the Babylonian is promised the plunder of Egypt as a recompense:—"Son of man, Nebuchadrezzar king of Babylon caused his army to serve a great service against Tyrus: every head was made bald, and every shoulder was peeled: yet had he no wages, nor his army, for Tyrus, for the service that he served against it. Therefore, thus saith the Lord God, Behold I will give the land of Egypt unto Nebuchadrezzar king of Babylon; and he shall take her multitude, and take her spoil, and take her prey; and it shall be the wages for his army. I have given him the land of Egypt for his labour (or, hire) wherewith he served against it, because they wrought for me, saith the Lord God" (Ezek. xxix. 18–20).

It is very probable that Nebuchadnezzar took only the city of "Old Tyre" on the mainland; but, being destitute of a naval force, failed in the attempt, which Alexander found so arduous, to drive a mole to the island city, in which were stored the treasures that should have rewarded his army. At all events, the whole coast of Phœnicia was subdued; and the stories of his conquests as far as the Pillars of Hercules may be based on his claims of sovereignty over the colonies of the conquered cities. The result of these campaigns was the submission of all the countries of Western Asia, from the Euphrates to the frontier of Egypt, to the Babylonian yoke, with a completeness of conquest never attained by Assyria.

Next came the turn of Egypt, whose fate had been predicted by Ezekiel, in language as striking as that of Nahum concerning the Assyrian conquest.[14] Seventeen years before the prophecy just quoted, Ezekiel had confirmed Jeremiah's prediction of the conquest

<hr>

[12] See the repeated allusions in Jeremiah and Ezekiel, and Psalm cxxxvii. 7.

[13] The fact that he was holding his court at Riblah, in Hamath, when Jerusalem fell, seems to point to operations in Phœnicia. Comp. Chap. XL.

[14] See Chapter XXVII.

of Egypt by Nebuchadnezzar;[15] prophesying its utter desolation
"from Migdol to Syene," and its restoration as the vassal of
Babylon, "the basest of the kingdoms," never to "exalt itself any
more above the nations."   And, just after the remnant of the Jews
had fled to Egypt, Jeremiah had foretold her punishment, like
that of Jerusalem, by the sword, by the famine, and by the pesti-
lence; and had denounced the fate of Pharaoh-Hophra by name
(Jerem. xliv.).

These prophecies furnish us with the truest history of the real
conquest of Egypt, which Berosus expressly claims for Nebuchadnezzar, but which the Egyptians concealed under their story of the
fall of Apries.[16]   As the latest of these prophecies was delivered in
B.C. 571, and the Egyptian chronology places the accession of Amasis
about B.C. 569, we must place within these limits the conquest
of Egypt, which is the last known of the wars of Nebuchadnezzar.
He had now reigned 35 years, and 8 years remained for him to
enjoy, as he thought, the wealth, state, and glory, which his sword
had won.

[15] Jerem. xlvi., referred to above, p. 83; Ezek. xxix. 1–16.   Observe the distinction between this prophecy, which was delivered in the 10th month of the 10th year
of the Captivity (early in B.C. 587), and that which follows (Ezek. xxix. 17, xxx.).
belonging to the 1st month of the 27th year (the spring of B.C. 571).   To these are
added the prophecies in Ezek. xxxi. (Mids. B.C. 587) and xxxii. (spring of B.C. 585).
All should be carefully read.
[16] See Chapter XIII.

Babylonian Brick, with a Cuneiform Inscription.

View of the *Kasr*, or Palace of Nebuchadnezzar.

CHAPTER XXX.
THE BABYLONIAN OR CHALDÆAN EMPIRE.
B.C. 625 TO B.C. 538.

PART II.—ITS CLIMAX AND FALL.

THE great works of Nebuchadnezzar at Babylon and in the whole land had gone on during his wars, which had also furnished the means for their execution in the spoil of the conquered nations, and the forced labour of the people deported in mass to Chaldæa.

A summary of these great works is given by the historian of the ancient monarchies of the East: "He built the great wall of Babylon, which, according to the lowest estimate, must have contained 500,000,000 cubic feet of solid masonry, and must have required three or four times that number of bricks [1] He constructed a new and magnificent palace in the neighbourhood of the ancient

---

[1] Not such bricks as ours. The Babylonian bricks are about a foot square, and from 3 to 4 inches thick.

residence of the kings. He made the celebrated *Hanging Garden* for the gratification of his wife Amyitis. He repaired and beautified the great temple of Belus at Babylon. He dug the huge reservoir near Sippara, said to have been 140 miles in circumference and 180 feet deep, furnishing it with flood-gates, through which its waters could be drawn off for purposes of irrigation. He constructed a number of canals, among them the *Nahr Malcha*, or "Royal River," a broad and deep channel, which connects the Euphrates with the Tigris. He built quays and breakwaters along the shores of the Persian Gulf, and he at the same time founded the city of Diridotis, or Teredon, in the vicinity of that sea. To these constructions may be added, on the authority of Nebuchadnezzar's own inscriptions or of the existing remains, the *Birs-i-Nimrud* or great temple of Nebo at Borsippa; a vast reservoir in Babylon itself, called the *Yapur-Shapu*; an extensive embankment along the course of the Tigris near Bagdad; and almost innumerable temples, walls, and other public buildings, at Cutha, Sippara, Borsippa, Babylon, &c. The indefatigable monarch seems to have either rebuilt, or at least repaired, almost every city and temple throughout the entire country. There are said to be at least a hundred sites in the tract immediately about Babylon, which give evidence, by inscribed bricks bearing his legend, of the marvellous activity and energy of this king." [2]

His inscriptions celebrate the power given him to execute these works by the gods whose servant and son he boasts himself. But these religious professions, which are common to all the Assyrian and Babylonian documents, did not exclude the proudest glorification of himself; and the abasement of his pride forms the last of the three great lessons which taught him to confess the power of the God before whom "Bel boweth down, Nebo stoopeth." For the true element of grandeur in his history consists in those dealings which brought the destroyer of the Jewish nation not only to learn— but to be the *conscious* instrument of teaching the world—to give glory where only it is due.

First, Daniel's interpretation of the vision of the colossal image rebuked the king's dream of universal empire (Dan. ii.). Next, the escape of the three Hebrew youths from the flames which slew their persecutors, drew from him a formal decree, confessing that "no other god can deliver after this sort," and securing toleration for those who would not "serve nor worship any god except their own god" (Dan. iii.). Thus Bel was humbled; but it needed a

Rawlinson, 'Five Monarchies,' vol. iii. pp. 496-9.

third lesson to humble the king himself: and of that lesson we have *his own formal record* in a public decree.[3]

It was "when he was at rest in his house, and flourishing in his palace"—amidst the empire he had won and the capital he had finished—that the self-glorifying thought shaped itself as before into a dream, and the dream was made a warning revelation. There is no need to explain the image—which we have already seen applied to Assyria—of the stately tree, which gave a home to all the birds of heaven, shelter to the beasts of the earth, and food to the inhabitants of the world; or of its fate as expounded by Daniel. One year of grace was granted to the king "to break off his sins by righteousness, and his iniquities by shewing mercy to the poor, if it might be a lengthening of his tranquillity."

But the prosperity and magnificence around him were too captivating. "At the end of twelve months he walked in the palace of the kingdom of Babylon. The king spake and said, Is not this great Babylon, that I have built for the house of the kingdom by the might of my power, and for the honour of my majesty? While the word was in the king's mouth, there fell a voice from heaven, O king Nebuchadnezzar, to thee it is spoken; the kingdom is departed from thee: and they shall drive thee from men, and thy dwelling shall be with the beasts of the field: they shall make thee to eat grass as oxen, and seven times shall pass over thee, until thou know that the Most High ruleth in the kingdom of men, and giveth it to whomsoever he will. The same hour was the thing fulfilled upon Nebuchadnezzar: and he was driven from men, and did eat grass as oxen, and his body was wet with the dew of heaven, till his hairs grew like eagles' feathers, and his nails like birds' claws" (Daniel iv. 29–33).

Madness is the frequent penalty of despotism, and it seized upon Nebuchadnezzar in the strange and degrading form called *Lycan-thropy*.[4] The patient, fancying himself a beast, rejects clothing and ordinary food, and even (as in this case) the shelter of a roof; disuses articulate speech, and sometimes persists in going on all-fours. We may assume that Nebuchadnezzar was allowed the range of the private gardens of his palace, and that his condition was concealed from his subjects. But he himself formally

---

[3] Daniel iv. It is not enough (though that would be much) to say that this chapter is a *translation* of the king's own proclamation, made when there was *no doubt* about the interpretation of cuneiform writing: but it has really the force of an *original*. For we may be sure that, according to custom, like the trilingual inscriptions of the Persian kings, and like the previous decree, it was published in versions intelligible to "all the peoples, nations, and languages," to whom it is addressed (ver. 1).

[4] From λυκάνθρωπος, the *were-wolf*.

proclaimed it to them on his recovery, to teach the lesson he had learnt, "that the heavens do rule," and to "praise and extol and honour the King of heaven, all whose works are truth, and his ways judgment; *and those that walk in pride he is able to abase.*"

It seems, from an inscription, that the government was carried on by the father of the king's son-in-law, who was probably the *Rab-Mag*, or chief of the order of Chaldæans. Though, of course, only regent, he assumed the title of "King," like "Darius the Median" under Cyrus. We may suspect some intrigue for seizing the crown, which was disconcerted by Nebuchadnezzar's return to reason, apparently as suddenly as he had lost it. For he says, "*I was established in my kingdom, and excellent majesty was added unto me*" (Daniel iv. 36).

How long this greater brightness of his closing days lasted, depends upon the meaning of the "seven times" appointed for his humiliation. They are commonly interpreted, as by the Jewish historian Josephus, *seven years;* though some understand but *seven months.* The former supposition would leave but two or three years before this great king—to use the simple language of Berosus—fell ill and departed this life, after a reign of just 43 years (B.C. 561).

The real greatness of the Babylonian empire ended, as it had begun, with Nebuchadnezzar. A moderate degree of political foresight might have hazarded the prediction, which some ascribe to the dying king, of the destruction of Babylon by the Medes and Persians. For the Median empire, now at its climax, passed into the more vigorous hands of the Persian Cyrus two years after the death of Nebuchadnezzar.

Nor was there any adequate power within, to resist the well organized military strength of the Aryan tribes. The chief force of Babylon consisted in the fiery cavalry of *Irak-Araby* and Lower Chaldæa, well described by the prophet as "terrible and dreadful, swifter than leopards, and sharper than evening wolves"—a "bitter and hostile nation, to possess the dwelling-places that are not theirs" (Habakkuk i. 6–10)—an admirable instrument of rapid conquest, but not of lasting dominion.

The end was hastened by court intrigues and dynastic revolutions. The son of Nebuchadnezzar, EVIL-MERODACH, had reigned but two years (B.C. 561–559), when he fell the victim of a conspiracy headed by his brother-in-law, Neriglissar. He had reigned lawlessly and profligately, says Berosus; but one interesting fact is recorded of him in Scripture. He released Jehoiachin, the captive king of Judah, from his 37 years' imprisonment, and gave him a daily allowance, and a place at his own table above all the other kings that were in captivity at Babylon (B.C. 560).   (2 Kings xxv. 27–30; Jerem. lii. 31, 32.)

NERIGLISSAR [5] was the son-in-law of Nebuchadnezzar, and the son of the regent during that king's madness. His descent, and his hereditary dignity of *Rab-Mag* (or *Rabu-emga*), the chief of the Chaldæan order, are known from inscriptions on the bricks of the "smaller palace" of Babylon, which he built on the western bank of the Euphrates. After a reign of 3 or 4 years (B.C. 559–556), he died quietly in his palace, according to the prevailing account, or, as others say, in a battle which he fought with Cyrus for the possession of Media. His son, LABOROSOARCHOD, a mere boy, reigned nominally for 9 months (B.C. 556–555), when his near connections put him to death with tortures, on the plea that he gave signs of a vicious disposition. His murderers, the chiefs of the Chaldæan order, conferred the crown on one of their own number.

NABONADIUS [6] (B.C. 555–538), may appear a strange name for the last king of Babylon, to our young readers who are familiar with the grand story of that night when Babylon was taken, and "BELSHAZZAR, king of the Chaldæans was slain" (Daniel v. 30). But this is now made clear by the inscribed cylinders found at *Mugheir*, in Lower Chaldæa, where the protection of the gods is asked for "*Nabu-nahid* and his son *Bil-shar-uzur*." [7] The names are coupled in a way which implies the son's association in his father's throne; and the mention of Belshazzar's 3rd year in the book of Daniel proves that the association was made at least as early as B. c. 510. [8]

Its motive was probably one which we often find in the Oriental dynasties, the descent of Belshazzar from the old royal line. In Daniel, Nebuchadnezzar is seven times called the father of Belshazzar; by the historian and prophet, by the king himself, and by the queen. [9] This queen was, in all probability the queen-mother,

<hr>

[5] Properly *Nergal-sar-uzur*, i. e. "Nergal, protect the king." The name also occurs in "*Nergal-sharezer*, the Rab-Mag," who was one of the princes left by Nebuchadnezzar to finish the siege of Jerusalem (Jerem. xxxix. 3, 13), and probably the grandfather of the usurper. The latter calls his father by a name which is doubtfully read as *Bel-sum-iskar*, or *Bel-mu-ingar*, or *Bellabarisrouk*.

[6] The name is *Nabu-nahid* (*i. e.* "Nebo, make prosperous"), of which *Nabu-induk* is supposed to be a dialectic variety. Besides the various classical forms beginning with *Nabo-*, Herodotus gives *Labynetus* (Herod. i. 188), a form which he seems to use for different Babylonian kings whose name began with *Nabu* (comp. i. 74). *Nabu-nahid* calls himself on his inscriptions "son of *Nabu-bala-tirib*, the Rab-Mag" (but the middle element is doubtful).

[7] The name signifies "Bel, protect the king."

[8] Dan. viii. 1. But it might have been earlier.

[9] Dan. v. 2, 11, 13, 18, 22. It is scarcely necessary to call to mind the use of "father" for any lineal ancestor.

Nitocris, the daughter of Nebuchadnezzar by an Egyptian princess of the same name. Hence the authority with which she rebukes her unworthy son by the example left him by his illustrious grandfather.

This Nitocris is celebrated by Herodotus for the great defences of Babylon against the Medes, which other writers ascribe to Nabonadius. His name is still read upon the bricks of the quays along the Euphrates within the city; the neglect of which, by his rash son, let in the army of the Persians. He added upper storeys, and other embellishments and restorations, to the primeval temple-towers of Chaldæa.[10] A curious testimony to the hopeless condition of his kingdom is given by an inscription of his last year, at Calneh in Lower Chaldæa, confessing his neglect of the worship of the gods, to obtain whose protection he undertakes to restore the temple of *Sin* (the Moon-god). His alliance with Crœsus, king of Lydia, against the Persians, will be related in the history of Cyrus.

In the 16th year of Nabonadius (B.C. 539), the Persian conqueror marched from Ecbatana. Having wintered on the banks of the Gyndes, he crossed the Tigris, and overran all the country as far as Babylon. The Chaldæan army, which was posted in front of the city under the king in person, was routed in a single battle; and Nabonadius threw himself into the fortress of Borsippa. The defence of Babylon was left to Belshazzar, aided by the counsels of the queen-mother. For some time, the city was so well guarded as to drive Cyrus almost to despair. As a last effort, he diverted the course of the Euphrates above the city, either into the reservoir of Nitocris, or by a canal returning to the river lower down.

His opportunity came with the license of that festival, of which the vivid drama is so familiar to us in the book of Daniel (Dan. v.). That night's revelry in the palace was imitated throughout the city. The Persians, marching along the dried bed of the Euphrates, entered the neglected river-gates: had these been closed, they would have been caught, as Herodotus says, "in a trap." Then followed the tumultuous scene of hurry, confusion, fire, and massacre, which Jeremiah had foretold in one of those marvellous prophecies which only differ from minute history by their vivid poetic colouring (Jerem. li.). Caught in the midst of dance and revelry, "the mighty men of Babylon forebore to fight: they became as women." In vain did "one post run to meet another, and one messenger to meet another, to shew the king of Babylon that his city was taken at one end, and that the passages were stopped." None were ready to repel the foe; for "her princes were made drunk, her captains, her rulers, and her mighty men: they slept a perpetual sleep."

<hr>

10 See Chapter XVII.

"The broad walls of Babylon were utterly broken, and her high gates were burnt with fire:" and "in that night was Belshazzar the king of the Chaldæans slain."

Nabonadius surrendered at Borsippa on the approach of Cyrus, who admitted him not only to mercy, but to his favour, and assigned him an abode in Carmania.   Only the outer wall of Babylon was dismantled; and the book of Daniel represents the government as carried on under the new masters by "Darius the Median" who "took the kingdom, at the age of 62" (Dan. v. 31), and whom he elsewhere speaks of as "Darius, the son of Ahasuerus of the seed of the Medes, which was made king over the realm of the Chaldæans."[11]   These phrases seem to describe a viceroy, of the Median royal family, who exercised kingly authority at Babylon during the interval of two years before Cyrus came to reign there in person (B.C. 538–536).   The captive Jews, who were subject to the direct rule of Darius at Babylon, naturally and properly spoke of him as *king*, and reckoned the years of Cyrus from the epoch of his personal reign at Babylon, where his first act was to issue the order for their restoration to their land (B.C. 536).[12]

From this time Babylon became the second capital of the Persian Empire, and the ordinary royal residence in winter.   Though it suffered severely in consequence of its revolts under Darius and Xerxes, it retained its greatness to the time of Alexander, who destined it for his eastern seat of empire.   The transfer of its population to Seleucia, on the Tigris, by the Greek kings of Syria, began that long decay which has fulfilled the most awfully sublime picture of desolation that was ever drawn even by an inspired pen, and has left "Babylon, the glory of kingdoms, the beauty of the Chaldees' excellency, as when God overthrew Sodom and Gomorrha:"—*a type of the doom reserved for every scheme of universal empire* (Isaiah xiii.; Jerem. l., li.).

Not to weaken by mere extracts the force of the prophecies, which we ask the reader to peruse, let us hear the testimony of travellers to their fulfilment.   Besides the great mound of *Babil*, and some undulating heaps, one of which bears the expressive name of

---

[11] Dan. ix. 1.   Some of the older writers, misled by Xenophon's historical *romance*, the *Cyropædia*, make Darius a reigning king of Media, the son of Astyages, and the ally of Cyrus, who quietly succeeds him in B.C. 536.   But there is no doubt that Cyrus had dethroned Astyages 20 years before the capture of Babylon (see below, (Chapter XXXIV.); and Xenophon's son of Astyages, named Cyaxares, is either a prince who never came to the throne, or an imaginary person, who is introduced into the romance as a foil to the virtues of Cyrus.

[12] 2 Chron. xxxvi. 22; Ezra i. 1; Dan. x. 21: comp. x. 1, where the 3rd year of Cyrus is specified.   In Dan. vii. 28, there is a clear distinction between "the reign of Darius" (the Mede) and "the reign of Cyrus the Persian."

Mujelibé, " the overturned "—" Other shapeless heaps of rubbish cover for many an acre the face of the land. The lofty banks of ancient canals fret the country like natural ridges of hills. Some have long been choked with sand; others still carry the waters of the river to distant villages and palm-groves. On all sides, fragments of glass, marble, pottery, and inscribed bricks are mingled with that peculiar nitrous and blanched soil, which, bred from the remains of ancient habitations, checks or destroys vegetation, and renders the site of Babylon a naked and hideous waste. Owls start from the scanty thickets, and the foul jackal skulks through the furrows." [13]

" Various ranges of smaller mounds fill up the intervening space to the eastern angle of the walls. The pyramidal mass of El-Heimar, far distant in the same direction, and the still more extraordinary pile of the Birs-Nimrud in the south-west, across the Euphrates, rise from the surrounding plain like two mighty tumuli, designed to mark the end of departed greatness. Midway between them, the river Euphrates, wending her silent course towards the sea, is lost amid the extensive date-groves which conceal from sight the little Arab town of Hillah. All else around is a blank waste, recalling the words of Jeremiah : " Her cities are a desolation, a dry land and a wilderness, a land wherein no man dwelleth, neither doth any son of man pass thereby.' " [14]

To these descriptions we may add the poetic view of the same scene, pointing the truth to which it bears a constant witness :—

> " Slumber is there, but not of rest ;
> There her forlorn and weary nest
>   The famish'd hawk has found :
> The wild dog howls at fall of night ;
> The serpent's rustling coils affright
>   The traveller on his round.
>
> " What shapeless form, half lost on high, [15]
> Half seen against the evening sky,
>   Seems like a ghost to glide,
> And watch, from Babel's crumbling heap,
> Where in her shadow, fast asleep,
>   Lies fall'n imperial pride?
>
> " With half-closed eye a lion there
> Is basking in his noontide lair,
>   Or prowls in twilight gloom.
> The golden city's king he seems,
> Such as, in old prophetic dreams,
>   Sprang from rough ocean's womb. [16]

---

[13] Layard, ' Nineveh and Babylon,' p. 484.
[14] Loftus, ' Chaldæa and Susiana,' p. 20.
[15] The allusion is to a group of lions seen by Sir R. K. Porter on the summit of the Birs-Nimrud.   [16] Daniel vii. 4.

" But where are now his eagle wings,
    That shelter'd erst a thousand kin
        Hiding the glorious sky
    From half the nations, till they own
    No holier name, no mightier throne ?—
        That vision is gone by.

" Quench'd is the golden statue's ray;
    The breath of heaven has blown away
        What toiling earth had piled,
    Scattering wise heart and crafty hand,
    As breezes strew on ocean's strand
        The fabrics of a child." [17]

Still the renowned *name* of Babel has lingered about that " plain
in the land of Shinar;" and the successive capitals of the Syrian
Greeks, the Parthians, and the Mohammedans—Seleucia, Ctesi-
phon, and Bagdad—have all been spoken of as *Babylon*.[18]
The fall of Babylon marks the epoch when the empire of the
East was wrested from the Semitic race, till they recovered it,
about 12 centuries later, by the Mohammedan conquest.

In order to set the history of Assyria and Babylon in the full
light of recent discovery, we have had to make such constant
reference to the monuments of Chaldæa, Babylonia, and Assyria, to
the scenes portrayed on them, and to the inscriptions and annals
of the kings, as to render a separate account of the civilization and
arts of these countries unnecessary. An explanation of the system
of cuneiform writing would be out of place in this elementary
work: it will be found in the 'Student's Manual of the Ancient
History of the East.'

[17] Keble.   [18] See, for example, 1 Peter v. 13.

Men and Monsters (from a Cylinder).

Aryan Physiognomy (*Persepolis*).

BOOK III.
THE MEDO-PERSIAN EMPIRE, AND ITS SUBJECT COUNTRIES IN ASIA.

CHAPTER XXXI.

IRAN AND THE PRIMITIVE ARYANS.

THE conquest of Babylon by Cyrus, at the head of the united forces of the Medes and Persians, completed the transfer of the empire of Western Asia from the Semitic to the Aryan race.   The family of Japheth, " enlarged" by increase and conquest, had now begun to make Ham his " servant," and to " dwell in the tents of Shem."   The former races, settling in the two great fertile plains which were ready to nourish the earliest civilization, had built up kingdoms on a vast scale of despotic power and rude magnificence; and they had cultivated the arts and sciences which minister to the material wants of man : but their despotisms had grown effete, and their science was the handmaid of superstition.

At this juncture, the third race—the hardy natives of the ruder climate and the freer air of highlands, trained to war by conflicts with the nomad Turanian tribes and animated by a religion based on pure and spiritual principles—took possession of the fruits of civilization prepared for it, and reorganized an empire destined in its turn to succumb before the more vigorous spirit of Western freedom.   To trace that conflict to its source was the motive which impelled the " father of history " to compose his picture of the nations included in the Persian Empire; and the undying interest, to all freemen, of the great issues which were fought out at Marathon and Salamis, is enhanced by the fact that the combatants on both sides were of kindred race.

Whatever may have been the first cradle of that race, the branch with which we have now to do traced its earliest known origin to the region of Central Asia which lies on the further margin of the great table-land of *Iran.*   The part of Asia with which we have been concerned, as the region of the Assyrian and Babylonian empires, is the low count.y enclosed on the north and east by the mountains of Armenia and Zagrus.   Now we have to ascend the latter; and we find ourselves on a vast table-land, supported on the north and south by the prolongations of those ranges, and on the east by the *Suleiman* mountains, which divide it from the valley of the Indus.   This is the table-land of *Iran,* the ancient *Ariana,*[1] a collective name for the abode of those various races of Aryan origin which we now call *Iranian* as distinguished from the kindred Indians.   Beyond its northern boundary (the range called by the general name of the Indian Caucasus), the table-land of *Turan* (*Turkestan*) was the region of the nomad races called *Turanian,*

---

[1] The correspondence of names is put thus generally for the sake of a first clear impression; but they are not coextensive. The ancient *Ariana* (at least usually) excluded Media and Persia, but included the eastern slopes of the mountains down to the Indus, and the specially Aryan regions of Bactriana, Sogdiana, and Margiana, on the northern side of the Indian Caucasus. The Persian name of Iran is found on the coins of the Sassanidæ, the new Persian dynasty who expelled the Parthian Arsacidæ in A.D. 226.

Mongol, or *Turkish,* who formerly disputed the possession of all Asia with the Semites and Iranians.

The table-land of Iran is a vast elevated region between 46° and 68° of East longitude and 26° and 36° of North latitude,[2] rising nowhere so much as 3000 feet above the sea. The central part, lying on what geographers call " the rainless zone," forms the great salt desert of *Khorassan,* which extends south-east, in the form of an oblique parallelogram, to the shores of the Indian Ocean. Here was the desert of Gedrosia (*Beloochistan*), in which the army of Alexander almost perished from thirst.

The other margins of the region derive a more varied character from the mountains and their streams. Of Media and Persia, on the west, we shall have to speak more particularly. In the north and north-east, the rivers flowing from the Indian Caucasus and Paropamisus redeem from the desert regions of more or less fertility, forming the districts of Parthia, Aria, Draugiana, and Arachosia (*Northern Khorassan,* and *Afghanistan*). But these streams, as well as those flowing from the eastern slopes of Zagrus, are lost in the central desert, forming an exception to the law—

> " As to the sea returning rivers roll."

Not such, however, is the state of those districts on the northern slope of the table-land, which were among the earliest abodes of the Aryan race. In the angle between the *Hindoo Koosh* and the ranges which strike off to the north (the *Bolor-Tagh,* &c.), the valley watered by the upper streams of the great rivers Oxus and Jaxartes (*Jihun* or *Amu-daria,* and *Sihun* or *Syr-daria*) formed the surpassingly beautiful and fertile regions of Bactria and Sogdiana (*Bokhara* and *Khokhan*). To the west lay Margiana, the land watered by the river Margus (*Moorghab*), where stands the city of *Meru,* famed in Oriental legends.

These lands, north of the Indian Caucasus, are marked as the primitive abode of the Iranian race in their own traditions, preserved in their sacred Books, called the *Zendavesta.* One of the oldest portions of those books enumerates the regions which were fitted for the successive abodes of the race by the blessings of Ahuramazda (the good deity), but blighted by Ahriman (the evil deity). At the head of these stands an unknown country, called *Airyanem vaejo,* the " source " or " native land of the Aryans;" and the next is " Bactria with the lofty banner."

The limits of this work barely permit us to allude to the tradi-

---

[2] These limits are of course stated roughly, as the natural boundaries do not run in straight lines.

tions which make these regions the cradle of the whole Indo-European race; of which the *Yavanas*,[3] or "younger" branch, migrated westward to Europe; while the *Aryas*, or elder branch, remained in Asia, and were divided into the *Iranians*, who spread to the west and south-west over Iran, and the *Indians*, who crossed the Hindoo Koosh into the great valley of the Indus and its tributaries (the *Punjab* and *Scinde*).   The latter separation is ascribed to religious disputes; and the doctrines of the two peoples are found in their religious books, the Old Persian *Zendavesta* and the Hindoo *Vedas*.   Ancient history is only concerned incidentally with the Indians, when their country was invaded by Alexander the Greek.   But the Iranians were the stock from which the Medes and Persians sprang, and their states formed the eastern half of the Medo-Persian Empire.

Whatever may be the truth about these early traditions, we possess in ourselves and our kindred races a living witness to the mode of life, customs, and social institutions of the primitive Aryan race.   That witness is furnished by the words common to all the languages of the Indo-European family.   From the essential identity [4] in the leading terms relating to the life of the shepherd and the herdsman, and in the names of the chief domestic animals —the ox, sheep, goat, swine, horse, dog, goose—we infer that the primitive Aryans were a pastoral people, who possessed and tended these animals.   On similar evidence we conclude that they harnessed horses and oxen to carriages, but that riding on horseback was unknown to them; as, indeed, it was still rare among the Greeks and Trojans of the Homeric age.

They had acquired the art of working in gold, silver, and bronze, but not yet in iron: their arms were furbished; and they made ornaments of metal.   Though a pastoral people, they were not nomad dwellers in tents (like the Turanians); but they had fixed abodes, and built themselves houses.   They tilled the soil, but only by the rudest methods; and it was in the course of their subsequent migrations that they learned, from races more advanced in agriculture, the use of the plough, the culture of various kinds of grain and vegetables, and the production of wine and oil.   Still they raised corn enough to form the staple of their diet, and to dis-

---

[3] In this name some recognise the *Javan* of Gen. x., and the Greek *Ionians*, besides the common root of the words signifying *young* in the various Indo-European languages.

[4] There are certain changes of letters which are found to occur by regular laws, when we compare different cognate languages.   Allowing for these changes, a certain difference is a stronger proof of *essential identity* than a superficial likeness would be.   (The teacher may illustrate this from 'Grimm's Law.')

tinguish them, as they advanced westward and northward, from the aborigines who fed on acorns and berries. They also ate meat, and they seasoned it with salt. They had begun to venture on rivers and lakes in skiffs: but masts and sails were as yet unknown.

Still more important is the evidence borne by language to their social life, morals, and religion. Marriage was contracted with solemn ceremonies and by the sign of joining hands; and polygamy was unknown. The wife was treated with the honour which has been transmitted to modern times by that Teutonic branch of the race which preserved its primitive simplicity longest. The happiness of possessing children, their mutual help and love, and the reward reaped from their industry, shine forth in most expressive terms. A boy is the "giver of joy," the "increase of happiness," the "dispeller of vexation;" a girl is "she that causes rejoicing." The brother is "he who supports," and the sister is "the good, the friendly:" the son is the "protector," and "nourisher" of the family; the daughter is the "keeper of the flocks," the "tender of the cows."

The family constitution formed the basis of that wider union of the *tribe*, the *brotherhood*, the *clan*, which has survived to the present day at the eastern and western extremities of the chain of Aryan nations, among the Persians and our own Celts. The authority of the patriarch or chief rested on a law of nature; but was kept from arbitrary abuse by a council of elders, or heads of families. The chief of these patriarchs was the KING, who was chosen for his wisdom and courage. His first function was to lead in war, for the early Aryans were a martial race. They used weapons, and some defensive armour—the sword and pike, the javelin and arrow, the bow and quiver, the helmet, shield, and breastplate. They fortified towns, though but rudely. The prisoner taken in battle was made a slave. The king was also the chief judge; but there was an appeal to the judgment of God, in those very forms of ordeal by fire and water, which are familiar to us as the customs of the Teutonic races, and among the rest in our own early history.

The primitive religion of the Aryans acknowledged one supreme God, "the living"—"the divine and eternal spirit that pervades the universe;" "by whom the heaven and earth, space and the firmament, have been solidly founded; who spread abroad the light in the atmosphere." He was worshipped with hymns and bloodless sacrifices. The process by which this primitive belief was corrupted into the doctrine of two opposite divine principles of good and evil, known by the famous names of *Ormuzd* and *Ahriman*—and the history of the religious reform ascribed to ZOROASTER,—are beyond the limits of this work. It is, indeed, still a matter of dispute, whether Zoroaster (if the name denote a real person) lived in Bactria before the westward migration of the Iranians, or many centuries later in Media under Darius the son of Hystaspes.

It is, however, probable that, in the great conflict with the Turanians, which is the subject of ancient Aryan tradition, the purer form of religion, or *Mazdeism*, was corrupted by that worship of the powers of nature, and especially of *fire*, which formed the element of the Medo-Persian religion called *Magism*, from the *Magi*, who were the priestly caste of Media. Further and grosser corruptions were borrowed from the idolatry of the Semitic nations, when the Medes and Persians occupied Mesopotamia. The earliest Persian kings were zealous Zoroastrians; but in process of time Magism prevailed throughout both nations.[5]

[5] A fuller account of the early Aryan and Zoroastrian religions, and of the relations between Mazdeism and Magism, will be found in the 'Student's Ancient History of the East,' chap. xviii.

A Mede or Persian, wearing a Collar and Ear-rings (*Persepolis*).

The Rock of Behistun.

CHAPTER XXXII.

RISE OF THE MEDIAN KINGDOM.

IN the westward migrations of the Aryans, two great nations (or confederacies of tribes) advanced to the western borders of the table-land of Iran, and occupied the countries called MEDIA and PERSIA. These countries may be roughly described as formed by the mountain belt, so often mentioned under the name of Zagrus, with a portion of the table-land to the East.

The mountains (as they are now called) of *Kurdistan*, *Luristan*, and *Farsistan*, dividing the table-land from the valley of the Tigris and Euphrates and the Persian Gulf, consist of six or seven

parallel ranges, which all converge at their northern extremity in
the central knot of the highlands of Armenia.   Here they join the
chain now called *Elburz*, which skirts the south-western and
southern margin of the Caspian, and in which the snowy peak of
Demavend (the highest in Asia west of the Himalayas) overlooks
the modern Persian capital of *Teheran*.

A line drawn a little to the east of this peak, nearly along the
meridian of $52\frac{1}{2}°$ of E. longitude, may serve to mark the rather
indefinite limit, at which Media merged on the east into Parthia
and the salt-desert of *Khorassan*.   The two divisions of Media
Atropatene on the north, and Media Magna (*Great Media*) on
the south, corresponded nearly to the modern provinces of *Azerbijan*
and *Irak-Ajemi*.   On the north-east, the strip of coast between
Mount Elburz and the Caspian (the modern *Ghilan* and *Mazanderan*),
nominally included in Media, was held by tribes (the Cadusii, &c.)
which generally maintained their independence; and the eastern
part merged into Hyrcania.

The boundary between Irak-Ajemi and *Luristan* answers to
the division between Media and Persia, as fixed by some of the
ancient geographers; but some place it much lower, at the northern
limit of *Farsistan*,[1] a name which still preserves the name of Persia,
or *Persis* as some called the country to distinguish it from the
empire.   This country, including *Luristan* to the south, is a knot
of noble and healthy highlands; separated from the Persian Gulf
by a narrow alluvial shore, which is almost uninhabitable from
heat; and merging on the east into the desert, where Carmania
(*Kerman*) always appears as a dependency of Persia.   We may
here observe that the modern kingdom of Persia corresponds very
nearly to the western and larger half of the Iranian plateau, including the ancient Media, Susiana, Persis and Carmania, with Parthia
and Hyrcania to the north.   The eastern part of the plateau (which
was included in the *empire* of Persia) forms the countries of
Afghanistan, Seistan, and *Beloochistan*.

The varied surface and climate of Media and Persia fitted them
for the abode of a hardy and warlike, but a civilized and wealthy
people.   The bare rocky regions, sterile downs, and sandy valleys
of the highlands, scantily supplied with water, and lying but a
little beyond the tropic, are exposed to great extremes of heat and
cold, which are still more severe on the margin of the desert.   But
the two spring months of April and May form a delicious exception
to the rigour of the climate and the sterility of the soil.   " In the
worst parts of the region there is a time, after the spring rains,

---

[1] In these geographical names the termination *stan* means " place " or " country."

when Nature puts on a holiday dress, and the country becomes gay and cheerful. The slopes at the base of the rocky ranges are tinged with an emerald green; a richer vegetation springs up over the plains, which are covered with a fine herbage, or with a variety of crops. The orchards are a mass of blossoms; the rose-gardens come into bloom; the cultivated lands are covered with springing crops; the desert itself wears a light livery of green. Every sense is gratified: the nightingale bursts into a full gush of song; the air plays softly upon the cheek, and comes loaded with fragrance." [2]

Some favoured spots, however, enjoy constant fertility and beauty. Such is the basin of the great salt lake *Urumiyeh*, in Azerbijan (a sort of Median Dead Sea), and the valleys of its tributary streams, on one of which stands the royal summer residence of *Tabreez*. Such, too, is the plain of the lower Araxes (*Aras*), on the northern border towards Armenia, where the Persians say that the grass is tall enough to hide an army in its camp. Such are the valleys of the few considerable rivers: the *Kizil-Uzen* (Amardus) in Azerbijan; the *Zenderud*, which waters the valley of the modern capital *Isfahan* (Aspadana),[3] and then redeems a part of the desert by a curious system of artificial irrigation; and the southern Araxes (the *Bendamir*), with its tributary the Cyrus (*Kur*), on which stood the old Persian capitals of Pasargadæ and Persepolis. Fruit and forest trees abound in the sheltered parts of Azerbijan, and on the slopes and valleys of Zagrus; and the upland plains of this range in the south of Media Magna, near *Bagistan*, furnished pasturage to thousands of horses, including the far-famed Nisæan breed. Media gave 3000 horses as an annual tribute to the Persian kings.

Before the Aryan migration from the East, these regions were inhabited by Turanian tribes, who still formed so large a part of the population in historic times, that the trilingual inscriptions of the Persian kings have one column in their dialect.[4] In fact, the Aryan tribes, who are known in history by the collective name of MEDES (*Mada*), seem to have first acquired that name on their settlement in the country.[5] When that event took place, and whether the migration of the Persians was made at the same time, or later, are questions the discussion of which is unsuited to this work. It seems probable that there were successive waves of migration from the East, till, in the 7th century, B.C., the Aryan

---

[2] Rawlinson, 'Five Monarchies,' vol. iii. pp. 7, 8, 46.

[3] That is, "the place of horses," from its vicinity to the great horse-pastures.

[4] This dialect is called the *Medo-Scythic*.

[5] *Mad*, of which *Media* is the Greek form, is said to be a Turanian word, signifying " the land" or "country."

tribes obtained the mastery over the Turanians, and began to threaten Assyria.   The annals of Esar-haddon's campaigns in Media mention the conquest of several independent tribes, the names of whose chieftains are unmistakably Aryan.

There are, indeed, two traditional stories, in the books of Ctesias and Herodotus, which represent Media as an organized and aggressive kingdom long before this time; but sound criticism has now rejected both accounts.   The system of Ctesias,—who makes a series of eight kings before Astyages, with Arbaces, the first destroyer of Nineveh, at their head (about B.C. 876)—is proved to be artificial.   Herodotus gives only four kings inclusive of Astyages. But his story of the consolidation of the Median tribes and the foundation of the monarchy by DEJOCES is a legend conceived in a Greek spirit; and its date falls at the very time when the annals of Sargon begin to boast of conquests in Media.[6]   It is worth notice, however, as the legendary account of that organization of Media, the true history of which is unknown, as well as for the elements of truth which *may* be wrapt up in it.

The Assyrians—says Herodotus—had held the empire of Upper Asia for the space of 520 years, when the Medes set the example of revolt from their authority.   They took up arms for the recovery of their freedom, and fought a battle with the Assyrians, in which they behaved with such gallantry as to shake off the yoke of servitude, and to become a free people.   For a time they enjoyed self-government in their scattered villages; but the lawlessness resulting from the absence of any central authority enabled Dejoces, the son of Phraortes, to bring them again under the kingly yoke. Having thus secured his election to the crown, he gathered the six Median tribes into one political body.   He compelled them to neglect their several towns, and to build him a capital and palace. Here he lived secluded from his subjects' eyes, and surrounded by his body guard, but diligently transacting all public business, and informed by spies of all that passed in his dominions.

The legend includes the whole growth of the despotic monarchy of Media, such as we find it described in Xenophon's picture of the court of Astyages in the 'Cyropædia.'   In the six tribes, which Dejoces is said to have welded together, we recognize the four original Aryan classes of the *priests* (whose place is filled by the Magi), the *warriors*, the *agriculturists*, and the *shepherds* or " those

---

[6] The name of *Dejoces* seems to be the Turanian word *dahak*, "biting," which appears in various forms in the Aryan legends of conflicts with the Turanians, whose emblem is the destroying serpent.   As the title of a chief, it seems to have been adopted by the Aryan conquerors; and it appears again in *Astyages*, that is *Aj-dahak*, "the biting snake."

living under tents." The other two may perhaps represent the conquered Turanians, in the two classes of tillers and mountaineers.

In the description of the capital, Ecbatana (more properly, Agbatana), with its citadel surrounded by seven walls, with battlements rising one above the other, plated and painted with the metals and colours of the seven heavenly bodies—like the Chaldæan temple towers—we see the admixture of Sabæism with the purer Aryan religion. The historical Ecbatana, in Media Magna, which was the Median capital under the whole Medo-Persian empire, is represented by the ruins at *Hamadan*.[7]

After a reign of 53 years, Herodotus goes on to say, Dejoces was succeeded by his son PHRAORTES,[8] who began to extend the Median dominion by conquering the *Persians*, and then attacked the Assyrians of Nineveh; but (as we have related above) he perished in this expedition, after reigning over the Medes 22 years.[9]

His son CYAXARES[10] led back the shattered relics of the army into Media, and there pursued the work, ascribed to him by Herodotus, of converting his warlike hordes into a disciplined army. "He is said to have been far more warlike than his ancestors, and he was the first who arranged his Asiatic subjects in military bands, and organized the several bodies of spearmen, archers, and cavalry, who had been formerly mixed confusedly together" (Herod. i. 103). Such an organization of his forces would naturally involve the full establishment of his royal authority, for the Median kingdom was essentially military. At all events, there is a concurrence of proofs that CYAXARES *was the real founder of the Medo-Persian kingdom*.[11]

We say *Medo-Persian* rather than *Median*, because there is no doubt that the Persians were now closely connected with the

---

[7] The name in the cuneiform inscriptions is *Hagmatána* or *Hagmatán*, which signifies "the place of assemblage." In the description of Herodotus some writers of high authority see another Ecbatana, the capital of the northern province of Media Atropatene (*Azerbijan*), in which they suppose the Aryan Medes to have first settled.

[8] *Fravartish*, which signifies in old Persian "a protector," appears, in the great historical inscription of Darius I. at Behistun, as the name of a rebel, who was for a time recognised as king of Media, and whom the native tradition may have confounded with the father of Cyaxares. Both this Fravartish and another rebel trace their hereditary claim to *Cyaxares*, not to Phraortes or Deioces.

[9] According to the chronology of Herodotus, his death would fall in B.C. 634.

[10] In old Persian '*Uvakhshatara*, "with very beautiful eyes." The name should be pronounced (as, indeed, the great majority of Oriental names) with the accent on the penult, Cyaxáres. So Sardanapálus, Arbáces, Arsáces, &c. The Latin poets are of no authority in such cases: they made the quantity suit their metres.

[11] The view that Phraortes and Cyaxares led a new migration of Aryans from the East deserves mention as an ingenious speculation.

Medes.   There are still earlier traces in the Assyrian inscriptions
of that union, which was already a proverb in their earliest history.
They had the same language and religion, the same customs and
dress; and Herodotus, in mentioning the identity of their equip-
ments, observes that the dress common to both was rather Median
than Persian.   Their common institutions are attested by their own
celebrated formula, " The law of the Medes and Persians, which
altereth not " (Dan. vi. 8, 12, 15).   We shall presently see that the
Persians had their own hereditary line of kings.

Whether the secondary position of the Persians in the alliance
was due to a conquest, such as Herodotus ascribes to Phraortes, or
was simply the result of their numerical inferiority, is a question
hardly to be decided.   All that we really know on this point is
summed up in the prophet Daniel's impersonation of the Medo-
Persian kingdom as a powerful "ram which had *two horns:* and
the two horns were high, but the one was higher than the other,
and *the higher came up last.*   I saw the ram pushing westward, and
northward and southward; so that no beasts might stand before
him, neither was there any that could deliver out of his hand"
(Dan. viii. 3, 4).

In order to follow the course of these conquests, we must now
look " westward " and " northward " to the nations with which the
Medes first came into contact under Cyaxares.

Sculptures on the Rock of Behistun.

Ruins of Sardis.

CHAPTER XXXIII.

RISE OF THE LYDIAN KINGDOM; AND ITS FIRST CONTACT WITH MEDIA.

THE Aryan race has always been distinguished by the love not only of dominion and martial fame, but of the risks of excitement of the game of war. Theirs is the very spirit of conquest for its own sake. The tribes of Media, organized into a military nation, looked down from the margin of their highlands upon the fertile plains that owned the power of Nineveh, at once a prize and a challenge. But, when that power proved still sufficient to hold the passes of Zagrus against their first great assault, other lands lay open in the natural direction of their progress to the West.

The table-land of Iran is linked by the mountain-system of Armenia to the other great plateau which runs out westward in the peninsula of Asia Minor; so that tribes might emigrate, and armies might march to and fro, over these elevated regions, without descending into the valley of the Tigris and Euphrates. The ancient geographers regarded the chain of Taurus, which skirts the southern shore of Asia Minor, as continuous with that of Zagrus; and a similar connection was established between the Indian Caucasus and the range which runs along the north shore of the peninsula.

Even when these ranges—as well as the spurs which fringe the western edge of the central plateau—seem to end in the long promontories that run out into the Ægæan Sea, they are continued in the islands which link them, as by a series of stepping-stones, to the shores of Greece. On the north-west the narrow straits divide Europe from Asia so slightly as to derive a name from the ease with which the pastoral inhabitants ferried over their oxen from shore to shore to seek fresh pasture.[1]

Towards Asia again, besides the continuity of the central highlands, there were passes between the shore and the mountains at both corners of the peninsula. That on the north-east formed an open door for the Cimmerians and Scythians, who successively inhabited the steppes beyond the Euxine. On the south-east the *Gates*[2]—as the passes were expressively called—after letting in the Semitic races from Syria to the rich plains of the southern coast, gave a passage to many an army to and fro, and, above the rest, to the Macedonian conqueror of Persia. By sea, too, there was an easy passage from Syria to Cilicia and Pamphylia, with Cyprus in the angle between; and we have clear evidence of a maritime connection between Egypt and the southern coast of Asia Minor during the climax of the kingdom of the Pharaohs.

The peninsula of Asia Minor lay thus like a bridge, along which the teeming races of the one continent might find a passage to the other; and, when prepared by the civilization brought to them by the same route, might go back to reconquer their primeval seats. By this way the chief portion of the races which peopled the south of Europe entered their new abodes. From the splendid harbours of the western coast, and by the stepping-stones of the Archipelago,

---

[1] Of course the remark applies specifically to the "Thracian Bosporus" (Straits of Constantinople). The *Hellespont* got its name from a mythical story The word *Bosporus* signifies *Ox-ford*, or rather, in this case, *Ox-ferry*. Let the young reader beware of the modern barbarism, *Bosphorus*, which would mean (if anything) "a man strong enough to carry an ox."

[2] This, the ordinary Greek term for a narrow mountain pass, often gained a new force from the practice of defending such passes with walls and gates. Such was the case with the passes now in question, through which lay the route round the Gulf of Issus.

they received the commerce of Asia, with its wealth and civilizing power. And when, by a reflex movement, large bodies of the Greeks settled on those western shores, it was there that they first cultivated, under Asiatic influences, commerce and art, philosophy, and literature.

By a necessary consequence of its position, the population of Asia Minor contained a mixture of all the primitive Asiatic races. To discuss its ethnology, however, lies far beyond our present purpose. It is enough to say that—about the time of the fall of Nineveh—a primitive Turanian people, the *Cappadocians*, held their ground in the central table-land and on the northern coast, to the east of the great boundary formed by the Halys. The western part of the table-land was occupied by the primeval Aryan race of the *Phrygians*, who had till lately formed a powerful kingdom;[3] but along the western half of the northern shore they had partly given way to, and were partly mingled with, the *Thracian* tribes which had recrossed from Europe. The southern shore was peopled by Semitic races, mingled with other waves of Turanian and Aryan populations, the former being perhaps represented by the *Carians*, the latter certainly by the *Lycians*. On the west coast the Greek colonies of the *Æolians* in the north, the *Ionians* in the centre, and the *Dorians* in the south, had returned to the land from which the *Pelasgians* had formerly crossed to Greece, and had planted great and flourishing cities on the shores thus reclaimed for their race.

But these centres of commerce, civility, and freedom were about to succumb to a power which made Asia Minor the seat of an empire rivalling the Medo-Persian. The LYDIANS were probably a Semitic race[4]—perhaps from northern Mesopotamia—who, having passed along the central table-land, displaced the Aryan Mæonians from the rich valley of the Hermus, where *Sardis* became the famous capital of their kingdom. The mythical story of their first two dynasties—the *Atyadæ* and the *Heraclidæ*—and the romantic legend of the transfer of the crown from Candaules, the last of the Heraclids, to the new dynasty of the *Mermnadæ*, may be read at the proper time in the fascinating pages of Herodotus. The true history of the Lydian monarchy begins with GYGES, at about the end of the 7th century B.C.

---

[3] We purposely omit the period of Phrygian supremacy (and still more the Trojan) as being chiefly mythical, and because the historical elements involve doubtful discussions. The existence, however, of a highly civilized Phrygian kingdom is attested not only by tradition, but by its influence on the Asiatic Greeks, and its existing monuments. (See further in the 'Student's Anc. Hist. of the East,' chap. xxii.)

[4] In Gen. x. 22. we have the Semites of Mesopotamia ascending from S. to N.:— "The children of Shem, Elam, and Asshur, and Arphaxad, and *Lud*, and Aram.'

According to the received chronology (which, however, is far from certain), the five kings of this dynasty reigned for 170 years as follows :[5]—

	B.C.	Years.
1. Gyges	716–678	38
2. Ardys	678–629	49
3. Sadyattes	629–617	12
4. Alyattes	617–560	57
5. Crœsus	560–546	14
Duration of the Monarchy		170

The story of these kings is told by Herodotus, in order to shew the origin of that great quarrel between Greece and Asia which was fought out at Marathon and Salamis. Illustrating this theme in the spirit of Greek poetry, rather than of sober history, he adorns the story with legends of the retributive fate that befel the enemies of his nation.

The attacks on the Greek colonies were begun from the first accession of the dynasty. As soon as Gyges became king, he made an inroad on Miletus and Smyrna, and took Colophon; but, the historian adds, he performed no other great deed during his reign of thirty-eight years. In another way these Lydian kings held close relations with the Greeks. They constantly consulted the oracles, both of Greece and Asia, and attested by costly gifts their sense of past and hope of future favours from the deities. Gyges is said to have been the first foreigner, except Midas king of Phrygia, who made offerings to the shrine of Delphi. His rich presents of gold and silver, which were preserved apart as " the Gygean offering," were the reward of a response which confirmed his usurpation. To this, however, the Pythian priestess added, that vengeance for the dethroned Heraclidæ should fall upon the fifth descendant of Gyges. On the East, the relations of Gyges with Assyria seem to be indicated by Asshur-bani-pal's record of the presents he received from " *Gougou*, king of the *Ludim*." [6]

The reign of ARDYS, the son of Gyges, is related by Herodotus in two short sentences: " Ardys took Priene and made war upon Miletus. In his reign the *Cimmerians*, driven from their homes by the nomads of Scythia, entered Asia, and captured Sardis, all but the citadel." [7] Elsewhere he says that " the Cimmerian attack upon Ionia, which was earlier than Crœsus, was not a conquest of

---

[5] The dates are those of Clinton.

[6] According to the Assyrian chronology, this was in B.C. 667 or 666, which brings down the reign of Gyges at least 11 or 12 years later than Clinton's date. The *Chronicle* of Eusebius gives Ardys only 38 years, instead of 49.

[7] Herod. i. 16.

the cities, but only an inroad for plundering."[8] The appearance of this new nation upon the scene derives a double interest from the probability that they were of the great Cymrian race, which spread over western Europe, sacked Rome, invaded northern Greece, and, returning to Asia Minor, effected a settlement under their other name of *Gauls* or *Galatians;* and who still form a large part of the population of our own islands, in one case under the same name, as the *Cumru* or *Cymry* of Wales. To discuss the truth of this view, or the accuracy of Herodotus's story of their invasion of Asia, is beyond the scope of this work.

The land from which they came was the great region of plains and steppes (now a part of southern Russia), surrounding the northern side of the Euxine from the Danube to the Don. Displaced thence by the wandering tribes of *Scythians* from the East —not, as Herodotus says, at a single blow, but wave upon wave—a part pursued their migration westward, and another part crossed the Danube, and joined the Thracian tribes in pouring across the Hellespont and Bosporus upon the rich lands and cities of Asia Minor. Herodotus, indeed, brings them in by the road round the Euxine at the north-eastern corner of the peninsula; but this, if not altogether a mistake, can only apply to one of their successive irruptions. The contemporary poet, Callinus of Ephesus, gives a vivid description of their ruthless cruelties, which are said to have laid waste all the provinces as far as the Taurus and Cilicia. Here the hardy mountaineers repulsed them with terrible slaughter ; and the death of their leader, Lygdamis, was regarded by the Greeks as the vengeance of Artemis for his attack on her temple at Ephesus.

The Cimmerian invasion lasted during the twelve years of SADYATTES, the son of Ardys. But its force must have been spent in the first half of his reign, for he rekindled the flame of war against Miletus, and made incursions into its territory during six years. The war was continued during the first five years of his son ALYATTES, who then granted Miletus an honourable peace. The romantic story of the causes which led to this result can only be properly read in the language of Herodotus. The other attempts of Alyattes upon the Greek cities, with vicissitudes of success and failure, seem to have been interrupted by the enterprise of driving the Cimmerians out of Asia. Their settlement, which remained at Sinope, indicates the direction in which they retired ; and it may have been in pursuing the war against them that Alyattes extended his conquests to the Halys, and was thus brought into collision with the westward progress of Cyaxares.

This is not the place to discuss the difficult question of the

<hr>

[8] Herod. i. 6.

relations of the Median conquests to the west with the Scythian domination in Western Asia; or whether the Lydian war preceded or followed the fall of Nineveh.   This war cannot have been earlier than B.C. 610; [9] and this year has been commonly fixed for the eclipse which broke off the great battle between the Medians and Lydians, "when the night was turned into day as they fought." [10] But the most careful astronomical calculations have left the date of this "Eclipse of Thales"—as it is called from the philosopher who foretold it—still doubtful.   The peace, which was mediated by "Syennesis the Cilician" and "Labynetus the Babylonian," [11] and cemented by the marriage of Aryénis, the daughter of Alyattes, to Astyages, the son of Cyaxares, fixed the river Halys as the boundary between the Median and Lydian empires.

According to the received chronology, Cyaxares died in B.C. 594; but the reign of Alyattes was prolonged almost to the fall of the Median empire under Astyages.   His tomb, which Herodotus calls the one noticeable structure in all Lydia, is still the most interesting monument in the land.

[9] That is, according to the date of B.C. 617, for the accession of Alyattes, whose first five years were occupied in the Milesian war, after which came the expulsion of the Cimmerians.

[10] Herod. i. 103.

[11] We have here a confirmation of the alliance between Media and Babylon, which Herodotus does not mention in his notice of the capture of Nineveh. Some suppose *Labynetus* to be Nabopolassar, others Nebuchadnezzar; and we have seen that Herodotus elsewhere applies the name to Nabonadius. It seems, indeed, to be his form of all the Babylonian royal names beginning with the element *Nabu*. One historian states that Cyaxares sent a Median contingent to aid Nebuchadnezzar in the war against Jehoiakim (B.C. 597).

Coin of Sardis (Greek Period), Reverse.

King seated on his Throne (*Persepolis*).

CHAPTER XXXIV.

ASTYAGES AND CYRUS. THE EMPIRE PASSES FROM MEDIA TO
PERSIA. FROM B.C. 594 TO B.C. 558.

THE settlement of Western Asia, effected by the destruction of
Nineveh, by the result of the war between Lydia and Media, by
the decisive victory of Nebuchadnezzar over Egypt, and later
by the establishment in that kingdom of a dynasty friendly to
Babylon, remained undisturbed till B.C. 560. The three great
monarchies of Western Asia, connected by treaties and inter-

marriages, made war only upon the lesser powers which they claimed as their respective subjects; while the peaceful policy of Amasis, who was also connected by marriage with Babylon, renewed the wealth of Egypt.

This period of repose was broken by one of the greatest revolutionary convulsions which have ever shaken the Eastern world, at the moment when its great conflict with the West was being prepared for by new events in Greece. The usurpation of Pisistratus at Athens took place in the same year as the accession of Crœsus in Lydia (B C. 560); [1] just before the time when Cyrus overthrew the Median kingdom, and established the supremacy of Persia as the head of the Medo-Persian empire (B.C. 558).

ASTYAGES or ASDAHAGES,[2] the son of Cyaxares (B.C. 594–558), lost the empire which his father had won. Its short duration is to be explained by the causes which are often seen at work in the East. The conquest of Cyaxares was purely military; and his successor sat down to enjoy the pomp and luxury of a despotic king. The character of Astyages, and the ceremonial of his court at Ecbatana, have been depicted for us by Herodotus and other writers, and especially by Xenophon.[3] His avowed purpose, of contrasting the luxury of Astyages with the hardy discipline in which Cyrus had been trained, may have coloured some of the details; but the broad outline is confirmed by the general likeness among all these Oriental courts, and by its resemblance to that of Assyria.

The picture has been well drawn by Professor Rawlinson: " The monarch lived secluded, and could only be seen by those who asked and obtained an audience. He was surrounded by guards and eunuchs, the latter of whom held most of the offices round the royal person. The court was magnificent in its apparel, in its banquets, and in the number and organisation of its attendants. The courtiers wore long flowing robes of many different colours, amongst which red and purple predominated, and adorned their necks with chains and collars of gold, and their wrists with bracelets of the same precious metal. Even the horses on which they rode had sometimes golden bits to their bridles. One officer of the court was especially called " the King's Eye;" another had the privilege of introducing strangers to him; a third was his cupbearer, a fourth his messenger. Guards, torch bearers, serving-men, ushers, and sweepers, were among the orders into which the lower sort of attendants were divided. While among the courtiers of the highest rank was a prominent class known as " the king's tablecompanions."

<hr>

[1] That is, according to the ordinary chronology.
[2] His name has been explained above, p. 203, note.   [3] In the 'Cyropædia.'

"The chief pastime in which the court indulged was hunting. Generally this took place in a park or 'paradise' near the capital; but sometimes the king and court went out on a grand hunt into the open country, where lions, leopards, bears, wild boars, wild asses, antelopes, stags, and wild sheep abounded; and, when the beasts had been driven by beaters into a confined space, despatched them with arrows and javelins. Prominent at the court, according to Herodotus, was the priestly caste of the Magi. Held in the highest honour by both king and people, they were in constant attendance, ready to expound omens or dreams, and to give their advice on all matters of state policy. The religious ceremonial was, as a matter of course, under their charge; and it is probable that high state offices were often conferred upon them. Of all classes of the people they were the only one that could feel they had a real influence over the monarch, and might claim to share in his sovereignty."[1]

Astyages himself is described as remarkably handsome, cautious in policy, and of a noble spirit. The legend of his fall, as related by Herodotus, conveys the impression of a self-indulgent king, secure in his despotic power, but wantonly cruel when his suspicion [is] aroused and in avenging disobedience. Herodotus makes his [illegible] the cause of the subjection of the Medes to the Persians; [illegible] He says that Cyrus was encouraged to attack him through [his] luxurious life and the weakness of his rule. Of [his] reign, before the final revolution, we have very [illegible] whose [illegible] clever policy is said to have gained the [illegible] wild and powerful Cadusii on the shores [of the] Caspian.

M[oses] [illegible] the [illegible] historian of Armenia, relates a [illegible] attempt of Astyages to circumvent the king [illegible] sister (Dikranuhr) the Median [illegible]. In [illegible] where [illegible], the [illegible] of Media and [illegible] is carried [illegible] Tigranes, by whom Astyages is put to death, and [illegible] appears the ally of the Armenian. The fact, which [illegible] vanity [illegible] deferred, [illegible] to be that a successful revolt of Armenia [illegible] a punish[illegible] that of Persia. The Armenian historian himself says that Tigranes became the vassal

[1] Rawlinson, 'Five Mon[archies],' vol. iii pp. [illegible] This description will serve also for the Persian court of t[he] [illegible] k[ing]; from which, indeed, the details seem to be drawn.

[2] The kingdom here referred to is th[at] of Eastern Armenia (the true *Ararat*), in the basin of *Lake Van*, with a capital of the same name. The cuneiform inscriptions of the kings contemporary with the Lower Assyrian dynasty are still to be read on the rocks of the Acropolis of Van. It seems that the Armenians had united with the Medes (as subordinate allies) against their old Assyrian enemy.

of Cyrus, and not only embraced the Zoroastrian faith, but zealously propagated it in his kingdom. At all events we find Armenia, from the very beginning of the Persian empire, one of its most faithful provinces, and Zoroastrianism the prevalent religion. The descendants of Tigranes continued to govern Armenia under the Persians without a single revolt; and the last of the dynasty, Vahé the son of Van, fell in defending the cause of Darius Codomannus against Alexander.

The true nature of the revolution, which transferred the supremacy from the Medes to the Persians, is obscured by the legends which glorified the person of its leader Cyrus. Nor, indeed, have we any very clear account of the relation of the Persians to the Medes before the revolution. We have seen that it was a close alliance, based on blood, language, and religion, in which the precedence belonged to Media. But the hardy Persians seem to have preserved, with their simplicity of life, a virtual independence among their highlands; growing in vigour as the Medes gave way to luxury, and equally disposed and prepared to resist the outrages of despotic power.

The Persians were still partially in the nomad state. They were divided into ten tribes, forming three social classes—the aristocracy of warriors, the agriculturists, and the nomads. The noblest of all were the Pasargadæ, whose name (in old Persian, *Parçauvâdâ*) is really that of the ancient capital, and means " the encampment of the Persians." In this tribe there was a royal clan, whose name (*Hakhámanishiya*) and that of their reputed ancestor (*Hakhamanish*),[6] appear in the Greek writers as *Achæmenid* and *Achæmenes*. The common descent of the two lines of Persian kings, who constantly boast this name on their inscriptions, is shown by the appended genealogy, as far as their union in the person of Xerxes.[7]

The great inscription of Darius at Behistun attests that the ancestors of Cyrus the Great were really " *Kings* of the Persians " as his father Cambyses is called by Xenophon. Nay more, a brick found at Senkereh, in Chaldæa, Cyrus styles himself the son of Cambyses, *the powerful king.* The story of the marriage

---

[6] The name signifies " friendly," or " possessing friends." As examples of its appearance in the inscriptions, we may cite those on the tombs of the first and second founders of the empire, " Adam KURUSH, Khsuáyathiya, *Hakhámanishiya*," that is, " I [am] Cyrus, the King, the *Achæmenid*:"—" Adam DARYAVUSH, &c. &c., *Hakhámanishiya*, " I am Darius, &c., the *Achæmenid*;" to which the latter king adds, " a *Persian*, the son of a *Persian*; an *Aryan*, of Aryan descent." Here is one of several original authorities for calling the Persians an Aryan race.

[7] See end of the chapter. The names of the royals shew the kings of the Medo-Persian empire.

of Cambyses to Mandane, the daughter of Astyages, and the con-
sequent position of Cyrus as heir to his grandfather, may be an
invention. Nothing is more usual than for a dynasty, established
by conquest or revolution, to trace a descent from the displaced
family; though there is no improbability in the marriage of the
King of Persia to the daughter of his Median suzerain.[8]

The marvellous legend of the superstitious motive for that marriage, the exposure and preservation of the young Cyrus, his recognition by his grandfather, the cruel vengeance which Astyages
takes upon Harpagus for preserving the boy, whom nevertheless,
lulled into security by the Magi, he brings up at his own court;
and the plot by which Harpagus at once gluts his own revenge,
and leads Cyrus on to seize the crown—all this, which would be
spoilt by telling in any other words than those of Herodotus, must
be dismissed to the realm of poetry, with the legend of Romulus
and Remus. The attempt to *rationalize* either the one or the other
is only (in the happy phrase of Professor Malden) to " spoil a good
poem, without making a good history."

All we know for certain is, that the Persians revolted under
Cyrus, who defeated and dethroned Astyages, after what seems to
have been a sharply contested war.[9] The title, by which one
writer says that Cyrus was saluted by his army on the field of
[illegible]—" King of Media and Persia "—describes the true nature
[illegible] empire which he won. It was not a conquest by a foreign
[illegible] but the transfer of supremacy from one to the other of the
two nations, [illegible] maintained their close union, and the government of [illegible] still shared between Medes and Persians. An
[illegible] administration was at once given in the
[illegible] with which Astyages was treated by the conqueror.[10]

Not only has the rise of Cyrus been adorned by patriotic legends,
[illegible] conspicuous in the higher poetry, which
reveals its true [illegible] in the scheme of divine Providence. As

<hr>

[8] Some of the ancient writers distinctly affirm that Cyrus was in no wa[illegible]
to [illegible].

[9] For the account of this, and for some curious details of the war, given on
uncertain authority by [illegible] of the time of Augustus, as well as a discussion of
the probable motives of [illegible] in the ' Student's Anc. Hist. of the East,'
chap. xxiv. § 15.

[10] It is particularly worthy of note that not only does the name of the Medes keep
precedence in the title of the [illegible]; but it is [illegible] used alone, where the
whole empire is meant. Thus the Hebrew prophet [illegible] the *Medes* as the destroyers of Babylon; Greek writers speak of the [illegible] and brand treacherous
intrigues with Persia as *Medism*; and the Roman poets [illegible] to transfer the
name to the *Parthians*, who had succeeded to a great part of the Persian empire,
including Media itself.

the restorer of the Jews and the rebuilder of the Temple, as the
subduer of the nations and the destroyer of Babylon, prophecy had
long since addressed him *by his very name* (Isa. xliv. 28; xlv. 1–5).
But the significantly repeated phrase, "I have surnamed thee,
though thou hast not known me," should serve to correct the religious
fondness which has thrown a halo of sanctity about the prince
whom Xenophon has adorned with the spirit of the Socratic philosophy.   With all his real greatness, Cyrus was but the best type
of the true Asiatic conqueror and the leader of a rude military
people; to whom it was given, in the happy words of Æschylus, to
fulfil the destiny that "one man should rule over all Asia, nourisher
of flocks, holding the sceptre of government;" or, as a modern
ethnologist would say, to bring the Semitic nations under the new
and invigorating influence of Aryan rule.

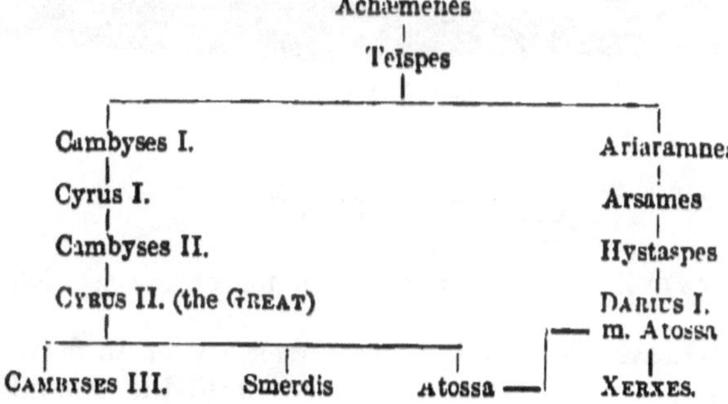

Staircase of Artaxerxes (*Persepolis*)

Tomb of Cyrus.

CHAPTER XXXV.

CRŒSUS AND CYRUS.   FALL OF LYDIA AND BABYLON.   B.C. 560—529.

CYRUS THE GREAT[1] is said by one Greek writer to have been exactly forty years old, when he succeeded to the dominion of Astyages over all the tribes from the Halys to the desert of *Khorassan* (B.C. 558).   Two years before (according to the received chronology), CRŒSUS succeeded his father Alyattes on the throne of Lydia, in the thirty-fifth year of his age (B.C. 560).   So nearly matched, in time and age, were the two new candidates for the empire of Western Asia.

CRŒSUS is distinguished by Herodotus as the prime mover of the great assault of Asia upon Greece.   Treating the partial attacks of former Lydian kings on the Ionian colonies as of little permanent importance, he says of Crœsus: " He was the first of the barbarians, so far as we know, who held relations with the Greeks, forcing some of them to become his tributaries, and entering into alliance with others.   He conquered the Æolians, Ionians, and Dorians of

---

[1] In old Persian *Kurush*, an old Aryan title of doubtful meaning.   The Greeks interpret it as " the Sun."

Asia, and made a treaty with the Lacedæmonians. Up to that time all the Greeks had been free." [2]

Having made successful war, on various pretences, upon all the colonies on the mainland, he began, says Herodotus, to think of building ships, and attacking the islanders. But he was diverted from the project by the ingenious apologue of one of the " Seven Sages of Greece." Bias, or as some said Pittacus, on arriving at Sardis, was asked by the king if there was any news from Greece. " O king," said he, " the islanders are collecting a myriad of horse, with the intention of marching against Sardis and thee." Crœsus took the news in earnest, and exclaimed, " I only wish that the gods would put such a thought into the minds of the islanders, to come on horseback against the sons of the Lydians"—for the Lydians were esteemed at this time the best horse-soldiers in Asia. Upon this the sage suggested that the islanders would be just as eager to catch the Lydians on the sea, and to avenge themselves on the enslavers of their continental brethren. So Crœsus left off building ships, and made a treaty of friendship with the Ionians of the islands.

This story is rather an illustration of the growing influence of Greek ideas on Lydia than an historical fact. A palpable anachronism is involved in that other and very beautiful episode of Solon's preaching to the king, who had shewn him all his wealth, the lesson which is the key-note to Herodotus's tale of Crœsus :— " He who unites the greatest number of advantages, and, retaining them to the day of his death, then dies peaceably—that man alone is entitled to the name of happy. But in every thing it behoves us to mark well the end ; for oftentimes God gives men a gleam of happiness, and then plunges them into ruin." To this fate, incurred in the eyes of the Greek by the king's aggressions upon his countrymen, Crœsus was hurried on through his ambition to measure his strength with Cyrus, and to check the growing power of the Persians before it came to a head.

He had conquered all the nations within (that is, to the west of) the river Halys, except the Lycians and the Cilicians, when he heard that Cyrus had destroyed the empire of Astyages, and that the Persians were becoming more powerful every day.[3] His first object was to add Cappadocia to his dominions, and he claimed to be the avenger of his brother-in-law Astyages. His command of the fertile regions of Asia Minor, the gold-yielding streams of

<hr>

[2] Herod. i. 6.

[3] This statement of Herodotus is the only light we have on the proceedings of Cyrus before the Lydian war, the date of which is not certainly fixed ; nor, indeed, is that of Crœsus's accession.

Lydia, and the commerce of the Ionian states, made the riches of Crœsus a proverb to all antiquity; and these resources might well seem adequate to the enterprise, to which the Delphic oracle had given the divine sanction, though with characteristic ambiguity.

The curious chapter in the history of superstition, which tells how Crœsus first shrewdly tested, and then blindly trusted, the oracle which finally lured him to his fate, should be read in the charming story of Herodotus. Such was the intercourse now carried on among the states of the Levant, that the Lydian messengers were sent, not only to the Milesian oracle in Asia, to those of Bœotia, Phocis, and Epirus, and especially of the Delphians at Pytho, in Northern Greece, but even to that of Ammon in the Lybian desert. The Pythian oracle alone—mindful, doubtless, of former gifts from Lydia, and not grudging to scatter among the envoys the seeds of future golden harvests—was able to tell the grotesque and improbable occupation, which formed the test fixed by Crœsus. Thereupon, with an amusing mixture of credulity and scepticism, he decided that the Delphic was the only real oracular shrine. The offerings, which attested his faith, make the page of Herodotus glitter with gold; and they deserved a better reward than the two-fold assurance, that "if Crœsus attacked the Persians he would destroy a mighty empire," and that "when a mule should be king of Media, the Lydian need not be ashamed to fly like a coward to the pebbles of Hermus." Even so was Macbeth assured of his safety

"Till Birnam wood shall come to Dunsinane."

Confident in the promise of the first response and the impossibility of the second, the fated Lydian resolved to be the first to cross the Halys—thus measuring himself against the "mule" of mixed Persian and Median birth, and bringing destruction on *his own* mighty empire. Before the Lacedæmonian alliance, which he contracted by the advice of the Pythian oracle, Crœsus had made a league with Amasis king of Egypt, which was now strengthened by the accession of "Labynetus," King of Babylon.[4] But he was too eager to give these powerful allies time to send their contingents to his aid. In the remonstrance of a prudent Lydian counsellor, Sandanis, Herodotus draws a picture of the state of the Persians:—

"Thou art about, O king, to make war against men who wear leathern trousers, and have all their other garments of leather; who feed not on what they like, but on what they can get from a soil that is sterile and unkindly; who do not indulge in wine, but

---

[4] Comp. Chapters XIV., XXX. Supposing this Labynetus to be Nabonadius, we have an upward limit of time for the ensuing war, as he came to the throne in B.C. 555.

drink water; who possess no figs, nor anything else that is good to eat. If, then, thou conquerest them, what canst thou get from them, seeing that they have nothing at all? But if they conquer thee, consider how much that is precious thou wilt lose. If they once get a taste of our pleasant things, they will keep such hold of them that we shall never be able to make them loose their grasp. For my part, I am thankful to the gods that they have not put it into the hearts of the Persians to invade Lydia." Though this speech failed to persuade Crœsus, the historian adds that "it was quite true; for before the conquest of Lydia the Persians possessed none of the luxuries or delights of life." [5]

CYRUS, on his part, was equally ready to take the offensive. He had led forth his hardy horsemen from their native hills in the true spirit of a conqueror; and from him may be traced the fixed maxim of Persian policy: "For Asia, with all the various tribes of barbarians that inhabit it, is regarded by the Persians as their own." [6] But the ambition of the conqueror was tempered by the prudence of the consummate general and statesman. Aiming to disturb his enemy at home, he sent heralds to the Ionians, inviting them to revolt from the Lydian king; but they refused compliance. He then collected his army, and marched apparently through Media and Armenia, increasing his numbers at every step by the forces of the nations that lay on his route.

He came face to face with the Lydian army in the district of Pteria, near Sinope, where Crœsûs was ravaging the country. A long and bloody battle, in which both armies fought valiantly, with great slaughter on both sides, was ended by the fall of night. The Lydians, though overmatched in numbers, sustained the reputation, that "in all Asia there was not at that time a braver or more warlike people." [7] Crœsus retreated to Sardis, disbanded his army, and summoned his allies for the spring. But Cyrus pursued with such speed, that he was the first to announce his coming to the Lydian king.

In this emergency Crœsus led out from Sardis his Lydian lancers —then the best cavalry in Asia—to meet the enemy in the valley of the Hermus. Cyrus placed his baggage-camels in front of his line, "because the horse has a natural dread of the camel, and cannot abide either the sight or the smell of that animal." [8] The horses fled; but the Lydians leaped out of their saddles and engaged the Persians on foot. The fight was long, but numbers prevailed, and after great slaughter on both sides the Lydians took shelter behind the walls of Sardis.

[5] Herod. i. 71.   [6] Herod. i. 4.   [7] Herod. i. 79.   [8] Herod. i. 80.

That capital [9]—with its citadel built on a precipitous rock, at a point in the valley of the Hermus where the hills approach each other closely—had been made doubly impregnable by nature and a charm. But, as in all such cases—from the heel of Achilles downwards—the ancient king had left out one point which seemed safe through the steepness of the rock. Here a Persian soldier, who had seen a Lydian descend the cliff to fetch his helmet which had rolled down, and climb up again, made the ascent, followed by his companions. Sardis was surprised and taken; and Crœsus was made prisoner. Leaving the fabulous incidents that ensued to be read in Herodotus, we need only add that Crœsus was received, like Astyages, into the favour of Cyrus; and became a sage adviser to him and his headstrong son.

The subjugation of the Ionian colonies and of Lycia by Harpagus belongs to the history of Greece. Cyrus himself returned to Ecbatana, bent on larger schemes of conquest:—"He wished to make war in person against Babylon, the Bactrians, the Sacæ (Asiatic Scythians), and Egypt." [10]   The interval before his march against Babylon was occupied with the campaigns which are thus summed up by Herodotus:—"While the lower parts of Asia were brought under by Harpagus, Cyrus in person subjected the upper regions, conquering every nation, and not suffering any to escape." These conquests extended as far as Afghanistan on the East, and Sogdiana on the North. The full establishment of the Persian empire may be dated from the fall of Babylon (B.C. 538).

Of the last seven years of Cyrus all we know for certain is that he fell in battle with the Massagetæ, or some other Scythian tribe of Central Asia; where probably the frontier needed constant protection against the Turanians (B.C. 529). The romantic legend of his fate is another of the choice "readings from Herodotus," which lie before the young student. His body was recovered and buried at the old capital, Pasargadæ, where his tomb is identified by the inscription, I AM CYRUS THE KING, THE ACHÆMENIAN. The character of his conquests is thus summed up by Mr. Grote:—"In what we read respecting him, there seems, amidst constant fighting, very little cruelty. His extraordinary activity and conquests admit of no doubt. He left the Persian empire extending from Sogdiana and the rivers Jaxartes and Indus, eastward, to the Hellespont and the Syrian coast, westward; and his successors made no permanent addition to it, except that of Egypt."

<hr>

[9] Its ruins still bear the name of *Sart*.   [10] Herod. i. 153.

Mound of Susa.

CHAPTER XXXVI.

CAMBYSES AND THE MAGIAN USURPER.   FROM JANUARY B.C. 529
TO THE END OF B.C. 522.

The Persian Empire, like the Roman, proved how soon the *personal government*, established and adorned by a great warrior or politician. is apt to pass into a despotism so cruel, as only to be accounted for by the madness which is the revenge of outraged nature on un- bridled self-will.   The type of Caligula and Nero in the ancient world, and of the Czars Paul and Nicholas in the modern, is seen in Cambyses, the eldest son of Cyrus.[1]   Having been appointed by his father to succeed him, he was sent back with Crœsus to Persia before the battle in which Cyrus fell.[2]   His first deeds of lust and cruelty require some account of the royal family.

Cyrus had but one wife, Cassandané, an Achæmenid, who died before her husband, and was greatly lamented by him.   They left

[1] This comparison is admirably worked out in a chapter of the late Mr. Arthur Malkin's most interesting work entitled ‘Historical Parallels;’ published in the ‘Library of Entertaining Knowledge,’ and in ‘Knight's Shilling Volumes.’

[2] His accession is fixed by the *Canon* to Jan. 5, B.C. 529.

two sons and three daughters. The sons were *Kabujiya* and *Bardiya*,[3] names transformed by Greek organs into *Cambyses* and *Smerdis*. Of the daughters, *Atossa* became famous as the wife, first of Cambyses, next of the Magian who personated Smerdis, and lastly of Darius; and as the mother of Xerxes, who is said to have killed her in a fit of passion.

The second daughter, who is not named, was also married by Cambyses, after consulting the royal judges, who gave an opinion which Herodotus slily calls, " at once true and safe." They did not find any law allowing a brother to take his sister to wife; but they found a law that the king of the Persians might do whatever he pleased. So early did courtly judges maintain " the dispensing power." And it pleased Cambyses to put to death this sister-wife, when she covertly reproached him about his brother, whom it had pleased him to murder. Thus Cambyses set the example of the polygamy, incest, and fratricide, which have stained the annals of Persia, perhaps above every other despotic monarchy.[4]

The murder of his brother was doubtless due to jealousy and fear; but we have no trustworthy details. Some writers of inferior authority say that Cyrus bequeathed to his younger son the government of several important provinces. All concur in ascribing to Smerdis noble qualities, the report of which may have been enhanced by hatred for the memory of Cambyses. Herodotus says that Smerdis was the only man of the Persian army in Egypt, who could draw the bow which the Ethiopians had sent as a challenge to Cambyses. Having therefore sent him back to Persia out of envy, Cambyses dreamed that his brother sat upon the royal throne, with his head reaching to the heavens. Thereupon he employed a trusty Persian, named Prexaspes, to go and kill Smerdis at Susa.

The romance of this legend is exposed by the one original testimony, which also proves the crime; for it was committed *before* Cambyses went to Egypt. The great inscription of Darius at

---

[3] *Kabuyija* is interpreted "one who speaks praises," that is, "a bard;" or perhaps " praised by those who speak (of him"). *Bardiya* probably means "elevated" or "glorious." In both names the *m* comes in as the *nasalization of b*, by the same euphonic law which connects "*mors*" (*death*), "*mortal*" and "*ambrosial*" with the Greek "*brotos*" (*mortal*). The *s* in ".*Smerdis*" is due to the same law which gives us "*smelt*" as a form of "*melt*." Æschylus calls the younger brother "*Mardus*," without the *s*. Readers who have learned Greek will recognize the same laws in λαμβάνω and λανθάνω from the roots λαβ and λαθ, and in such double forms as μίκρος and σμίκρος. Further on, we use *Bardes* simply as a convenient form of the Persian *Bardiya*.

[4] The remaining daughter of Cyrus, Artystoné, who was perhaps too young to be married by Cambyses, became the favourite wife of Darius, the son of Hystaspes.

Behistun (of which we have presently to speak more particularly)
tells the story thus :—" A man named Cambyses, son of Cyrus, of
our race, he was here king before me. Of that Cambyses there was
a brother; Bardes (*Bardiya*) was his name, of the same mother, of
the same father, with Cambyses. Afterwards Cambyses slew that
Bardes. When Cambyses had slain Bardes, it was not known to
the people that Bardes had been slain.[5] Afterwards Cambyses
proceeded to Egypt."

His conquest of that land, which has been related in its place,[6]
was effected with the aid of the Phœnician fleet, which was hence-
forward the chief maritime force of Persia. It seems that the submission of Phœnicia, which would be a result of the conquest of
Babylon, was actually made under Cambyses. Herodotus says
that, in the time of Cyrus, "Phœnicia was still independent of
Persia, and the Persians themselves were not a sea-faring people;"[7]
but, under Cambyses "the Phœnicians had *yielded themselves* to
the Persians, and upon them all his sea-service depended."[8] He
also mentions the voluntary submission of Cyprus, which was an
old dependency of Phœnicia, but had lately been conquered by
Amasis. Hence the courtiers of Cambyses said that "he surpassed
his father, for he was lord of all that his father ever ruled, and
further had made himself master of Egypt, *and* the sea."[9] The
flattery added by Crœsus is worth quoting, as an example of the
"fantastic tricks" which even wise men play before the despots
whom they are condemned to serve :—"In my judgment, son of
Cyrus, thou art not equal to thy father, for thou hast not yet such
a son as he left behind in thee."

How much reason Persia had to be thankful that he had not,
may be seen from the samples we have given of his outrages in
Egypt,—the combined fruits of despotic rage, religious fanaticism,
habitual drunkenness, and a natural tendency to epilepsy. It
cannot be doubted that his excesses of tyranny aided the revolution for which his long absence in Egypt gave the opportunity.
But its real cause was deeper, and the Behistun inscription has
enabled us to see this event in its true light. "When Cambyses
had proceeded to Egypt, then *the state became wicked.* Then the
LIE became abounding in the land, both in Persia and Media, and
in the other provinces. Other parts of the inscription shew that
this "lie" was the religious heresy of *Magism*, as opposed to pure
Mazdeism; a heresy which was especially rife in Media, and always
struggling for the upper hand; and to which there is reason to

---

[5] This testimony to the secrecy of the murder is important with reference to the
imposture of the Pseudo-Smerdis.

[6] See Chapter XIV.   [7] Herod. i. 143.   [8] Herod. iii. 19.   [9] Herod. iii. 34.

believe that Cambyses had himself given some encouragement.[10] The ensuing rebellion is not that lie itself, but its later consequence.

For Darius goes on to say in a separate paragraph,—"*Afterwards* there arose a certain man, a Magian (*Magush*), named GOMATES (*Gaumata*). He arose from Pissiachada" (in the east of *Persia*). "He thus lied to the state :—'I am Bardes, the son of Cyrus, the brother of Cambyses.' Then *the whole state became rebellious.* From Cambyses it went over to him, both *Persia and Media*, and *the other provinces.* He seized the empire"—(then the Persian *date* is given). "Afterwards Cambyses, unable to endure (or, *self-wishing to die*) died." It is clear that this was no mere *Median* revolt; and, though the plot originated with the Magi, it was recommended to the whole empire by the popularity of Bardes (Smerdis). Cambyses was virtually dethroned when he received the news in Syria, on his return from Egypt; and his accidental wound from his own dirk, as he mounted his horse to march against the rebels, looks like a figment to gloss over the despairing suicide which seems implied in the inscription.

The popular story of his death is adorned by more than one example of that *irony of fate*, on which the Greeks loved to dwell. His wound was in the thigh, at the very spot where he had stabbed the Apis. Cambyses, acknowledging the retribution, and, feeling that his hour was come, asked the name of the city where the accident had befallen him. "They told him," says Herodotus, "that it was *Ecbatana ;* whereas the oracle at Buto had warned him before that he would end his life at Ecbatana. Now he thought to die in old age at the Median Ecbatana, where all his treasures were ; but the oracle meant forsooth the Ecbatana in Syria.[11] So when he learnt the name of the city, struck with the double calamity inflicted by the Magian and by his wound, he came to his senses ; and understanding the oracle he said :—"Here Cambyses, the son of Cyrus, is doomed to die." [12]

---

[10] Herodotus tells us that Cambyses had left behind in Persia, as comptroller of his household, a *Magian,* named Patizeithes, who, struck with the likeness of his brother to the murdered Smerdis, set him on the throne. This is not at all contradicted by the mention of only one Magian, the usurper himself, in the very brief story of the inscription.

[11] This Syrian Ecbatana has not been identified.

[12] There is a well-known parallel in Shakspere's scene of Henry's IV.'s death in the Jerusalem Chamber at Westminster :—

> " *King.* Doth any name particularly belong
> Unto the lodging where I first did swoon ?
> *Warwick.* 'Tis called *Jerusalem,* my noble lord.
> *King.* Laud be to God ! even there my life must end.

Now,. too, he understood, and first revealed to the chiefs of the Persians who were around him, the true meaning of his dream about the exaltation of Smerdis, and the useless crime he had committed in murdering his brother. In that brother he had lost, he said, his true avenger on the Magians ; but he adjured the Persians, and especially the Achæmenians, not to suffer the kingdom to go out of their line.   But his dying words were ascribed only to hatred of his brother ; the story of whose murder was denied by Prexaspes. This may be all a legend ; but it expresses the favourite Greek doctrine, that a man's destined fate is only more terribly ensured by the sins done by him to prevent it.

Cambyses had reigned seven years and five months ; and the remaining seven months of the year, B.C. 522, belong to the Magian usurper, GOMATES, or, as he is usually called, the PSEUDO-SMERDIS. The completeness with which his power was established is proved by the Behistun Inscription :—" After Gomates the Magian had dispossessed Cambyses both of Persia and Media and the dependent provinces, *he did according to his desire :* he became king. There was not a man, neither Persian, nor Median, nor any of our family. who would dispossess that Gomates the Magian of the crown. *The state feared him exceedingly.*" So Herodotus :—" The Magian now reigned in security." The historian's account of the concealment which was used to help out the impostor's likeness to Smerdis is confirmed in the same manner :—" He slew many people who had known the old Bardes : for that reason he slew them, ' lest they should recognise me, that I am not Bardes, the son of Cyrus.' " [13]

The complete religious revolution which he effected—destroying the temples, and abolishing the religious chaunts and worship—is attested by Darius in declaring his own restoration of what Gomates had taken away.[14] The support of the provinces was purchased by immunities, and Herodotus says, " His subjects, while his reign

> It hath been prophesied to me many years,
> I should not die, but in Jerusalem ;
> Which vainly I supposed the Holy Land :
> But bear me to that chamber ; there I'll lie ;
> In that Jerusalem shall Harry die."
> *K. Henry IV.*, Pt. II. Act IV. Sc. V.

[13] According to Herodotus, the Magian, for some crime, had had his ears cut off ; no unusual punishment in Persia : and it was this that led to his detection by his wife, Phædima, at the instigation of her father, Otanes.

[14] The reversal of the religious policy of his predecessors was extended to Jerusalem ; for the order of the narrative in Ezra (iv. 7–24) seems to require the identification of the usurper with " Artaxerxes," a title which he may very probably have assumed, for it simply means " king," with the extensive prefix " arta." The " Ahasuerus " of Ezra iv. 6 is evidently Cambyses, who seems to have *inclined* to a policy of suspicion towards the Jews, perhaps under Magian influence.

lasted, received great benefits from him, insomuch that, when he died, all the dwellers in Asia mourned his loss exceedingly, *except only the* Persians. For no sooner did he come to the throne, than forthwith he sent round to every nation under his rule, and granted them freedom from war-service and from taxes for the space of three years." The Persians were already exempt from taxation; and though they at first adhered to the usurper, supposing him to be the son of Cyrus, for this very reason their indignation would be the greater when the imposture was discovered.

Meanwhile this Magian revolution must have excited disaffection among the Zoroastrians; and the continued seclusion of the pretended Smerdis must have roused suspicion. Accordingly Herodotus represents a band of seven Persian chiefs (natural leaders of the Zoroastrians) as conspiring against him, detecting his imposture, and slaying him at Susa; after which they conferred the crown on one of themselves, Darius, the son of Hystaspes.[15] That king thus tells the story for himself:—"No one dared to say anything concerning Gomates the Magian till I arrived. Then I prayed to Ormazd : Ormazd brought help to me. On the 10th of the month *Bagayadish*, then it was, *with my faithful men*, I slew that Gomates the Magian, and those who were his chief followers. The fort Sictachotes, in the district of Media called Nisæa, there I slew him. I dispossessed him of the empire. By the grace of Ormazd I became king : Ormazd granted me the sceptre."

Darius here acts in the character which he claims most emphatically through the whole inscription, as the undoubted heir of the royal house of Achæmenes :—"As it was before,. so I arranged it, by the grace of Ormazd, *that the Magian should not supersede our family.*" But he does not claim to have done this deed alone : only the aiders, whom Herodotus represents as conspirators with him on equal terms, are his "faithful men," or loyal followers. Their service is emphatically acknowledged in the concluding paragraph of the inscription :—"Says DARIUS the king: these are the men who alone were there, when I slew Gomates the Magian, who was

---

[15] Once more we leave the legendary story to be read in the graphic pages of Herodotus. Some of his details are probably derived from good authority; and we can judge how well he was informed by his accurate repetition of the conspirators' names. The one exception is so easily accounted for, as to confirm his accuracy. But the *speeches*, as usual, express the historian's own views,—a sort of reflections on the events themselves. He never wished his readers to believe that Persian chiefs would discuss the forms of government which had divided the Greeks. But he seems not to have been aware of the true position of Darius as heir to the throne. Hystaspes (the father of Darius), who was absent in Persia, probably devolved his claims upon his son, as fitter than himself for the enterprize. (See the genealogical table on p. 217.)

called Bardes. *These men alone laboured in my service;*" and then he names them — *Vidafrana, Outana, Gaubaruva, Vidarna, Bagabukhsha, Ardumanish;* all Persians. The six conspirators with Darius, in Herodotus, are *Intaphernes, Otanes, Gobryas, Hydarnes, Megabyzus,* and *Aspathines.*[16] The names are all identical, except the last; and *Aspathines* may well have been present, for he appears as the quiver-bearer of Darius in the inscription on the king's tomb.

Most of these "faithful men" appear in the inscription as the lieutenants of Darius in subsequent wars; and the names of some are conspicuous in the history of the attack on Greece.[17] If, as some have supposed, they, with Darius, were the heads of the seven Persian clans, the privileges, which Herodotus represents the other six as exacting from Darius as the price of his crown, may have been ancient rights, which the Magian has annulled. These were free access to the palace and the intermarriage of the king with their families alone. The still higher privileges said to have been granted to Otanes, as the reward of his abstaining from competition for the crown, may have been bestowed upon him as an Achæmenid in the female line.

Herodotus describes the plot as concocted by Otanes; but he agrees with the inscription, that nothing was actually done till Darius arrived. Even then, in the Greek story, Darius forces the conspirators into action against their will; and he takes the lead in the execution of the plan. He gained entrance to the palace (or rather, as appears from the inscription, to the fort in Media, where the Magian had shut himself up) as the bearer of a despatch from his father, Hystaspes, who was governor of Persia. The six "faithful men" rushed in with him, and two of them were wounded in the desperate conflict which ensued. The Magian usurper was slain by the hand of Darius, his brother having been killed before him; and the victors rushed out to shew the heads of the two impostors to the people.

The deception was forthwith avenged by a general massacre of the Magians, which only ended with the fall of night; and the event was commemorated by the great festival called *Magophonia,*

<hr>

[16] The initial *V* in Persian names is generally replaced in Greek by the aspirate , and thus *Vidarna* becomes *Hydarnes,* just as *Vishtaspa* (the father of Darius) becomes *Hystaspes.* In *Intaphernes* (for *Vidafrana*) the *V* seems to be dropped in consideration of the strengthening of the syllable by the *n*, which comes in before the *t*, like the *m* in *Cambyses* before the *b.* So *Bagabukhsha* becomes *Megabyzus,* just as *Bardiya* becomes *Mardus* and *Smerdis.*

[17] Besides Megabyzus, for example, Gobryas, who is called in the inscription the the son of Mardonius (*Marduniya*), was the father of the celebrated Mardonius

when no Magian might stir abroad during the whole day, on pain of death. According to "the law of the Medes and Persians, which changeth not," this festival was observed as the strictest of the whole year, even when the Magi became the priest-caste of the Persians. The massacre of the Magians illustrates, and is illustrated by, Haman's intended massacre of the Jews, and that which they inflicted on their assailants instead (Esther, cc. iii., viii., ix.).

Ordinary Persian Costume.

Persian King hunting the Lion.   (From Signet-Cylinder of Darius Hystaspis.)

CHAPTER XXXVII.

CLIMAX OF THE PERSIAN EMPIRE.   DARIUS THE SON OF HYSTASPES.
B.C. 521 TO B.C. 486 INCLUSIVE.

DARIUS I.,[1] the son of Hystaspes, is rightly regarded as the second founder of the Persian Empire. He was scarcely twenty years of age when Cyrus is said to have seen him, in a dream, with wings upon his shoulders, overshadowing Asia with the one wing and Europe with the other (B.C. 530). He would therefore be 28 at his accession, which is dated on the first day of B.C. 521, and 64 when he died, on the 23rd of December, B.C. 486, after a reign of 36 years.

In the epitaph upon his tomb he describes himself as "Darius, the Great King, the King of Kings; the king of all inhabited countries; the king of this great earth, far and near; the son of Hystaspes, an Achæmenian; a Persian, the son of a Persian; an Aryan, of Aryan descent." Throughout the Behistun inscription, he represents himself as the champion of the Achæmenid house against Gomates and all other rebels. After naming his ancestors up to Achæmenes,[2] he adds, "From antiquity our family have been kings. . . . Nine of us have been kings in a double line." He

---

[1] In old Persian the name is *Daryavush* (Heb. *Daryavesh*), which is interpreted "holder" or "restrainer." His father's name, *Vishtaspa*, means "possessor of horses."   [2] See the table on p. 217.

united his own line with the elder branch by marrying both the surviving daughters of Cyrus, and also the daughter of Smerdis; and with the younger branch by marrying the daughter of Otanes. He had previously married a daughter of Gobryas, and he also married the daughter of his brother Arsames.

The events of his first five years are recorded by the king himself in the great inscription already referred to, and of which it is time to give some account. Near the south-western frontier of Media, on the high road from Babylon to Ecbatana, there is a precipitous rock about 1700 feet in height. Standing out from the chain of Zagrus, it overlooks a plain, watered by a fountain, where the Persian Kings had a garden or "paradise," with a palace and a city. The old Persian name of *Bagistan* is retained in the present *Behistun*, *Bisitun*, or *Bostan*.[3] The spot, which appears to have been a primeval sanctuary, was famous in antiquity, from the legend of Semiramis to the visit of Alexander; and it was again a royal residence under the Sassanidæ. The face of the cliff is carved with sculptures and inscriptions of four different ages: the first is of unknown antiquity (perhaps Assyrian and the same which the ancients ascribed to Semiramis). The second is the great record of Darius. The third celebrates the victory of a Parthian king over his rival (probably in the time of the emperor Claudius). The fourth is a comparatively modern inscription in Arabic, of merely local interest. No spot affords a better example of "words graven with an iron pen and lead in the rock for ever" (Job. xix. 24).

The trilingual inscription of Darius is carved at the height of 300 feet above the plain; and it was with no small difficulty that Sir Henry Rawlinson obtained the copy, his translation of which formed the decisive epoch of cuneiform interpretation (A.D. 1846). It is in the three languages, in which the Persian kings were wont to issue their edicts to their Aryan, Semitic, and Turanian subjects, —the Persian, Babylonian, and "Median" or Scythic.[4] Four such threefold columns contain the complete record of the first five years of Darius; the fifth, which is very imperfect, is evidently supplemental, but added very shortly after the other four. The date of the inscription is assigned (from its own notices of time) to the sixth year of Darius (B.C. 516).

The events recorded are the overthrow of the Magian usurper; the restoration of the Zoroastrian worship; and the suppression of

<hr>

[3] The classical writers call the town *Bagistana* or *Bastana*, and the hill *Bagistanus Mons.* It is said to have been sacred to Jove, and the name probably means "the place of God" (*Baga*). See Vignettes on pp. 200 and 205.

[4] The rock itself stands near the confines of Persia, Babylonia, and Media (the chief seat of the old Turanian population).

a series of rebellions, which prove that Darius had to reconquer the whole empire. He expressly says that much had been done by him besides, that was not recorded in this tablet; and he sums up what he has recorded, in the conquest and capture of nine "kings," the leaders of rebellions, and the winning of nineteen battles. All the battles are of course victories; but a critical eye can detect reverses, which prove how arduous the struggle was. The campaigns of Darius in person are distinguished from those of his generals, who receive due honour by the mention of their names. But their exploits are appropriated by the king, with that curious mixture of the third and first persons, which we have noticed in the monuments of Assyria.[5]

All the central provinces constituting the original empire, from the mountains of Armenia to the head of the Persian Gulf, as well as several of those of the Iranian table-land, had to be reconquered. The only important provinces not thus named are Lydia and Egypt; and even their satraps (as we learn from Herodotus) seized the opportunity of these troubles to assume an insolent air of independence, which only stopped short of rebellion through the swift vengeance inflicted on them by Darius. His treatment of the defeated kings sternly illustrates the profession—"He who has laboured for my family, him well cherished I have cherished: he who has been hostile to me, him well destroyed I have destroyed."[6] The rebel kings, except one killed by his own followers, were put to death when taken, three at least by crucifixion; and two of these were first mutilated of nose, ears, and tongue, and chained at the palace-gates of Darius.

The object of this exposure was probably to prevent the future personation of the insurgents, both of whom professed to represent the Median royal line, calling themselves "of the race of Cyaxares." For both the Medes and Persians were disposed to rise at the call of pretenders to the old royal blood; and a revolt of Persia was led by another Pseudo-Smerdis, who was taken and crucified. That the Magian religion, too, was one source of these rebellions, may be inferred from the king's reiteration of what he had done to suppress "lying," and his adjuration of his successors to destroy it everywhere. Throughout the inscription he appears as the champion of Zoroastrianism, quite as much as of the Achæmenids, and the

---

[5] For example, when the satrap Vibanus defeats the Arachosian rebel, we read. "Then *he* took him, &c. Then the province submitted to *me*. This is what was done *by me* in Arachotia." In fact, the style is appropriate to a sovereign; and Queen Victoria might say: "Lord Clyde quelled the mutiny. Then the provinces submitted to me. This is what was done by me in India."

[6] Observe the form, which biblical critics call a "Hebraism."

devoted servant of Ormazd. "By the grace of Ormazd," he says, "I am king;" and all his victories are gained "by the grace of Ormazd." The record concludes with a prayer to Ormazd for protection to himself, his house, and his kingdom, and with the solemn charge to his subjects:—"Oh, people! the law of Ormazd, that having returned to you, let it not perish. Beware, lest ye abandon the true doctrine!"

Herodotus only mentions two of these rebellions, the Babylonian and the Median; with which, indeed, we find most of the others to have had some connection. The simultaneous revolts of Babylonia and Susiana were movements of national independence, taking advantage of the dynastic troubles in Persia. The leaders of both claimed to represent the old royal lines.[7] "During all the time," says Herodotus, "that the Magus was king, and while the seven were conspiring, the Babylonians had profited by the troubles, and made themselves ready against a siege." It is uncertain whether his details (some of them highly romantic) of the twenty months' siege and of the treacherous capture of the city, refer to this occasion, or to the later revolt recorded in the inscription. The crucifixion of the pretender and his chief adherents on the latter occasion agrees with the crucifixion of 3000 citizens recorded by Herodotus; and that the first siege, which was conducted by Darius in person, lasted a long time, is clear from the consequences it involved elsewhere.

"While I was at Babylon," says Darius, "these are the countries which revolted against me: Persia, Susiana, Media, Assyria. Armenia, Parthia, Margiana, Sattagydia, Sacia"—pretty well the whole empire east of the Euphrates. Assyria and Armenia seem to have joined the revolt of Media, in favour of Phraortes (*Fravartish*), who assumed the name of "Xathrites (perhaps *emperor*) of the race of Cyaxares." He was at once accepted as king, not only by Media, but by the adjoining provinces of Iran, especially Parthia and Hyrcania.

While Hystaspes, the king's father, held his ground in these provinces, two of Darius's lieutenants, sent to Assyria and Armenia, fought no less than five great battles. Of course they were victories! but of what sort, we may judge from the result : both the generals "waited for (Darius's) arrival in Media." At length the king defeated Phraortes in a great battle, by which he recovered Ecbatana. The Median fled with his horsemen to Rhages (a famous city at the foot of *Mt. Elburz*), where he was taken by a pursuing

<hr>

[7] Both in this and the subsequent revolt of Babylon, the pretender called himself "Nebuchadrezzar (*Nabukudrachara*) the son of Nabonidus." The Susianian rebel was put to death by his own followers on the approach of Darius.

force, brought back to Ecbatana, and there mutilated, exposed, and crucified, as we have told above[8] (Probably b.c. 518). We need not dwell on the remaining revolts noticed in this invaluable document.

When Darius carved this record on the monumental rock of Behistun, he had re-established his authority over the 23 provinces which he enumerates as given to him by Ormazd. But the great and distant satrapies of Lydia and Egypt were on the verge of revolt, through the air of arrogant independence assumed by their governors. Orœtes, who ruled at Sardis, had dared, during the last illness of Cambyses, to put to death his master's ally Polycrates of Samos.[9] He not only abstained from aiding Darius against the Magian, but he took advantage of " the troubles of the season " (says Herodotus) to slay his private enemy, Mitrobates, and to add his satrapy of Phrygia to those of Lydia and Ionia. He kept up a body-guard of 1000 Persians ; and, when Darius sent him a mandate of recal, he caused the courier to be waylaid on his return, and neither man nor horse was heard of again.

Not wishing, in the unsettled state of the empire, to make war on so powerful a vassal, Darius appealed to the chief men of the Persians to accomplish the affair by skill, without force or tumult. One, chosen by lot from among thirty who offered themselves, set out from Sardis with a budget of despatches sealed with the king's signet. Delivering them one by one to the royal secretary in the satrap's full court, he first tested the temper of the guards by the reverence they showed for the king's letters. Then he handed the two decisive mandates to the secretary, who read—" Persians, king Darius forbids you to guard Orœtes :" and the soldiers laid down their spears :—" King Darius commands the Persians who are in Sardis to kill Orœtes :" and the guards drew their swords and slew him on the spot.

The punishment of Aryandes, the satrap of Egypt, with death, for daring to issue a silver coinage of his own in imitation of the king's gold, is referred by Herodotus to a later period. But we must not omit one of the earliest and most important acts of Darius in the south-western part of his empire. In his second year he issued an edict for the resumption of the building of the temple at Jerusalem, which the Magian had interrupted (b.c. 520).

---

[8] Rhages (in Persian *Rhaga*) was one of the oldest Aryan settlements in Media. It occupies a prominent place in the apocryphal books of Tobit and Judith. The statement in Judith i. 15 is thought to refer to the event now in question, though the *names* are strangely altered.

[9] The romantic story of Polycrates, and of his vain offering to envious fortune belongs to Greek history.

Besides its sound policy, this act may be viewed as a part of the restoration of the religious institutions annulled by the usurper; and the conduct both of Cyrus and Darius seems to shew the sympathy of those zealous Zoroastrians for the pure monotheism of the Jews. At the opposite extremity of the empire, Darius extended his power over the valley of the Indus, after the river had been explored for him by Scylax, a Greek of Caryanda in Caria, who reached the head of the Red Sea in a voyage of thirty months. The part of India,[10] thus added to the empire, including the *Punjab* and *Scinde*, yielded a tribute exceeding that of any other province,[11] and added a body of brave soldiers to the army. These troops from the farthest East appeared in the army of Xerxes in their cotton dresses, with their bows of cane and arrows of cane tipped with iron, and so met the Greeks on the field of Platæa.

The great conflict, which was decided on that field in his son's reign, was contemplated by Darius, as it seems, not long after he had restored and consolidated his Asiatic empire; but he postponed it to another expedition. Conquest, in some direction, was the spirit with which Cyrus had imbued the empire; and Darius justly feared that quiet might breed new revolts. Herodotus says that he was urged to the conquest of Greece by his queen Atossa, at the instigation of the Greek physician, Democedes;[12] while he himself was minded to construct a bridge which should join Asia to Europe, and so to carry war into Scythia. It seems to have been according to an Oriental idea of right, and not as a mere pretext, that he claimed to punish the Scythians for their invasion of Media in the time of Cyaxares.

The name of SCYTHIANS, or, as the Persians called them SACIANS (*Saka*) described, in general, the wild tribes of pastoral horsemen (*nomads*), with " houses on wheeled carts "—as Æschylus says— who dwelt beyond the northern frontier of the empire. They belonged, for the most part, if not wholly, to the great Turanian or Mongol race; but this is not the place to discuss their ethnology, or whether the *Sacæ* on the northern confines of Iran were the same race as the Scyths against whom Darius now marched. The latter inhabited the plains and steppes to the north of the Euxine (*Black Sea*) and the Palus Mæotis (*Sea of Azov*), whence they had displaced the Cimmerians. The Greeks knew much of them through commercial settlements established on those coasts; and Herodotus

<hr>

[10] It was then the only part called *India* (*Sind*), from its river.

[11] This tribute was 360 talents of gold-dust.

[12] All the steps that led to the invasion of Greece, as well as the whole story of the wars between Greece and Persia, are referred to the history of Greece.

takes this occasion to give a very interesting account of their tribes and customs.

It was probably about B.C. 508, that Darius, having collected a fleet of about 600 ships from the Greeks of Asia, and an army of 700,000 or 800,000 men from all the nations of his empire, crossed the Hellespont by a bridge of boats. On his march to the Danube, he conquered the Thracians within, and the Getæ beyond, Mt. Hæmus (the *Great Balkan*). The Danube was crossed by a bridge formed of the ships of the Ionians, just about the point where its mouths divide.

The Scythians retreated before Darius, avoiding a pitched battle, and using every stratagem to detain the Persians in the country till they should perish of famine. When the army seemed inextricably involved, a herald arrived with strange presents to Darius from the Scythian princes—a bird, a mouse, a frog, and five arrows. The king saw in this a surrender, signified by the symbols of earth, water, the means of motion, and the weapons of war. But Gobryas, the former conspirator, gave the true interpretation :—" Unless, Persians, ye can turn into birds, and fly up into the sky, or make yourselves frogs, and take refuge in the fens, ye will never make escape from this land, but die pierced by our arrows."

Darius saw that it was full time to try the surer means of escape supplied by his own military genius. He retreated in the night, leaving his sick behind, with the camp-fires lighted and the asses tethered, to make the enemy believe that he was still in their front. The pursuing Scythians missed his line of march, and came first to the place where the Ionian ships bridged the Danube. Failing to persuade the Greek generals to break by the same act both the bridge and the yoke of Darius, they marched back to encounter the Persian army. But their own previous destruction of the wells forced them into a different route; and Darius got safe, though with difficulty, to the Danube. It was dark night when the army reached the bank, and found no bridge; for the Ionians had withdrawn the nearest ships, at once to prevent an attack from the Scythians and to make them believe that the bridge was broken. But a certain Egyptian, who had a louder voice than any man in the world, shouted across the gap to Histiæus, the Milesian general. His call was heard: the bridge was restored; and the army passed to the southern bank.

The Hellespont was crossed by means of the fleet with which the strait had been guarded by Megabazus (or Megabyzus); and the second opportunity was barred against a rising of the Greek colonies. Darius knew how to discern between the policy of Histiæus and the loyalty of Megabazus. Being once asked, as he broke a pomegranate, "what he would like to have in as great plenty as the seeds of the pomegranate?" he answered, "Had I as many men like Megabazus as there are seeds here, it would please me better than to be lord of all Greece." Megabazus, left in Europe with 80,000 troops to complete the conquest of Thrace, effected also the reduction of Macedonia to a vassal kingdom; and he rejoined Darius at Sardis (B.C. 506). The king returned to Susa, which was now the chief capital of his empire, to gloss over his failure by adding to the list of his subjects on his tomb, "the Scythians beyond the sea."

How his repose was broken by the Ionian Revolt, in the first year of the 5th century B.C.—the epoch of the great struggle which transferred the dominion of the world from the despotism of the East to the free spirit of the West—is written in the pages of Greek history. From the repulse of the army of the first Darius, on the plain where

> "The mountains look on Marathon,
> And Marathon looks on the sea,"

to the day when the victor of Issus and Arbela threw his cloak in pity over the corpse of Darius Codomannus, the interest of Persian history centres in her relations towards Greece. The "Persian Wars" mark the epoch when Oriental civilization had prepared the harvest to be reaped by European liberty; and the great events of general history, even when acted in the East, are henceforth to be looked at from the West.

In fact, though the Persian Empire survived the battle of Marathon for 160 years, and even dictated terms of peace to the rival Hellenic republics, the collision with Greece gave it its death-blow from the very hand which had founded and organized it anew. After devoting three years to collecting all the resources of his empire, in order to avenge in person the disaster of his generals at Marathon, Darius found his enterprise interrupted by the revolt of Egypt (B.C. 487); and he died at the end of the following year, having, as required by the Persian law, appointed his son Xerxes to succeed him (Dec. 23, B.C. 486). He was buried in a splendid tomb near Persepolis (at *Naksh-i-Rustam*), the frontispiece of which is engraved with a cuneiform inscription only second in importance to that of *Behistun*.[13] Of his organization of the Persian Empire, according to satrapies, we shall speak at the close of the next chapter.

[13] See the vignette in the 'Smaller Scripture History,' chap. xii.

Ruins of a Massive Gateway (*Istakr*).

CHAPTER XXXVIII.

THE DECLINE AND FALL OF THE PERSIAN EMPIRE. XERXES I. TO DARIUS III. FROM B.C. 486 TO B.C. 330.

XERXES I. (B.C. 486–465)[1] was the son of Darius and Atossa, the daughter of Cyrus, and on this account, probably, he was preferred to his elder brother Artabazanes, who was the son of the daughter of Gobryas. His age was now not more than 35, and he possessed in a high degree the noble personal beauty for which the Achæmenids were famous. Having reconquered Egypt in his first year, he was led on, against his wish, by the persuasions of Mardonius and of the exiled Athenian Pisistratids, to the fatal enterprise which ended at Salamis, Platæa, and Mycale. Historians differ as to whether it was before or after his return from Greece, that Xerxes, by his acts of impiety, provoked a new revolt of

---

[1] In old Persian *Khshayárshá*, and in Hebrew *Achashverosh* or *Ahasuerus* (in the book of Esther). The first element, *Khshaya*, means "king" or "royal;" but the second is doubtful; some making it "venerable," others "eye." Thus the name means either "the venerable (or majestic) King," or the "King Seer" or "Ruling Eye." We shall see presently that *Arta-xerxes* is not formed from *Xerxes*.

Babylon, which was put down by Megabyzus, the son of Zopyrus, when the temple of Belus and other shrines were plundered of their most sacred objects.

The disastrous issue of the attempt against Greece stript Persia of her European provinces, and drained off the strength of all the rest. While the tide of war rolled back to the shores of Asia Minor, Xerxes retired to his seraglio; and the Book of Esther furnishes an interesting picture of the domestic and political intrigues of his court at Susa. The Jewish queen must not be confounded with Amestris, the chief wife of Xerxes, whose savage and jealous temper caused horrible scenes of cruelty. In fact, from this time to the fall of the empire, the history of the Persian court forms one series of intrigues and conspiracies, executions and assassinations, in which the kings were often the victims. Xerxes was murdered in his bed-chamber by Artabanus, the chief of his guard, and the eunuch Aspamitres, his chamberlain (B.C. 465). He left the empire exhausted and depopulated. Both conspirators were put to death by the late king's third son, Artaxerxes, at the end of seven months, during which ARTABANUS appears to have reigned in his name.

ARTAXERXES I.,[2] surnamed by the Greeks "the *Long-handed*" (in Latin LONGIMANUS), had the long reign of forty years (Dec. 7th, B.C. 465 to Dec. 17th, B.C. 425). He had murdered his eldest brother Darius, at the instigation of Artabanus. The second brother, Hystaspes, raised his satrapy of Bactria in support of his claim to the throne; but he was defeated by Artaxerxes. In this reign the first series of the wars between Greece and Persia was brought to an end, and the Greek colonies recovered their independence, just fifty years after the Ionian revolt (B.C. 449).

The great rebellion of Egypt under Inarus and Amyrtæus, which has been related in its place,[3] led to another most formidable revolt in Syria. Megabyzus, the satrap of that province, and the conqueror of Egypt, took up arms to avenge the breach of his promise of life to Inarus. His successful resistance, and his final reconciliation to Artaxerxes on easy terms, furnished other satraps with a dangerous-precedent, which his son Zopyrus attempted to follow in Lycia and Caria towards the close of this reign; but the rebellion was frustrated by the firm loyalty of the Caunians.

Artaxerxes is memorable in Jewish history as the king who gave EZRA and NEHEMIAH their commissions (B.C. 458 and 444.)

---

[2] The Persian name *Artakhshatra* is *Khshatra*, "king" or "warrior," with the intensive prefix *Arta*. The king's by-name is derived from the circumstance that his right hand was longer than the left.

[3] Chapter XIV.

The intrigues of the harem, which were ever tending to the destruction of the royal house, broke out in full force on the death of Artaxerxes Longimanus.   The only legitimate heir among his eighteen sons, XERXES II., was murdered in his drunkenness, after a reign of only forty-five days, by his half-brother SOGDIANUS or Secydianus.   Another half-brother, *Ochus*, the satrap of Hyrcania, declared war against the usurper, with the support of the satraps of Egypt and Armenia.   Sogdianus surrendered and was put to death, after a reign of six months and a half.

DARIUS II. (surnamed by the Greeks NOTHUS) was the name under which Ochus reigned (B.C. 424-405).   His wife *Parysatis* was the daughter of Xerxes I.; and many of our young readers will recognise the sentence, "Darius and Parysatis had two sons, the elder named *Artaxerxes* and the younger *Cyrus*."   Till his accession, Artaxerxes bore his own name of *Arsaces*, which was afterwards rendered famous by the great line of Parthian kings.   He was born before, but Cyrus after, Darius came to the throne; and herein lay the germ of a disputed succession.   The childhood of Cyrus, however, postponed the question till the last illness of Darius.

Meanwhile the king gave himself up to the influence of his eunuchs and of his wife, who surpassed her mother Amestris in wickedness and cruelty.   His reign was marked by one continued series of rebellions, which pushed on the empire to its fate; but the greatest blow was the complete loss of Egypt, which regained her independence and maintained it for another half century.[4]   Amidst these troubles Darius died, having for once resisted the desire of Parysatis, that he would confer the succession on his younger son, whom he had made satrap of Lydia, Phrygia, and Cappadocia, and commander of the western coast of Asia Minor.

The elder son succeeded to the throne by the name of ARTA-XERXES II., and held it for the long period of forty-six years (B.C. 405-359).   He was surnamed, in Greek, MNEMON, from his retentive memory.   How his reign was almost cut short at its beginning by the rebellion of Cyrus is related in Greek history, of which the part played by Xenophon and the "Ten Thousand" makes the campaign an essential chapter.   To that history also belong the transactions of the satraps of Asia Minor (especially the crafty Tissaphernes) with the Greek states, during this reign and the preceding, the brilliant campaigns of Agesilaus, and the sacrifice of the Asiatic Greeks by the disgraceful "Peace of Antalcidas" (B.C. 387).[5]

The proud position in which Artaxerxes thus appeared, as the arbiter of Greece, threw a false lustre over his utter weakness wherever his authority was withstood.   Evagoras, the Greek tyrant

---

of Salamis in Cyprus, in alliance with the kings of Egypt and Caria, maintained a powerful fleet and took Tyre. When he was at last defeated and shut up in Salamis by the Persian fleet, and compelled to surrender after a six years' siege, he obtained a confirmation in his government as a tributary king (B.C. 380 or 379). A mighty effort to recover Egypt miscarried through the delays of the Persian general, and a general rising of the satraps and native princes of Asia Minor and Phœnicia could only be frustrated by the bribery of the satrap of Phrygia.

To this confusion in the empire were added domestic horrors, which took their rise from the savage temper of Parysatis, and continued long after her death. We need not relate the complicated intrigues, treasons, executions, and murders in the royal family. At length the assassination of the king's favourite son, Arsames, killed Artaxerxes himself with grief at the age of ninety-four (B.C. 359). His character is drawn as mild, affable, and kind; but his weakness hastened the dissolution of the empire, which was only postponed by the abilities of his son, of whom Plutarch says that "he surpassed all the other Persian kings in cruelty and blood-thirstiness." [6]

Ochus,[7] the son of Artaxerxes and his first and favourite wife Statira, having obtained his inheritance by a series of ruthless murders, confirmed it by the massacre of all the royal princes within his reach. He reigned with vigour for twenty-one years (B.C. 359–338); but much of his success is ascribed to his able and unscrupulous minister, the eunuch Bagoas, and to Mentor, the commander of his Greek mercenaries.

This Mentor and his brother Memnon were Rhodians, whose sister was the wife of Artabazus, the satrap of Western Asia Minor. With their aid, and the support first of the Athenians and afterwards of the Thebans, Artabazus revolted against Ochus, and long resisted all the force of the neighbouring satraps. At length Artabazus and Memnon fled to Philip king of Macedonia, and Mentor found a new field for his hostility to Persia in the service of Nectanebo II. the last king of Egypt.

It was by means of the Greek mercenaries that the first attack of Ochus upon Egypt was repulsed. Upon this success Phœnicia and Cyprus revolted, and Nectanebo sent Mentor with 4000 Greek mercenaries to the aid of Sidon. Cyprus was reduced by the king of Caria, with the aid of Greek mercenaries under Phocion; but

[6] In Plutarch's ' Lives' there is a biography of Artaxerxes Mnemon.

[7] *Ochus*, which we have already met with as the proper name of Darius Nothus, is variously interpreted as *good tempered* and *rich*. This Ochus is less often called by his assumed name of ARTAXERXES III.

Mentor and the king of Sidon, Tennes, defeated the satraps of
Syria and Cilicia. When, however, Ochus marched against Sidon.
with an army of 300,000 foot and 30,000 horse, the king turned
traitor to his people, without saving his own life. The Sidonians.
after a foretaste of the cruelty of Ochus, in his butchery of some
hundreds of the citizens whom Tennes had betrayed into the
Persian's hands, chose a voluntary death in the conflagration of
their city. Its ruins were sold to a company of adventurers, who
hoped to find quantities of gold and silver in the ashes; but Ochus
gained a greater treasure in the transfer of Mentor's services to
Persia. As joint commander with Bagoas, he effected that reconquest of Egypt, which is characterized by Mr. Grote as " one of the
most impressive events of the age " (B.C. 346).[8]

Still more impressive events were preparing from the growing
power of Philip of Macedon; nor was Persia insensible to the
danger. Ochus, or his able ministers, Bagoas and Mentor.
despatched letters of warning to the satraps of Western Asia Minor;
and a Persian force seems to have been sent into Thrace to aid its
king against Philip. But any idea of combined action between
Greece and Persia against the common enemy was frustrated by
the *Battle of Chæronea*, which was fought in Greece just after
Ochus had been poisoned by Bagoas at Susa (B.C. 338).

The minister, who had been urged to this crime by the king's
unbridled cruelty, and doubtless by fear for his own safety, murdered also the other sons of Ochus, excepting the youngest, ARSES,
whom he set upon the throne. But, as the young king began to
feel his power, he was heard to utter threats against the exter-
minator of his father's house; and Bagoas murdered him, with
his infant children, in the third year of his reign (B.C. 336).

The vengeance due to so many crimes was already on the way,
and was hastened by another murder, which seemed at first likely
to postpone it. Philip, appointed after the battle of Chæronea
general of all the Greeks for the war with Persia, had completed
his preparations, and had sent over a body of troops under Parmenion
to rouse the Asiatic Greeks, when he was assassinated at his
daughter's wedding festival at Ægæ, shortly after the death of
Arses (July, B.C. 336).

Meanwhile Bagoas had raised to the throne his friend Codomannus, who assumed the name of Darius, and is known in history
as DARIUS III. CODOMANNUS, the last king of Persia (B.C. 336-330).
His tall and singularly beautiful person, and his amiable disposition,
befit the hero of one of the most tragic catastrophes in the drama of
man's history. He had proved his bravery by killing a gigantic

8 See Chapter XIV.

R 2

warrior of the wild Cadusii in single combat; and Ochus had rewarded him with the satrapy of Armenia. But his flight from Issus and Arbela betrayed the lack of that higher courage, which can uphold, or perish beneath, a falling cause; and his few acts of good generalship do not reverse the sentence of history on his whole military career.

Scarcely had his reign begun, when Bagoas was detected in another plot to remove the king he had set up; but this time the king-maker and king-slayer was forced to drink the poison he had mixed for Codomannus. While thus ridding himself of the nearer danger, Darius trusted that fate had averted the greater by the death of Philip and the difficulties which seemed to rise up round Alexander. How soon he was undeceived, and how "the great Emathian conqueror" overthrew Darius in the decisive battles of Issus and Arbela, and overran the Persian empire, from the Hellespont to the Indus, and from the Oasis of Ammon to the deserts beyond the Jaxartes;—and how, in the midst of these conquests, Darius was murdered by the treacherous satraps who had carried him away, a prisoner bound with golden chains, into Hyrcania;—all this is related in Greek history, and vividly depicted in the symbolic prophecy of Daniel: "And, as I was considering, behold *an he-goat came from the west* on the face of the whole earth, and touched not the ground"—a striking image of the rapidity of Alexander's conquest. "And he came to the ram that had two horns, which I had seen standing before the river, and ran unto him in the fury of his power. And I saw him come close unto the ram, and he was moved with choler against him, and smote the ram, and brake his two horns: *and there was no power in the ram to stand before him, but he cast him down to the ground and stamped upon him*: and there was none that could deliver the ram out of his hand" (Dan. viii. 5–7).

The story of the Persian Empire, virtually ended at Arbela in the autumn of B.C. 331, closes with the pathetic scene in which Alexander threw his own cloak over the body of Darius (B.C. 330).

The marvellous rapidity, with which the conqueror led his small band of warriors through the almost unresisting body of the Persian Empire, demands a further explanation besides the genius of Alexander, the disciplined valour of his phalanx and the resistless shock of his "companions," or even the decrepitude of Persia. The organization of the empire under the first Darius—though probably the best that could have been devised for such a mixture of Asiatic nations—prepared for its collapse under Codomannus.

The many nations which dwelt from the Indus to the Ister, and from the Sea of Aral to the shores of the Greater Syrtis, retained their own languages, laws, manners, and religion. In some lands the native princes held the honour and part of the power of royalty. The Greek cities of Asia Minor administered their own internal government; but the tyrants who rose to power in them were generally favourable to Persia. The old boundaries of the nations marked out for the most part the new provinces, or *satrapies*, as they were called from the officer who ruled each as the lieutenant of the king.[9] When the levy of the empire was called out, the soldiers of each satrapy appeared in their own national equipment.[10] But this was only when a great effort was required: the ordinary defence and restraint of the provinces was committed to garrisons of Persian and Median soldiers. The king delegated as much of his absolute authority as he pleased to the satrap, whom he appointed from any nation or rank, and degraded or put to death at his will.

A check was provided on the power of the satrap by placing the command of the forces in separate hands, while, sometimes at least, the commandants of garrisons were independent of both. The satrap, however, was often the military commander, especially in the frontier provinces.

The administration of justice, too, was committed to officers independent of the satraps—the *Royal Judges*. They were appointed by the king, who called them most rigorously to account for any corruption in their office. Cambyses had one such offender put to death and flayed, and his skin made a covering for the judgment-seat. The proverbial unchangeableness of the Medo-Persian laws must have added no small security against judicial oppression; but we have seen how ingeniously the principle could be evaded.[11]

In reference to that function which is always most tempting to provincial tyranny, each province was assessed to a regular amount

<hr>

[9] Herodotus gives a full account of the satrapies established by Darius the son of Hystaspes; but the name of *satrap* is already found in the Behistun inscription. It is probable that this sort of vice-regal government was introduced at the beginning of the empire, and perfected by Darius. As to the name *Khshatrapa*, all we can say with certainty is that it is akin to *Khshatram*, "kingdom," and *Khshaya*, the abbreviated form for "king," whence the modern Persian *shah*. The "127 provinces from India to Ethiopia," with a "prince" over each, must have been subdivisions of the satrapies. (See Esther i. 1, viii. 9; Daniel vi. 1.)

[10] In describing the levy of the empire by Xerxes for the invasion of Greece, Herodotus gives a most interesting account of the dress and equipment of the several nations.

[11] In their memorable answer to Cambyses (see Chapter XXXVI.). Again, under Xerxes, the decree for the massacre of the Jews, which could not be recalled, was nullified by another authorizing them to slay their assailants (Esther viii.).

of *tribute*. The satrap might, indeed, levy for his own use as much as his power or prudence permitted; but there was a check upon his extortion, in the interest which the king had to prevent the impoverishment of the provinces. All these checks, however, did not prevent gross abuse of the enormous power entrusted to the satraps; and there are glaring instances, not only of extortion, but even of personal outrage upon Persians of the highest rank.

So long, in fact, as the province was orderly and flourishing, the tribute regularly paid, and no suspicion of the satrap's fidelity excited by his own conduct or by the machinations of his rivals, he enjoyed the state and much of the power of an independent sovereign. This was especially the case in the satrapies of Asia Minor, which, besides being remote from the capital, were involved in the restless intrigues of Greek politics. Here we find embassies received and sent, and alliances and wars made, not only without reference to the king, but by the different satraps taking different sides. Each enlisted his own body of Greek mercenaries, with whose aid they made war upon one another.

Such a system involved the constant danger of rebellion; and various means were taken to guard against the risk. The satrapies were assigned, as far as possible, to members of the royal family, and to nobles connected with it by marriage. Watch was kept upon the satrap by a *Royal Secretary*, who reported all his proceedings to the king, and received despatches and edicts from the capital by means of "posts on horseback and riders on mules, camels, and young dromedaries" (Esther viii. 10). Sometimes, as we have seen in the case of Orœtes, the secretary was the organ of a royal decree for the deposition, or even the death, of the satrap. Special commissioners, also, were sent every year to make enquiries into the state of each satrapy.

These precautions seem, upon the whole, not to have been ineffective. Excluding the revolts against the new power of Darius, the chief risings recorded are purely national, as those of Babylonia and Egypt. The attempt of the younger Cyrus was a struggle for the succession to the throne, not a provincial rebellion. In process of time, however, some of the more distant or less accessible provinces seem to have fallen off quietly from the empire, which was certainly of less extent under the last Darius than under the first.

The position of the Great King, as the Greeks called him, differed in no material respect from that of an Asiatic despot at the present day, such as the Shah of modern Persia. We have already had occasion to describe the state in which he held his court,[12] residing in the spring at Susa, in the summer at Ecbatana, and in the

<hr>

[12] See Chapter XXXIV.

winter at Babylon; as well as at Persepolis, which several of the
kings adorned with splendid palaces.   He appears to have governed
without a council, except when of his mere motion he summoned the
nobles to aid him with their advice, which even then he was under
no obligation to follow.   If his courtiers ventured to appeal to the
unchanging laws of the Medes and Persians, the Royal Judges
pronounced the law which overrode all others, that the king might
do whatever he pleased.   The only effective check on his despotism
was assassination, the fate of Xerxes I., Xerxes II., and Ochus.

Interior view of the Parapet Wall of a Staircase at Persepolis.   (Restored.)

Grand Range of Lebanon.

CHAPTER XXXIX.

THE HISTORY OF PHŒNICIA.

PART I.—TO THE TIME OF TYRE'S SUPREMACY.

One of the smallest provinces of the Persian Empire demands our special notice, from its very ancient civilization, its extensive colonies, and the vast development of its commerce, which on the one side enriched the great empires of the East, and, on the other, carried the civilization of Asia to the shores of Europe; and, lastly, from the part played in history by its great colony of Carthage. In the oldest biblical records, and in the earliest monuments of Assyria, Phœnicia appears as the seat of trade; the mythical history of Greece looks to that shore for her earliest civilization, and, whatever may be the value of those legends, whether Cadmus ever lived or not, the very forms of the *letters* in which we now write attest the truth of the tradition that they were brought from Phœnicia.

Phœnicia is nothing more than a narrow strip of coast, partly level and partly hilly. It lies among the foot hills of the great chain of Lebanon, the projecting headlands of which, with the detached islands, form some excellent harbours. The average width of the undulating plain between the sea and the mountains is only about a mile, increasing at Sidon to two miles, and near Tyre to five; the whole breadth of the land, inclusive of the slopes of Lebanon, nowhere exceeds 20 miles, the average being about 12. Its northern limit is usually fixed at the island of Aradus, and the city of Antaradus nearly opposite on the mainland; the southern at the " White Cape " (*Ras el Abiad*), about 6 miles south of Tyre. This coast line is about 120 miles in length. The southern limit is often carried as far as Mount Carmel; for Acco (afterwards Ptolemais, and the modern *'Akka* or *St. Jean d'Acre*) was an old Phœnician settlement.

This narrow region had abundant resources within itself, besides its advantageous position for commerce. Its varied surface is watered by the numerous streams, short but copious, which run down across it from Lebanon to the sea, and some of these have interesting associations. The largest of them is the river now called *Nahr-el-Kasimieh* or *Nahr-el-Litany*, and supposed to be the ancient Leontes, which drains the great valley of Cœle-Syria ("Hollow Syria") between the two ranges of Lebanon. and falls into the sea north of Tyre. At the northern part of the country in like manner, though on a much smaller scale, the valley between Mounts Bargylus and Lebanon is drained by the " Great River " (*Nahr-el-Kebir*), the ancient Eleutherus, which falls into the large bay between Aradus and Tripolis. Of the rivers having their sources on the western slope of Lebanon, the most important is the Bostrenus (*Nahr-el-Auly*), which watered the plain of Sidon. Proceeding to the north, across the Tamyras (*Nahr-el-Damur*) and the Magoras (*Nahr-Beyrut*) just beyond Berytus. we come to the Lycus (*Nahr-el-Kelb*), famous for the *stelæ*, or sculptured tablets, of Rameses II. (or, as the Greeks said, Sesostris), and of several Assyrian kings, on the face of the rocks which overhang its stream. A more poetical celebrity belongs to the stream just south of Byblus, from the legend (derived perhaps from the blood-red colour of the water in flood time) which gave the river its name of Adonis (*Nahr Ibrahim*), and as the seat of the elemental worship of Thammuz—

> " Whose annual wound in Lebanon allured
> The Syrian damsels to lament his fate
> In amorous ditties all a summer's day;
> While smooth Adonis from his native rock
> Ran purple to the sea, supposed with blood
> Of Thammuz yearly wounded."

The last river deserving to be mentioned (for the lesser streams and mountain torrents are innumerable) is that of Tripolis (the *Nahr-Kadisha* or " Holy River "), which has its chief source just opposite that of the Orontes on the other slope of Lebanon.

A coast road was carried across these rivers by many bridges, and over the intervening promontories by means of zigzags or, as the Greeks called them, *climaces* (*stairs* or *ladders*), the most remarkable of which was the *Climax Tyriorum*, across the *White Cape*, which rises to the height of 300 feet.   But in earlier times the valleys must have been severed in a way which goes far to account for the independence of the original states among themselves.   The land lay out of the great highways trodden by the oriental armies.   The military road from Egypt to the Euphrates struck inland from the maritime plain of Palestine south of Damascus ; while that which led to Hamath and the valley of the Orontes—the land of the martial Hittites—and in later ages to Antioch, passed through Cœle-Syria behind Lebanon.   This great mountain rampart severed the Phœnician coast from that constantly disputed region of Syria.

Lying in the fairest part of the temperate zone, between the breezes of the Mediterranean and the heights of Lebanon, which are snow-clad for the greater part of the year, and with a surface varying from level plains, through undulating hills, to high and rugged mountains, Phœnicia possesses a climate and productions equally remarkable for excellence and diversity.   Its exposure to the west gives it a high temperature, especially on the sea-level.   The prevailing winds are westerly, bringing rain in the winter, and violent storms in October and November, from the very quarter (N.W.) to which the harbours are most exposed.   The winter rains fall in November and December.   In January and February, if the winter be at all severe, these rains become snow, and there is frost enough to cover the standing waters with a thin coat of ice, but not to harden the ground.   The winter rains are preceded and followed by lighter showers, the " early and latter rain " of Scripture.   The former, about the end of October, prepare the soil for autumn sowing : the latter, in March, bring forward the crops, which ripen in the delightful months of April and May.

The four summer months are rainless and almost cloudless ; with winds which follow the daily course of the sun, and a land breeze in the evening on the coast and about three miles out to sea.   The violent and parching east wind from the desert is felt, even across the barrier of Lebanon, from March to June, and the south wind, which blows in March, has the enervating effect of a *sirocco*.   When the heat is excessive, a few hours' journey affords a delightful retreat in the coolness and verdure of Lebanon, with its grand and beautiful scenery. In these mountains the winter is severe from November to March ; the snow usually falling heavily and lying deep. The summit of Lebanon retains the snow during the summer in its ravines only, giving the effect of silvery wreaths amidst the less brilliant white of the jagged points of lime-stone which mark its naked ridge.[1] Both these circumstances may have contributed to give the range its name of *Lebanon*, that is " White," the *Mont Blanc* of Palestine. In the higher chain of *Antilibanus* (which, however, is quite separate from Phœnicia), the culminating summit of Hermon, 10,000 feet high, is clad with perpetual snow. The climate is usually healthy, and the fevers, which prevail on the coast in the heat of summer, might probably be prevented. The whole region is subject to earthquakes.

The country thus described must needs have a great abundance and variety of vegetable products. The soil is fertile, although now generally ill-cultivated. In the rich gardens and orchards about Sidon may be seen oranges, lemons, figs, almonds, plums, apricots, peaches, pomegranates, pears, and bananas, all growing luxuriantly, and forming a forest of finely-tinted foliage. The fertile lowlands bore abundant crops of corn ; and the olive, vine, and fig-tree, were proverbial products of Phœnicia as well as of Palestine, where the inhabitant could " dip his feet in oil," and " sit under his own vine and under his own fig-tree." The former abundance of the date-palm attested, as some think, by the very name of Phœnicia, which is the Latin form of the Greek *Phœnicé* (Φοινίκη from φοῖνιξ), just as *Brasil* is named from its famous wood. Others, however, derive the name from the Syrian *purple*, of which we have presently to speak.

All readers are familiar with the proverbial fame of the forests which clothe the jagged sides of Lebanon, and of the spurs which it throws out to form the bold headlands of the coast. " Lebanon is not sufficient to burn, nor the beasts thereof for a burnt offering." [2] The average height of the chain of Lebanon is from 6000 to 8000 feet, and the upper line of vegetation runs along at about 6000 feet. The forests, which furnished timber not only for the Phœnician navy, but for the Assyrian palaces, as well as for the temple and palaces of Solomon, consist of pine, fir, cypress, and evergreen oak, as well as the famous " cedar of Lebanon." As far as is at present known, the cedar of Lebanon is confined to one valley of the range, that of the *Kadisha*, or river of Tripoli. The grove stands quite alone in a depression at the upper part of the valley, about 15 miles

<hr>

[1] Jeremiah (xviii. 14) speaks of " the snow of Lebanon.

[2] Isaiah xl. 16 ; lx. 13 ; comp. Ps. lxxii. 16 ; Hos. xiv. 5 ; Zech. xi. 1

from the sea, and 6172 feet above its level, beyond the elevation reached by all the other trees of this mountain range. There are about 400 trees, of which eleven or twelve are very large and old, fifty of middle size, and the rest younger and smaller. The older trees have each several trunks, and spread themselves widely round, but most of the others are cone-like in form, and do not send out wide lateral branches. They are still regarded with as great reverence as in ancient times, when one of them was affirmed to be as old as the creation, or at least as the time of Abraham.

The ravines and caverns in the rugged sides of the limestone range give shelter to many wild beasts—jackals, hyenas, wolves, bears, and panthers. "The beasts, thereof," mentioned by Isaiah, must have been cattle fed upon the lower hills. Antilibanus, which is now more thinly peopled, is more abundantly stocked with wild beasts; and it was the scene of many of the hunting exploits commemorated in the Assyrian annals and sculptures. The lower formation of sandstone contains iron ore in sufficient abundance to have been worked in some parts, when wood was more plentiful than now; but Phœnicia appears to have obtained her metals chiefly from abroad.

Such a coast of course supplied important *fisheries;* and a very probable etymology derives the name of its oldest city, *Sidon*, from its being a fishing-station, like *Beth-saida* (the " house of fish ") on the Lake of Galilee. Most famous of all was the fishery for the *murex*, the mollusk which supplied the famous "Tyrian purple" from which, indeed, some derive the very name of Phœnicia. The writings of the Assyrian kings often mention the skins of sea-calves which they obtained from the Phœnician coast, to use as hangings and coverings in their palaces.

Whether as " the land of the date-palm," or as " the land of purple," Phœnicia is known, like so many other countries of the ancient and modern world, by a foreign appellation; an appellation which recals its primeval connection with Greece. But the Phœnicians called themselves *Canaanites* and their land Canaan. In the ethnic table of *Genesis X.*, we are told that " *Canaan* begat *Sidon*, his first-born," the oldest and long the most important of the Phœnician states; and, among the other Canaanites, the *Arkite*, the *Sinite*, the *Arvadite*, the *Zemarite*, and the *Hamathite*, represent the cities of Arca, Sinna, Aradus, Simyra, and Hamath (the later Epiphania); the last being beyond the northern limit of Phœnicia. There are good grounds for believing that the Canaanite nations came as immigrants from the East, and displaced that older population which is mentioned in the Bible by the names of *Rephaim*,

Emim, Zuzim, Zamzummim, Anakim, and *Nephilim.* The native traditions of the Phœnicians derived their origin from the shores of the Persian Gulf; and the classification of their tribes in Scripture among the children of *Ham,* that is, "the swarthy," agrees with their migration from the native land of a dark race, such as the plain of Lower Mesopotamia. The migration may be fixed, with probability, to a time just before that of Abraham. There are also reasons for supposing that the *Hyksos* or Shepherd Kings of Egypt, whom Manetho expressly calls *Phœnicians,* were a branch of the Canaanite migration; and that, on their expulsion from Egypt, they took with them a mode of *writing,* from which were derived the *alphabetic characters,* which Phœnician commerce afterwards carried to the shores of Europe.

That the *Phœnician Language* was *Semitic* is abundantly proved by its remaining fragments and proper names, both in Phœnicia and the colonies, especially Carthage. To say that it had a near affinity with the Hebrew, is understating the case; for the two differed merely as dialects. In fact, the Hebrew immigrants from Mesopotamia, being at first but a wandering family among the surrounding Canaanites, adopted the language of their new country in place of their own Syriac tongue; and their speech is called the "language of Canaan" (Isaiah xix. 18).

The story of the native historian, Sanchoniathon, that the Phœnicians were *autochthons,* whose race was deduced from *Chaos,* through a succession of gods, to Chna, the first Phœnician, is of course a baseless assumption of national pride. Equally fictitious is the claim of Tyre to a very high antiquity, and to the title of "Mother of the Phœnicians." The Tyrian priests of Hercules (*Melcarth*) told Herodotus that the temple and city had then existed 2300 years, which would carry back their building to about 2750 B.C. To such a claim the want of any monumental or other historical evidence is fatal. Tyre is not mentioned in Scripture till the entrance of the Israelites into Canaan (Josh. xix. 29); nor does the name occur in Homer, though he speaks of the Phœnicians in general, and the Sidonians in particular, and calls Phœnicia *Sidonia;* and the older and higher authority of Scripture uses "Sidonians" and "all the Sidonians" for the Phœnicians in general (Josh. xiii. 4, 6; Judges xviii. 7).

This name truly represents the original Phœnicia as the territory of Sidon, its most ancient city. As such we have seen Sidon named in the ethnic table as the firstborn of Canaan, and it appears again in *Genesis* in the dying blessing of Jacob, as already famous for its maritime enterprise:—" Zebulun shall dwell at the *haven of the sea;* and he shall be for an *haven of ships;* and his border shall be unto

Zidon." [3] The maritime importance here promised depended wholly on the proximity of Sidon ; for the Jews were never great sailors. nor did Asher, to whom this coast was assigned, ever conquer his inheritance in Phœnicia. On the contrary, the Phœnicians planted their colony of Dora above 10 miles S. of Carmel; and the account which an old historian gives of its growth may stand for the supposed origin of the Phœnician cities in general. "The rocky nature of the coast, which abounded with the purple-fish, brought the Phœnicians together here. They built themselves huts, which they surrounded with a fosse, and, as their industry prospered, they hewed stones from the rock, surrounded themselves with a wall, and made their harbour safe and commodious." Doubtless this description is more from imagination than from knowledge ; but the very name of Sidon makes it probable that fishing industry preceded the commerce which is the first phase of her known history. In the books of Joshua and Judges Sidon has the epithet of " Great " or " The Capital " (*Tsidon-Rabbah*). It stood in 33° 34' N. lat., 2 miles south of the Bostrenus, in the most fertile plain of Phœnicia, which is prolonged 8 miles southward to Sarepta (O.T. Zarephath). The city was built on the N.W. slope of a small promontory, and had a harbour formed by three low ridges of rock, on which massive substructions are still seen.

The settlements of " the sons of Canaan," mentioned in the ethnic table of *Genesis* in connection with Sidon, lie at and near the northern part of the Phœnician coast, and some of them beyond the proper limits of Phœnicia. They are the *Arkite, Sinite, Arvadite, Zemarite*, and *Hamathite* (Genesis x. 17, 18 : comp. 1 Chron. i. 15).

Arca (now *Tel-Arka*), also called " Arca in Lebanon " [4] stood about 12 miles N. of Tripoli and 2 or 2½ hours from the shore, on the summit of a northern spur of Lebanon, which here sinks abruptly to the valley of the Eleutherus. As the birthplace of Alexander Severus, it obtained the name of *Cæsarea Libani ;* and it was famous in the crusading wars. Its inland site seems to have caused the Arkite capital to be transferred to Orthosia, as the Greeks called the port which appears in Assyrian documents by the name of *Simron.*

The *Sinites*, also, had their original cities in the mountain, namely Sinna, and Aphek (*Afka*) (Josh. xiii. 4, xix. 5 ; Judges i. 31), the chief sanctuary of Ashtoreth. Their capital, however, was the great sea-port of Gebal, the Byblus of the Greek writers (now *Jebeil*), north of the river Adonis (Psalm lxxxiii. 7 ; Ezek. xxvii. 9).

---

[3] Gen. xlix. 13. The form *Zidon*, used in our version of the O. T. (except in Gen. x. 15, 19), represents the Phœnician *Tsidon*, which becomes in Greek *Sidon*, the usual form in the Apocrypha and New T., as well as in the Greek and Latin authors.   [4] Joseph. ' Ant.' i. 6, § 2.

This was one of the most ancient religious cities of Phœnicia; the burial-place of Adonis, and the seat of his mysteries. The *Giblites*, or Byblians, were famous artificers, and aided in preparing the trees and stone-work for the temple of Solomon (Josh. xiii. 5: 1 Kings v. 18). They founded the great city of BERYTUS, *i.e.*, "wells" or "cisterns" (now *Beyrût*), south of the Lycus, on the border of the Sidonians.

The other three peoples of this group had their abodes north of the Eleutherus; and they seem in the oldest times to have been connected politically rather with Syria than with Phœnicia. Accordingly the *Arvadite* and *Zemarite* appear with the Hittites of the Orontes (on which *Hamath* stood), in the great wars of the Pharaohs of the XVIIIth and XIXth dynasties, whose monuments make no mention of Sidon among the confederates. ARADUS was in later times a member of the Phœnician league, its king being a vassal of the King of Sidon. The town occupied the whole island of Aradus (*Ruad*), lying in the same latitude as Citium, the southern point of Cyprus. It was surrounded by a wall, serving also as a dyke, in the remains of which are stones of 5 and 6 yards in length. It possessed on the mainland the two towns of Antaradus (*Tartus*) with the necropolis of the island city, and Marathus (*Amrit*) the site of some important monuments of Phœnician architecture. Very near to them, and further inland, was SIMYRA (*Shumra*), the chief city of the *Zemarites*, who appear never to have joined the Phœnician league.

Last named, because at the extreme north of the Canaanite settlements, was HAMATH, the Epiphania of the Greeks, which still retains the name of *Hamah*, and has a population of between forty and fifty thousand. Lying in the valley of the Orontes, at the junction of all the routes from Antioch, Phœnicia, and Cœle-Syria, on the one side, to Damascus, Palmyra, Northern Syria, and Mesopotamia, on the other, Hamath was a great centre of the commerce of Phœnicia with Syria, Assyria, and Babylonia. Its situation gave it the command of the valley of the Orontes, from the defile of Daphne below Antioch to the watershed between it and the Leontes. This valley, which includes the northern half of Cœle-Syria, appears to have formed the region and (usually) the kingdom of Hamath; and the watershed formed "the entrance of Hamath," which was the northern limit of the promised land" (Numbers xxxiv. 8; Josh. xiii. 5, &c.).

The political connections of Hamath appear always to have been with Syria rather than with Phœnicia; and the Hamathites formed a part of the Hittite confederacy, with which the great Theban Pharaohs made war. In the time of David it was the seat of an independent kingdom, which sought David's protection against the King of Zobah (2 Sam. viii. 9). It was included in the empire of Solomon, and its commercial importance, especially for the traffic by way of Palmyra, is attested by his foundation of "Tadmor in the wilderness, and all the store-cities which he built in Hamath" (2 Chron. viii. 8; Josh. xiii. 5, &c.). On the disruption of Israel, Hamath seems to have regained its independence. In the Assyrian inscriptions of the time of Ahab (B.C. 900), it appears as a separate power, in alliance with the Syrians of Damascus, the Hittites, and the Phœnicians. About three-quarters of a century later, Jeroboam II. recovered Hamath (2 Kings xiv. 28): he seems to have dismantled the place, whence the prophet Amos couples "Hamath the Great" with Gath, as an instance of desolation (Amos vi. 2). Its importance ceased with its conquest by Sargon, who transplanted its inhabitants to Samaria (2 Kings xvii. 24, xviii. 34, xix. 13). The city received the Greek name of *Epiphania* from Antiochus Epiphanes. These notices of the Syrian states bordering Phœnicia on the north are important in themselves, and serve to define the limits of Phœnicia. It remains to speak of the city which ultimately acquired the supremacy.

Tyrus is the Greek and Latin form of the Phœnician and Hebrew *Tsur* or *Tzôr* (that is, "a rock"), now softened into *Sûr*. The general opinion of the ancients made Tyre a colony of Sidon; and it certainly lies within the original territory of Sidon. It is worthy of notice that, in Scripture, the Tyrians are sometimes called Zidonians, but the Zidonians are never called Tyrians. The usual mention of "Tyre and Sidon," in that order, belongs to a time when the greater importance of the former was established; and it is reversed at the period of Sidon's supremacy under the Persians (Ezra iii. 7).

Tyre is first mentioned in Scripture as "the strong city Tyre" (Josh. xix. 29); and its position made it one of the strongest in the world. The "rock," from which it had its name, was an island about half a mile from the shore and nearly a mile in length, in lat. 33° 17' N., just 20 miles south of Sidon. On the shore of the mainland, about 3 geographical miles to the south, there stood in Greek times a city called "Old Tyre" (Palætyrus). As early as the time of Rameses II., we find a clear notice both of the island city of Tyre, and of *Sarra* on the mainland, a little further to the south (see below p. 258). It is quite clear, from the scriptural allusions and from other evidence, that the island city was *the Tyre* of the flourishing period down to Alexander.

The last founded of the great Phœnician cities was TRIPOLIS (*Tripoli* or *Tarabulus*), the name of which points to its origin. It

was not only a common foundation of the *three cities* of Tyre
Sidon, and Aradus; but the respective colonies formed three distinct quarters (which the old geographer calls *cities*), at distances
of about 600 feet, each having its own wall, though united under
a common government. The city occupied a splendid site, on a
promontory about half a mile broad, jutting out about a mile into
the sea, in 34° 26' N. latitude. The harbour is sheltered from the
violent north-west winds by a chain of seven small islands, extending 10 miles out to sea. The city stood on what is now called
the "Holy River" (*El Kadisha*), in one of whose upper valleys
are the famous cedars. Among its remains is an aqueduct, which
brings down the water from Lebanon.

To sum up. The chief cities of Phœnicia, in their order from
north to south, were these ten: Aradus, Simyra, Orthosia, Tripolis,
Gebal or Byblus, Berytus, Sidon, Sarepta, Tyre, and Acco (afterwards Ptolemais). Their varying relations to each other, as members of the Phœnician confederacy, will appear from the ensuing
history.

The whole history of the Phœnicians may be divided, speaking
generally, into the periods of *Sidonian* and *Tyrian* supremacy.
The traditions already noticed seem to place their first settlements
on the Syrian coast about the age of Abraham and the Shepherd
Kings of Egypt. Their condition under the domination of the
great Theban kings confirms the statement of Herodotus, that they
soon began to apply themselves to distant voyages. The conquests
of the XVIIIth and XIXth dynasties in Syria and Northern Phœnicia are attested both by their inscriptions and by the *stelæ* set
up by Rameses II. at the *Nahr-el-Kelb*, and at *Adlun*, near Tyre.
In these records the Sidonians never appear as enemies, but they
seem to have purchased peace by placing their maritime enterprise
and manufacturing industry at the service of the Pharaohs. The
tributes, the arts, and the riches of Phœnicia are often mentioned
in the hieroglyphic inscriptions of this age.

We possess a more particular account of Phœnicia under the
great Rameses, and consequently in the age before the Exodus.
A papyrus in the British Museum contains the description of an
imaginary journey made into Syria by an Egyptian functionary, at
the end of the reign of Rameses II., after the conclusion of the
final peace with the Hittites. The hero is supposed to have been
in the country of the Hittites, and to have travelled as far as Helbon,
the present Aleppo. On his return, before entering Palestine,
where he describes the Canaanitish cities, he is supposed to pass
through Phœnicia. The narrative describes him as first stopping
at Gebal: he records the religious importance of the city, and the

mysteries celebrated there; he then visits Berytus, Sidon, Sarepta, and Avata (*Adlun*). He is then supposed to arrive at "TYRE the maritime," and describes it as *a little town situated on a rock in the midst of the waves.* "They carry water there in boats," says he, "and it is very rich in fish." Close to Tyre, a little further south on the mainland, the Egyptian traveller arrives at *Seraa*, the *Sarra* of classical geographers, and his account contains a pun on the name of Seraa (in the Phœnician language, "the wasp"); he speaks of the bad lodgings found there, and adds "the sting is very sharp." After traversing this part of the country, he visits Caïera (now *Um-el-Awamid*), then Achzib, where he quits the sea-coast, and enters the mountain region to reach Hazor. The traveller has been on Egyptian ground all this time, travelling with as much freedom and security as if he had been in the Nile valley, and even, by virtue of his functions, exercising some authority.

"From these statements," observes M. Lenormant, "it seems to us clearly proved that, from the date of the establishment of Egyptian dominion in Syria, the Sidonians and the Sinites of Gebal had completely separated their interests from those of the other Canaanite nations, and pursued quite a different line of action. Instead of seeking to recover a full independence, they became perfectly submissive to the Pharaonic supremacy, and remained faithful to Egypt under all circumstances. Doubtless the kings of Egypt, whose people were neither merchants nor seamen, needed and used the services of the Phœnicians, and therefore treated them with more favour than other nations of the same race, and granted them great privileges in order to secure their fidelity. They themselves, with true mercantile spirit, preferred to reap the material advantages arising from the protection of a great empire, rather than to indulge their pride by an empty assertion of independence, with its contingent disadvantages and dangers from foreign invasion. . . . Trade flourished and was profitable; and, contented with this result, the Phœnicians submitted to a state of vassallage with scarcely any opposition, provided always that the foreign suzerain did not interfere with their local self-government, and permitted them to preserve their own laws, and their own traditional worship, manners, and customs." It is during this period of the subjection of Phœnicia to Egypt, that we find the latter powerful at sea, under Thothmes III. and other Pharaohs; and the inference is highly probable, that this maritime power rested, as in later times, on the command of the Phœnician fleet.

The policy of Egypt towards her subject states made her suzerainty quite compatible with the existence of a native dynasty of

Sidonian kings, who themselves exercised sovereignty over the other Phœnician cities, except Gebal, which had its own kings. The highest commercial prosperity of Sidon belongs to this very period of the supremacy of the Pharaohs. She carried on trade in the eastern part of the Mediterranean, the Archipelago, and the Black Sea, where no rival navy yet existed.

During this period, the Sidonians seem to have planted colonies at Citium in Cyprus, at Itanum in Crete, and along the southern shores of Asia Minor, where a large part of the Semitic population claimed a Phœnician origin. In the south of the Ægean, they formed naval stations at Rhodes, Thera, and Cythera; and the famous worship of Aphrodite in the latter island, as in Crete, was at first that of the Phœnician Ashtoreth. In the Cyclades, they may be traced at Antiparos, Ios, and Syros: and to them is ascribed the first working of the silver mines of Siphnos and Cimolus, and of the gold mines of Thasos, where Herodotus saw the remains of their immense works. They also visited the neighbouring shores of Thrace, and bartered with the natives for the gold of Mount Pangæus. Entering the Euxine, they obtained the gold washed down by the rivers of Colchis; the tin of the Caucasus, which all the nations of that age required for their bronze implements, weapons, and armour; iron from the mines worked by the Chalybes, and, it seems, steel also; besides lead and silver. For these and other products of their voyages—which extended as far west along the shores of Europe as Epirus, southern Italy, and Sicily, they found markets on their own coast—whence caravans traded with Syria and the region beyond the Euphrates,—and also in Egypt.

Along the northern coast of Lybia, they pursued their voyages as far as the shore about *Cape Bon* (the Africa Proper of later times); and there they founded the famous colony of Hippo (that is, "a walled city"), and Cambe on the site afterwards occupied by Carthage. Berytus shared with Sidon in this colonizing work; but Gebal (Byblus) founded its own settlements, some of which were perhaps earlier than those of Sidon, as Paphos in Cyprus, and Melos in the Ægean.

The attacks from the sea, which we have seen made from the north and west upon Egypt and the Syrian coast, under Rameses II. and his successors, seem to imply a decline of the maritime power of Sidon about the 14th century B.C. It appears to have been about this time that the Pelasgo-Tyrrhenians began to acquire their naval supremacy in the Mediterranean, while commerce was assailed by that piracy which is one of the earliest Greek traditions. The same revolution may be implied in the two fables of the Argonautic expedition to Colchis, and of Greek voyages to the lake Triton, at the bottom of the Great Syrtis—the very shores which formed the north-eastern and south-western limits of Phœnician commerce.

To the same region of fable—at least so far as our present knowledge extends—we must leave the settlements said to have been formed on the shores of Greece and Africa by the redundant population of Canaan, which, displaced by the Israelitish conquest, found a temporary and insufficient refuge on the Phœnician coast, and thence overflowed in a new wave of colonization. But, obscure as are the causes, we know, as certain facts, that letters were carried from Phœnicia into Greece; and that Phœnician colonies were thickly planted on the shores of Zeugitana and Byzacium long before the foundation of Carthage.

For the rest, it is quite clear that the conquest of Canaan by the Israelites stopped at the Phœnician border; and that its only direct effect was the more complete isolation of Phœnicia from the country beyond Lebanon. So far from being subdued by the Israelites, the Sidonians are named among their oppressors (Judges x. 12); but their generally peaceful policy, the fruit of commercial prosperity, is indicated by the mention of the men of Laish, "how they dwelt careless, after the manner of the Zidonians, quiet and secure" (Judges xviii. 7). About the same time, the southern part of the maritime region was occupied by a new and large settlement of the Philistines, who in about a century grew strong enough to impose their yoke upon the Israelites, and not only to deprive the Phœnicians of much of the land traffic with Egypt, Assyria, and Arabia, of which Azotus and Gaza became great emporia, but even to vie with them at sea. There is a tradition that the Philistines, under the leadership of Ascalon, sent a fleet against Sidon, which was taken by storm and razed to the ground, about the end of the 13th century B.C. It is added, that the inhabitants of Sidon withdrew to Tyre, to which city the supremacy was now transferred. The Philistines did not pursue their success, and the Sidonians recovered from the blow; and henceforth the names of Tyre and Sidon constantly appear together in the history of Phœnicia. Under the supremacy of Tyre, the people were still called *Sidonian;* and on inscriptions, referred to this early period, the King of Tyre styles himself "King of the Sidonians," while "the King of Sidon" is his vassal.[5]

For the century and a half down to the distinct appearance of

---

[5] In 1 Kings v. 6, Solomon requests Hiram, King of *Tyre,* to command his servants to hew cedar-trees out of Lebanon, because "there is not among us any that can skill to hew timber like the *Sidonians.*"

Tyre in history as a powerful kingdom, in alliance with David and Solomon, we have only fragmentary traditions of the state of Phœnicia.   The isolation in which the people were left by the conquests of the Israelites and the Philistines, on the south, and of the Aramæan Syrians on the north and east, appears to have caused them to unite in a league of common defence, which embraced the cities from Simyra to Acco.   Each town preserved its ancient form of government, which was a monarchy, controlled by general assemblies of the wealthiest and most influential citizens, and by councils of priests and magistrates, who were on an equality with the king in all public ceremonies.   The institutions of Gebal (Byblus) were considered the most perfect type of these governments,—partly monarchical, but pre-eminently aristocratic.   The kings of the various cities were all subject to the King of Tyre as their suzerain.   He decided all business respecting the general interests of Phœnicia, its commerce, and its colonies.   He concluded treaties with foreign states, and disposed of the military and naval forces of the confederation.   He was assisted by deputies from the other towns; and the annual embassies to the temple of Melcarth henceforth assumed a political character.

The *Arvadites* alone remained isolated.   Doubtless they were in close alliance with the other Phœnicians, and shared in their commerce and their maritime expeditions; but there are reasons to believe that they were not subject to the authority of the kings of Tyre.   They served as sailors on board the ships of Tyre, whose population was inadequate to man her fleets, and as soldiers in her armies, which were composed entirely of mercenaries.   A body of Arvadites formed the garrison of Tyre itself.   The other recruits were drawn chiefly from the Liby-Phœnicians and other Africans. There were also in her service hardy mountaineers from Persia; Lydians, whether from Asia Minor, or a branch of the people from the Armenian highlands; and Ethiopians, obtained probably through her commerce with Egypt (Ezek. xxvii. 8, 10, 11; xxxviii. 5).

This was also the period in which Tyre began her more distant voyages to the West, for the Carians and Tyrrhenians held the supremacy in the seas of Asia Minor, Greece, and Italy.   From Utica, the chief of their new settlements on the African coast, they proceeded westward along the coasts of Numidia and Mauretania (*Algeria* and *Marocco*); till, as their traditions say, after twice failing in the attempt to pass beyond the Straits, they founded the famous colony of Gades (*Cadiz*—in Phœnician, *Gadir*—" a fortified enclosure "), a few years after Utica.   This was the great emporium for their commerce with the south of Spain, the *Tarshish* of Scripture, where they obtained the gold, silver, iron, lead, copper, tin, and cinnabar of the Andalusian mines, besides honey, wax, and pitch. "Tarshish was thy merchant by reason of the multitude of riches; with silver, iron, tin, and lead they traded in thy fairs" (Ezek. xxvii. 12). Besides Gades, they founded Calpe and Carteia (*Gibraltar* and *Algesiras*) on the Straits, and numerous settlements on the southern coast of Spain, of which Malaca (*Malaga*) and Abdera were the chief. These remote colonies were connected with the mother-country by the midway station of Melita (*Malta*), with Gaulos (*Gozo*), where are found the only remains of Phœnician temples. In Sardinia a splendid harbour invited them to found Caralis (*Cagliari*); and at Nora (near *Pula*), which bore the name of an old city in Phœnicia, Phœnician inscriptions have been found. They established commercial factories on the coast of Sicily, which were connected with Africa by a station on the little island of Cossyra (*Pantellaria*). It will be seen that these settlements commanded the whole shores of the Western Mediterranean, except the great bay between Spain and Italy, of which the Tyrrhenians were masters. The naval power of the latter was not broken till both Carthage and the Sicilian Greeks were strong enough to encounter them with success.

Phœnician Bireme (*Koyunjik*).

Ruins of the Roman city of Palmyra on the site of Solomon's Tadmor.

CHAPTER XL.

THE HISTORY OF PHŒNICIA.

PART II.—FROM THE AGE OF DAVID AND HIRAM TO THE TAKING OF TYRE BY ALEXANDER.   ABOUT B.C. 1050 TO B.C. 332.

TYRE first appears distinctly on the page of recorded history, as a powerful kingdom, at the epoch of the great Jewish monarchy under David, in the middle of the eleventh century, B.C.; and, from the same period, Menander of Ephesus, in a fragment preserved by Josephus, traces the succession of the kings of Tyre for about 200 years as follows :—

1. ABIBAAL : from about B.C. 1050.
2. HIRAM, his son : from about B.C. 1025 : reigned 34 years.
3. BALEAZAR, his son :   „   991   „   7   „
4. ABDASTARTUS, his son; from about 984 to 975 ; murdered by a conspiracy.
5. One of the Conspirators reigned about B.C. 975–963.

6. Astartus; reigned about b.c. 963 to 951.
7. Aserymus (his brother): about b.c. 951 to 942; murdered by his brother,
8. Phales, who reigned only 8 months, and was murdered by the priest of Astarte.
9. Ethbaal or Ithobalus: b.c. 941–909, whose daughter *Jezebel* was the wife of *Ahab;* and in whose reign there was a great drought.
10. Badezor, his son: about b.c. 909 to 903.
11. Matgen, his son: „   903 to 871.
12. Pygmalion, his son: about b.c. 871 to 824; was the brother of Dido.   Carthage founded.

In the first historical mention of Tyre *as a kingdom,* we find Hiram in close alliance with David, to whom the King of Tyre sent cedar-trees and carpenters and masons to build his palace.[1] It is emphatically stated that "Hiram was ever a lover of David" (1 Kings v. 11).   This alliance, the perpetuation of which under Solomon is familiar to us from the Scripture history, was based on the natural principle of common interests and common dangers.

The Philistines on the south and the Syrians on the east were the enemies alike of Israel and Phœnicia, and both countries were protected by the conquests of David.   While the Jewish kings enjoyed the fruits of Phœnician commerce, Phœnicia depended on the agricultural wealth of Palestine, alike in the time when Solomon fed the servants of Hiram at their work in Lebanon (1 Kings v. 11; 2 Chron. ii. 10), and when Herod Agrippa could bring "them of Tyre and Sidon" to their senses "because their country was nourished by the king's country" (Acts xii. 20).   In the prophet's invaluable picture of the sources of Tyrian wealth we read, "Judah and the land of Israel . . . they traded in thy market wheat of Minnith and *pannag* (either some cereal or some aromatic product), and honey, and oil, and balm" (Ezek. xxvii. 17). The value of Palestine to Tyre as a wheat country was greatly enhanced by its proximity, as there was scarcely a part of the kingdom of Israel, west of Jordan, which was distant more than a hundred miles from that great commercial city.   The fact that Palestine was the granary of Phœnicia helps to account for the peace between the two countries, of which there is no recorded interruption, notwithstanding Hiram's anger at Solomon's ingrati-

---

[1] 2 Sam. xxiv. 7.—If this statement be taken strictly where it stands, at the beginning of David's reign, it would seem to refer to a Hiram who may have been the father of Abibaal, and grandfather of Solomon's Hiram; and some writers accordingly distinguish them as Hiram I. and Hiram II.

tude (1 Kings ix. 13), and the provocation given to Ethbaal by the slaughter of his daughter's Phœnician priests at Carmel, almost on his own frontier (1 Kings xviii.).

In the aid rendered by Hiram to Solomon, Tyre appears as the seat, not only of commerce, but of manufacturing art, especially in works of metal, for which the Sidonians are equally conspicuous in the Homeric poems. In the fragments of the Phœnician historians, the reign of Hiram is represented as the great epoch when Tyre reached the climax of her power, and was strengthened and adorned anew. He is said to have quelled in person a revolt of Citium, in Cyprus. He undertook great works at Tyre in the beginning of his reign, and entirely altered the appearance of the city. He rebuilt, with unexampled splendour, the great temple of Melcarth and the adjacent temple of Ashtoreth. The little arm of the sea, which had hitherto separated the sacred islet of Melcarth from insular Tyre itself, was filled up, so as to make one island, the extent of which was more than doubled southwards by the formation of an artificial embankment, on which was built a new quarter of the city, called by the Greeks *Eurychoron*, "the spacious." Insular Tyre, thus transformed, was protected on all sides by dykes, and surrounded by a strongly fortified enclosure. Quays bordered the whole of the ancient harbour, and a second port was formed on the south side of the island, and thus shelter was obtained for more than double the number of ships that could have been accommodated before. Hiram also built a royal palace in the insular city, which henceforth became the true Tyre, while Palætyrus on the mainland gradually declined.

The completion of these works, about the time of David's death, set Hiram and his trained artificers at liberty to aid Solomon in those great works at Jerusalem, of which the account belongs to Scripture History. Solomon married a " Zidonian " princess, a daughter of Hiram, by whom the worship of Ashtoreth was set up at Jerusalem (1 Kings xi. 1, 5). His joint maritime adventures with the fleet of Hiram, described in Scripture history (1 Kings x. 11, 22; 2 Chron. xx. 36), attest both the distant voyages of the Tyrians from the Red Sea ports belonging to Israel, and the policy of Solomon in having his own sailors trained by the Phœnician mariners. When, however, on the partition of Solomon's kingdom, Phœnicia, maintaining her alliance with the northern kingdom, was shut out from those ports, the attempt of Jehoshaphat to reopen the Red Sea navigation proved too much for the skill of the Jewish mariners, and the ships were wrecked (1 Kings xxii. 48; 2 Chron. xx. 35-37).

The death of Hiram was soon followed by dynastic troubles at

Tyre; and his grandson was murdered through a conspiracy formed by the four sons of his nurse in the very year of the death of Solomon and the partition of his kingdom (B.C. 975). It is thought that Phœnicia, as well as Judah, may have felt the hostility of the Egyptian king Shishak; and the foundation of the kingdom of Damascus cannot but have affected the power of Tyre. The 30 or 40 succeeding years of disturbance and revolution coincide remarkably with the like troubles in Israel; and both kingdoms, obtaining settled governments about the same time, formed a new alliance. Ethbaal, the priest of Ashtoreth, established a new dynasty at Tyre, and married his daughter, Jezebel, to Ahab, son of Omri, with disastrous results to both the Hebrew kingdoms.

It was under Ethbaal's fourth successor that new dynastic troubles are said to have produced that great event, which has come down to us in the garb of the most favourite poetical legend of antiquity. The following is the historical version (real or supposed) which the classical writers gathered from the fragments of native tradition. The Tyrian king Matgen died, leaving two children—a son, aged eleven years, named *Pümelüa* (PYGMALION), and a daughter, some years older, named *Elissar* (ELISA). His last wish was that the two should reign conjointly. But the populace, desirous of changing the aristocratic form of government, proclaimed Pygmalion sole monarch, and surrounded him with councillors of the democratic party. Elisa, excluded from the throne, married *Zicharbaal* (in Virgil, Sichæus), the high-priest of Melcarth, whose position placed him at the head of the aristocratic party.

Some years later, Pygmalion caused his rival Zicharbaal to be assassinated; and Elisa formed a conspiracy with 300 senators, the heads of the patrician families, to avenge her husband and restore the aristocratic government. The democracy was too vigilant to give the conspirators any hope of success in Tyre; so they resolved upon a great secession. Seizing by surprise some ships, which lay in the port ready for sea, they embarked to the number of several thousands, and departed to found a new Tyre beneath other skies, under the guidance of Elisa, who, from this emigration, received the name of Dido, " the fugitive." Disembarking among the settlements of their countrymen at the north-eastern point of Zeugitana, they bought from the Libyan king the site of the old Sidonian colony of Cambe, which had long since fallen into ruins; and, whether in contrast with this older town or with the mother city, their settlement was called *Kiryath-Hadéshath* (that is, the " New City "). which became in Greek *Carchedon*, and in Latin Carthago. The migration of Dido is placed in the seventh year of Pygmalion's reign, B.C. 872 or 865.

From the time of Ethbaal, the great kings of the Old Assyrian Monarchy, whose monuments are found at *Nimrud*, began to extend their power as far as Phœnicia. About two centuries earlier, indeed, Tiglath-pileser I.[2] had reached as far as the northern end of Lebanon and Aradus, where his Annals state that he went on board a ship and killed a dolphin with his own hand! But it is not till now that we find conquests claimed in Phœnicia.

The great *Nimrud* king, Asshur-nasir-pal, records on his obelisk:—
" At this time I took possession of all around Mount Lebanon. I proceeded towards the great sea of Phœnicia. On the summits of the mountains I sang the praises of the great gods, and I offered sacrifices. I received tribute from the kings of the countries around the mountains, from *Tyre, Sidon, Gebal (Byblus)* . . . from Phœnicia, and from *Aradus* in the sea: these tributes consisted of silver, gold, tin, bronze, instruments of iron, stuffs dyed purple and saffron, sandal-wood, ebony, and seal-skins. They humbled themselves before me." In our Museum we still behold the cedar-wood, which this king himself tells us that he cut in Lebanon and carried to Nineveh, as well as the weights inscribed with their values in Phœnician terms (*manah* and *shekel*), both in Phœnician and cuneiform letters.[3]

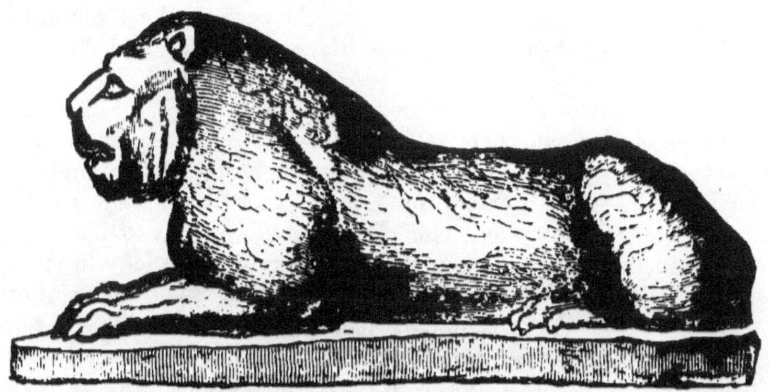

Bronze Lion Weight, from Nimrud.

This king's son, Shalmaneser II., the " Black Obelisk king," after his great campaign against Hazael, king of Syria (his 21st campaign), advanced into Phœnicia, and received the tribute of Tyre, Sidon, and Byblus ; and his grandson, Iva-lush (or Houli-Khus) IV. enumerates, among the countries paying him regular tributes, " the whole of Phœnicia, the lands of Tyre and of Sidon."[4]

<hr>

[2] See Chap. XX.   [3] See Chap. XXI.

Even taking these claims at their fullest meaning, the loose hold of Assyria on her tributary provinces, especially at so great a distance, would not interfere with their maritime power; and it is precisely at this period that a Greek tradition ascribes to the Phœnicians a dominion of the seas, from B.C. 824 to 786.

The founder of the New Assyrian Monarchy began, as we have seen, from his very accession, to reconquer the western provinces, which the fall of the Old Monarchy had restored to independence. Now also we find the relations of Phœnicia to Assyria continually referred to in Scripture and in the fragments of the old historians. The prophet Amos denounces Tyre among the nations which were to feel the weight of Assyrian conquest (Amos i. 9, 10); and Tiglath-pileser II. mentions *Hiram*, king of Tyre, and *Sibitbaal*, king of Gebal, in the list of kings who submitted to him in the campaign of B.C. 742.[5] The destruction of the kingdom of Damascus, the captivity of northern Israel, and the conquest of Hamath and the Philistines, must have left Phœnicia completely exposed : and Sibitbaal of Gebal again appears among the twenty-three vassal kings, who brought their tribute and homage to the conqueror at Damascus (B.C. 731). In the following year *Muthon* or *Mit'enna*, king of Tyre, leagued with Pekah, king of Israel, in refusing to pay tribute. The approach of an army, sent by Tiglath-pileser, appears to have given the occasion for the murder of Pekah by Hoshea, who made his submission, and Muthon followed the example.

About the same time, the Greek colonisation of Sicily displaced the Phœnicians from their settlements on the island, with three important exceptions. Their retention of Motya, "the muddy," Kepher, "the town" (Soluntum), and Machanath, "the camp" (Panormus), at the western end of the island, nearest to Carthage, secured them the powerful support of their great colony in maintaining their trade with the interior : and these same cities afterwards gave the Carthaginians a footing in Sicily. This loss in Sicily was partly compensated by the reduction of a rebellion of Citium, in Cyprus, by *Eluli* (Elulæus), who became king of Tyre about B.C. 726, at the time of the final effort of Hoshea to throw off the Assyrian yoke. We have seen the issue in the destruction of Samaria, and the decisive campaign of Sargon against the kings of Egypt and Ethiopia on the southern frontier of Palestine.[6]

From the victory of Raphia, Sargon returned to exact the tribute of Phœnicia, and received the submission of Sidon, Acco, and the other cities, including Palætyrus on the mainland. The island

---

⁴ See Chap. XXII.   ⁵ See Chap. XXIII.   ⁶ See Chap. XXIV.

city of Tyre alone, confident in its strength, defied a power which had no navy, and stood the first of its three memorable sieges.[7] The Assyrian pressed into his service the fleets of his Phœnician vassals; and the Tyrians were attacked by 60 ships, manned by 800 rowers, of their late confederates, Sidon, Acco, and Old Tyre. Putting to sea with only 12 vessels, they gained a complete victory, sank many ships, and took 500 prisoners. Sargon left his generals to reduce Tyre by blockade. They cut the aqueduct built by Hiram to bring water from the mainland; but the Tyrians sank wells in the rock till they reached springs. After five years the siege was abandoned (B.C. 715).

Tyre emerged from this contest with safety and glory; but that was all, for her supremacy was gone. The desertion of her confederates—nay, their appearance in the field against her—are facts of terrible import. Sidon, in particular, had the memory of old supremacy to inflame her jealousy; and we shall soon see her appearing as a separate centre of the resistance of Phœnicia to her foreign masters. While thus deprived of her sovereignty at home, Tyre was stripped of her last and most valuable possession in the Ægean—Thasos, with its gold mines,—which was seized by the people of Paros during the siege of Tyre. Some years later, Sargon used the Phœnician and Philistine fleets for an expedition against Cyprus, which was thus lost to Tyre (B.C. 708). The conquest was commemorated by a stela, which Sargon set up in Citium (now in the Berlin Museum), and it was probably with reference to this exploit that he boasts, "Arbiter of combats, I traversed the sea of Jamnia like a fish. I annexed Koui and Tyre."

The loose yoke of Assyria was again cast off during the troubles of Sargon's later years, and Sennacherib had to reconquer Phœnicia with the other western provinces. The conquest this time included Tyre, whence Elulæus fled, and was replaced by *Ethbaal*, or *Toubaal*, as a vassal of the Assyrian. Sennacherib commemorated his conquest of Phœnicia by the stela which he set up at the mouth of the *Nahr-el-Kelb*, beside those of Rameses II. So complete for the time was the subjection of Tyre, that it is Sidon, under the king, *Abdi-Milkut*, that heads the next revolt, on the opportunity of the murder of Sennacherib (B.C. 680). Esar-haddon, in his first campaign, quelled the revolt, sacked the city, and transported many of his Phœnician captives to Babylonia. He says, in an inscription, "I put all its grandees to death. I destroyed its walls and houses: I threw them into the sea. I destroyed the site of its temples."

---

[7] The other two were those by Nebuchadnezzar and Alexander the Great.

The next transfer of the Assyrian crown presented a special opportunity for revolt, in concert with Tirhakah's recovery of supremacy in Egypt; and the Phœnician cities, always ready to return to their ancient alliance, rose in rebellion (B.C. 667). But Asshur-bani-pal's complete victory in Egypt left him free to reduce Phœnicia in the following year. He first took Acco: then *Baal*, king of Tyre, earned his pardon by submission: and this time it was the island city of Aradus that made a desperate resistance. When it could hold out no longer, the king, *Yakinlu*, son of Kulubaal, put himself to death; and seven of his sons were killed by Asshur-bani-pal, who set the eighth, *Azbaal*, upon the throne.

His conquest of Phœnicia seems to have been as thorough as that of Egypt; but the decline and fall of the Assyrian empire restored the country to a virtual independence, which was rather confirmed than annulled by Egypt's temporary recovery of her dominion in Western Asia under Neco (B.C. 610). The Phœnician cities welcomed this vigorous Pharaoh as a deliverer from the Assyrian yoke; and their fleet, placed as of old at the service of Egypt, was employed in the maritime adventures which have been related in the reign of Neco.

But the decisive victory of Carchemish restored the lands west of the Euphrates to a harder yoke than that of Assyria; and "the king of Egypt came not any more out of his land" to help his allies. It was only, however, after some delay and a terrible struggle, that Nebuchadnezzar gained possession of Tyre. Meanwhile the impending fate of the proud city gave occasion to those wonderful prophecies, which paint to the life that prosperity which forms the mystic type of some future state, that should attain to the like height only to have as terrible a fall.[s]

In the historical picture of Tyre's resources (for such the passage really is), the prophet Ezekiel gives some most interesting details of the trade of "Tyre, the crowning city, whose merchants were princes, whose traffickers were the honourable of the earth"—"the isle whom the merchants of Zidon, that pass over the sea, had replenished" (Isaiah xxiii. 2, 8). Her gold came from Arabia by the Persian Gulf, just as in the time of Solomon it came from Arabia (Ophir) by the Red Sea. The silver, iron, lead, and tin of Tyre came from a very different quarter of the world, namely from the settlement of Tarshish, in the south of Spain. There seems reason

---

[s] Ezek. xxvi., xxvii., xxviii.; comp. Rev. xviii. The older prophecy in Isaiah xxiii. furnishes other touches to the fuller picture of Ezekiel, and may be used to illustrate the state in which Tyre doubtless existed for many centuries: its occasion would naturally be the siege by Sargon in B.C. 720.

to believe that this was the period when the diminishing produce of the Spanish tin-mines caused the Phœnicians to venture on the distant voyage to the *Cassiterides* (" tin-islands ") the *Scilly Isles* and the adjacent coasts of Cornwall.   Her copper is mentioned, not as coming from Cyprus (the *copper* island), but in connection with Javan, Tubal, and Meshech, in the neighbourhood of Armenia and the southern line of the Caucasus; and from this quarter slaves were procured as from Circassia and Georgia in later times.   From Palestine Tyre obtained oil, honey, and balm, but apparently not wine, which was imported from Damascus, as was also white wool. This city was the emporium for "a multitude of wares of Tyre's making, and for the multitude of all riches."   The Bedouin Arabs supplied Tyre with lambs and rams and goats.   Egypt furnished linen for sails, and doubtless for other purposes; and the dyes from shell-fish, which afterwards became such a source of profit to the Tyrians, were imported from the Peloponnesus.   Lastly, from Dedan in the Persian Gulf, an island occupied possibly by a Phœnician colony, horns of ivory and ebony were imported, which must originally have been obtained from India (Ezek. xxvii. 7, 10–13, 15, 17, 18, 21, 22).   Let the reader turn to the prophecy itself for the rest of the picture of " the renowned city, inhabited of seafaring men, that was strong in the sea, she and her inhabitants, which caused their terror to be on all that haunted it;" that said. "I am of perfect beauty," whose " borders were in the midst of the seas, her builders had perfected her beauty : whose prince said, in the pride of his uplifted heart, " Behold, I am God, I sit in the seat of God, in the midst of the seas; " who claimed to be " wiser than Daniel," and boasted as much of the " great wisdom and traffick by which his riches were increased," as of that wealth itself : while the vices of a commercial people, and their unbounded indulgence in luxury and sensual pleasure, cried to heaven for the coming vengeance which the prophet denounces in the most vivid poetic language (Ezek. xxvi. 17; xxvii. 3, 4; xxviii. 1-5 ; 16-18).

The first of these three prophecies is dated on the first day of the month in the 11th year of the Great Captivity (B.C. 588); its occasion is specified, as arising out of the exultation of Tyre over the fall of Jerusalem, " I shall be replenished now she is laid waste:" and Nebuchadnezzar, king of Babylon, is named as about to besiege and destroy the city (Ezek. xxvi. 1-14).   The exultation and malevolence of the Tyrians are to be explained by Josiah's religious reformation, when he uprooted the Phœnician worship in Judæa, slew its priests upon their altars (Ezek. xxvi. 1-4', burnt the images of their gods, and destroyed their high places—not excepting that near Jerusalem, which Solomon, the friend of Hiram, had built to Ashtoreth, the Queen of Heaven (2 Kings xxiii. 20). We can scarcely doubt that the death in battle of Josiah at Megiddo, and the subsequent destruction of the city and temple of Jerusalem, were hailed by them with triumphant joy as instances of divine retribution in human affairs.

The prophet warned them that this catastrophe was the prelude to their own; and it seems indeed to have been brought on by the same causes. Nothing is more likely than that Tyre, the ancient ally of Egypt, would join the league formed by Pharaoh-Hophra, which brought down this final ruin upon Judæa; and the siege of Tyre would probably be formed at the same time as that of Jerusalem (B.C. 588). And this agrees with the date of that remarkable prophecy of Ezekiel, which leaves it doubtful whether Tyre was actually taken by Nebuchadnezzar:[9] "Son of man, Nebuchadrezzar, king of Babylon, caused his army to *serve a great service* against Tyrus; every head was made bald, and every shoulder was peeled" (doubtless in " casting the mount against the city "); " yet *he had no wages*, nor his army, for Tyrus, for the service that he served against it:"—and therefore the land and spoil of Egypt are assigned as his reward. The natural inference—that Nebuchadnezzar, like Sargon, failed to take the island city, though he took and destroyed Old Tyre on the mainland—is confirmed by the silence of Josephus, who relates the siege from the Tyrian annals, and of all other Greek and Roman writers, as to the capture of Tyre.[10] It seems most probable that the firm resistance of the city secured a capitulation on moderate terms. This view is not inconsistent with the account that a part of the population sailed away at the last moment to Carthage, and that the king, *Ethbaal*, was led captive to Babylon, with all the most noted families, and that Nebuchadnezzar installed a new king, Baal, as his vassal.

This king is presently found, with the King of Sidon, fighting for his new sovereign against the attempts of Apries (Pharaoh-Hophra) to recover Phœnicia to Egypt. The power, which had once relied wholly on Phœnicia for its marine service, now gathered a great fleet by the aid of its Ionian and Carian mercenaries. They defeated the united Phœnician and Cyprian fleets, which perhaps fought with little zeal for Nebuchadnezzar, in a great battle off

<hr>

[9] Ezek. xix. 17–20.—The date is the first day of the first month of the 27th year of the Great Captivity, B.C. 571. Now B.C. 588—13 years = B.C. 575.

[10] The only exception is St. Jerome, who may have assumed the result from the prophecy on which he was commenting (Hieron. 'Com. in Ezech.' xxvi.). Ezekiel's prophecy looks forward to the final destruction of the city by Alexander, and its subsequent desolation. (See the whole question discussed in the 'Dict. of the Bible,' art. Tyre).

Cyprus. The fleet of Pharaoh levied contributions along the
Phœnician coast, and took Sidon by storm; but retired with their
plunder. Aradus alone was held for a time by an Egyptian garrison, as we learn from an inscription of Apries lately discovered
there.

After this war of Apries we may place the inscription of *Esmu-
n'zar*, king of Sidon, the longest yet discovered, on his sarcophagus
in the Museum of the Louvre. It is as follows:—"I am Esmunazar, king of Sidon, son of Tabnith, king of Sidon, grandson of
Esmunazar, king of Sidon; and my mother was Amashtoreth,
priestess of our lady Ashtoreth, the queen, daughter of the king
Esmunazar of Sidon. We have built the temple of the *Alonim*
(the great gods) at Sidon on the sea-shore, and all-powerful Heaven
has made Ashtoreth favourable to us. We also have built on the
mountain a temple to *Esmun*, whose hand rests on a serpent.
Lastly, we also built the temples of the Alonim of Sidon at Sidon,
of the Baal of Sidon, and of Ashtoreth, the glory of Baal. *May
the master of the kings always grant us possession of Dor, Japha,
and the magnificent corn-lands in the valley of Sharon, as a recompense for the great things I have done.*" The last sentence seems to
imply that Sidon had been specially favoured by Nebuchadnezzar,
"the master of kings," probably as the reward of her ready submission; and that her territory was enlarged by the rich lands
named in Palestine. From this time to her destruction by Artaxerxes Ochus, it is Sidon, not Tyre, that is found at the head of
Phœnicia: and this appears to have been the time of Sidon's
greatest prosperity.

Tyre, however, has still a separate history. In a fragment of
her annals, she appears divided by factions, and restlessly snatch-
ing at opportunities for change. Such an opportunity would be
presented by the madness of Nebuchadnezzar; and in B.C. 563 we
find his vassal, Baal, deposed in a popular tumult, monarchy abo-
lished, and the king replaced by a republican magistrate, afterwards
increased to two, with the title of *Suffetes* (*Shofetim*, "Judges"),
as at Carthage. After a period of anarchy, a king, Baalaton, was
set up again, but dethroned in one year; and Nabonadius, among
his measures for reorganizing the empire, sent Mcherbaal, a member
of the old royal house, to Tyre as vassal king (B.C. 555). After four
years, he was succeeded by his son Hiram (B.C. 551), whose reign
extended into the period of the Persian Empire, and who died in
B.C. 531, leaving the crown to his son Muthon, who was king of
Tyre when Xerxes gathered his forces against Greece.

We have had occasion already to notice the voluntary submission
of the Phœnicians to Persia, probably under Cambyses, and that

rather as allies than subjects; and we have seen that the Phœnician fleet rendered powerful aid in the conquest of Egypt, but refused to serve against their Carthaginian kinsmen, to whom it is stated that they were bound *by oaths* (chap. xxxvi.). Henceforth, Herodotus tells us, the sea service of Persia mainly depended on the Phœnicians; but a glance over his list of the navy of Xerxes will suffice to correct the error that they formed the only fleet of Persia.

The restoration of friendly relations with the restored Jews is indicated by the service rendered again by "them of Zidon and Tyre," in bringing cedar-trees from Lebanon (and, it is implied, hewn stones, for the rebuilding of the temple. As in the time of Solomon, the Jews paid the wages of the masons and carpenters, and supplied provisions, "meat, drink, and oil," and the materials were brought round by sea to Joppa (Ezra iii. 7).

The policy of Persia towards her provinces was eminently suited to foster the prosperity of Phœnicia, whose commerce still connected the whole empire with the Mediterranean. Tyre had regained a high state of prosperity when visited by Herodotus, who saw the ancient temple of Hercules (*Melcarth*, the "king of the city"), and its rich offerings, among which were two pillars, one of gold and one of emerald, which Sir Gardner Wilkinson conjectures to have been of glass. But it was Sidon that enjoyed the special favour of the Persian kings as the chief seat of their naval power. This comes out clearly in the expedition against Greece. When, from a hill near Abydos, Xerxes witnessed a boat race in his fleet, the prize was gained by the Sidonians. When he reviewed his fleet, he sat on the deck of a Sidonian ship, beneath a golden canopy. When he wished to examine the mouths of the river Peneus, he entrusted himself to a Sidonian galley, as was his wont on similar occasions; and the king of the Sidonians sat first among the vassal sovereigns, tyrants, and officers. Herodotus states that the Phœnicians supplied the best vessels of the whole fleet; and of the Phœnicians, the Sidonians; and the highest commendation he can give to the vessels of Artemisia is by saying that they were the most renowned in the whole fleet *after the* Sidonians.

The breaking up of the Persian Empire was felt in Phœnicia all the more, as her cities were drawn into the revolts of Asia Minor and Syria, on the one side, and of Egypt on the other. We have already noticed the capture of Tyre by Evagoras of Cyprus, the share of Phœnicia in the general revolt of the western satraps against Artaxerxes Mnemon (chap. xxxviii.), and the great rebellion of Cyprus and Phœnicia, in connection with Nectanebo, the last independent king of Egypt, which led to the utter destruction of Sidon by Artaxerxes Ochus (about B.C. 350).

The cruel revenge taken for this revolt had a disastrous effect upon the Persian cause in the ensuing conflict with Alexander. Sidon, recovering with that marvellous rapidity which we see in these commercial cities, opened her gates to the conqueror after the battle of Issus, from the avowed motive of hatred to the Persians (B.C. 333); and her fleet, thus placed at the disposal of Alexander, was a main element of his success in the siege of Tyre. The possession of Phœnicia was doubly essential to the invader's plans. The naval force, which it was most important for him to acquire for his own use, might have been the means, in the hands of Persia, of cutting off his communications with Macedonia and Greece. After rejecting the overtures of Darius, which reached him at Marathus (opposite to Aradus), Alexander advanced southwards through Phœnicia, receiving the submission of Aradus, Byblus, and the other cities; Sidon hailed him as a deliverer; and the seamen of these cities, serving in the Persian fleet, obeyed the summons to bring away their ships to join him. But Tyre, which had now regained the supremacy since the fall of Sidon, seems to have hoped to rally those ships to her defence. While offering a nominal submission, and sending the conqueror a crown of gold and provisions for his army, they resolved not to admit him into the island city. Alexander, on his part, accepted their surrender as unconditional, and informed them of his intention to sacrifice to Hercules (Melcarth) in his ancient temple. The Tyrians pleaded their law forbidding the admission of strangers within their walls, and invited him to sacrifice in a still more ancient shrine of the god upon the mainland. Upon this he dismissed their ambassadors and prepared for the siege, which is one of the most famous in history.

By constructing a mole, which to this day forms an isthmus, he joined the island to the main; and using the Cyprian navy on the north side, and the Sidonian on the south, to blockade the harbours and protect his works from the incessant attacks of the Tyrian fleet, he at length succeeded in bringing up his newly invented engines and effecting a breach. The city was taken in July, B.C. 332, after the siege had lasted seven months; and the Macedonians, exasperated by their long and immense labours, put 8000 of the people to the sword. The remainder, with the exception of the king and some of the chief citizens, who had taken refuge in the temple of Melcarth, were sold into slavery, to the number of 30,000, including women, children, and slaves.

It lies beyond our subject to trace the later history of the Phœnician cities. It is enough to say that they flourished again, and enjoyed their municipal privileges, under the Seleucidæ, the Romans, and the Mahometans; and both Tyre and Sidon were flourishing seats of learning, as well as of commerce and manufacture. And it is worthy of note that Tyre was still famous in the 12th century for the *glass*, which the Greeks believed to have been a Phœnician invention. Their final decline dates from the time of the Crusades, in which Sidon suffered from several sieges; while Tyre, after being held by the Christians for more than a century and a half, was utterly ruined by the secession of its inhabitants, to avoid the fate inflicted upon Acre by the sultan of Egypt and Damascus (March, 1291). The story is thus told by a contemporary: "On the same day on which Ptolemaïs (*Acre*) was taken, the Tyrians, at vespers, leaving the city empty, without the stroke of a sword, without the tumult of war, embarked on board their vessels, and abandoned the city to be occupied freely by their conquerors. On the morrow the Saracens entered, no one attempting to prevent them, and they did what they pleased."

From that time every traveller might well ask, "Is this your joyous city, whose antiquity is of ancient days?" (Isaiah xxii. 7). Here is one of many answers (in 1751): "None of these cities, which formerly were famous, are so totally ruined as this, except Troy. *Zur* now scarcely can be called a miserable village, though it was formerly Tyre, the queen of the sea. *Here are about ten inhabitants, Turks and Christians, who live by fishing.*" Compare this with the prophecy uttered just 2310 years before:—"I will make thee like the top of a rock"—as bare as the sea-girt rock from which the proud name was first taken—"*thou shalt be a place to spread nets upon; thou shalt be built no more*" (Ezek. xxvi. 14). In spite of some revival since, the site wears an aspect of desolation. "On approaching it we come first to a low sandy isthmus, the remains of Alexander's causeway, which converts what was once an island into a peninsula. The ruins of old walls and towers, formed of still older materials, are here seen. . . . The island (that was), on which the city stood, is a ledge of rock parallel to the shore, three-quarters of a mile long, half a mile broad, and about half a mile distant from the coast-line. It was low and flat, not more than from 10 to 15 feet above the sea; but the accumulation of rubbish has rendered it uneven, and has given it in places a greater elevation. The isthmus, when first formed, was probably narrow; the united action of the winds and waves, dashing up the loose sands, has gradually increased it to the breadth of nearly half a mile. . . . The harbour, now nearly filled up with sand and rubbish, is on the north side of the isthmus, where the ruins of old moles are yet visible. The present town is beside the harbour, occupying a small section of the north-western part of the peninsula. Along its western side is a broad strip of land cut up into little

gardens; and the whole southern section of the peninsula is without
a habitation. Here are modern burying-grounds, there patches of
gardens; but the greater part is covered with rubbish-heaps, intersected by deep pits and gullies, from which building-stones have
been carried off to Beyrut and 'Akka. The modern town, or rather
village, contains from 3000 to 4000 inhabitants, about one-half
being Metâwileh, and the other Christians. Most of the houses are
mere hovels; the streets are unusually narrow, crooked, and filthy;
and the walls, and a few houses of a superior class, are so shattered
by repeated shocks of earthquakes, that they look as if about to fall
to pieces. The palm and Pride of India trees, scattered among the
houses and gardens, relieve in some degree the aspect of desolation,
and contribute to hide Tyre's fallen glory. The ancient Mistress
of the Seas can at the present day only boast the possession of a
few crazy fishing-boats; and her whole trade consists in the yearly
export of a few bales of cotton and tobacco, and a few boat-loads of
mill-stones and charcoal. There is but one gate, and the numerous
breaches in the old wall render others unnecessary. One is reminded
at every footstep, and by every glance, of the prophecies uttered
against this city: ' And they shall make a spoil of thy riches, and
make a prey of thy merchandise; and they shall break down thy
walls, and destroy thy pleasant houses. . . . They shall lament
over thee, saying, *What city is like* Tyrus, *like the destroyed in the
midst of the sea?*' (Ezek. xxvi. 12, xxvii. 32)." [11]

Sidon (*Sayda*) never sank so low. It is still a place of considerable traffic, and important enough to have been bombarded in the
Syrian war of 1840. Its architectural remains are few and insignificant—some marble and granite columns, with here and there
a sculptured frieze, and some fragments of mosaic pavement—but
even these are more than exist at Tyre. In the neighbouring hill-
side, however, and scattered over the plain, are tombs, with many
sarcophagi, which are among the most interesting monuments of
old Phœnicia. Among these the sarcophagus of King Esmunazar
(already mentioned) was discovered in January, 1855, by the accidental opening of one of the sepulchral caves, and is now in the
Louvre at Paris. The sarcophagus is of black syenite, and the lid
is hewn in the form of a mummy with the face bare. The material,
the form, and the decidedly Egyptian cast of the features, make
it probable that it was executed in Egypt for the Sidonian king.
The inscription of 22 lines is on the upper part of the lid.

Of the present state of the other Phœnician cities, a bare reference
must suffice to the commercial importance still enjoyed by some,

[11] Porter, 'Handbook of Syria,' pp. 391, 302.

as *Tripoli*, and especially *Beyrut*, and the historic fame which has clung to Acco (now '*Akka*, or in the Frank tongue, *St. Jean d'Acre*) from the days of Richard Cœur de Lion to those of Napoleon and Sir Sidney Smith.

Eighty years after the siege of Tyre by Nebuchadnezzar, her chief daughter, Carthage, appears in history as a great maritime power, making a treaty of commerce with the infant republic of Rome (B.C. 509). Her destiny, as the rival of her old ally, attracts her history to that of Rome, rather than of the East. That rivalry made the West the new scene of the great struggle between the Semitic and Aryan races, in which the interest of oriental history culminates. The contest was finally decided by the fall of Carthage in B.C. 146; when the saddened victor repeated over the burning city the prophecy, which had foretold the issue of the first act in the same long drama, and which may still be applied to every work of human policy and human power :—

> " The day shall surely come, when sacred Troy will fall,
> And Priam, and the people of the warrior Priam all."

Coin of Tyre.

INDEX.

A

Aahmes, admiral, 44.
——, founder of the Theban monarchy, 50. His marriage with an Ethiopian princess, the ground of claims made by his successors to Ethiopia, 50. His Asiatic wars, 50.
Acco, 249, 270.
Achæmenes, the, 215.
Achæmenids, stem of the 217.
Achthoës, 33.
Actium, battle of, 94.
Africa, Phœnician settlements in, 259.
Agesilaus, campaigns of, 241.
Ahab marries Jezebel, daughter of Ethbaal, 266.
Ahaz, King of Judah, made tributary, 146.
Ahriman, the evil principle, 196.
Ahuramazda, the good spirit, 196.
Akkad, people of, 115.
Alexander the Great's conquest of the Persian empire, 94. His siege of Tyre, 275.
Alexandria, founded, 94. Its library, 94.
Alphabet, its probable Egyptian origin, 253. Brought to Phœnicia by the Hyksos, 253.
Alyattes, his long reign, 210. War with the Milesians, 210. Drives the Cimmerians out of Asia, 210. Tomb of, 211.
Amasis, 83. Anecdote illustrating his change of condition, 85. Prosperity of Egypt under him, 86, 87. Architectural works, 87. The ally of Croesus against Cyrus, 88, 89.
Amenemhe I., 33.
—— II., 34.
—— III., 34.
—— IV., 34.
Amenhotep III., identified with the Memnon of Homer, 53. His statue, the vocal Memnon, described, 53.
—— IV., his religious innovations, 53.
Ameni, pictures and epitaph on the tomb of, 37.
Amenti, realm of, 20.
Amestris, chief wife of Xerxes, 240.
Amun, the supreme god of Egypt, 100.
Amyrtæus, succeeds in re-restoring the independence of Egypt, 93.
Animal worship Egyptian, 100.
Antalcidas, peace of, 241.
Antilibanus, 251, 252.
Apepi, king, 44.
Apis, Egyptian worship of the bull, 100, 101. The incarnation of Phtha, 100. Wounded by Cambyses, 92.
Apries, King of Egypt, 82. His expedition against Cyrene, 83. The Pharaoh-Hophra of Scripture, 82; his death, 84.
Aradus, island and city of, 255. Taken by Asshurbani-pal, 270.
Arbela, the Persian empire ends at the battle of, 244.
Arca or Caesarea Libani, 254.
Architecture of ancient Egypt, 103, 104.
Ardys, son of Gyges, reign of, 209.
Ariana = the later Persian Iran, 195.
Armenia, province of Persia, 215.
Arsames, killed, 242.
Arses, King of Persia, murdered by Bagoas, 243.
Art, Egyptian, 27-29.
Artabanus, usurpation of, 240.
Artabazus's rebellion in the reign of Ochus, 242.
Artaxerxes I. (or Arsaces) Longimanus, 240. His commissions to Ezra and Nehemiah, 240. Explanation of the name Artaxerxes, 240 n.
—— II., Mnemon, 241; his character, 242.
Aryan language, 197. Divided into the older branch the Aryas, and the younger the Yavanas, 197. The primitive Aryans a pastoral people, 197. Their social life, morals, and religion, 198. Primitive religion, 198. Its monotheistic basis, 198. Corruption into dualism and pantheistic nature-worship, 198. Conflict of Aryans and Turanians, 199.
Aryandes put to death by Darius, 235.
Ascalon takes and destroys Sidon, 260.

Ashdod. *See* Azotus.

Ashtoreth, temple of, 265.

Asia, conquests in, by Theban kings, 50.

Asia Minor, its geographical structure, 207. Remarkable mixture of populations, 208.

Asshur, capital of Assyria, 128.

Asshur-bani-pal, his name suggestive of Sardanapalus, 166. A great conqueror and magnificent monarch, 166. His systematic care for literature, 166, 167. His annals, 167, 168. Homage to him by Gyges King of Lydia, 170, 171. Wars in Susiana and Babylon, 171. Horrible cruelty, 171. Domestic scene in his bas-reliefs, 172. His library, 167.

Asshur-nasir-pal, King of Assyria, 135. Plan of his palace, 131, 135. Conquests of, 136. His great inscription, 135.

Assyria, conquered by Theban kings, 51. Its geographical position, 107. Like Egypt, yielding up long-hidden history, 116. The Assyria of the Greek historians, 116. The Semitic Asshur, 121. Its oldest contemporary records, 127. Full establishment of old empire, 128. Extent of the empire, 129. Foundation of the new empire, 144, 145. Upper and Lower dynasties of, 126. Elements of royal names, 127. Their Semitic character, 127, n. System of chronology, 132. Cruelties of the kings, 136, 137. Light thrown on difficulty in connecting Assyrian records with Scripture history, 141, 142. Seven kings of the New or Lower Empire, 144, 145. Canon lately discovered, 142. Fall of, 175.

Astronomy, Egyptian knowledge of, 102.

Astyages, his reign, 213.

Description of his court, 213, 214. Dethroned by Cyrus, 216.

Athothis, 19.

Atossa, daughter of Cyrus, 224. Urges Darius to undertake the conquest of Greece, 236.

Avaris of the Shepherd kings, the Zoan of Scripture, 41. Proved to be Tanis, 42.

Azotus (Ashdod) taken after a siege of 29 years, the longest on record, 78.

B

Baal, King of Tyre, 272, 273.

Baalaton, 273.

Babel, city and tower of, 111, 112. Tower of Babel at Borsippa, and the ruins of Birs-Nimrud on its original foundation, 112.

Bab-il, mound of, 191.

Babylon, its rivalry to the empire of Assyria, 129. Fall of, 190, 191. Great works of Nebuchadnezzar at, 185, 186. Darius's first siege of, 234.

Babylonia, contrast between its ancient and present state, 106. Its temple towers, 113. Semitic dynasty in, 115.

Babylonian empire, its history begins, 178. Ruins, objects found in, 192. The early chronology of the Babylonians, 132.

Bactria, 196.

Bagoas, the eunuch, minister of Ochus, 242. Poisons Ochus, 243. Murders Arses, 243. Compelled to drink the poison he had mixed for Codomannus, 244.

Bardes. *See* Smerdis.

Behistun, inscription relating to Magism, 225. Transcription of the trilingual rock-inscription of, 232. The famous record of Darius, 215. Its account of the revolution of the pseudo-

Smerdis, 226. Its contents relating to Darius, 228, 229. Agreement of Herodotus with 229.

Belshazzar, 189. His defence of Babylon, 190.

Belus, temple of, 186.

Beni-hassan, tombs of, 37.

Berosus, his history of Babylon or Chaldæa, 115.

Berytus, city of, 255.

Birs-Nimrud, mound of, 112. Identified with the temple at Borsippa, 112. Inscription found among its ruins, 112, 114.

Bocchoris burnt alive by Sabaco, 73.

Borsippa, great temple of Nebo at, 186.

Bubastis, capital of Egypt, 70. The sacred city of the goddess Pasht, 70. Described by Herodotus, 70. Temple of the goddess Bubastis, 70. Her festival, 70.

Byblus or Gebal, an ancient religious city of Phœnicia, 254, 255.

C

Calah (Nimrud), ruins of, 122. At the height of its splendour, 134, 135.

Cambe, the site afterwards occupied by Carthage, 259.

Cambyses, father of Cyrus, and king of the Persians, 215, 216.

Cambyses, son of Cyrus, 223. Puts to death his sister-wife, 224. Formation of his name from the Persian original, 224. His attack on Egypt, 89. Takes Memphis, 90. Defeats Psammenitus, 89, 90. His sacrilege in killing the Apis, 92. He marches into Ethiopia, 91. Destruction in the desert of a detachment of his army sent against the Ammonians, 92. His madness ascribed to his sacrilege, 93. Secures the submission of Egypt, 93. His suicide, 226.

Canaanites, immigrants from the East, 252.
Cappadocians, 208.
Carchemish, city of, 79. Victory of Nebuchadnezzar over Neco at, 79.
Carians, the, 208.
Carthage, foundation of, 266. Its treaty of commerce with the infant republic of Rome, 278. Its fall decides the conflict between Eastern and Western civilisation. 278.
Cassandané, wife of Cyrus, 223.
Cassiterides (the Scilly Islands), Phœnician voyages to the, 271.
Caunians, their loyalty to Artaxerxes, 242.
Cephren, 25.
Chaeronea, battle of, 243.
Chaldæan monarchy, 115. The kings of Babylon Chaldæans, 178, 179. Priests, 179, 185.
Chedorlaomer, 115.
Cheops, builder of the Great Pyramid, 24.
Chev, branch of Royal family at, 65.
Cimmerian invasion of Asia, 209, 210. Conquest of the country by the Scythians, 210. The Cimmerians probably progenitors of the Cymry of Wales and even of all the Celtic races, 210.
Crœsus succeeds Alyattes, 218. Ambiguous reply of the Delphic Oracle to him, 220. A curious chapter in the history of superstition, 220. His retreat to Sardis after defeat, 421. Cyrus's treatment of the conquered king, 422.
Ctesias's history of Persia, 203.
Cush, 95.
Cyaxares takes Nineveh, 175. Overthrows the Assyrian empire, 175. The first who gave organization to an Asiatic army, 204. The true founder of the Medo-Persian kingdom, 204.

Cyprus, 225. Taken by Sargon, 269.
Cyrene, 83.
Cyrus the Great, legend of his birth and early life, 216. His rebellion, 216. His generosity to the conquered Astyages, 216. Accession, 218. Of mixed Persian and Median birth, 216. Invites the Ionians to revolt from Crœsus, 221. Conquers Lydia, 221, 222. Upper Asia, 222. Besieges Babylon, 190. Diverts the course of the Euphrates, 190. Conquers Babylon, 190, 191. Falls in battle with the Massagetæ, 222. His tomb at Pasargadæ identified, 222. His two sons and three daughters, 224.
Cyrus the younger, rebellion of, 241.

D

Damascus, foundation of the kingdom of, 132. Taken and destroyed, 146, 147.
Daniel, 181, 182.
Darius, the head of seven conspirators, slays the pseudo-Smerdis, 228. Names of his associates in the enterprise, 229. Behistun inscription relating to, 228, 229. His right to the crown by descent, 228. Privileges granted to his confederates, 229. Massacre of the Magians, 229. The second founder of the Persian empire, 231. His marriages, 232. In the Behistun Inscription represents himself as the hereditary champion of the Achæmenids, 231. The revolts against him while he was at Babylon, 234. Takes Babylon after a siege of twenty months, 234. Defeats, mutilates, and crucifies Phraortes, 234-235. His Zoroastrian zeal, 233,

234. Conquest of the Indians, 236. His Scythian expedition, 237, 238. Death of Darius, 238. His tomb, 238.
Darius II., Nothus, 241.
—— III., Codomannus, the last king of Persia, 243. His flight from Issus and Arbela, 244. Alexander throws his cloak over the corpse of, 244.
Deioces, king of Media, 203.
Delta of the Nile, 2. Its dimensions, 2.
Derceto, the great goddess of Ascalon, 117.
Dido = the fugitive, 266.
Diodorus on Egyptian history, 14.
Dora, colony of, 254.
Dynasties of Manetho. See Manetho.

E

Ecbatana, the capital city of Media, 204.
Egypt, upper and lower, 3. The granary of the ancient world, 4. Causes of its early prosperity, 5. Abundant supply of food, 5. Facility of communication, 5. Metals of, 8. Monuments of, 7-12. History begins with Egypt, 12. Traditional history of, 13, 14, 19. Two classes of records of especial historical value, 12. Succession of kings according to Herodotus, 16. Lists of Manetho, 17. Eight broad divisions of the whole history of Egypt, 17. First three dynasties, 18, 19. Antagonism between Upper and Lower, 32. Conquered by the Hyksos, 43. Its conflict with Western Asia, 52. Mistress of the Mediterranean, 52. Decline of power, 55. Falls under the dominion of Ethiopia, 73. Conquered by Cambyses, 89-93. Submits to Alexander the Great, 94. Becomes

a Roman province, 94. Judicial administration of, 99. Religion of, 100, 102. Origin of animal worship, 100. Conquered by Nebuchadnezzar, 183, 184. Revolts from Darius, 238. Reconquest of, 241. *See* Architecture, Sculpture, Painting, Hieroglyphics.

Egyptians, civilisation of the, 5. Their astronomical and geometrical knowledge, 5. Their symbols of life and death the Nile or Osiris, and the evil power or Typhon, 6. Speculations on their origin, 29. Their life represented on the tombs surrounding the pyramids, 27-29. Their agriculture and manufactures under the Middle Monarchy, 37. Razzias to kidnap negroes, 48, 51. Of the Hamitic race, 95. Seven classes enumerated by Herodotus, five by Diodorus, 97. Vast variety of classes of artizans seen on the monuments, 97. Priests the highest class, 96. The military class, 96, 97. Theory of the king's royalty, 98. His divinity and rules of daily life, 98.

Elam, land of, 109.

Enentefs, monuments of the, 33.

Esar-Haddon, king of Assyria and Babylonia, 162. Destroys Sidon, 269. Invades Egypt, 164. His palaces, 164.

Esmunazar, king of Sidon, inscription of, 273, 277.

Ethbaal forms a new dynasty at Tyre, 266.

Etesian winds of Egypt, 5.

Ethiopia, conquests in, by Theban kings, 50, 51. Its relations to Egypt, 68-74.

Euphrates, course of the, 106.

Evagoras, rebellion of, in Cyprus, 241, 242. Captures Tyre, 274.

Evil-Merodach, reign of, 188.

Exodus from Egypt, calamities attending it, 64.

F

Fyûm, valley of the, 33, 35.

G

Gades founded by the Phœnicians, 261.

Gebal. *See* Byblus.

Gomates, the true name of the Pseudo-Smerdis, 226. Usurps the crown of Persia, 227. Slain, 228.

Greeks, their intercourse with Egypt under Psammetichus, 76-78. Their influence attested by the monuments of the Säite age, 87. End of the first series of their wars with Persia, 240.

Gyges, king of Lydia, 208. Oracle that vengeance for the Heraclidæ would fall on his fifth descendant, 209.

H

Hamath, or Epiphania, city and kingdom of, 255, 256.

Hamitic race, 95.

Harpagus, 216; his conquests in Asia, 222.

Hatasou (queen), monument of her splendour in the palace of Karnak, 52.

Heracleopolis, 33

Her-Hor, high priest, 66. Line of, 69, 70.

Hermetic books of the Egyptians, 102.

Hermotybians and Calasirians, 97.

Herodotus's account of Egyptian life and manners, 13, 14.

Hezekiah, 151, 153, 156-160.

Hiddekel of Eden, the Tigris, 106.

Hieroglyphics, 9-12. Three forms of Egyptian writing, — hieroglyphic, hieratic, and demotic or enchorial, 102, 103. The characters partly phonetic and partly ideographic, 103. Illustrations of the system, 103.

Hiram, king of Tyre, his alliance with Solomon, 264. His great works at Tyre, 265. His relation with Solomon, 264, 265.

Histiæus, the Milesian General, 237.

Hittites, the, 51, 129, 130.

Hophra (Pharaoh) of Scripture, the Apries of Herodotus. *See* Apries.

Hoshea, 147, 148

Hyksos or Shepherd kings invade Egypt, 40. False identification with the Hebrews, 41. Their race Semitic, 41. Conquer Egypt, 43. Their expulsion, 44, 45.

Hystaspes, father of Darius, 218, 234.

I

Inarus and Amyrtæus, rebellion in Egypt under, 93.

Indo-European language, 197.

Ionian colonies in Asia Minor, 208.

Ionians revolt against Darius, 238.

Irac-Arabi, 106.

Iran, the table-land of, 195, 196, 206.

Iranians, 197.

Israel, oppressed by Rameses II., 58, 59. Exodus of, 63, 64. Under Solomon, empire of, 69. Captivity of the Israelites of Gilead, 146. The whole population removed to Mesopotamia, 147.

Issus, battle of, 244.

Iva-Lush or Vul-Lush, union of the two crowns of Mesopotamia under, 141.

J

Jebusites, 38.
Jehoiachin, 181.
Jehoiakim put to death by Nebuchadnezzar, 181.
Jeremiah's prophecies, 182.
Jerusalem, according to Manetho quoted by Josephus, built by the Shepherd-kings of Egypt, 40. The first capture of, by Nebuchadnezzar, 180. Siege and destruction of, 182. Besieged by Sennacherib and defended by Hezekiah, 157, 159.
Jezebel, 266.
Joseph's Pharaoh, 43. Joseph brought into Egypt under the Shepherd-king Aphophis, 44.
Josiah, his resistance to Nechao, 79
Judah, first captivity of, 180. Great captivity of, 181.

K

Kamês, king, 43, 44.
Karnak, temple of, 49. The numerical wall of, 52. Description of the Hall of Columns, the triumph of Egyptian architecture, 49.
Kheta, the, 51.
Khorsabad, M. Botta's discovery of inscriptions at, 123, 124. Palace of Sargon, 124, 154.
Khufu, 24, 25.
Khumneh, fortress of, 34.
Kileh-Sherghat (Asshur), 115, 122, 125, 127.
Kosseir, port of, 30.
Koyunjik, mound of, 123, 125. Palace at, 156.

L

Labaris, 37.
Labynetus, king of Babylon, 220.
Labyrinth, the Egyptian, 35, 36.
Lachish, siege of, 158-160.
Ladice, wife of Amasis, 87.

Lamps, feast of, in honour of the goddess Neith, 77.
Lebanon, cedars of, 251, 252.
Lydians, the, 208. Origin of the race, 208. Mythical story of their two first dynasties, 208. Three dynasties, 208, 209. Semitic origin of the Lydians, 208. The third dynasty, the Mermnadæ, 208, 209. War between Lydia and Media, 211.
Lygdamis, leader of the Cimmerians, killed, 410.

M

Magi, their influence at the court of Astyages, 214.
Magian religion, 199.
Magophonia, festival of, 229.
Manasseh's captivity, 163. Restoration, 163.
Mandopt I., 33.
Manetho's history of Egypt, 14. His List of Dynasties, 14-17.
Marathon, battle of, 238.
Margiana, 195.
Margen, king, 165.
Maxyes, the, 62.
Mazdeism, 199.
Media, limits of, 200, 201. Media Atropatene, and Media Magna, 201.
Medes, their final attack on Assyria, 175. And Persians both branches of the Aryan race, 195. Their affinity with races of northern India and with European races, 197. Origin of the Medes, 197. Foundation of the Median monarchy, 204. War with the Lydians, 211.
Medo-Persian empire, 194. Foundation of, 204.
Megabazus's conquest of Thrace and Macedonia, 238.
Megabyzus revolts, 240.
Melcarth, temple of, 265. The Phœnician Hercules, 274.
Melita, 262.

Memphian monarchy, the old, 18, 19. Life under the, 26.
Memphis, the earliest seat of the Egyptian kingdom, 15. Its site, 19, 20. The Memphite necropolis, 20, 21. Taken by Cambyses, 90.
Menephtha, the Pharaoh of the Exodus, 63, 64.
Menes, first (human) king of Egypt, 18. Turns the course of the Nile, 19. Builds Memphis, 19.
Menes, dyke of, 19.
Menkare, 25.
Mentor, 242. Transfers his services from Sidon to Persia, 243.
Mermnad kings of Lydia, 208, 209.
Merodach Baladan conquered by Sargon, 153. By Sennacherib, 160.
Meroë, island of, 2.
Mesopotamia, 51. The land of the two rivers, 106-109. Primitive kingdoms of, 110-115. Transfer of supremacy in, from Babylon to Assyria, 128.
"Middle monarchy," the, 15, 32.
Mizraim the Semitic name of the Egyptians, 3.
Mœris, king, 37.
Mœris, lake, 3, 35, 36.
Month, the Sun-God, 100.
Moses's initiation into the wisdom of the Egyptian priests and instruction as a soldier, 98.
Mycerinus, 25.

N

Nabonadius or Nabonidus, last king of Babylon, 189. His alliance with Crœsus, 190. Defeated by Cyrus, 190. His flight to Borsippa, 190. Motive for associating Belshazzar in the sovereignty, 189. Surrenders to and is favoured by Cyrus, 191.
Nabopolassar, accession of, 179.
Naharain, land of, 51, 106.

Nahum, striking prophecy of, 170. His warning of Nineveh, 176.

Naïri, the, 129.

Napata, city of, 72.

Nebo, his statues, 141.

Nebuchadnezzar, king of Babylon, 79. Without him the Babylonians would have had no place in history, 178. Created the empire of Babylon by the victory of Carchemish, 180. Campaign against Tyre, 183. Takes Jerusalem, 180, 181. His vision of the colossal image of the empires of the world, 181, 182. Destroys Jerusalem, 182. Conquers Egypt, 183, 184. His great works at Babylon, 185, 186. His madness, 187. Recovery and death, 188. Decline of the Babylonian empire after his death, 188.

Nechao, the Pharaoh-Necho of the Bible, 79. His attempt to complete the canal connecting the Mediterranean and the Red Sea, 80. His fleets in the two seas, 79.

Nectanebo, the last king of independent Egypt, 94.

Neith identified with Athena or Minerva, 77. Temple of, 77.

Neriglissar, his reign, 189

Nile, "Egypt the gift of the Nile," 1. Cataracts, 2. Physical phenomena, 2. Formed by the junction of the White and Blue rivers, 2. Junction with the Black River, 2. Periodical inundation, 4, 5. Its cause, 4.

Nilometers, 4.

Nimrud, mound of, 112. Plan of the mound, 133. Mr. Layard's excavations at, 124, 125. Discovery of the North-West palace at, 135. Standard inscription of, 135, 136. Pyramid of, 138. Nimrud identified with Calah, 132.

Nin and Nergal, deities

who correspond nearly to Hercules and Mars, 130.

Nineveh or Niniveh, site of, 120. Its description by Jonah, 120. The epoch of its fall, 119. Still unsettled, 173, 176. Contents of the Royal Library of, 167. Nineveh taken by Cyaxares, 175.

Ninus, the hero-eponymus of Nineveh, 117.

Ninyas, son of Semiramis, 118. A politic and self-indulgent ruler, 119. His profound policy, 119.

Nitocris, queen, 31. Regarded as a queen regnant by Herodotus, 31. Her vengeance and suicide, 31. Her defence of Babylon, 190.

Notre-t-ari, princess, 50.

Nomes, division of Egypt into, 3.

O

Oasis of Ammon, 92. And the Greater, 92. The Lesser, 92.

Obelisk (the Black) of Shalmaneser II., 138, 139.

Ochus, Satrap of Hyrcania. See Darius II.

Ochus or Artaxerxes III., his cruelty and bloodthirstiness, 242. His ministers Bagoas and Mentor, 242. Poisoned by Bagoas, 243.

Ormazd, 198.

Orœtes, treason and punishment of, 235.

Orthosia. See Simron.

Osiris and Typhon, the good and evil principles, 6. Osiris, Isis, and their son Horus, 100.

Osorchon, I., 72.

P

Padan-Aram, 106.

Painting, Egyptian chiefly a decorative art, 104. Illustrations of the Ritual of the Dead, 104.

Palestine, a tributary of Assyria, 145, 146. The Granary of Phœnicia, 264.

Papyri, 10.

Papyrus reed, description of writing on it, 10.

Parysatis, wife of Darius II., 241. Her wickedness and cruelty, 241.

Pasargadæ, the Persian capital, 202. Tribe, the, 215.

Pentaour, the poet, 56, 61.

Persepolis, 202.

Persia or Persis, 201.

Persians, position of, under the Median supremacy, 215. Their ten tribes and three social classes, 215. Reconquest of Egypt, 243. Constitution of the empire, 245. Royal judges of Persia, 245. Despotism of the Great King, 246.

Persian empire, climax of the, 231-238. Fall of the, 244.

Phanes of Halicarnassus, his sons killed before their father's eyes, 89.

Pharaoh, title of, 98.

Philip of Macedon, death of, 243.

Phiops, 31.

Phios, king, 30.

Philistines, conflict of Israel with the, 68.

Phœnicia, description of, 249. Climate, 250. Etymology of the word, 251, 252. Its population before the migration of the Canaanites, 252, 253. Chief cities, 252. Its history divided into periods of Sidonian and Tyrian supremacy, 257. Phœnicia before the Exodus described in an Egyptian papyrus, 257. Phœnician fleet the great maritime force of the Persian empire, 225.

Phœnicians, the, called themselves Canaanites, 252. The Hyksos or Shepherds called Phœnicians, 253. Their language and the Hebrew differed only as dialects, 253. Sidonian colonies,

259. Relations to Assyria, 262. Conquered by Asshur-bani-pal, 267. Colonies in Africa and Greece, 260.

Phraortes attacks Assyria, 175. Succeeds Deioces, 204. A Mede of the same name heads a rebellion against Darius, 234. A pretender to the crown of Darius, 234. His punishment, 234, 235.

Phrygians of Aryan origin, 208.

Phtha, the Egyptian deity, the worker by the energy of fire, 100. His temple, 18. The patron deity of Memphis, 20.

Pithom, built by the Israelites, 8, 59.

Polycrates of Samos, 235.

Priests, Egyptian, 13, 14.

Psamatik II., 81.

Psammenitus defeated and put to death by Cambyses, 90.

Psammetichus, his fulfilment of an oracle, 76. Makes himself king of Egypt, 76. His Hellenizing policy, 77. Favours heaped on his mercenaries, 78. Deserted by the Egyptian class of warriors, in number 200,000, 78.

Pteria, battle of, 221.

Ptolemais. See Acco.

Ptolemies, Egypt under the, 94.

Pul of Scripture (the), question concerning, 141, 142.

Pygmalion and Elisa (Dido), 266.

Pyramid of Cheops, the first monumental link in not only Egyptian but universal history, 13.

Pyramid, the Great, records on, 9.

Pyramids, description of the, 21 25. Plan of the pyramids, 22, 23. Artistic motives for their size and form, 21 Dimensions of, 24. Skill and art in building the pyramids, evidence of high civilisation, 27. The

Pyramid of Degrees at Sakkara, 113.

Pyramids of Jizeh, 21.

R

Ra, the Sun god, 98.

Raamses, built by the Israelites, 8.

Rab-Mag, the, 188.

Rameses, the city of, papyri recording the Hebrews by name as its builders, 59.

—— I., or Rhamses, 54.

—— II., son of Seti I., 54. His exploits recorded in the Greek legend of Sesostris, 55. The Rameseïd, an epic by Pentaour, 56. Personal exploit of Rameses told in a true Homeric spirit, 56. His enormous harem, 60. The great oppressor, of the Israelites, 58, 59. His great buildings, 56-58. His colossal statues, 58. Bust of one of them in the British Museum, 58.

—— III., restores the Egyptian empire, 65 His campaigns, 65. Victory of his fleet, 65, 66.

—— XII., collecting tribute in Mesopotamia, marries a chief's daughter, 66.

Raphia, battle of, 151.

Rosetta stone, the, 94, 103.

Rotno, the, 51.

S

Sabaco I., 73.

—— II., identified with the priest-king Sethos of Herodotus, 73

Sabæism, 204.

Sacians, the Persian name for Scythians, 236.

Sadyattes, reign of, 210.

Saïs, capital of Egypt, 77. Its remains, 77. Connection with Athens, 77.

Saïte kings of Egypt, 75.

Samaria, the kingdom of, destroyed, 147, 148.

Sanchoniathon's Phœnician history, 253.

Sandanis's expostulation to Crœsus, 220, 221.

Saracus burns himself with his palace, 175.

Sardanapalus collects his treasures, constructs a funeral pile, and perishes with his wives and concubines, 119.

Sardis, 208. Captured by Cyrus, 222.

Sarepta, 257.

Sargon, founder of the dynasty of Bubastis, 70.

Sargon, or Sarkin, a military adventurer, 149. His campaigns, 150. His annals on the walls at Khorsabad, etc., 154. Victory over the Egyptians at Raphia, 151. Expeditions against the Medes, Parthians, and other nations, 153, 154. Capture of Ashdod, 152. Embassy to him from Cyprus, 151. Assassinated, 153. His description of his palace at Khorsabad, 154. Fruitless siege of Tyre, 269. Expedition against Cyprus, 269.

Satrapies, Persian, 245, 246. Explanation of the word satrap, 245, n.

Sculpture, Egyptian style of, 104. Its spirit symbolism and repose, 104.

Scylax's voyage down the Indus, 236.

Scythian domination over Asia, 175. Their dominion lasted for twenty-eight years, 175.

Semiramis, legend of, 117. Her divine birth, 117. Exploit for which Ninus married her, 117. Becomes sole queen, 117. Her prodigious edifices, 118. Reproached for her debaucheries and threatened with crucifixion by the Indian king, 118. Her own record of her deeds, 118. Apotheosis of, 118. An historical Semiramis, 141.

Semitic race, 177, 195.

Semneh, fortress of, 34.

Sennacherib, reign of, 155. His recovery of a signet-ring of an ancient predecessor, 128. Reconquers Babylon, 156. And Phœnicia, 156. Victory at Altaku over Egypt and Ethiopia, 157. Besieges Jerusalem, 158. And Lachish, 158. His army destroyed by a miracle, 159. His fleet built on Phœnician models, 160. Murdered by his two sons, 161. The worst type of an oriental despot, 161. His inscriptions at Nineveh, 161.

Serapis, worship of, 101.

Sesortasen I., 33.

—— II., his deification, 34.

—— III., 34.

Sesostris of the Greeks traced in Sesortasen and in Rameses II., 34.

Set or Soutekh, the god, 43.

Seti I., king of Egypt, 54. His magnificent buildings, 54, 55. Reliefs and inscriptions in the Hall of Columns, in the palace of Karnak, a Sethe'd of his exploits, 55. Began the canal uniting the Nile to the Red Sea, 55.

—— II. (son of Menephtha), regains the throne from the kings of Chev, 65.

Shafre, 25.

Shalmaneser I., founder of Calah, 128.

—— II., statue of, 129. The Black Obelisk king, 138. His campaigns, 140. Rebellion of his eldest son subdued by a younger, 141.

Shalmanezer III., expeditions of, 142, 143.

—— IV. destroys the kingdom of Samaria, 147, 148.

"Shepherd kings." See Hyksos.

Sheshonk I. the first Pharaoh mentioned in Scripture by his personal name (Shishak), 69, 71.

Shinar, land of, 107.

Shishak. See Sheshonk.

Sicily, Greek colonisation of, 268.

Sidon, the most ancient city of Phœnicia, 252,

251. Its colonies and commerce, 254, 255, 257. Destroyed by Esarhaddon, 269. By Artaxerxes Ochus, 243. Still a place of considerable traffic, 277. At the head of Phœnicia, 273.

Sidonian, generic use of the name for Phœnician, 253. Colonies, 259. Superiority of the fleet, 274. The Sidonians burn their own city, 243.

Silsilis, breaking of the rocky bar of the Nile at, 35, 36.

Simron, 254.

Simyra (Shumra), 255.

Sinai, mines of, 8.

Sippara, huge reservoir near, 186.

Smerdis, formation of his name from the Persian original, 224. Murdered by Cambyses, 224. Personated by Gomates, 225.

Sogdianus, reign of, 241.

Solomon's great commercial empire, 69. His relations with Hiram, 264, 255.

Solon's preaching to Crœsus an anachronism, 219.

Stibium, 38.

Stranger kings of Egypt, 53.

Suffetes at Carthage and Tyre, 273.

Susa, chief capital of the Persian empire, 109.

Syene, granite found near, 7.

Syria, a tributary of Assyria, 145, 146.

——, Cœle, 50.

T

Tanis, the Greek form of Zoan, the Avaris of the Shepherd kings, 42. Its ruins, 42. Description of its site, 42. Becomes the capital of Lower Egypt, 68.

Taylor cylinder in the British Museum, 156.

Temple - towers (Babylonian), their astronomical character, 112-114.

Thebes (Egyptian), 3. In-

fancy of the monarchy of, 15, 33. Its epithet hecatompylos, 46. Gates and war - chariots, 46. Various names, 47. Its site, 47. Marked by the villages of Karnak, Luxor, etc., 48. Vast necropolis, 49. Trade, manufactures, and religion, 48. Linen fabric, 48. The sacerdotal capital of all who worship Ammon, 47. Its fall, 48. Principal edifices, 49. Succession of its kings, 50.

Theban monarchy, new, 54.

Thinite kings, first dynasty of, 18. Second dynasty of, 19.

Thirty, Egyptian supreme court of, 99.

This, city of, 19.

Thothmes III., his reign the climax of the power of Egypt, 51. Extent of her empire under him, 51, 52. The Numerical wall of Karnak the record of his exploits, 52. His victory over the Assyrians at Megiddo, 51. Conquest of Cœle-Syria in his sixth expedition, 51. Conquest of Nineveh and Babylon, 51. Maritime power, 52.

Thracians, conquered by Darius, 237.

Tinaken, king, 43, 44.

Tiglath-pileser, meaning of the name, 12.

—— I., annals of, 127-130. Campaigns, 129, 130. First organised Assyria as an empire, 130.

—— II., an obscure adventurer, 145. Records of his wars, 145. Reduction of Syria and Palestine, 145-147.

Tiglathi-Nin, 128.

Tigranes of Armenia, 214. Story of his conquest of, Astyages, 214.

Tigris, 106. Identified with the Hiddekel of Eden, 106. Its junction with the Euphrates, 106.

Tirhakah, king of Ethiopia, 73, 159, 168, 169.

Tissaphernes, policy of,

among the Greek States, 241.

Tnephachthus, curse on Menes pronounced by, 18, 72.

Tripolis, the threefold Phœnician colony of, 256, 57.

Turanian race, 195, 202.

Tyre, Nebuchadnezzar marches against, 181. Siege of, 183. Its antiquity inferior to that of Sidon, 253. Old Tyre, 254. Distant voyages to the West, 261. Succession of kings, 263, 264. Climax of her power, 265. Three sieges by Sargon, Nebuchadnezzar, and Alexander, 269, 272, 275. Ezekiel's historical picture of its resources, 270. Its exultation over the fall of Jerusalem, 271. Wealth and power before its fall, 270, 271. Captured by the Saracens, 276. Its present state, 276, 277.

Tyrian purple, 252.

Tyrrhenians, 261, 263.

Tyrrheno-Pelasgians, 62.

U

Urumiyeh, lake, 202.

Utica, 261.

X

Xerxes, preferred to his elder half-brother by the influence of his mother Atossa, 239. His attempt against Greece, 239. Murdered by Artabanus, 240.

—— II. murdered, 241.

Y

Yakindu, king, 270.

Yavanas, the branch of the Aryan family which spread over Europe, 197.

Z

Zab, the Great and Lesser, 107.

Zedekiah, rebellion of, against Nebuchadnezzar, 182.

Zend-avesta, the, 196, 197.

Zerah the Cushite, 15, 72.

Zicharbaal, the Sichæus of Virgil, 266.

Ziggurat at Calah, 134.

Zoan, field of, 63.

Zopyrus, rebellion of, against Artaxerxes, 240.

Zoroaster, great religious reform of, 198.

THE END.

DR. WM. SMITH'S

SMALLER HISTORIES & MANUALS.

These Smaller Histories have been drawn up chiefly for the lower forms in Schools, at the request of several teachers, who require for their pupils more elementary books than the STUDENT'S MANUALS.

---

1. A SMALLER HISTORY OF ENGLAND. With 68 Woodcuts. 16mo. 3*s.* 6*d.*

2. A SMALLER HISTORY OF GREECE. With 74 Woodcuts. 16mo. 3*s.* 6*d.*

3. A SMALLER HISTORY OF ROME. With 79 Woodcuts. 16mo. 3*s.* 6*d.*

4. A SMALLER CLASSICAL MYTHOLOGY. Illustrated with Translations from the Ancient Poets, and Questions on the Work. With 90 Woodcuts. 16mo. 3*s.* 6*d.*

5. A SMALLER SCRIPTURE HISTORY OF THE OLD AND NEW TESTAMENT. With Woodcuts. 16mo. 3*s.* 6*d.*

6. A SMALLER HISTORY OF ENGLISH LITERATURE. 16mo. 3*s.* 6*d.* Also SELECT SPECIMENS, 16mo. 3*s.* 6*d.*

7. A SMALLER MANUAL OF ANCIENT GEOGRAPHY. 16mo. *[In the press.*

8. A SMALLER MANUAL OF MODERN GEOGRAPHY. 16mo.

SEPTEMBER, 1871.

STANDARD SCHOOL BOOKS

PUBLISHED BY MR. MURRAY.

DR. WM. SMITH'S DICTIONARIES.

A COMPLETE LATIN-ENGLISH DIC-
TIONARY. Medium 8vo. 21*s.*

A SMALLER LATIN-ENGLISH DIC-
TIONARY. Abridged from the above. Square 12mo. 7*s.* 6*d.*

A COPIOUS AND CRITICAL ENGLISH-
LATIN DICTIONARY. Medium 8vo. 21*s.*

A SMALLER ENGLISH-LATIN DIC-
TIONARY. Abridged from the above. Square 12mo. 7*s.* 6*d.*

A CLASSICAL DICTIONARY OF MYTHO-
LOGY, BIOGRAPHY, AND GEOGRAPHY. With 750
Woodcuts. 8vo. 18*s.*

A SMALLER CLASSICAL DICTIONARY.
Abridged from the above. With 200 Woodcuts. Crown 8vo.
7*s.* 6*d.*

A SMALLER DICTIONARY OF GREEK AND
ROMAN ANTIQUITIES. Abridged from the larger Work.
With 200 Woodcuts. Crown 8vo. 7*s.* 6*d.*

A CONCISE DICTIONARY OF THE BIBLE.
Its Antiquities, Biography, Geography, and Natural History.
With Maps and 300 Illustrations. Medium 8vo. 21*s.*

A SMALLER DICTIONARY OF THE BIBLE.
Abridged from the above. With Illustrations. Crown 8vo. 7*s.* 6*d.*

DR. WM. SMITH'S LATIN COURSE.

PRINCIPIA LATINA, Part I. A First Latin
Course. A Grammar, Delectus, and Exercise Book with Vocabularies. 13th Edition. 12mo. 3s. 6d.

₊ This Edition contains the Accidence arranged for the
"Public School Latin Primer."

PRINCIPIA LATINA, Part II. Latin Reading
Book. An Introduction to Ancient Mythology, Geography,
Roman Antiquities, and History. With Notes and a Dictionary.
12mo. 3s. 6d.

PRINCIPIA LATINA, Part III. Latin Poetry.
1. Easy Hexameters and Pentameters. 2. Eclogæ Ovidianæ.
3. Prosody and Metre. 4. First Latin Verse Book. 12mo. 3s. 6d.

PRINCIPIA LATINA, Part IV. Latin Prose
Composition. Rules of Syntax, with Examples, Explanations of
Synonyms, and Exercises on the Syntax. 12mo. 3s. 6d.

PRINCIPIA LATINA, Part V. Short Tales
and Anecdotes from Ancient History, for Translation
into Latin Prose. 12mo. 3s.

A LATIN-ENGLISH VOCABULARY, arranged
according to Subjects and Etymology; with a Latin-English
Dictionary to Phædrus, Cornelius Nepos, and Cæsar's "Gallic
War." 12mo. 3s. 6d.

THE STUDENT'S LATIN GRAMMAR. By
WM. SMITH, D.C.L., and THEOPHILUS D. HALL.
Post 8vo. 6s.

A SMALLER LATIN GRAMMAR. Abridged
from the above. 12mo. 3s. 6d.

DR. WM. SMITH'S GREEK COURSE.

INITIA GRÆCA, PART I. A FIRST GREEK COURSE, containing Grammar, Delectus, Exercise Book, and Vocabularies. 12mo. 3s. 6d.

INITIA GRÆCA, PART II. A READING BOOK; containing short Tales, Anecdotes, Fables, Mythology, and Grecian History. With a Lexicon. 12mo. 3s. 6d.

INITIA GRÆCA, PART III. GREEK PROSE COMPOSITION; containing the Rules of Syntax, with copious Examples and Exercises. 12mo. 3s. 6d.

THE STUDENT'S GREEK GRAMMAR. By PROFESSOR CURTIUS and WM. SMITH, LL.D. Post 8vo. 6s.

A SMALLER GREEK GRAMMAR. Abridged from the above work. 12mo. 3s. 6d.

HUTTON'S PRINCIPIA GRÆCA. A FIRST GREEK COURSE. A Grammar, Delectus, and Exercise Book, with Vocabularies. 12mo. 3s. 6d.

MATTHIÆ'S GREEK GRAMMAR. Abridged by BLOMFIELD. A New Edition, revised and enlarged, by E. S. CROOKE, B.A. Post 8vo. 4s.

LEATHES' PRACTICAL HEBREW GRAMMAR. With an Appendix, containing the Hebrew text of Genesis i.—vi., and Psalms i.—vi. Grammatical Analysis and Vocabulary. Post 8vo. 7s. 6d.

MURRAY'S STUDENT'S MANUALS:

A Series of Historical Class-books for advanced Scholars.

"This series of 'STUDENT'S MANUALS,' edited for the most part by DR. WM. SMITH, and published by Mr. MURRAY, possess several distinctive features which render them singularly valuable as educational works. While there is an utter absence of flippancy in them, there is thought in every page, which cannot fail to excite thought in those who study them, and we are glad of an opportunity of directing the attention of such teachers as are not familiar with them *to these admirable school-books.*"—*The Museum.*

THE STUDENT'S MANUALS, *after many years' use, have proved the most valuable aids both to Pupils and Masters engaged in preparing for the* **CIVIL SERVICE** and other Competitive **Examinations.**

I.—ENGLAND.

THE STUDENT'S HUME; A HISTORY OF ENGLAND, FROM THE EARLIEST TIMES. By DAVID HUME. Corrected and continued to 1868. Woodcuts. Post 8vo. 7s. 6d.

**** *Questions on the " Student's Hume."* 12mo. 2s.

THE STUDENT'S CONSTITUTIONAL HISTORY OF ENGLAND. By HENRY HALLAM, LL.D. With the Author's latest Additions and Corrections. Post 8vo.
[In the Press.

II.—EUROPE.

THE STUDENT'S HISTORY OF THE MIDDLE AGES, including the Supplemental Notes. By HENRY HALLAM, LL.D. With the Author's latest corrections and additions. Post 8vo. 7s. 6d.

III.—FRANCE.

THE STUDENT'S HISTORY OF FRANCE. FROM THE EARLIEST TIMES TO THE ESTABLISHMENT OF THE SECOND EMPIRE, 1852. Woodcuts. Post 8vo. 7s. 6d.

IV.—ROME.

(1) THE REPUBLIC.

THE STUDENT'S HISTORY OF ROME. FROM THE EARLIEST TIMES TO THE ESTABLISHMENT OF THE EMPIRE. By DEAN LIDDELL. Woodcuts. Post 8vo. 7s. 6d.

(2) THE EMPIRE.

THE STUDENT'S GIBBON; AN EPITOME OF THE HISTORY OF THE DECLINE AND FALL OF THE ROMAN EMPIRE. By EDWARD GIBBON. Woodcuts. Post 8vo. 7s. 6d.

V.—GREECE.

THE STUDENT'S HISTORY OF GREECE. FROM THE EARLIEST TIMES TO THE ROMAN CONQUEST. By WM. SMITH, LL.D. Woodcuts. Post 8vo. 7s. 6d.

. *Questions on the "Student's Greece."* 12mo. 2s.

VI.—ANCIENT HISTORY.

THE STUDENT'S ANCIENT HISTORY OF THE EAST. From the Earliest Times to the Conquests of Alexander the Great, including Egypt, Assyria, Babylonia, Media, Persia, Asia Minor, and Phœnicia. Woodcuts. Post 8vo. 7s. 6d.

VII.—SCRIPTURE HISTORY.

THE STUDENT'S OLD TESTAMENT HISTORY. FROM THE CREATION TO THE RETURN OF THE JEWS FROM CAPTIVITY. With 50 Maps and Woodcuts. Post 8vo. 7s. 6d.

THE STUDENT'S NEW TESTAMENT HISTORY. With an Introduction, containing the connection of the Old and New Testament. With 40 Maps and Woodcuts. Post 8vo. 7s. 6d.

VIII.—LANGUAGE, LITERATURE, &c.

THE STUDENT'S MANUAL OF ENGLISH LITERATURE. By T. B. SHAW, M.A. Edited with Notes and Illustrations. Post 8vo. 7s. 6d.

THE STUDENT'S SPECIMENS OF ENGLISH LITERATURE. Selected from 'the BEST WRITERS. By THOS. B. SHAW, M.A. Edited with Additions. Post 8vo. 7s. 6d.

THE STUDENT'S MANUAL OF THE ENG- LISH LANGUAGE. By GEORGE P. MARSH. Edited with additional Chapters and Notes. Post 8vo. 7s. 6d.

IX.—GEOGRAPHY.

THE STUDENT'S MANUAL OF ANCIENT GEOGRAPHY. By REV. W. L. BEVAN, M.A. Woodcuts. Post 8vo. 7s. 6d.

THE STUDENT'S MANUAL OF MODERN GEOGRAPHY. By REV. W. L. BEVAN, M.A. Woodcuts. Post 8vo. 7s. 6d.

X.—SCIENCE.

THE STUDENT'S ELEMENTS OF GEOLOGY. By SIR CHARLES LYELL, F.R.S. With 600 Woodcuts. Post 8vo. 9s.

XI.—PHILOSOPHY AND LAW.

THE STUDENT'S MANUAL OF MORAL PHILOSOPHY. With Quotations and References. By WIL-LIAM FLEMING, D.D. Post 8vo. 7s. 6d.

THE STUDENT'S BLACKSTONE. AN ABRIDG-MENT OF THE COMMENTARIES, ADAPTED TO THE PRESENT STATE OF THE LAW. By R. MALCOLM KERR, LL.D. Post 8vo. 7s. 6d.

MRS. MARKHAM'S HISTORIES.

HISTORY OF ENGLAND, FROM THE FIRST INVASION BY THE ROMANS. Continued down to 1865. With Conversations at the end of each Chapter. New and revised Edition. With 100 Woodcuts. 12mo. 4s.

HISTORY OF FRANCE, FROM THE CONQUEST BY THE GAULS. Continued down to 1867. With Conversations at the end of each Chapter. New and revised Edition. With 70 Woodcuts. 12mo. 4s.

HISTORY OF GERMANY, FROM THE INVASION OF THE KINGDOM BY THE ROMANS UNDER MARIUS. Continued down to 1867. New and revised Edition. With 50 Woodcuts. 12mo. 4s.

LITTLE ARTHUR'S HISTORY OF ENGLAND. By LADY CALLCOTT. New Edition. Continued down to the year 1864. With 28 Woodcuts. 16mo. 2s. 6d.

ÆSOP'S FABLES. A New Version, chiefly from Original Sources. By REV. THOMAS JAMES. 62nd Thousand. With 100 Woodcuts. Post 8vo. 2s. 6d.

NATURAL PHILOSOPHY.

1. **FIRST BOOK OF NATURAL PHILOSOPHY;** an Introduction to the Study of Statics, Dynamics, Hydrostatics, Optics and Acoustics, with numerous Examples. By SAMUEL NEWTH, M.A., Fellow of University College, London. Seventeenth Thousand. Small 8vo. 3s. 6d.

⁎ *This work embraces all the subjects in Natural Philosophy required at the Matriculation Examination of the University of London.*

BY THE SAME AUTHOR.

2. **ELEMENTS OF MECHANICS,** including Hydrostatics, with numerous Examples. Fifth Edition, revised and enlarged. Small 8vo. 8s. 6d. cloth.

⁎ *The First Part contains all the subjects in Mechanics and Hydrostatics required for the B.A. and B.Sc. Examinations of the University of London.*

3. **MATHEMATICAL EXAMPLES.** A Graduated Series of Elementary Examples in Arithmetic, Algebra, Logarithms, Trigonometry, and Mechanics. Small 8vo. 8s. 6d. cloth.

JOHN MURRAY, ALBEMARLE STREET.

Bradbury, Evans, & Co., Printers, Whitefriars.

www.ingramcontent.com/pod-product-compliance
Lightning Source LLC
Chambersburg PA
CBHW031026120726
47905CB00007B/2067